# DIRECT MARKETING

# EDWARD L. NASH

# DIRECT MARKETING

*Strategy, Planning, Execution*

WITHDRAWN

## McGRAW-HILL BOOK COMPANY

New York   St. Louis   San Francisco   Auckland
Bogotá   Hamburg   Johannesburg   London   Madrid   Mexico
Montreal   New Delhi   Panama   Paris   São Paulo
Singapore   Sydney   Tokyo   Toronto

*Library of Congress Cataloging in Publication Data*

Nash, Edward L.
Direct marketing.

Includes index.
1. Direct selling.   2. Marketing.   I. Title.
HF5438.25.N37        658.8′4        81-8141
                                     AACR2

3 4 5 6 7 8 9 0   DODO   8 9 8 7 6 5 4 3 2

ISBN 0-07-046019-1

The editors for this book were William Newton and Georgia
Kornbluth, the designer was Elliot Epstein, and the production supervisor was Thomas G. Kowalczyk. It was set
in Melior by J. M. Post Graphics.

# DEDICATION

To my teachers—everyone for whom I have ever worked, or who has ever worked with me or for me. Each has taught me something new about direct marketing or, more important, about life.

# EDWARD L. NASH

**ABOUT THE AUTHOR**

Edward L. Nash is president of BBDO Direct, Inc., the direct marketing subsidiary of one of the largest advertising agencies in the world. He had previously been executive vice president of Rapp & Collins, where he helped develop direct marketing programs for companies such as Avis, Burpee, Citicorp, Consumers Union, Doubleday, Equitable Life, International Gold, Knapp, Lanier, National Liberty, Save the Children, and Time Life Books. Ed Nash has been in the industry for twenty years, starting as a copywriter for Schwab & Beatty and serving as vice president, marketing, for LaSalle Extension University and president of Capitol Record Club. Ed has been called "the master strategist" of direct marketing. He has addressed direct marketing groups in New York, Minneapolis, Los Angeles, Dallas, San Francisco, and Boston, and has lectured on direct marketing at New York University and Fordham University. Nash is a featured speaker at the International Direct Marketing Symposium in Lausanne. He is chairman of the DMMA Awards Committee and the DMMA Marketing Council.

# CONTENTS

# PREFACE

Direct marketing is not only a technology, it is a process. It not only seeks to make a sale, it builds profitable customer relationships.

In doing this, any medium may be used—not only direct mail, but newspapers, magazines, radio, television, matchbook covers, and other media not yet dreamed of. The defining characteristic is not the method of reaching the prospect, or even the method by which the prospect responds to us. It makes no difference whether the inquiry or order comes to us by mail, phone, Mailgram, interactive cable, or a visit to a retail location.

What is essential is that the customer's name and address be "captured," to be recorded on a list which becomes the heart of the marketing process. The mailing list is the means by which we fulfill our obligations to the customer or prospect; provide satisfactory service; collect payments due us; and make subsequent offers of products, services, or information.

Those of us who make our living in direct marketing entered the field from widely divergent directions. Among us are mail-order entrepreneurs seeking profits from the amazing leverage of direct marketing; advertising executives fascinated by its measurability; academicians captivated by its logical and scientific foundations; writers and artists pursuing its virginal creative opportunities; and suppliers of paper, printing, and other services who have discovered its present immensity and its future potential.

Lately our ranks have been joined by skilled practitioners in financial, packaged goods, retail, and other marketing methods who have suddenly been called upon to apply the direct marketing process in one way or another to their own fields.

In the advertising agency business I have worked with people who have approached this business from all these varied perspectives. There has always been the need to train new people who voluntarily choose or accidently stumble into this unique and immensely satisfying field.

I originally conceived this book as a means of sparing myself the trouble of explaining the basic principles of direct marketing over and over again. The book gradually expanded into a guide for anyone who must conceive, plan, or execute all or part of a direct marketing program.

My intention is to take the reader step by step along the road to eventual success in any direct marketing endeavor. For novices, it is the basic training needed to succeed in this fast-moving field. For specialists, I do not presume to teach about their own field, but to provide a sense of context—how their speciality interrelates with every other area of this business. For everyone, I offer some new insight and wide abstractions about my particular forte, direct marketing strategy. Though not every reader may agree with all my hypotheses on strategy, it is my expectation that this book will at least initiate starting points for the identification of each reader's own strategic conclusions.

In addition, I have tried to apply some of the writing principles of the field to the book itself. If the book is interesting and fast-moving, that is because the subject is interesting and fast-moving. If the book is long, that is only because there is a lot to say. If the book is lively and conversational, that is because I believe that the style of the written word should not differ significantly from that of the spoken word.

I welcome you, the reader, to *Direct Marketing*, the book. If you are new to the field, I welcome you to that, as well. May you find both as stimulating and satisfying as I do.

*Ed Nash*

New York, NY

# A STATEMENT OF APPRECIATION

Where does one begin to thank those who have taught the lessons or provided the opportunities to enable one to write a book like this?

There are the people who trained me at various points in my own career: Tom Collins, Mel Fauer, Lee Friend, Ray Hagel, Alan Livingston, Stan Rapp, Dave Reider, Vic Schwab, Warren Smith, Sam Sugar, Aaron Sussman, and George Violante. They can be said to have been my teachers; but so was every client with whom I have ever worked, every specialist and staff member who has ever worked with me or for me. So are the authors of the books which came before mine, the lecturers whose talks I attended, and the brilliant men and women who invented some of the theories I only report. These include Richard Benson, Mike Fabian, Jerry Hardy, Rose Harper, Si Levy, Ben Ordover, Maxwell Sackheim, Robin Smith, Robert Stone, Frank Vos, and Lester Wunderman.

I must extend my warmest appreciation to the staff of the Direct Mail Marketing Association, whose manuals, materials, and advice proved invaluable. These include, among many others, Richard Brennan, Karen Burns, Bob DeLay, Bonnie DeLay, Richard Montesi, Ed Pfeiffer, Bonnie Rodriquez, Marilyn Ross, Laurie Spar, Donna Sweeney, Merrill Tomlinson, Ruth Troiani, Sue White, and Dante Zacovish. Pete Hoke, the publisher of *Direct Marketing* magazine, offered not only advice and information, but also encouragement when I needed it most.

More immediately, there are those who provided specific information or who helped me by reviewing specific sections of the manuscript: Renee Birnbaum, Sol Blumenfeld, Susan Bynum, Tom Collins, Joel Feldman, Tom Garbett, Hal Glantz, Lloyd Kieran, Ellen Kraus, Carol Ladanyi, Marge Landrau, Jeramy Lanigan, Craig Mansfield, Walter Marshall, Fran McCown, Murray Miller, Charles Orlowski, Fred Rola, Murray Roman, Joe Shain, David Shepard, Iris Shokoff, and Mike Vigil.

My executive assistant, Caroline Cohen, supervised the endless hours of typing, proofing, and working with the editorial and production specialists at McGraw-Hill. I would never have met the final deadlines without her help. I would like to thank my editor, as well, who has been superb; I omit his name only in deference to his company's preferences. As they put it, their people are "just doing their job."

Having saved the most important for last, I now thank my patient and loving wife, Diana, who provided the inspiration and encouragement to start this project in the first place, and to keep it going night after night, week after week, as what started as a labor of love seemed to become a monstrous burden and an impossible chore. She made it all worthwhile, and still does.

A word of apology to my five-year-old daughter, Amy. When she's old enough to read this passage, perhaps then she'll understand why Daddy was spending so much time at "the typewriter" (sic) instead of with her.

To all of you, for all your contributions, thank you.

## CHAPTER ONE

# INTRODUCTION

Direct marketing is a powerful and fast-growing science. It is the fundamental marketing precept of corporations doing over $100 billion in sales. And it is becoming an essential supplementary marketing tool in virtually every type of industry in the world today.

It is being discovered by banks, insurance companies, office equipment manufacturers, the travel industry, and the telecommunications industry. It is often the first marketing tool employed by new industries—such as prerecorded videocassettes—or by new entries in established industries. Direct marketing executives are being positioned alongside advertising, sales, and public relations as major components of corporate marketing organizations.

Yet, even as direct marketing is being discovered, it is still discovering itself.

## A BRIEF BACKGROUND

Only ten years ago direct marketing was considered to be a specialty to be employed by book publishers, record clubs, magazines seeking subscriptions, correspondence schools, and sellers of kitchen gadgets and low-priced fashions. No one, then, would have guessed that it was destined to become a marketing tool utilized by more than half the companies listed in Fortune's list, "500 Largest Corporations."

Anyone looking through antique magazines will find early examples of what was then called mail-order advertising. Many of the classic advertisements of all times were mail-order ads: "They laughed when I sat down to play . . . " or Charles Atlas' bully kicking sand in our hero's face, or "Do you make these mistakes in English?"

Advertisements were crowded with small-type copy, appealing to every human desire. The most mundane products were offered as keys to fame, success, popularity, riches, admiration, sex appeal, security, and eternal happiness. Mailing pieces began to utilize the simplest kinds of personalization, such as a prospect's handwritten name on an invitation to subscribe to *Business Week*. And mailing lists progressed, slowly and painfully, from typed labels to Scriptomatic cards to rooms filled with trays of ink-covered Elliott addressing stencils. Clerks pushed long metal rods through trays of hole-punched stencils to select prospects by elementary categories, and then refiled them manually.

It all seems primitive today, and yet in those early efforts a solid foundation was already being laid for direct marketing as it is today. The earliest advertisements, as far back as I have been able to search, all include the one tiny element that has made it possible for a copywriter's art to become a marketer's science, that has enabled modern writers to declare what works and what doesn't with a sense of certainty unknown to most other kinds of advertising.

### The Incredible Key Number

That tiny element is, simply, the key number. This is the common denominator of every type of direct marketing activity, in every medium, for every product, in the years that have passed as well as those that are yet to come.

The incredible key number, carried in coupons, reply cards and, today, in television announcements, is what makes direct marketing unique. It is the foundation of our knowledge, the key to our science, the signpost to our future.

The early giants of our field—Maxwell Sackheim, Victor Schwab, John Caples—did not have to rely on a client's subjective opinion to gain acceptance and fame for their advertising. They *knew* it worked. The clients knew it when the responses, bearing key numbers of advertisements they or their agencies prepared, poured out of mail sacks. The advertising community knew those ads were "great" the same way we do today—by seeing them repeated, over and over again, in ever-expanding media schedules.

As the reservoir of knowledge grew, copy-oriented executives looked to other areas for response improvement: price testing, media testing, and premiums. Products began to be created just for mail-order advertising. Sherman & Sackheim created the Little Leather Library and then another innovative proposition, the Book-of-the-Month Club. An innovative retailer named Sears started developing a catalog offering merchandise to railroad station agents, and another industry was born.

In later years, Lester Wunderman helped Columbia Broadcasting System (CBS) create the now-famous concept called the Columbia Record Club. Jerry Hardy, creator of the original Time-Life Books concept, later became president of the Dreyfus Fund and revolutionized the financial industry by selling mutual funds by mail without using stockbrokers.

As the industry emerged, computers and optical scanning devices counted the same incredible key numbers and produced a wealth of data showing marketers not only how many coupons were returned from a particular advertisement but how many people bought how much, and paid for it. Simple concepts like cost per order gave way to precise forecasts of return on advertising investment. The key number led not only to new ads and new mailing lists, but to the creation of entire new businesses.

## The Miracle of Statistical Projectability

One reason for the rapid evolution of the industry is its unique ability to test new ideas with minimal downside risk. The key to this ability is statistical projectability. Direct marketing is a statistician's paradise, for all the practices of this mathematical application are used daily as an intrinsic part of its marketing and its operations.

If a test mailing to a valid sample produces a 5 percent response, there is a reasonable probability that the rest of the list or similar lists will, within a predictable margin of error, produce the same result. It is therefore possible, by spending relatively small amounts, to accurately determine the best copy, offer, or list for a given proposition, or even to test one product against another. The same principle is present in magazine advertising, where regional editions and split runs can provide a very accurate reading of which ad "pulls" best or whether the publication itself is potentially profitable.

To make this miracle possible, thousands of prospective customers turn the pages of a magazine or look in their mailboxes in a frighteningly predictable manner. They elect to rush to the phone or put our coupon aside—each acting independently—until a precisely graphable "later." The total pattern makes it possible for direct marketing to be more of a science than any other field of advertising or marketing.

## OTHER ADVANTAGES OF DIRECT MARKETING

The predictability of direct marketing, arising out of its measurability and the science of statistics, is only one of the unique elements of this field. Others are (1) concentration, (2) personalization, and (3) immediacy. Businesses built on direct marketing live with these advantages every day, for they are what makes the existence of such businesses possible. And any company planning to apply direct marketing techniques to its established business or to enter the direct marketing field must first understand how these advantages work and how to apply them to their objectives.

## Concentration

Concentration is a media concept. It is the ability to take promotional dollars and direct them to the most likely prospects with great accuracy.

When general advertisers, seeking a larger share of market, blanket entire communities with newspaper, magazine, and television messages, selectivity is necessarily very limited. Readership surveys and Simmons data make it possible to achieve relative efficiencies, but not anywhere near the precision targeting available to direct marketers.

Our successful campaign for Starrett City is an excellent example of this capability. Previously the conventional approach had been used—ads in the real estate section of the prestigious *New York Times*. The fixed budget produced low awareness, no perceptible attitude changes, and—most important—a lack of new leases from the target audience: middle-income families with children.

The new effort switched the same dollars into a different media pattern. Instead of the *Times*, with distribution throughout the metropolitan New York area including its affluent suburbs, we switched to the mass-audience *New York Sunday News*, using preprints distributed only in those areas of Queens and Brooklyn where our client's development presented a distinct advantage. Instead of being just one ad among many, the preprint format gave us a full-color, high-impact story and a response coupon asking for an appointment.

Within the same budget that was previously spread thinly over a large area, we were able to use preprints to give us greater penetration and awareness among our audience than even a Procter & Gamble (P&G) product could achieve.

Direct mail offers even greater concentration, by offering even greater selectivity. From tens of thousands of mailing lists an advertiser can select those people who have identified themselves as being interested in buying products of a certain type in a particular price range, and buying them through the mail. In addition, one can select—instead of or in addition to so-called "Buyer's" lists—an incredible range of community and individual characteristics compiled from census, Simmons, and telephone directory data. Chapter 5 will review these possibilities in detail.

## Personalization

Another cornerstone of direct marketing, particularly within the direct-mail media, is the ability to personalize communications. Not only can we select very specific audiences for concentrated promotions, but we can address them in a manner that dramatizes our conviction that the product or service we are offering is particularly right for each person who gets our message.

Addressing a person by name is one obvious example, which can range from a label showing through an envelope window to much more dramatic display: giant ink-jet letters, computer-addressed salutations, or handwritten fill-ins on envelopes or invitations.

Of much greater effectiveness is personalization incorporated in the concept of the mailing itself. A *Newsweek* mailing talks openly about the kinds of subscribers they are looking for, and the characteristics indicated by the address of the recipient. *Reader's Digest*, in a sweepstakes promotion, lists the names of winners in the same or nearby towns. Business mailings refer to the industry type of sales volume or employee count, as indicated by Dun & Bradstreet (D&B) mailing lists.

One mailing we did to promote weekend car rentals for Avis included one paragraph which showed through the envelope and dramatized the kinds of weekends the prospect might take. The examples changed depending on the location of the prospect. Different weekend suggestions were written for each zip code group to make the appeal as real as possible.

A Lanier promotion for word-processing equipment used not only computer personalization but a half-dozen variations in the printed brochure to illustrate the specific applications of a new product to each of several industries. Only the cover and a couple of pages changed, but the mailing became more relevant when the recipient's industry type was boldly displayed. "How this new product can save time and money for advertising agencies (or engineering firms, or law offices)" is much more likely to be read than any general appeal.

## Immediacy

The third and most vital element of direct marketing is immediacy. Conventional advertising invests millions of dollars to establish product awareness and positive attitudes. It can establish a desire; but it can't fulfill it.

On the way to buy an advertised product our prospects may be exposed to competing messages, conflicting desires, alternative uses of discretionary spending power. The store may not have our client's product, or the salesclerk may not know where it is, how to use it, or why the customer should buy it.

The decline of selling skills in retailing is one of the great forces propelling the growth of direct marketing. Advertisers who count on the wisdom of store buyers or the ability of store salespeople to move their products may find that even the finest products can become marketing casualties.

Direct marketing messages, in all media, ask for the order now, or at least for a response that enables us to ask for an order on the next communication. If general advertising's objective is awareness and attitude, direct marketing's is the third A—action.

There is a wide spectrum of actions we can ask for. The ultimate is to ask for a sale—a mail order, a subscription, a membership, or a contribution. We can ask for it on a loose "send-no-money-now" trial basis or on a hard "check-with-order" basis.

We can establish a contact, by making an appointment or providing a less specific motivation to bring our prospect to a retail outlet or a showroom, or we can arrange to have our salesperson visit the prospect's home or office.

On the less committed end of the spectrum we can offer a booklet or sample as a means of identifying prospects who are worth the expense of additional mailings, phone contacts, or personal visits.

Immediacy is a strength of direct marketing, but it is also a requirement. Our promotions are successful only to the extent that we facilitate immediate action. It is for this reason that our copy disciplines find ways to urge action now, rather than later; that our offer disciplines require simple, easy-to-use, sometimes pre-filled-out reply forms; that our media planners place a premium on bound-in insert cards or other easy-to-use reply devices. A sacred rule of direct marketing is that response devices must be easy to use, for if they are not used immediately, they may never be used. In direct marketing, as we'll explain in Chapter 2, procrastination is as serious a challenge as conscious decisions to decline your offer, and in some ways it is an even more serious challenge.

## THE REVOLUTION IN DIRECT MARKETING

Earlier I pointed out that direct marketing is being accepted as a fundamental marketing tool in a growing variety of businesses—from giant multinational financial corporations to local retailers offering an interesting new product to their customer lists or a specialized item in the shopping sections of national magazines.

The greatest attention has been given to the companies starting or acquiring direct marketing businesses, or deciding to offer their existing product line by mail order. But the most important development, and one that I predict will have the greatest role in the widening importance of this field, is the rapidly emerging acceptance of the fact that the techniques of direct marketers can be valuable even for businesses that do not utilize any type of direct marketing distribution. The principles of direct marketing are already widely in use by financial institutions of every kind. The largest manufacturers of office equipment are rapidly discovering how lead selling can increase the efficiency of the most powerful sales organizations who never needed it before. Oil companies, telephone companies, and hotel chains are using it. Applications of direct marketing have been investigated, and in most cases are being developed, for automobile companies, appliance manufacturers, toy makers, and camera manufacturers. The list is unlimited.

### The Two-Way Discovery

Just as the world of general marketers is discovering the tools of direct marketers, we in direct marketing have made a discovery of our own. We, as an industry, have looked down our noses at the undefinable, unmeasurable, seemingly unscientific methods of general advertising. Suddenly each of us has, in our own way, waked up, rubbed our eyes, and looked around to make an incredible discovery: We didn't know all the answers!

As we educated the barbarian practitioners of communications techniques which lacked the mighty key number, our pontifications were interrupted by the startling realization that maybe, just maybe, all these giant marketing organizations with years of experience investing larger budgets than direct marketers even dream of might just have something to teach us after all.

Little by little, direct marketing specialists became exposed to the workings of general advertising. Executives with packaged-goods experience came to work for direct marketing agencies and clients. Realizing the growing importance of direct marketing as a tool for every kind of advertiser, major advertising agencies such as Young & Rubicam (Y&R) and Doyle Dane Bernbach (DDB) purchased the most famous specialized agencies in this field and worked with them to bring both general and direct marketing clients the combined expertise of both disciplines.

Today the field has changed completely. Yes, the basic principles are still intact—and still correct. The old books are still correct; they're just not complete. Today there are new tools and new sciences which enable us to reach new levels of professionalism never before attainable. There are five such areas which I consider extremely important: computer technology, strategic planning, structured creativity, predictive research, and multimedia planning.

## The Coming of the Computer

The availability of computer systems has been to the direct marketing industry what airplanes have been to transportation. No development has had such far-reaching, truly revolutionary impact on our way of doing business.

The computer's first applications in our field were similar to those in every other field of business. They saved us time. Mailing lists were transferred from clumsy mechanical techniques to punched cards which could be sorted and filed easily. Customer records could be maintained on magnetic tape and, later, instantly recalled for billing, shipping, and promotional mailings. The cards gave way to tape, and the tape to floppy discs. Punched cards became high-speed printouts and ink-jet labelers which operated faster than the eye could see. Labels became heat-transfer fill-ins, and then became computer letters.

The ability to file and retrieve data changed the procedures, the personnel, and the profitability of direct marketing. But this was only the beginning. These first applications of the computer were, in effect, only simpler, faster ways to do everything we always used to do before. The real excitement was yet to come.

Responses, once laboriously entered on ledger cards, are now not only tallied but compared to expectations, compared to test cells, forecast to infinity, factored for relative customer quality, analyzed for trends, and tracked for profitability through the life of the customer relationship.

Sophisticated firms now operate in the field of "modeling," printing out scenarios based on subtle changes in pricing or renewals—most often in the magazine field, but in other direct marketing fields as well.

Both customer lists and prospect lists can now be subjected to infinite selectivity, merging, purging, matching, elimination of present customers, and screening of individual names or census tracts for likely bad credit risks.

A merchandiser now, for instance, can go through the company's customer list and make an offer only to those who have purchased an item in a specific category, in a specific time frame, and within a chosen price range. The customer can be selected by neighborhood, credit experience, sex, or any other deducible factor. Once the customer has been selected, a computer letter can refer to past purchases or known interests.

**Direct Marketing Flow Chart**

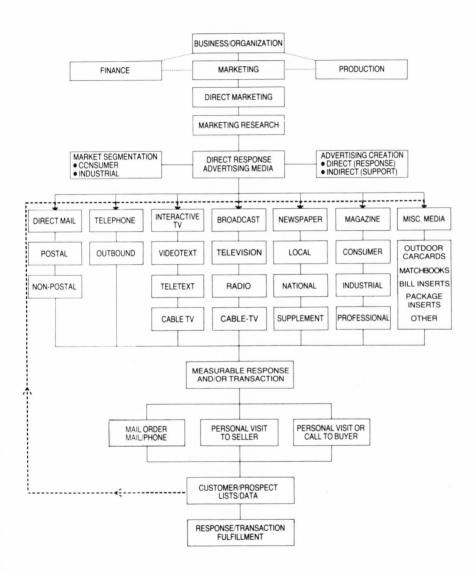

**Direct marketing flowchart.**    (Source: Direct Marketing, *Garden City, New York. Reprinted by permission.*)

Computerized list segmentation has made it possible for mailings to be directed to those most likely to respond, sparing others from unwanted offers and advertisers from unnecessary expense.

Credit can now be extended more easily, on the basis of more reliable data. Screening of bad credit risks can be based on past experiences in a half-dozen areas. And we can be more creative than ever in displaying our customer's name and other data with dramatic computer-driven printing methods.

Thanks to the computer, our industry can be not only more accurate than ever but also more personal. The technology invented to process enormous volumes of data and keep track of millions of customers has made it possible for us to treat each one individually, and to be more personal than ever in our offers, our appeals, and even the products we develop.

## The Emergence of Strategic Planning

Another great evolution has been the growth of strategy as a recognized factor in direct marketing.

When the bulk of mail-order ads promoted a single product or self-help book, each advertisement stood on its own to a much greater extent than today. We concerned ourselves with building sales, not reputations, with very few exceptions. The occasional farsighted advertiser—such as the Book-of-the-Month Club—established an identity in copy style and layout. The legendary Oscar Ogg painstakingly drafted calligraphic-style layouts for Book-of-the-Month Club which accurately portrayed the respectability and sincerity of this mail-order institution.

Most firms, however, searched for the elusive "hot product," wrote headlines and copy which promised the moon, and relied on research methods which can be fully described as "Let's run it somewhere and see if it works."

It's very different today. The market is bigger. The options are more numerous, and the stakes are gigantic. There are at least two dozen direct marketers with sales volumes over $100 million, and many more aiming to join their ranks. The rewards are greater, and so are the risks. Fortunately, the tools to work with have improved also.

The success of a product today begins in its very design. You can't take a product off a retail shelf and expect it to succeed in a mail-order ad without some special advantage. That's why many products are designed especially for mail-order markets and are "Not available through stores."

The offer is more than just a good price. It involves calculations of market potential and advertising cost. It requires consideration of returns, credit, premiums, trade-ups, and additional items which can be sold.

Media are much more complex also. What's the size of the "universe"? Can multimedia support methods expand it? Is there a core market that can be segmented out for special attention? Should our strategy "skim off" the most likely prospects from a large audience, or concentrate on squeezing every sale out of a smaller target market with what we call a "high-penetration" strategy?

Creative copy is no longer the starting point. Brilliant headlines are no longer enough. Professionals in this field resolve questions of positioning, emotional appeal, benefit extension, and credibility before the first word of copy comes out of a typewriter.

Today marketing strategy involves long-range objectives seldom considered in the past. Every advertisement not only brings in orders, but creates impressions which will influence the result of future offers by your firm. Every customer relationship is a value in itself, to be treated as carefully as if you were running an exclusive retail shop. Furthermore, it is likely that you will face direct, effective competition within months after your success becomes well known.

### Structured Creativity

Another great change which is rapidly sweeping this industry, and many other industries as well, is the emergence of structured creativity.

When I was running the Capitol Record Club, I remember Capitol's president, Alan Livingston, telling our board, "You can't have a hundred-million-dollar corporation dependent on whether or not four dope addicts get their act together and give us a hit single."

The same advice applies to direct marketers. We can't build and maintain multi-million-dollar businesses on the occasional brainstorm of the rare and unpredictable genius who comes along from time to time. If you're running a Doubleday or a Time-Life or a CBS, you need new ideas and new products when you need them, not when an idea happens to be available.

The solution to this dilemma was found in the development of techniques to stimulate and evaluate new ideas on a reliable, dependable basis. Some of the early attempts at this included "positive thinking" and what we now call "brainstorming" in various forms. "Synectics" developed a fascinating approach to problem definition and formal creativity.

The approach I am most familiar with is the one used at Rapp & Collins and developed by one of our founders, Stan Rapp, in association with Liz Forrest, an educator who runs Innovation Labs. This approach is called Effective Problem Solving (EPS).

EPS involves a formal approach to organizing idea meetings, defining problem statements, and delegating specific responsibilities to members of the idea-forming group. The participants are asked to "wish" for solutions to the problem at hand, which may involve anything from a search for a premium or product benefit to the creation of whole new businesses for a major corporation. Idea forming is stimulated not only by a unique positive-thinking environment but by devices to stimulate fantasy and break mental blocks.

I have seen hundreds of ideas created for a client, most of them—by necessity—unusable, but always—by design—including one or two brilliant approaches which would not have emerged in any other way. Some have resulted in spectacular direct marketing successes.

### Seeing the Future: Predictive Research

The fourth major revolution has been the recognition of the potential of predictive research.

In a field where, for years, only "split-run testing" was respected, research is coming into its own.

I'm not talking about fact-finding research—questionnaires and interviews to help define a market or determine a product's previous positioning. And I don't mean creative research—the use of focus panels and similar techniques to get reactions to a proposition and zero in on customer vocabulary. Neither of these techniques has been effective in determining which advertising approach will work best in the media marketplace.

The new development, predictive research, does tell us just this. Now that there is so much invested in a major campaign, when speed is so often part of the marketing strategy—to test a proposition and roll it out before a competitor can react—some type of advance research has become essential. In addition the high cost of full-color plates and small-quantity direct-mail executions made its use an economic necessity.

Chapter 9 will reveal some of the techniques used today, not necessarily to pick winners, but to eliminate the losers and give our split-run tests a better chance to come up with a winner.

### Other Important Developments

The four developments discussed above are not the only major changes going on. They are, however, the ones responsible for the present scientific and professional level of direct marketing. Even as I write this, new changes are emerging with dramatic and far-reaching consequences in the direct marketing world of the future.

The telephone is one change, as both an ordering opportunity and a selling tool. Credit cards are another, bringing advertisers the ability to offer "credit" terms while getting cash payments. Independent delivery systems are another, offering direct marketers at least the hope that we might someday have an alternative to the costly, inefficient, slow, wasteful, and bureaucratically frustrating postal system.

## THE SCIENTIFIC ERA OF DIRECT MARKETING

Today direct marketing is a science, but it is still an art also. It has harnessed the tools of twentieth-century technology to the traditions and skills of its nineteenth-century origins. Today we offer selling arguments built on logic as well as emotional appeals built on modern psychology. Today we aim to build long-range reputations for our companies and our industry as well as to strive for short-range sales goals.

David Ogilvy describes direct marketing as his "secret weapon." Bill Bernbach calls it the essential craft of "asking for the order." Direct marketing has earned the respect of the greatest of contemporary general advertisers even while it is just beginning to learn to respect the tools of conventional advertising.

Direct marketing is the purest form of marketing. A business which fully accepts its philosophy will develop its products to meet the desires of the marketplace, rather than the other way around.

Direct marketing is one of the last sanctuaries for the corporate entrepreneur. It is still a field where good ideas can be tested with minimal investment and grow rapidly into a Publisher's Clearing House, a World of Beauty, a Monex, or a Margrace—all giant enterprises which started with a single successful idea.

This book reveals the rules of direct marketing. Learn them. Use them. Respect them. And as soon as you've mastered them, find new ways to break them—for that is where the new methods, the new traditions, will come from.

Just as a Picasso had to master realistic depiction in order to create startlingly simple abstractions, so must direct marketers learn the basics of this business before we can successfully innovate. But then innovate we must. Add even one new idea, one new technique, and you become part of the continuum of our art, our science, our field of direct marketing.

## CHAPTER TWO

# STRATEGIC PLANNING

If you hand a mail piece to a group of direct marketers, you will have a scene reminiscent of the Indian tale of several blind men describing an elephant. Somebody will comment on a brilliant letter, another on a clever headline, still another on an original format or an exciting layout. Someone else might overlook the communications vehicle altogether and note an attractive offer or appealing product.

Direct marketing is no one of these things. It is all of them together— a sum more powerful than its ingredients, a harnessing of the forces of art, science, psychology, and common sense to achieve a marketing objective.

## STRATEGY DEFINED

What brings it all together is strategy. Am I using "strategy" in the sense that military planners use it when planning or discussing wars won or lost? Yes. In the sense that Machiavelli wrote about in his advice on how to manipulate masses and topple princes? Yes. Will we deal with it in the dictionary sense of harnessing combined resources to achieve a selected goal? Yes. Further, we will see how and why strategic planning is the great essential difference between amateurism and professionalism in direct marketing particularly, and probably in most other fields as well.

## FOUR ESSENTIAL ELEMENTS OF STRATEGIC PLANNING

The first step in any marketing endeavor is to determine a basic strategy. There are four elements of strategic planning in direct marketing—the product, the offer, the media, and the creative strategy. No one of these is all-important. No one of these is unimportant. Each of these four elements demands careful study, perceptive problem definition, innovative solutions, and logical decision-making.

The tendency in most organizations is to emphasize one or the other of these four elements, depending on the strengths and interests of a corporation's management. That is how they eventually get into trouble, providing opportunities for new management to become heroes by coming up with new solutions in a neglected area.

These principles apply whether one is planning a major launch of a giant new program or preparing one mailing piece for a kitchen table mail-order business. They are universal and, used with some imagination and lots of hard work, can increase the profitability of any size or type of direct marketing endeavor.

## PRODUCT STRATEGY

Originally, most businesses were based on the idea that a product is a fixed, inflexible entity which is developed by one area of business management, then handed to a sales or marketing department with the order: "Now you guys figure out how to sell it!"

Today the emphasis has reversed, with product-development teams directed to find products or services to meet marketing opportunities. Instead of the old dictum "We made it, you (the consumer) should buy it," we now have "You want it, we'll make it."

Direct marketing has been a pioneer in this approach. The ultimate application is, unfortunately, one that is not available to everyone: the development of brand-new products "from scratch," designed and priced exclusively for direct marketing.

Such products are *designed* to provide appealing offers that can be sent on a trial basis, with both product and packaging that looks good on a printed page. They are *priced* to permit credit sales, introductory offers, and repeat sales in subscription or club programs. They are *exclusively* direct marketing in that, at least in the version offered, they are "Not available in stores."

The giants of industry have their best marketing teams develop and test new products for their house lists—products that benefit from the reputation and expertise of the originating company.

For most direct marketers, the options are more limited. A retail product can be adapted for mail-order sales. A group of printed publications can be repackaged as a direct marketing program. A successful overseas proposition can be tailored for introduction in another country.

An even more challenging situation is the stale product which has to be revitalized—a process akin to reopening "dry" oil wells or "mined-out" gold veins. That is a more common objective. The principles remain the same.

### Changing a Product Without Changing It

The most economical way to revise a product is to change it without actually adding anything to it. There are several ways to make these "changes" in direct marketing.

Positioning is a whole subscience, so important that Chapter 11 is devoted to it. Briefly, it involves "repositioning" the product or service by presenting it in a different placement vis-à-vis competition, by aiming it at a different market segment, or by selling it at a different point in the buyer's decision-making process—my own innovation, which I have named "horizontal positioning."

One example of conventional or "vertical" positioning is a campaign to sell Avis used cars as "The New Car Alternative," appealing to new-car buyers instead of the conventional used-car market. An example of horizontal positioning is Doubleday Book Club's "Fantasy" advertisements, selling prospects on the idea of reading itself rather than on book clubs in general or on their particular book club offer.

The "breakout" technique is another valuable tool of the trade. This involves taking a component of the basic package and isolating it to be featured as part of the offer. You'll spot the breakout technique in mailings or advertisements that take a packaging element—such as the plastic case in card file offers, or a reference service's binder or index section—and sells it as "Included at no extra cost."

Many products have attachments, accessories, manuals, or even service contracts which can be broken out and featured as ways of giving new life to old offers.

Multiple-part products can be taken apart, or put back together, to make what appear to be entirely different offers. A catalog of socket wrenches and tools with individual prices would probably not be successful in general markets; yet "100-Piece Tool Sets" including assorted sockets, taps, tools, and—as a bonus for fast action—1000 assorted nuts and bolts are offered in full-page ads in dozens of publications.

I remember a variation I once did for Walter Black's Classics Club, which basically offered three books for $1 with a subscription to others. I added a 6-square-inch panel which dramatized the end product:

"Build a fine collection of great classics like this," showing a shelf of the beautifully bound books. It worked so well that the panel eventually became the headline for an ad which is still running many years later.

On the other hand, a set of encyclopedias can be taken apart and sold volume by volume, or a Barbie doll can be sold on an offer which brings new doll outfits each month. A manufacturer of pots and pans, for example, can sell a deluxe set of pots, or a subscription to a pot-a-month club, or a basic set with other kitchen equipment added, or can offer a set of pots along with "The coffee pot free just for trying this amazing. . . . "

None of these products in these examples have changed. They have just been repositioned, redescribed, or recombined to make them seem fresh and different.

## Making Lemons into Lemonade

One of the most interesting approaches to revitalizing a stale proposition is the dramatization of a product feature that may have been either buried in body copy or left out of advertisements completely. You can build an ad around any aspect of a product or service. This includes not only the major features but the minor ones, not only the new improvements but the features that have been taken for granted.

Don't presume the customer knows everything there is to know about your product. Reintroduce it, and look for every product benefit that can legitimately be dramatized.

Is the product small? Stress space saving and portability. Does it lack controls that its competitors offer? Talk about simplicity and ease of operation. Is it an older model? Write that they don't make products like this anymore, and that this model is in limited supply.

Is your company not the largest in its field? Then you might be able to stress personal service or family ownership or the idea that the principals are intimately involved, read every letter, and personally stand behind their product.

Are your prices a bit high? Then make a plus out of it and feature the idea that not everyone appreciates extra quality and this offer is only for those who do, and are willing to pay for it.

Is your magazine thinner? Then perhaps it is fast to read with more selective editorial matter. Is your charity the smallest in its field? Then its work is probably more personal. I have never seen a marketing product where there wasn't something that could be pulled out and dramatized.

All this presumes that the claims given in the examples above are legitimate. If your product doesn't offer real value of some sort—if being different doesn't have some advantage to offer the consumer—then maybe you should start all over again with a new product. You can turn lemons into lemonade, just as long as you include some sweetener in the mixture.

### Enhancing Perceived Value

Your product strategy isn't limited to the extremes of developing whole new projects on one hand and repositioning or reassessing your product on the other. It often pays to invest in adding some genuine value to enhance the product's perception. Such additions are "paid for" by reduced order cost resulting from greater advertising response, and they can be tested easily and inexpensively.

Premiums are a simple addition. So is utilitarian packaging (such as a carrying case or storage container). If you're planning to send follow-up mailings anyway, why not include a newsletter which you can mention as an added benefit in your initial offer? Sarah Coventry's Personal Beauty Plan, for instance, planned an *Insider's Fashion Forecast* newsletter as an attractive feature of a customized beauty makeover. O. M. Scott's plants-by-mail service includes a magazine, *The Greenery*, which doubles as a catalog and adds value to the basic proposition.

Some other value add-ons include a really strong, long-term guarantee, which can become a powerful advertising appeal in itself. Or you can offer a follow-up telephone service, such as the call-for-assistance recipe preparation service offered toll-free by My Great Recipes.

One of the most interesting product evolutions took place at GRI's World of Beauty. Increasingly challenged by Cosmetique, these beauty sampler distributors escalated offers until the initial shipments contained products valued at as much as $100. GRI successfully outflanked its competitor by switching from price competition to the unique, exclusive Butterfly Collection, which put a new face on the offer as well as on the customer.

The essence of strategic product planning requires basic decision making—a commitment about what your product or service is and how you want it perceived. You can't have it be all things to all people. It can be the best or the cheapest, traditional or innovative, entertaining or educational. To try to be everything at once is to be nothing.

Whether you reposition your product, change it, dramatize a new feature, or invent something entirely new, the product itself must respond to research and test results in the same manner as every other ingredient of the four-part marketing equation. Unfortunately, the product is often the last consideration of many advertisers who prefer to place blame on the ad or the media rather than look objectively at their own product.

## OFFER STRATEGY

Though it is only one of the four critical elements, offer strategy is the element most easily revised for a fast result improvement. Even the slightest change in the price, though buried in body copy or coupon, can have dramatic effects on front-end performance.

### Expressing the Price

Not only the price itself but the way the price is expressed can drastically influence the cost per order. For example, let's say a monthly magazine has a newsstand value of $1 per copy, or $12 a year. The subscription offer is set at $6 per year. Here are some of the ways this offer can be expressed:

- One year for only $6    Basic price statement

- 50 cents per copy    Basic price expressed by unit

- Half price    Price expressed in fractions

- Six issues free    Savings dramatized by units

- Save $6    Savings expressed numerically

- Save 50 percent    Savings expressed in percentages

Note that all these offers represent exactly the same price. Only the means of expression varies. Of course, most of these statements will require qualification to comply with Better Business Bureau (BBB) standards and Federal Trade Commission (FTC) regulations and, if presented in a magazine, will be subject to the additional standards of the Audit Bureau of Circulation (ABC) codes.

### Price Sensitivity

One test I conducted for a film-processing client shows how sensitive pricing and price expression can be. The numbers are altered for confidentiality, but the relationships are correct. The offer is an introductory film-processing order, with a sliding scale of prices ranging from $1.99 for a twelve-exposure roll up to twice that for thirty-six-picture

TABLE 2-1
TEST RESULTS OF A FILM-PROCESSING OFFER

| Price statement | Twenty-print price | Average price (all sizes) | Cost per order | Margin | Units | Net | Contribution |
|---|---|---|---|---|---|---|---|
| Basic $1.99 up | $1.99 | $3.50 | $19 | $10.00 | 6,315 | ($9.00) | ($56,835) |
| Film, only 39 cents | 1.39 | 2.50 | 14 | 9.00 | 8,571 | ( 5.00) | ( 42,855) |
| 1-cent sale | 1.00 | 2.50 | 12 | 9.00 | 10,000 | ( 3.00) | ( 30,000) |
| $1 off | 0.99 | 2.50 | 9 | 9.00 | 13,333 | | |
| 99-cent offer | 0.99 | 2.50 | 8 | 9.00 | 15,000 | 1.00 | 15,000 |
| Half price | 0.99 | 1.75 | 5 | 8.25 | 24,000 | 3.25 | 78,000 |
| 39-cent limited offer | 0.39 | 2.20 | 2 | 8.70 | 60,000 | 6.70 | 402,000 |

35mm rolls. The objective was to attract film-processing customers who could then be sold additional processing at progressively higher prices. Table 2-1 shows what happened.

This test demonstrates several important lessons. In the first place, you can see how offer expression can be so important. The same average price produced a cost per order ranging from $5 to $12 or $14. (The discounted film offer was simply another way of offering savings.) If the 1-cent sale was your control offer and produced 10,000 orders at a cost of $12 each, the half-price offer would have produced 24,000 orders at $5 each. If your allowable margin at $3.50 was $10 per order, the 1-cent sale offer would have produced a $30,000 loss; the half-price offer would have produced a $78,000 profit, even after reducing the margin by 75 cents per order.

The 99-cent offer, which had a higher average price but a $3 higher cost per order, would have resulted in a profit of $15,000. It is often the case that a client finds a satisfactory offer like this one and stops experimenting, therefore never finding a more profitable offer, such as the half-price one in this example.

The more daring 39-cent offer would produce far more orders— 60,000 in this example—and a very dramatic $402,000 profit. This is true if the "back end" doesn't deteriorate and the margin holds up despite the poorer-quality orders. In most cases, there would be some deterioration of quality, but not enough to offset the dramatically higher number of responses at a much lower order cost.

## Elasticity of Price

In setting a pricing strategy, price elasticity must be taken into account. There are customers who must have your product and will pay almost any price to get it. If there are enough of them, you may be able to set your price very high.

However, inelasticity is more often the rule. If you are selling a product or service that people can live without—a strictly discretionary purchase—then it is likely that you are asking your customer to make an impulse purchase.

Just look at some of those executive toys in the airline gift catalogs. Let's face it. No one really *needs* a battery-operated travel alarm that plays your favorite tune and tells you what the time is in two time zones. However, for $5 or $10 few of us would have trouble justifying such a purchase in our own minds. We could probably talk ourselves into it at $29.95 as well. But what about $129.95? Suddenly, it's a considered purchase for most of us, and while we wouldn't mind getting it as a gift, it's not something we'd rush out to buy. This is an example of an inelastic price. It can only stretch so far, and no further.

## Price Break Points

In setting a price, the key break points are related to currency units. Prices should be just under currency break points. In the United States, 99 cents will do better than $1.20, $4.99 much better than $5.50, $10 better than $11, and $19.95 much better than $21.

On the other hand, you can often approach such a break point with no noticeable decline in results. If you're at $8.95 you can often move up to $9.95 with a negligible decline in response rate. But go to $10.95 and watch for a 20 to 30 percent drop-off.

You'll notice in this example that I use both rounded (i.e., $5) and broken (i.e., $4.95) prices. Frankly, I suspect that the consumer is smarter than most people think and that no one is fooled by the nickel change, or perceives it as a lower price. However, I have no definitive recommendation. There have always been more important things to test, and none of my clients have ever had a test cell to spare for this question. Whether the client with the $10 subscription price should charge $9.95 or whether the $9.95 marketer has unnecessarily sacrificed a treasure in nickels is a question I'll leave for others to solve. My feeling is that prestige-related offers should use the rounded figures, price-appeal offers the broken prices. My advice is to decide what's appropriate for your own business and stick to it.

## Add-On Pricing

I'm often asked about shipping and handling costs, which are a frequent complaint raised in customer correspondence. Should you set your price at $10 plus $1.50 postage and handling, or should it be $10 or $11.50? I have tested this, and it is a perfect example of where the consumer has a way of surprising us. The tests indicate that a price of $10 will do about the same as $10 plus shipping and handling, without statistical significance one way or the other. The only "bad" price would be the $11.50, which would do about 20 percent worse than either alternative.

It appears that consumers don't mind paying for shipping costs as an add-on, just as they don't seem to object to paying sales tax on modest purchases. Some do object later and express their wrath when the U.S. Postal Service or United Parcel Service (UPS) stamp clearly says 45 cents and the accompanying invoice reads $1.50 for postage and handling.

### The Almighty "Free!"

No discussion of pricing would be complete without homage to the almighty word "Free!" I call it almighty because, when I was a young copywriter at Schwab & Beatty, no use of the word ever escaped being capitalized by my copy chief, as if the word represented a deity deserving of respect.

In a way, the treatment is deserved, because even in this day of FTC-specified qualifications and rampant consumer skepticism, "Free!" is still the single most powerful word in the vocabulary of direct marketing offers.

The film-processing price test I described earlier was an exercise necessitated because the most famous film offer of all time—the one developed for Film Corporation of America—was specifically barred by the FTC. That offer: "Free film—send $1.00 for postage and handling." The customer was sent film only to discover that it apparently had to be processed by the same company for additional costs.

The power of the word "free" is such that it often makes possible two-step offers where a customer is offered a free booklet, free information, a free trial, or a free short-term subscription in order to build a mailing list for later solicitation.

The enormously successful Time-Life Books operation limits itself to one offer: free examination—of the first book in a series.

One variation is what magazines call the "comp-copy offer," which is shorthand for complimentary initial copy sent on trial. Most comp-copy offers are free only to respondents who do not eventually subscribe. If they do, the first issue is made part of the subscription. In my view, this isn't really "free." As a result, we have evolved the "true comp-copy offer" which makes the first issue free whether or not the respondent elects to cancel. The problem is that ABC rules will not count this first copy in the magazine's circulation figures.

A healthy solution to this dilemma is that used by *Geo* magazine, published by Gruner & Jahr, a subsidiary of Bertelsmann. They developed an initial "collector's issue" which is offered as the free incentive. These can be printed in quantity and sent out to new subscribers promptly without waiting for the next issue date. The regular issues then all count as circulation for advertising purposes.

*Time* magazine's development of exciting premiums like almanacs are offered in much the same way, and enable the magazine to make an honest free offer.

## Other Considerations

There are many other matters besides price to be considered when planning offer strategy. Many of them are discussed in Chapter 4, The Proposition.

One question is credit. Depending on the nature of the product and the audience, you may or may not want to establish a credit relationship with your customer. "Send no money now" is a powerful result builder, especially when used with a full guarantee, but it involves sending out bills, setting up credit-evaluation procedures, and writing off some percentage of bad debt. Installment sales and credit cards have their own unique problems, as do cash-on-delivery (COD) shipments.

Contests and sweepstakes are another aspect of offer strategy, which has dynamic and dangerous consequences. The "lift" of a sweepstakes can be like a narcotic. It makes you feel good for the moment, but you can get hooked on it. While sweepstakes have been very important for many advertisers, they create a whole new set of problems in terms of poor quality, high costs, and the need to come up with bigger and better contests in order to maintain the hyped sales level. The effects show up in everything from bad debt to poor renewals to lower list-rental income. "Sweepstakes-sold" is, to a sophisticated advertiser, a warning that the magazine or list whose circulation is offered consists largely of people who like to enter contests, not necessarily of people truly involved in the type of magazine, product, or service sold.

## Evaluating the Time Factor

The most overlooked factor in planning offer strategy is time. Usually an advertiser must make some type of advertising or premium investment (such as a loss-leader sale) to attract a customer. We often refer to "buying" a customer, as it is not uncommon to deliberately lose money by selling an item for $10 which cost us $5, at a cost per order of $20. In this case we have "bought" a customer for $15—the order cost less the net income from the initial sale.

How fast we get back that $15 depends on what type of proposition we set up, the popularity of our products, and the effectiveness of our creative material. In other words, the same factors that go into planning customer acquisition strategy go into back-end strategy.

Many advertisers aim for a first-year break-even. That is, they want to recover their initial investment within twelve months of the initial solicitation. They then start pulling ahead and developing a satisfactory return on investment in the second, third, and subsequent years. Renewals, repeat purchases, list-rental income, trade-ups, and cross-sell projects (discussed in Chapter 18) bring in profits over a period of years. Sometimes the break-even point is not within the first year, but after two, three, or even four years.

This time factor accounts for the great profitability of magazines, mail-order catalogs, and club operations which have been in business for many years. They control the "mix" of old and new customers to produce a stable profit. Too many new customers in one year may bring the profit for that year down. To be a "hero" all one has to do is cut back on new-customer acquisition and let the profits from old customers overwhelm losses from the new ones.

A similar trick of the trade is the enactment of an unwarranted price increase. New customers come in at a higher price. Long-term models look good. But the balloon often bursts when customers who came in at an old, lower price are asked to renew at the new, higher one. Buyer resistance from old customers can set back any gains for a period of two or three years, until the mix of new customers, brought in at the higher price, catches up.

## Mathematical Models

All these approaches can be evaluated with the aid of mathematical models. While it can be done manually, fine companies like Kobak and PDC can do it on computer at very reasonable fees. These companies often work by placing a computer terminal in your office and, sometimes, in your agency. The basic data of your operation is programmed and entered, taking into account order cost, promotion expenses, conversion rates, renewal rates, cancellations, and bad debts. With magazines they add advertising space sales and newsstand circulation as well. At the touch of the right buttons, a model of the next few years can be printed out, showing profitability, cash flow, circulation or volume levels, and even production requirements. At any time, day or night, you can change an element of the model and see what happens.

For example, let's say you want to consider tightening an offer but you expect that cost per order will increase. You advise the model that you are changing conversion and payment expectations up 5 percent but you expect response rates to go down 10 percent. The entire business plan, utilizing these revised figures, is printed out in minutes. You can try out any scenario until you find the one that best suits your company's objectives and capabilities.

Whether you forecast the effects of offer changes manually or by computer, you will see that subtle changes will have the most profound—and sometimes most surprising—impact on your entire business. Any company which fails to think through offers and try new ones independently of what they do in the product, media, and creative areas is missing a bet. Any company which presumes that the best offer for one product line is automatically the best for every product line is going to be unnecessarily writing off some very good products. In the mysterious alchemy of direct marketing, the right offer is the indispensable catalyst that activates every other ingredient. It is the key ingredient in turning the paper we write our plans on into gold.

## MEDIA STRATEGY

In direct marketing, the medium is the market. We do not generally use lists or publications to reach predetermined market segments; each list or publication or broadcast audience is a market in itself.

Conventional advertisers pick out cities or market segments and plan schedules to build awareness within these target groups in the most efficient manner possible. Readership studies, audience profiles, and Simmons data are correlated with circulation figures in order to obtain a cost per page per target audience which might be 200 or 300 percent higher than a publication's cost per page per thousand circulation, depending on the need for selectivity.

In direct marketing, we usually don't care whether a new customer comes to us from one city or another or even in one month or another (except for circulation guarantees or fiscal year profitability goals). A customer is a customer is a customer. Since UPS or the U.S. Postal Service is our distribution system, we do not have to worry about proximity to retail outlets or distributor routes. Therefore our strategies are concerned not with markets but with media as markets. Since every medium is subject to precise testing and result measurement, we can determine the most effective medium objectively instead of subjectively.

## The Media Universe

Direct marketers often refer to a media "universe," meaning the maximum of known lists, publications, and other media that can be expected to be productive for a given product or service. The planning of strategy requires a full understanding and precise identification of the media universe for a given product.

With a new product, this universe is determined by logic alone. With one that has been tested, it is defined by previous testing and by grouping publications or lists into categories similar to those used previously.

No product has an unlimited universe, for no product appeals to everyone. A universe is limited in its width by the range of lists and publications available, in its depth by the intrinsic appeal of the product, the offer, and the creative strategy.

Consumer Reports presents a classic example. In 1977 and 1978 their universe consisted of about 10 million names on mailing lists and one national publication—TV Guide. A new creative approach enabled them to dramatically increase the number of publications that were profitable. At one point, over thirty magazines and dozens of newspapers were on their media list. Both radio and television became major media sources as well.

A media universe, like the planetary universe, contracts and expands. In fact, "expand the media universe" is the general strategic objective of many major new offer and creative tests.

For a large advertiser intent on maximizing its facilitaties and reputation, planning may begin with the availability of a media category which has not responded to otherwise successful propositions. Direct marketers will, for example, develop short-term offers for some media, special products for others, and different credit terms for still others. A magazine might try a short-term offer in an impulse medium such as package inserts. A book club might offer a preselected group of books instead of a choice in a television offer which requires phone response. A mail-order firm might require credit card payments or ask for additional information when advertising in a publication that has previously produced poor credit experience.

"Support" is another way of expanding a universe. Support will be fully discussed in Chapter 7, Broadcast Media. Broadcast is the most common support medium, but not the only one.

## Core Lists and Publications

In direct marketing, media and list-buying strategies are not as concerned with numbers as they are with relevance. If you are selling fishing reels, a small list of known buyers of fishing equipment is worth more than ten times that circulation consisting of demographically selected prospects—i.e., males, 35 and up, nonurban. A list of people who have bought such products through the mails is worth more than a list of patrons of local sporting-goods shops.

Magazine audiences are selected the same way. A publication directed at fishing enthusiasts is likely to do well for the fishing-reel proposition. If the bulk of its readers are "direct-mail-sold," they are more likely to respond than readers of a publication who bought it primarily through newsstand circulation.

Interestingly, this is the opposite criterion from that used by packaged-goods advertisers, who generally prefer newsstand readers. Such readers go out to buy their purchases in retail stores and so are more likely to buy a retail-distributed product.

Lists of relevant buyers of related products, or other lists composed of the most logical or previously most productive prospects, are called core lists. Similar publications are called core publications. These core media are usually the most productive for any product or service.

## Pilot Testing

In a typical media schedule, lists and publications are assembled into categories related to the potential markets for a product or service. Such categories might include, for a female-oriented product, "Women's Homemaking," "Women's Career," Women's Lifestyle" (such as Cosmopolitan or Viva), and "Women's Special Interests." In mailing lists it might include "Subscribers to Women's Magazines," "Cosmetics Plan Expires," and "Book Club Members."

These categories are assembled according to the logical relationships affecting the particular product being sold. If the product is particularly costly, price range might be more relevant than product type in assembling a list universe.

If you were selling a power saw, a media universe might include "Mail-Order Tool Buyers," "Mechanics-Type Magazine Subscribers," and "Home Repair Catalog Inquirers." Usually advertisers would devote the bulk of their media plan to repeat insertions in lists or proven publications. Test advertisements or mailings would be scheduled in new lists or publications within the same category. Other tests would be dedicated to probing related categories not previously tested.

The objective here is to limit downside risk. We want to test the new categories without committing so much of our budget that the new categories, if unsuccessful, would offset the profitability of the rollouts and test extensions.

## Risk Limitation

It is important to limit the number of untested variables. What is being tested—the X factor—is the category of publication. This is, therefore, not the place to also test untried space units, new formats, or new creative strategy.

If your control ads have worked with a full page, small space is not the way to test a new category. In space the way to minimize risk is, usually, to use a publication in the proper category which has small circulation but has been proved for other direct marketers. If you must use a larger-circulation, more costly magazine, then look into regional editions. Providing you are not penalized with a "back-of-the-book" position, a regional insertion should be projectable (with some geographic adjustments if run in a particularly poor or effective part of the country) to indicate what the cost per order would be on a national basis. It is important to adjust your cost figures to reflect the difference between the higher regional rate and the national rate.

Mailing lists are much more flexible, as it is less costly to test each new list. However, the principles are the same. The lists tested should be proven ones within each category. The type of lists should be comparable. For instance, don't use "hot-line" names if the bulk of the lists are year-old names. When analyzing results, adjust test printing costs for what the mailings would have cost on a large-quantity rollout basis.

Testing will be more fully explored in Chapter 10. For now, it is only necessary to understand how a media program is put together—a very different process than that used by general advertisers.

## CPM, OPM, and CPO

When planning a media program for your proposition, don't fall into the trap of presuming that cheap is good. A low CPM (cost per thousand circulation) is no bargain if the list or publication doesn't pull in buyers. The question to ask is cost per thousand what? If the publication is subscription-originated, without using a sweepstakes, with a high renewal rate, and with relevant editorial matter, the chances are that it will be very productive providing the cost hasn't been set too high.

That's where OPM (orders per thousand) comes in. OPM is an index of how many orders (or inquiries or donations or subscriptions) were produced by using the same mailing or advertisement in a given publication. This is the index of responsiveness.

The CPM and OPM figures together are combined by one basic and overriding index: cost per order. The CPO figure is the basic, but not final, index of the relationship between responsiveness and cost.

## Other Considerations

A media strategy must consider all the above factors and build a logical testing plan which reflects the acceptable degree of risk as compared with the need to exploit a productive campaign as quickly as possible. Time is a major aspect of strategy.

One must consider turnaround time—how long it will take to get the results from one effort and whether you can then act fast enough to exploit the next peak season.

Response formats are an important factor in publication advertising. Does your proposition need a bind-in card to facilitate a quick, impulsive response? That limits your options somewhat. Does it need an envelope to facilitate payment? That knocks out more than three-fourths of your potential magazine circulation.

Visibility is important. If you are testing a new product, use direct mail outside your competitor's home base. It is less likely to be noted and they have no way to determine how big your test is.

Competition is another factor. You don't want to be in the same issue with a direct competitor and, often, not even in the issue immediately following, unless you have a much more powerful offer. Mailing lists are usually rented on a protected basis, meaning that no competitor can use the same list in the same thirty-day period.

You must consider what type of space unit is needed to present the creative story. If you are offering a choice of fifty books or magazines or records, you'll obviously need a larger unit than if you have a simple story.

A media strategy usually must combine caution in testing with aggressive risk taking in exploiting a success before competition "rips it off." Your media strategy must be uniquely tailored to your own product, your market, and current availabilities.

## CREATIVE STRATEGY

No aspect of direct marketing is more discussed than the creative side. This is the glamor part of the industry. This is what makes direct marketing an art as well as a science. However, for purposes of planning strategy, the creative approach—meaning the copy, layout, and either media unit or direct-mail format—is the last consideration, not because it is the least important but because it is the most flexible.

### The Need for Flexibility

The crafts of the writer and the artist demand versatility. It is no trick to produce every advertisement in one distinctive style, no matter how effective it might be. This kind of creativity is like an actor who plays himself or herself no matter what the role calls for, or the artist who paints the same subject in the same style over and over again. True genius requires the ability, and more important, the willingness, to adapt one's skills to fulfill any objective.

A creative department must be able to solve the creative requirements of any product, any offer, any media. It must be able to adjust style and vocabulary to any market segment; to adjust length to any size advertisement or letter; to write headlines and conceive illustrations that attract any desired audience.

## Nonverbal Communication

In the old days, when copy was the undisputed king of all advertising, a copywriter's task was clear-cut. Benefits were offered, dramatized, guaranteed. Attributes were proclaimed, proved, glorified. Selling propositions were stated, restated, and stated again—in visual presentations crowded with copy and liberally sprinkled with exclamation points.

Today the creative process is infinitely more subtle. The old-fashioned "hard-sell" approaches can still work in the short run, but they are shortsighted. Hard-sell copy picks up core markets—the easy prospects—but fails to build credibility or positive attitudes for the future. Today we not only look at the 2 to 5 percent of people who respond to a mailing piece, or the much smaller percentage of magazine audiences who respond to an advertisement. We must consider that our advertisement is being seen and noted by a much larger percentage of readers or viewers who, though not responding now, are prospects for future promotions by the same company. Today, just as general or "awareness" advertisers find situations where it is desirable for them to ask for the order with direct marketing techniques, we in direct marketing must consider the awareness and attitude-building factors in our response-seeking advertising.

International Silver's American Archives division happened to run a half-page list-building advertisement offering a condiment set for $4.99 in the same issue as a full-page advertisement picturing an elegant silverware service available at retail outlets. Starch reports for the issue indicated that the half-page mail-order advertisement had higher "Noted" and "Read Most" scores than the full-page advertisement intended solely for those purposes.

Ninety percent of communication is nonverbal, and "first impressions" are based not only on what you say but how you say it. An analogy I have used frequently is that copy style is like tone of voice whereas layout is like body language. Both communicate credibility or lack of it, and say as much about your company and its product as anything in your basic copy platform.

When planning a creative strategy, you must consider not only those who respond today but those who may respond in the future.

## CHOOSING A STRATEGY

In preparing a strategy, it is important to consider all four of the basic elements and to make definite, clear-cut decisions. Many of the choices will be difficult, but they must be made. I have found that the worst strategy, in any of these four areas, is the so-called "safe" strategy. If you are competing against General Motors it is folly to produce cars just like theirs at the same kinds of prices. Somewhere you have to take a chance and be different in as many respects as possible. Volkswagen did not achieve its great marketing success in the United States by being the same as everyone else.

There are many ways to help make these decisions. A written plan is essential. Research can help. And when the alternatives are boiled down to a few significant fundamentals, you can always use split-run testing to let the consumer tell you the best way to go or which market is the best to aim for.

If you are introducing a new product, saving an old one, or looking for a major breakthrough or market expansion, then you must be willing to rethink all four main strategic areas.

Your strategy will, of course, be influenced by your corporate personality. In World War II British Field Marshall Bernard Montgomery was known for his cautious, logical, carefully planned campaigns, based on the best intelligence available. America's General George Patton had a radically different style. His armored divisions would plunge ahead as fast as his tanks could go, seizing bridges, bypassing pockets of resistance, exploiting opportunities as they occurred. I won't venture here into opinions about which approach was the best then, or which would be best for your company now. But I will urge you to consider not only the directions you want to go in, but how fast or how cautiously you want to proceed once you set your direction.

Strategy requires the selection of goals, the defining of objectives. Tactics are the methods of achieving those goals. Planning is the conscious decision-making process that must precede any act of creation.

## CHAPTER THREE

# THE MARKETING PLAN

You now know the many alternatives involved in planning for a successful combination of product, offer, media, and creative strategy. Now, let's see what it takes to work out the best combination of strategies for your particular business.

## WHY IS A WRITTEN PLAN IMPORTANT?

It is a common practice for individual entrepreneurs to carry their marketing plan "under their hats." Often such a business thrives at its inception, as a lucky choice of product is snapped up by a waiting but limited "core" market. I have met several such successful entrepreneurs. Most of them are now in different businesses. They might have remained successful and grown "rich beyond the dreams of avarice" if they had employed written marketing plans.

Only a written plan makes it possible to obtain useful professional advice from coworkers and consultants. Without it, any expert is only reacting to the scanty information and predigested prejudices of his or her client.

Only a written plan brings everyone involved into the total strategy. The greatest media buyers or copywriters cannot do their best work in a vacuum.

Most important, only a written plan enables its preparer to fully think through every essential element which affects decision making—not only the big decisions, but countless day-to-day implementation choices which are vital to the final result.

## HOW SHOULD A PLAN BE PREPARED?

In the following sections I'll describe the "what" of a marketing plan. But "who" should write it, and "how" should it be assembled?

Ideally the head planner should be a marketing strategist, no matter what the title, and regardless of whether the planner is the boss, a product manager, or an outside advertising executive or consultant. One person has to be responsible for assembling and coordinating the preparation of the plan, but a team is needed to write it.

Each component of the overall plan should be prepared by a specialist in the area being covered, after an overall briefing and with frequent consultation with others on the marketing planning team.

Much of the detailed assembly of information can be delegated. The decision making cannot be delegated, nor should one person make the decisions unilaterally. Just as it is impossible for most writers to be objective about their own writing, so it is with marketers. Planning must be an open, honest dialogue among professionals whose integrity precludes pleasing a client or the boss with "lip service."

The head planner who is too directive will not get honest opinions. But if the planner is not directive enough, the plan will be aimless or contradictory. An honest exchange is needed. As William Wrigley said, "When two people in a business agree, one of them is unnecessary."

At our advertising agency, marketing plans are written for (and with) clients by account supervisors who are assisted by team members recruited from the creative and media departments, as well as their own staffs of account executives and assistants. In almost every case, outside research, list-buying, and fulfillment specialists are brought in, as well as other staff members or consultants with experience in the specific product field.

At various stages, it is submitted for my approval and our client's. If the process of writing the plan is correct, the plan is right. To the extent anyone takes shortcuts, the plan may be off target. It is worth the time and care to write a plan from the ground up.

The format of the plan is not critical. It can be written in simple outline form, with elements listed, or in an exhaustive narrative format with charts, tables, and exhibits. I have endorsed excellent plans written in a few pages, as well as one for a major national corporation which required 300 pages to summarize a year of research and planning.

Once written, the plan is relatively simple to update from year to year. Segments should be in a loose-leaf binder to facilitate adding new competitive information, new marketing data, and the hard facts of research and testing.

The basic elements of a marketing plan are, in the broadest sense: (1) product description, (2) marketing environment, (3) objective, and (4) strategies.

I.
## PRODUCT DESCRIPTION

The first section of a marketing plan is ordinarily a statement describing the product or service. It sounds a great deal simpler than it is.

The obvious first level of product description is the physical. What exactly are we offering? What is the size, the material, the function? How does it work? Although you might attach samples or photographs of the product, it helps to verbalize each and every attribute, including the color, the feel, the weight, even the sound it makes when it operates. (Ogilvy's famous Rolls Royce ad about its loudest sound being the electric clock might never have been written if someone hadn't first verbalized this attribute.)

Then there is the scientific level. How was the product made? How does it work electronically, chemically, or mechanically? Exactly what does happen inside, where the customer can't see but the writer can describe? Is the product made of a scarce material? Tell about it. Is there hand craftsmanship, or exacting precision tooling, or rigorous quality control? How long will it last? How long will it operate? How is it better than competition?

The third level, and in some ways the most important, is the emotional. What real or imagined need does the product fill? What will it do for the buyer? How might it change the customer's self-image or image to others? What benefit might it add to the customer's life—comfort, convenience, spare time, confidence, prestige, wealth, romance, beauty?

There are intangibles to be considered also. Is there a guarantee or service contract? Is the company well known? Is there an endorser or other authority? How is it delivered? (Fast delivery is an asset, for instance.)

Perhaps the best way to dramatize the levels of product description is to share with you an exercise that is sometimes used to train copywriters. The assignment: Describe a pencil.

### The Classic Product-Description Example

"It's yellow. There's black lead inside a wooden tube. There's a point on one end and an eraser on another." How many writers would stop right there?

Another might go on to describe how the pencil lead is made, what kind of wood it's encased in, or the country of origin of the rubber eraser. Still another writer might describe the manufacturing process, tell how long the manufacturer has been in business, or dramatize the many types of pencils offered by the company.

Better. But then, along comes the scientific writer, who has painstakingly used up a pencil to find out how many times it can be sharpened, how long it will hold a fine point, and—after hours of work—exactly how many words can be written with a single pencil.

Much better. But we can still do more, by trying out competing pencils, and determining whether ours "lasts 20 percent longer." That's a lot of work, surely, but nobody has ever said advertising is easy.

Even with all this, we've only just begun, for advertising is an art as well as a science, and our prospective customer is emotional, as well as logical. Imagine for a moment the psychic satisfactions: the security of being able to erase errors easily, the peace of mind in knowing that the pencil will not leak or stain or smear.

Further, imagine what using a pencil says about our customers. They will impress their friends with practicality, conservatism, frugality, and the courage to admit that they can make mistakes.

Let's carry the copywriting art one step further and, adding a sense of poetry, suggest that such a pencil as ours might enable its possessor to script a beautiful play, describe a brilliant business idea, or compose a touching love sonnet. Thus our buyer might achieve—by buying a pencil—fame, riches, and romance. Want to buy a pencil?

## How Is the Product Perceived?

The product description section is also the place to include relevant research on how your product is presently perceived by various components of your customer base. Both quantitative and evaluative research, such as focus panel sessions, should be summarized here. The purpose is not to summarize the research itself, but the conclusions the marketing plan preparer is drawing from this research.

What consumers think your product is can be just as important as what it really is. Perception is an aspect of reality. If the product is perceived as better than it really is, you may face returns and complaints unless you either change the product or reveal the shortcomings in your promotions. The well-known Joe Sugarman, founder of JS&A, often includes a sentence in his long-copy advertisements pointing out features that a product is lacking, then adding a line making light of it, such as "Of course, at this price you can't expect everything."

If your product is perceived as worse than it really is, or if there are fears that have to be overcome, a good writer can make sure that every concern is overcome in the copy presentation. The knowledge that these perceptions exist and the decision to deal with them must be elements of the marketing plan.

## II.
## MARKETING ENVIRONMENT

The marketing environment is the cumulative total of every factor that might influence the development of marketing strategy. As you'll see, it includes competition, media, distribution, government regulations, and economic trends.

### Competition

The competitive situation is a constant and continuing factor in your own strategy development. Every legitimate information-gathering process should be used and all information recorded. In my own experience, recording information is a greater challenge than getting it in the first place. I have frequently seen clients or staff members vainly trying to recall which magazine they saw a competitor's ad in, or failing to find a tear sheet or news clipping.

That's why the marketing plan should summarize the current knowledge about competitors' activity and draw conclusions about what appear to be trends, their strategies, their offers, and their copy platforms.

The first step is obvious. Start collecting every tear sheet and direct-mail sample that falls into your possession from any source. Ask media representatives for back issues containing competitive advertising. Ask your staff, your suppliers, and even your friends and relatives to send you anything they get in the mail in the particular product category.

When you get the samples, "break them down." Spell out, in writing, what audience they seem to be aimed at and how they are positioned against your product. Reconstruct their copy platform, by listing each and every point used in the copy of each competitor. If there are many competitors, set up a chart and compare who is saying what.

Look for the evolution of the appeals, offers, and copy claims. This is often very revealing, especially if you don't make the common mistake of underestimating your competition. The safest course is to presume that if point A has been added or point B left out since last year, it may have been done because of research, testing, or results which would apply just as well to your product.

Go to a newsstand and look at several copies of a magazine. You might see ads being split-run. You may spot key numbers indicating subtle copy changes you might otherwise fail to notice.

There's no way to learn what lists are being used, except when your own orders are being blocked because of a mailing conflict, but whatever information you do get should be recorded.

It's easier to learn about a competitor's activity in print and broadcast. Publishers' Information Bureau is a service designed primarily for publications selling advertising space. Their publication, *PIB*, lists the exact magazine schedules of virtually every advertiser who uses national magazines. Most advertising agencies subscribe to this as well. If yours doesn't, a friendly space representative from a magazine you use might help you. Broadcast schedules are listed in *Broadcast Advertising Report*, a similar publication.

By all means order the product, subscribe to the service, or join the club or plan offered by your competitor. In fact, join it several times, through different people in your office, and see how they respond to different actions on your part, such as prompt payment, slow payment, and no payment. Keep track of every date you receive or send something. While you're at it, send in similar dummy memberships for your own product or service. You may be surprised, particularly if your fulfillment is being done at another location or by an outside service.

On top of this, use all the conventional research techniques for business information. Get annual reports. Look up articles that may have appeared in the business press or newspapers. Read books, articles, and interviews written by your competitors or their agencies.

It's amazing what people sometimes "drop" in the course of seminars or business meetings. In the direct marketing field, a unique and valuable source of information is the enormous library of cassettes available from the principal industry publication, *Direct Marketing* (Garden City, New York). Order and listen to every cassette of talks by your competitors and by their advertising agencies. Also, of course, subscribe to both this magazine and *Friday Report* (also located in Garden City, New York) to find out what's happening in the direct marketing field.

The Direct Mail Marketing Association (DMMA) (New York City) is a gold mine of valuable information about the industry in general, and well worth the membership fee. One of their lesser-known services is a library of contest entries which can be visited in New York or purchased on microfiche. These entries are in bound books which include statements of objectives, mailing plans, samples, and results. If your competitor has submitted campaigns for awards, this can be a surprisingly beneficial reference source.

Another valuable source is the list-rental cards issued by your competitors. Often they indicate the number of customers brought in within a given period of time, the size of their total list, the average sale, the source of the names, and a demographic breakdown. Some allowances are necessary because they are presenting the data in the most favorable light to rent their lists, but some valuable data can still be deduced.

## The Media Universe

This marketing environment section is also the place to record the media universe—a speculative, highly optimistic compilation of the mailing lists and publications that might be relevant to your particular proposition.

Standard Rate and Data Service (SRDS) publishes various catalogs of publications and mailing lists. Go through these SRDS publications and begin to assemble, in categories, the various media that you might someday use. Indicate the basic costs for print media, presuming a standard space unit. Also indicate what you might spend on mailing lists, figuring the list cost and an estimated package cost. You may find that some media categories are so large that it's worthwhile to tailor strategies to find ways of making those categories work.

Certainly the information on what media your competition has used, and repeated, should be taken into account here, as well as the media they tried and evidently discontinued. There's no dishonor in learning from someone else's experience. Don't make the mistake, however, of presuming that a medium has been "used up" by a competitor. Skandinavisk Press has followed Betty Crocker into markets all over the world and found that a quality product, the right offer, and good creative strategy can make even the most saturated media pay off. Don't let the competition scare you off. Go where the action is; just find ways to be better than they are.

Time is a factor in media selection, as well as cost. While you are formulating your marketing plan is the time to estimate how long it will take to get into the various media categories with your ad or mailing—and how long it will take to read the results. "Turn-around time" will be important, as you will always want to read the results of one mailing or ad in time to make decisions on the next.

To summarize, you should, for each media listed, estimate cost for a standard unit, record apparent competitive experience, indicate the lead time in preparing an ad or mailing, and finally, indicate how fast you should be able to read results.

## Distribution

Even if fulfillment is a different department in your corporate structure, information about how the product is going to be distributed should be available as part of the marketing plan.

Here's where we "weigh in" our product and calculate exactly what it will cost to get it to the customer. If the postal system is your distributor, then the weight will tell you the cost at current postal rates. But there's more to it. Here again, send out test packages to friends across the country, and determine how long it will take and what condition the packages arrive in.

Investigate UPS distribution, even if it raises your cost somewhat. And look into alternatives, such as private delivery systems, catalog outlets, and pickup stations through your own or third-party outlets.

In some parts of the world, where postal systems have seriously deteriorated, it is customary to require customers to pick up their products (and make payment) at specific locations. Everything else is done through the mail, up to the point of notifying the customer that a package is ready or a payment is due. The only exception is that neither money nor merchandise is ever entrusted to the hands of the postal worker. At least Europe and the United States do not have this problem.

All distribution options should be considered, including postal insurance, certified mail, and the possible role of the telephone. CODs should be studied, if they are an option being considered, and costs calculated not only for postal charges but for handling and refusals.

Distribution includes packaging—often an area that can influence not only safe arrival, but also acceptance and continued sales. Distribution also includes the efficiencies of the fulfillment system itself: shipping labels, invoices, and provision for returns. All these elements should be noted and recorded in this section of the marketing plan.

## Government Regulations

Another area that must not be taken for granted is government regulations. If your company is a member of the DMMA, your manual will include summaries of pertinent regulations affecting the direct marketing industry in general. The FTC is very concerned about being sure companies spell out commitments, make honest representations, and use words such as "free" or "guaranteed" within precise and accurate limits. These are matters of law which change rapidly, and so I deliberately did not attempt to record them here in a book whose use is intended to span a number of years.

Your lawyer should obtain all relevant regulations from the Federal Trade Commission and from any other regulatory bodies which affect your business. If you're selling on credit, you'll be governed by Regulation Z of the Treasury Department. If you're in the financial investment industry, the Securities and Exchange Commission (SEC) will have much power over what you can say.

It is extremely important to consult the dos and don'ts published by the Better Business Bureau and by the DMMA Committee on Ethical Standards. The U.S. Postal Service, of course, has life-and-death power over companies, for it can stop delivery for any business engaging in unethical practices. If this isn't enough, let me point out that mail fraud is a federal offense. Just look at the FBI "wanted" posters in any post office.

Any strategies you devise will have to be within the confines of government regulations, industry ethical standards, and simple fairness to the customer. Define those limits now, before you've worked out your strategies, so you won't risk going over the line in the letter or spirit of your marketing proposition.

## Economic Trends

Are there economic trends that affect your business, or other trends? Here's the place to spell them out, in narrative, figures, and charts. If your product is sensitive to the economy as a whole, include pertinent economic indicators such as the Consumer Confidence Index, the Dow-Jones Index, and Housing Starts. These are the tables I most often find relevant to mail-order predictions.

Is your product related to a specific hobby, interest, or fashion? Then spell out available information, and speculate about the life cycle of the interest. Usually, the best time to ride in on a new fad is near the beginning. Once it becomes so popular that general magazines and Sunday supplements deal with it, the fad is usually almost over.

CBS brought out *Popular Gardening Indoors* just in time for indoor gardening to be yesterday's enthusiasm. International Silver introduced a CB (citizens-band) necklace and a gorilla pendant just in time for CB radio to fade and for the movie *King Kong* to have come and gone.

Unless your product can be issued on a timely basis, with fast turn-around media, save your money. You can make a fortune if you're one of the first to offer mood rings or collectibles, but you can lose your shirt if you're one of the last.

## III.
## THE MARKET

In direct marketing, we deal with "media universes," "target markets," or "audiences." We try to quantify these markets by age, education, and income; by zip code and census tract; by demographics and psychographics. But this is just the beginning of defining a market.

### Your Customer Is Not a Statistic

All market data can tell us is who our audience has been, based on previously selected product, offer, and media choices. It shouldn't be a surprise, but often is, that years of positioning a product toward older people, for example, eventually results in a research study showing that older people have been buying the product. It doesn't show what could have been, or still could be, if the total market potential were considered and if different creative efforts were aimed at alternate lists or media.

The first lesson to remember is this: Your customer is not a statistic. The buyer is not packaged in neat demographic profiles waiting for your message to arrive. There is only one common denominator that you can count on: interest in your product.

Interest can be developed, with the help of the right creative strategy, among people who compose virtually any statistical unit; but their interest is individual. What they do have in common is that they are *accessible at an economic cost through a common list or medium.*

An average age or income is useless unless it is related to the accessibility of those characteristics through various media. Too narrow a definition, such as "people who like hummingbirds," is also useless, unless there are substantial numbers of publications or lists directed to such people. Inaccessible statistical profiles are academic exercises.

This is a fundamental difference between a typical packaged-goods marketing plan and a direct marketing plan. Although statistical data is a keystone of packaged goods marketing, it is usually idle curiosity for direct marketers. Available data should be included, of course, if it is known, but it should be precisely identified. The typical market study included in such a plan should not be called "Market for Our Product" when, in literal truth, it should be titled "Statistical Survey of Questionnaire Respondents by People Who Bought Our Product as a Result of Previous Creative Efforts in Previous Media."

## The Lifestyle Approach

Logical reasoning will take you further than statistics in a direct marketing plan, and should be the starting place for the market section of a plan.

Begin with the product—its function, its purpose, its benefits. Who needs it? Who might be persuaded to need it? What absolute limitations are there? What essential prerequisites exist with regard to where the prospective customer is in his or her life, career, or avocation?

One exercise used by some major agencies is the "ideal-prospect" scenario. Imagine an ideal buyer. Make up a story about where he lives, what he does, how his job is going, how he's getting along with his wife, what his ambitions are, what he does in his spare time. Does he have a beer after work at the local pub? Does he build craft projects in his workshop on Sunday afternoons? What are his political preferences? What's his favorite movie, TV show, or magazine?

Just letting your imagination go wild in this way will help you, and the copywriter, zero in on what's really important and relevant about the market characteristics for your particular product. In case the point hasn't been made yet, what's the chance that the defining characteristics of the ideal buyer are age, income, and education? Not very likely.

There are common denominators, and they should be taken into account, but these common denominators are, usually, pure speculation until after a full range of list and media and positioning tests have been run.

### Common Media Characteristics

Reading media and list results is an art form in itself. If media universes are assembled somewhat arbitrarily at the beginning of a marketing program, they require reshaping by the hard cold reality of result figures.

After adjustments are made for media format, competition, regionalization, date, and position (in print media), a clear picture starts coming into focus. Usually some list or publication categories are clear winners, others are clear losers, and some are marginal.

The art comes in looking beneath the obvious and searching out what winners and losers have in common. Often it is not the obvious publication title or list name, but characteristics beneath the surface. Barry Mark of Doubleday, one of the most astute analysts and strategic planners in the field, insists on reviewing editorial content of magazines, media sources of mailing lists, and the entire competitive environment before drawing conclusions about what works and what doesn't.

Common sense goes a long way in identifying abstractions about successful media. Direct marketing results are always subject to logical analysis and interpretation.

Beware of the glaring exception to logic. Every time I have been stumped by a seeming contradiction to an otherwise clear pattern, the villain has not been logic but the reliability of available testing procedures. I've found that a magazine which was supposedly a split run sent most of ad A to newsstand dealers and ad B to subscribers. Though the print run was 50-50, a large percentage of the newsstand copies were returned unsold, thus depressing that side of the split.

In mailing lists, I've seen list suppliers—accidentally or intentionally—provide the most recent names rather than a typical cross section, thus making a marginal list look better than it really is. If something looks odd, don't act on the test results until the contradiction can be explained, or until a retest can be arranged under tight supervision.

All test results, and the abstractions drawn from them, should be summarized in the marketing plan. The market portion of the plan should include all relevant data, and all speculation, about who the ideal buyer seems to be and what possible buyer profiles might be added. It should include the history, the interpretation, and a statement of objectives for the future. And it should all be spelled out in writing.

**IV.**
**THE STRATEGIES**

Strategic planning is possible only when the product, the market, and the environment have been clearly identified. There is always more than one possible strategy. Alternatives should be developed and then reviewed according to preestablished criteria, and the best strategy should be selected. Often it is possible to test more than one fundamental strategy. The consumer's response will determine which is the most effective. The selection of strategies depends on several considerations: budget, timing, market conditions, and the inherent personality of the corporation making the decision.

One important determinant is a substatement of the objective: the goal. Both should have been listed in the preliminary material. The objective is usually general, such as "Expand media universe," "Open youth market for product," or "Lower cost per order." The goal, however, is specific: "Expand media universe by $500,000" or "Reduce cost per order by 25 percent." The more ambitious the goal, the more daring a strategy can be justified, and the greater the downside risk merited. If the goal is modest, strategies should avoid daring new concepts or bold offers and stick to logical progressions from existing control ads and packages.

### Comprehensive Testing

Let's say, for example, that we are dealing with an existing and reasonably successful proposition that is ready to break into the big time. Our survey of the product, the environment, and the possible markets have identified several areas for possible improvement. Maybe the proposition has worked well in women's magazines in full-page black-and-white ads. The goal is to double sales for the next year.

We would probably list a variety of possible strategies, including a price change, a premium addition, the use of credit cards, new creative approaches to widen the appeal of the product, and some new media and formats. The trick is to test all these approaches in a short period of time to permit a massive rollout in a later prime season.

The first step would be to list and evaluate all of the possible strategies for testing. The key factor would be the likelihood, in the judgment of the people who have to make the decision, that the change would result in the desired improvement. At this point, some possibilities would be ruled out in favor of others. Perhaps some form of predictive research (discussed in Chapter 9) would be used to help select those variations most likely to involve the potential customer.

## Grid Testing

It is likely that, no matter how tight the decision-making process has been, there will be a variety of possibilities to be tested. At this point, a testing strategy should be established.

The testing strategy, generally, isolates test ads or mailings into three categories: media or list tests, simple offer or format tests, and basic creative concepts.

One creative concept, generally the most logical and proven approach, is selected—by past results or arbitrarily—to be the control ad or mailing piece. This control is the vehicle for testing one medium or list against another. Where possible, all offer and format variations are also tested within one or two media: a core list and an expansion probe list, for example. The basic control might run in ten or twenty purely media test cells. The variations might take two of the media and test four or five variations against each, and then the basic creative format testing might be tried. The result would form a grid like the one shown in Table 3-1.

In this case, lists A and B and publication L are pure split runs of the basic package against the new creative variation. Lists C and D and publication M are basically the same as the control except for the variation indicated. Lists E, F, G, and H and publication N are to give us readings of the new media.

One consideration in publication testing is the normal inability of publications to match split-run advertisements to bind-in cards. In this

TABLE 3-1

| | Mailing lists (10,000 names in each cell) | | | | | | | Publications | | |
|---|---|---|---|---|---|---|---|---|---|---|
| | A | B | C | D | E | F | G | H | L | M | N |
| Basic control | * | * | * | * | * | * | * | * | * | * | * |
| New concept | * | * | | | | | | | * | | |
| Offer variation | | | * | * | | | | | | * | |
| Price test A | | | * | * | | | | | | * | |
| Price test B | | | * | * | | | | | | * | |
| Add lift letter | | | * | * | | | | | | | |

test, the L publication might be a split run of a full-page advertisement, while the M publication is the control ad with a bound-in card. All variation testing is confined to the card itself. In this way an infinite number of variations on the card can be accommodated simply by preprinting and premixing the cards before supplying them to the publication.

With simple adjustments and interpolation, it is possible to calculate what any of the ads or mailings would have done in any of the lists or publications.

## The Product Viability Test

One frequent consideration is the need to prepare a test strategy for a brand-new product or concept. Under such circumstances budgets are generally more limited, and the need for more information is less demanding. What is needed here is not an estimate of the best copy or the ultimate media universe, but a quick answer to the query "Does this product have any life at all?"

In such a case the test program is confined to larger samples of four or five very logical media, usually in direct mail. Only lists which represent categories large enough to sustain the business by themselves are tested. It will do the client no good to learn that a small core list is highly successful if there is no place to go from there—if the list category cannot supply the needed volume.

It is vital to determine at what price the product can sell. Usually the creative concepts are limited to very basic approaches, perhaps a general discount certificate package and a sweepstakes approach. Within each basic list, both approaches are tested as well as some basic product or price concept.

One purpose of the test is to produce a large enough customer base to get a reading on back-end performance. If a 5 percent response is expected and a 10,000-customer base is considered minimal to get a valid reading, then this initial mailing would be 200,000 pieces. This might be spread over five lists of 40,000 names, each to be sent four different mailing packages, thus giving us 20 test cells of 10,000 names each.

If the test is going to be a "one-shot," now-or-never decision on a new product, then it is also necessary to test any basic alternate media. For instance, if previous competitors have used package inserts and broadcast to a larger extent than direct mail, then the control approach should be adapted for these media and the tests run simultaneously. While direct mail may be the best medium for testing variations, it is still necessary to include basic media categories which could produce a viable business in themselves. Both the broadcast and package insert markets are, independently of direct mail or publications, large enough markets to support enormous businesses.

## V.
## ECONOMIC CONSIDERATIONS

A marketing plan should stand by itself as a source document and as a working plan. Therefore the plan should include, perhaps in an appendix, all pertinent economic considerations.

All information on costs, allowable margins and past results should be recorded. I also find it helpful to do a simple chart showing the response needed to produce a break-even cost per order at different mailing package costs.

Such a chart is helpful to creative people, who occasionally have to be reminded that the more expensive the package, the larger the response must be just to break even. Sometimes, in a product with a limited market and a large unit sale, the reverse is true, and the same chart will justify spending the money on a high-penetration, multiple-part mailing program.

Another piece of information that should be included here is a statistical validity indicator. A simple table is called for, listing the minimum size sample that is needed to produce a 90 or 95 percent confidence level at various response rates and allowable error margins. This requirement will be covered in Chapter 10, Testing, in more detail.

All the economic assumptions should be detailed here as well. What are the basic costs for product and premium? What return, trade-up and collection assumptions are being made? What overall budgets are established and what profit and loss (P&L) is it expected to produce?

The availability of such economic considerations in the marketing plan makes it possible for everyone concerned in promotion to look at the overall picture. It might, for example, show that a modest back-end improvement in units sold per customer or in renewal rate might have more significant profit improvement than lowering the cost per order. This data would lead to appropriate strategies for back-end improvement.

## VI.
## IMPLEMENTATION

Now, at last, it's time to get down to action. The background has been clarified and the strategies chosen. All that remains is to implement the plan. This section of the marketing plan includes all the basics which, in less professional approaches, are likely to compose the entire plan. This section is not so much a logical, step-by-step, decision-making process as it is a blueprint for action.

## The Introduction

This section should start off with a simple statement of the purpose of the plan. If the purpose is a viability test, a universe probe, a search for breakthrough creative concepts, or a rollout of a proven approach, this is the point to say it, in so many words. Then set up the plan to do it.

Media schedules, timetables, and budgets are basics which should be included here in appropriate detail. If testing grids or keying systems are called for, include them. If product changes or revisions in the fulfillment system are necessary, this is the place to lay them out.

Further, with each step, this is the place for detailing exactly who is responsible for what—who will do it, who will approve it, and by what date.

## Creative and Offer Concepts

Creative and offer concepts should be separately outlined. They should approximate the same form as an advertising agency work assignment, containing everything copywriters need to start their work. For each offer and creative concept, there should be a simple statement of the objective and goal for that one version, and an explanation of the strategy chosen for this specific ad or mailing piece.

Any revisions in the basic copy platform should also be mentioned next to each creative concept, as well as any special economic considerations, cost limitations, timing problems, etc. Sensitivities—legal matters, styling considerations, and subjective client preferences—should also be noted, so that all concerned can agree on what they are.

A positioning statement should also be included, with special emphasis on any ways advertisements are expected to differ from previously established positioning. This positioning statement should refer specifically to copy style, level, and tone, as well as to graphic style and image. Often this type of detail is not part of the basic marketing plan but is added later in the form of individual strategy statements for specific advertisements, mailings, and broadcast commercials.

The final step is a statement of result targets—how the program as a whole is expected to affect the profit and loss sheet. This is the place to temper the goals and make allowances for the probability that not every new format is going to beat the control.

## Budgeting

The budget should be prepared on the "task method," meaning that recommended cost estimates should be provided for achieving the objectives stated in the plan. Possible budget shortcuts and abridgments should be included if it is possible that the task-based budget is in excess of management's expectations. However, the task-based budget should be stated, even if it is unlikely that the necessary monies will be appropriated.

Where there are alternatives, their effect should be clearly expressed. If a smaller test budget will require a second stage of extension testing and a season's delay in the rollout, it should be graphically depicted along with the risks and economic effect of such a delay.

If it is not yet possible to forecast results from recommended mailings or media insertions, a range of possible CPOs should be shown, with the economic effect of each worked out and shown.

It is a mistake to end a marketing plan with the cost of implementing the plan, for many executives scan the last pages first. The final wrap-up should restate the sales and profit expectations, to keep the final focus on what is to be gained, not on what investment is required.

## Timetable

The wrap-up is the schedule. How long will everything take? What are the key decision points? What answers are needed, at what dates, in order to move everything along? Who is expected to do what?

More marketing plans are killed by inaction than by deliberate rejection. If you want your marketing plan to have the approval of your management, then make it very clear who is expected to approve what by when, so that at least the blame will be clear if someone sits on your proposal.

Perhaps a note about overtime factors would be in order. Often as little as a one-week delay in the early stages of a program will result in adding 50 percent or more to production costs incurred for overtime and rush services. If you have the figures available, they make a dramatic footnote for the timetable section of a marketing plan.

\*    \*    \*

Whether your plan is a complete statement of every element and alternative, as outlined here, or a simple design for the next mailing, put it in writing, and add data as you go along. The simplest plan is better than none, providing it is a written document that everyone can agree upon in advance and look back upon later.

## THE MARKETING PLAN FORMAT

In the previous pages of this chapter, I have outlined what kind of information should go into a marketing plan, and explained why the background data is as important as the strategy itself—both in creating the strategy and in reviewing it.

Now, let me summarize the format of the plan in more conventional marketing language.

*Title*

Marketing Plan for PERIOD for XYZ COMPANY Product Line. Prepared by NAME. DATE.

*Introduction*

How and why the plan was prepared, at whose request, and with whose endorsement. The qualifications or point of view of the preparers. The process, if relevant. The data and briefings that were or were not available for inclusion in the plan.

*Product Description*

Physical description

Scientific data

Emotional data

Benefits

Present positioning

Possible variations

*Marketing Environment*

Competitive situation summarized

Competitive media utilization

Competitive copy point breakdown

Miscellaneous competitive information

Media availabilities

Media cost, timing, and testing factors

Distribution—cost, timing, effectiveness

Government regulations—dos and don'ts

Economic trends; fads and fashions

Known problems and opportunities

*Market Potential*

The media universe

Profile of prospective customer

Product, offer, or positioning changes needed to appeal to other likely market segments

Results of previous list and media tests

Available demographic or psychographic data

*Strategic Planning*

Objectives of marketing program

Goals: quantified objectives, within time frame

Strategic alternatives

Criteria for selection

Recommended prioritized strategies

*Implementation*

Basic campaign outline

Test grid, if applicable

Media or list recommendation

Offer or creative concept

Budgets

Timetables

Result targets

The writing style for a marketing plan should be as simple as possible. The object is to impress the boss or client with the soundness of the thinking, not with the number of words. An outline form, with bulleted points and telegraphic copy style, is very appropriate, as long as it is clear.

Loose-leaf binders are recommended as well, to permit updating, revision, and addition during the course of a campaign. New data, new ideas, and result reports should all be added to the basic marketing plan during the course of the year, so that the plan is not just a historical record of an original intention but a living, working document of a campaign in progress.


## EVALUATING A MARKETING PLAN

For many executives, particularly in larger businesses, the preparation of a marketing plan is left to an advertising agency, a consultant, or staff members. The real problem for such executives—one that is just as important as writing the plan—is its evaluation.

If the plan has been prepared as outlined here, or in any similar format, it is a self-contained document that includes all relevant background material. The evaluator should be able to take one binder on an airplane or to a poolside lounge chair and read through the plan without reference to outside data.

The first thing evaluators should note is whether all pertinent considerations have been taken into account. If they have, the other pieces should logically fall into place. The evaluators should then ask whether the plan looks ahead. Does it provide marketing and creative direction for the future?

If the plan is for a presently successful campaign, are there provisions for testing ads and mailing pieces for future seasons when the present control will eventually wear out?

The budget will be important, of course, especially as it fits into overall corporate budgets. However, it should be considered only in terms of downside risk. Even the unsuccessful portions of a campaign produce some orders.

Is the plan legal? Does it follow the letter as well as the spirit of the law? Sending the copy platform to lawyers for review now instead of waiting for finished copy may be helpful.

Most important, is it unique? Does it present fresh, original creative thinking? Or could it be your competitor's plan by just changing the product name? You should expect some new approaches and some challenging ideas, as well as obvious marketing logic.

After the plan has been completely reviewed, one final test remains. In some ways, this may be the most important. Call in the people who wrote the plan and approved it. Look them in the eye, and ask them this one question: "Do you really think this plan will be successful?" The people who wrote the plan should really believe in it. You have a right to expect them to believe in it and to have enthusiasm about it. If they don't, start looking for new people.

CHAPTER FOUR

# THE PROPOSITION

A much-talked-about series of TV commericals of the 1970s featured a retail store owner with a construction hat and a heavy Brooklyn accent answering a question from typical customers: "So Jerry, what's da story?" "Da story" in that case was heavily discounted loss leaders on home appliances, and the result was an outstanding retail success. In direct marketing, "da story" is no less important, except that we tend to call it "the proposition" or "the offer."

Except for changing the product itself, nothing can make as big a difference as a change in the basic proposition. There are exceptions, but this is still the rule. Changes in the price, the terms, the guarantee, the way the product is combined or segmented—all of these will show up faster in result tabulations than most changes in copy and layout. The rule: *The substance of the offer outweighs the form of its presentation.*

## PRICE OFFERS

Does price make a difference? You bet it does. We'll start with the simplest category: the types of propositions available to a business selling a single product or service directly to the consumer in a "one-step" approach which asks for the order on the initial contact.

### Hidden Price

If the product is new, has a new feature, or answers a real need, you may want to deemphasize price until after the benefits have been fully presented. In such a case the price may be buried in the last paragraphs of the main copy. LaSalle Extension University concealed its tuition under a flap on the enrollment form. Geo magazine used a sealed envelope to be sure the price was the last and not the first information communicated.

## Featured Price

"Giant wall map, only $1" can be a powerhouse offer. If the price is the news, then scream it out at the beginning, right in the headline of an ad, the superscription of a letter, or superimposed on a television commercial. Most general advertising can't feature price because of Robinson-Patman restrictions, but direct marketers—like retailers—can and should.

## Comparative Price

Did the product sell for more at an earlier time? Is it the equivalent of a retail product that sells for a higher price? Would your book club titles cost more in "publishers' original editions"? Then by all means let the consumer in on this fact. The more striking the comparison, the more prominent it should be. But make sure it's legitimate and make sure you can prove the claim. Government and industry self-regulators are frowning on stretched comparisons justified by a few token sales at a higher price.

## Introductory Price

If you're offering a new product or service, the introductory offer is a great way to get attention and encourage immediate action.

## Discount Offers

If the offer can be expressed in terms of a comparison with a previous price, a retail price, a newsstand price, etc., then consider expressing that price in percentages or fractions. "Half-price" will usually do better than "Originally $10, now $5."

## Savings Feature

Consider featuring the savings in a price comparison rather than the low price. "Save $11" can be a stronger lead than "Now only $19" if price is the feature.

**Split-run price test on film envelopes expresses similar offer in dramatically different ways.**   (Source: Fotomat Corporation, Wilton, Connecticut.)

## CREDIT PROPOSITIONS

The availability of credit in its many forms can be as valuable a sales stimulus as a product enhancement or price reduction. Credit is costly, not only in "no-pay" sales but in interest costs if you carry your own receivables, or in financing discounts or credit card charges if you don't. Don't forget paperwork processing, billing, postage, and the cost of added returns.

Whether or not you offer credit is a fundamental decision that will be affected by the value of your product and the nature of your market. In some product-market combinations, it is not an option; other propositions will not work at all without it. With still others it may be a marginal consideration requiring extensive testing of whether the front-end lift is worth the back-end cost and complications.

### Free Trial Offer

Credit combined with a guarantee is the strongest credit proposition available. Its powerful benefit is the implication that you have such confidence in your product that you are willing to let the consumer use, read, examine, or try it before deciding whether to return or pay for it.

As returns will be significant, it is necessary to consider the cost of the product before trying this offer. If you do try it, then make the most of it by using "Free trial," "Send no money now," and "Use it for 10 days at our risk." If you plan to refurbish and reship returned merchandise, use the term "Free examination." There are legal problems in shipping "tried" merchandise.

### Conditional Free Trial

Essentially the same as the previous offer, the conditional free trial has one vital difference: The offer is subject to acceptance. A clause in the coupon can state this reservation. The marketer can then apply a variety of credit-screening techniques. Here are some examples.

- *Internal match.* Previous bad-pay customers or those who have already taken advantage of a "one-time only" or "one-to-a-family" offer can be eliminated by computer matching, usually by address.

- *External match.* Prospective customers can be checked against lists maintained by credit compilers such as TRW, Hooper-Holmes, and local credit bureaus.

- *Zip code characteristics.* The credit history of previous respondents from the specific postal area or like postal areas, defined in clusters, can be checked. This data is sometimes tempered by media source data leading to accepting quality publication or list respondents despite the overall record of the zip code.

- *Individual indicators.* Substantial credit differences can result from the types of information provided in the coupon. Although a full credit application—inquiring about employment and banking histories—might be theoretically desirable, it would depress response rate severely. The bulk of bad-pay prospects can often be spotted simply by asking for additional information, such as a phone number or a signature.

A separate question is what to do with customers whose orders are rejected. The orders should be acknowledged in the interest of courtesy if not profitability. I prefer honest replies, advising the customers that previous history prevents shipping their orders on credit and asking for prepayment, credit card payment, or additional information.

## Installment Sales

With a large enough unit sale, or where a credit relationship already exists, installment sales can often be profitable. The most common application of installment sales is a simple three- or four-part billing, usually used with a trial offer. Installment sales can also require that a deposit be paid or that the order be charged to a credit card, a charge card, or a new or existing charge account.

Care should be taken to comply with applicable Regulation Z requirements regarding full disclosure of interest terms. Even if there is no interest but you give a premium or discount for cash, there is a presumption that the installment payments include interest and a disclosure statement is still required. I personally negotiated a waiver for magazine offers, but other products may still be subject to this requirement.

## Charge Credit Cards

One of the greatest changes in the entire direct marketing industry is the ability to utilize charge and credit cards in direct marketing. As of 1980, American Express, Diners Club, Carte Blanche, Visa, Mastercard, and other credit cards totaled an astounding 57 million cards in the United States. While this may not represent a majority of the population, it probably represents the majority of consumer spending power. The utilization of credit cards can be expanded still further for some purposes, by arranging for acceptance of oil company, telephone, hotel, airline, and other specific-purpose cards.

Obviously cards will be most effective when used with offers that are appropriate in both market and price range, but there is another important consideration—the response element itself. A credit card offer requires space for number, expiration dates, and the name of the card used. The customer may get frustrated trying to squeeze the fifteen digits into a tiny space. A solution for print-media advertisers is to offer a conventional coupon asking for check with order, and then combine credit cards with phone ordering, as in "Credit card holders may order by phone. Call 800. . . ."

Broadcast offers an excellent opportunity to "trade up" a send-no-money proposition to a credit card order by having the incoming phone operator offer a premium for such an order.

## COD Sales

Cash-on-delivery sales are a form of credit only in that the consumer is able to order without enclosing payment in advance. In this method, either the U.S. Postal Service or United Parcel delivers the package and collects payment. It is one alternative that some marketers use when selling impulse products to people who do not have an appropriate credit card, especially when orders are taken by telephone.

COD requires extensive and costly paperwork. More important, refusals tend to be excessive for several reasons. Sometimes the customer doesn't have the cash available when the order is delivered. At other times, no one is home and it is too much trouble to arrange redelivery or to pick the package up at the post office. More often, the impulse to buy has simply cooled off, particularly as the COD collection process usually presents an anonymous package with no presell, a request for immediate payment, and unexpectedly high postal charges. Even when all COD costs are passed on to the customer, the refusal rate is generally so high that most advertisers in the United States avoid this technique.

## Easy or Preapproved Credit

An age-old retail technique that is very effective for offers to demographic groups that traditionally have trouble getting credit at all is offering easy or preapproved credit. A more recent innovation is the utilization of preapproved credit offers to lists which have been computer prechecked by TRW and local credit bureaus. Such mailings have been overused by banks offering checkbook loans, with the cliché opening "You have already been approved for $2000 in credit."

An application of this technique which has still not been fully exploited is the offer of preapproved credit to prospective mail-order buyers of jewelry, collectibles, or similar high-ticket items.

## Low Down Payment

If you're offering credit or installment sales, a low down payment can be as important as a low price, particularly if it reflects an advantage to the consumer. One correspondence school, to add news value to its series of enrollment mailings, announced lower down payments at three different points in the series.

## Low Interest

As an alternative to a price reduction, a dramatic low interest rate can get attention and stimulate sales. If you are competing with department stores which carry their accounts at 12 or 18 percent interest, an offer of an installment item at 6 percent, for instance, might have greater appeal than an equivalent price reduction.

## GUARANTEES

In direct marketing, a guarantee of some sort is not an option. It is a necessity. We are asking consumers to trust us by placing orders and, sometimes, sending payment for items they have never actually handled. It is necessary to return that trust by standing behind the product and services we offer with the most liberal return or refund policies possible.

I believe it is not at all coincidental that the companies with the most generous policies seem to be consistently among the most successful.

Norm Thompson, a very professional catalog house featuring classic casual wear, makes this guarantee:

"YOU BE THE JUDGE℠"

When we say "You be the Judge℠", we mean just that! Every product you purchase from Norm Thompson must live up to YOUR expectations, not ours. If at any time a product fails to satisfy you, return it to us, postage prepaid, and we'll either replace the item, or refund your money in full, whichever you wish.

This is definitely not a 2-week guarantee. It's good for the normal life of the product. (You being the judge of what that normal life should be.) We'll stand behind everything we sell to the fullest extent . . . no ifs, ands, or buts.

Sears Roebuck & Company puts the same idea in more succinct language with this guarantee statement which they credit as a major contribution to Sears success:

SATISFACTION GUARANTEED OR
YOUR MONEY BACK.

### Unconditional Guarantee

The two statements quoted above are examples of unconditional guarantees. While some small minority of customers may abuse such a guarantee by returning obviously used and abused merchandise or by falsely claiming dissatisfaction, the guarantor is usually more than compensated by good will and added sales from the majority of its customers.

### Conditional Guarantees

If you must limit your guarantee, the law requires that you label limitations precisely. Some types of guarantees are:

- *Time limit.* The most common type of guarantee, the time limit is stated in a sentence such as "If not satisfied return within ten days for full refund."

- *Repair or replacement only.* This form of guarantee includes an assurance that the item will work, rather than that the customer will be satisfied with it.

- *Liability limit.* Where a customer might claim secondary damages, the guarantee takes the form of a limit on liability—for example, "Liability limited to replacement of film," as used by a film processor.

- *Usage condition.* For some products, including fragile items, the guarantee may be written in a form such as "When used according to instructions" or "Providing it has not been dropped or abused."

## Double Guarantee

While most financial officers will welcome this idea like an attack of eczema, its "lift" power is so substantial as to merit its consideration with most products offered to civilized audiences. "Double your money back" will be abused, but by so few people that you still come out ahead. Like any other offer, it must be tested first.

## Competitive Guarantee

If you believe your product is as good as any competitor's, try this: Offer to send them your competitor's product as a replacement or free, if they don't like yours. One variation of this was tried by *Newsweek:* "Try *Newsweek* for 3 weeks without cost. If you don't like it, we'll ask *Time* to send you their best offer."

## Dramatized Guarantee

You may not want to offer to eat your hat or roll a peanut down the street with your nose if your customer isn't satisfied, but there are more appropriate ways to dramatize your guarantee. For example, "Bring this coupon to our store; if our prices are not the best in town, we'll even pay for the gas you used to drive here."

## "Keeper" Offer

When you're offering a premium, you can dramatize your confidence in your product by telling buyers they can keep the premium, even if they elect to return the purchase.

## Trial Subscription

If your product is sold serially, as are magazine subscriptions and continuity programs, you can give buyers the right to cancel either "at any time" or after examining the first shipment.

## Value Protection Guarantee

Some organizations selling collectibles or investments have advertised a willingness to buy back the item at some future time if it has lost value or has not achieved a specific gain in value. Such offers should only be made by large, well-financed companies who can make good this claim. Anyone making this kind of guarantee recklessly may run into a personal charge of mail fraud. The "limited liability" protection of a corporation won't help anyone charged with fraud.

## CONTINUITY PROGRAMS

The most successful mail-order proposition generally involves the establishment of a customer relationship which extends beyond the initial transaction. Continuity is one of the most critical, and unfortunately most neglected, aspects of the direct marketing profitability equation.

A retailer can establish good customer relationships by providing the service, quality, and environment to support the simple invitation "Come again." A catalog marketer accomplishes repeat sales in the same manner, except that the marketer's image is created by the catalog and service facility.

In many direct marketing propositions, particularly those developed expressly to develop continuity, the product is segmented or serialized to facilitate continuity programs. Anyone promoting via direct marketing should look for ways to combine, break apart, or add to existing products in order to make possible some type of continuity offer.

### Subscription

The word "subscription" is most frequently associated with magazines. This form of publishing is not only the most common user of this proposition; it is also one of the most sophisticated. However, the technique can be applied to other products as well.

Basically a magazine is an information or entertainment product sold in installments over a period of time. The most common time period is a year, but most publications are willing to discount rates for longer subscriptions—two, three, or more years.

Shorter subscriptions are often used as introductory offers, to make a trial inexpensive for a new customer. One innovation is the variable-term introductory subscription, which permits a new subscriber to choose any number of copies at a low price per copy.

Subscription selling is probably the longest customer relationship in direct marketing. As a general rule, 50 to 60 percent of first-year subscribers will renew for a second term; 70 to 90 percent of renewed subscribers will then renew again for subsequent terms—on to infinity. This renewal rate is influenced by the professionalism of the renewal series but, obviously, depends to a much greater extent on the reader's satisfaction with the magazine's editorial content.

Subscription propositions are sometimes offered to the consumer as "item-a-month" or "pay-as-you-go" plans, where the total price is committed but payable in monthly installments.

The defining characteristics of subscription sales are that the term is fixed and the service is billable at its inception. The same technique can be applied to a library of books, a set of collectibles, or even linens or tablewear.

## Automatic Shipment Plans

Unlike subscription selling, the automatic shipment plan seeks not one sales transaction but a series of individual ones.

The customer is asked to participate in a sales plan which provides for the sale of individual units at a predetermined interval—a month, or six weeks, or even annually. The most famous examples are the various libraries or sets of books offered by Time-Life Books, Grolier, Greystone, Hearst, and other major publishers.

In this type of continuity plan the customer agrees to buy a unit per interval. The units could be books in an encyclopedia set, cosmetic samples, components of a teaching plan for children, parts of a desk set or matched luggage, annual diaries or yearbooks, or issues in a collectible series. A unit could even be a service such as furnace inspection or window cleaning. The possibilities are infinite.

A typical automatic shipment offer, from a Grolier ad, follows:

> I am enclosing (check) (money order) for one dollar. Please enroll my child as a trial member and send me the four Bright and Early Beginner Books shown here plus the free book, In A People's House and the free booklet. If not delighted, I may keep the free book and booklet and return the four books within 14 days and my one dollar will be fully refunded. Otherwise approximately every 4 weeks hereafter, please send 2 other Beginner Books at only $2.75 each (instead of the retail price of $3.95) plus delivery. I may cancel at any time.

Note that in this case, the customer is offered the first volumes at a substantially reduced price, with return privileges, and may cancel at any time. The free book and booklet is a "keeper"—a premium which may be retained whether or not the customer decides to continue with the program. Sometimes such coupons provide for accelerated shipments at a later date or the right to "load up" subsequent books once credit is established.

The essential principle is that the customer authorizes automatic shipments and agrees to pay for them or return them. Usually, the customer does not have the right to return a single shipment without canceling the program—a pressure to induce acceptance of the entire series.

The psychology of this principle is that inertia—one of the most powerful elements of human psychology—is converted from a negative buying force to a positive one. Customers no longer have to say "yes" to buy the product; instead, they must say "no" to not buy it. This is the underlying psychological principle of all continuity plans.

### Club Plans

Though some firms use the word "club" rather liberally to describe any type of continuity plan and even non-continuity membership plans, the technical usage of the term should be reserved for the club concept as originated by Book-of-the-Month Club.

The defining characteristic of the club concept is its addition of choice to the basic automatic shipment plan. In a conventional club, automatic shipment is not limited to one preselected product each interval, but a choice is provided—usually in a club bulletin or advance announcement. The club "member" is free to accept a recommended item (often called a selection of the month), choose no item that month, or select an alternative.

When you consider that there is generally not only advertising expense but also some type of inducement offered to persuade people to join such a club, some serious concerns must come to mind.

1. How do you get the members to respond to each announcement bulletin?

2. What is to keep members from always declining purchases?

These are very valid concerns, and they led to some ingenious solutions which now apply to many types of direct marketing propositions: (1) the negative option, (2) the positive option, (3) the commitment, and (4) the membership plan.

### Negative Option

Basically, the negative option refers to the customer's need to say "no" in order to keep a preselected shipment from arriving in the mailbox. It applies to continuity programs in which the definition of "no" can be "Pass this shipment only," "Cancel entirely," or a choice between the two types of refusal. In clubs, the negative applies only to the selection. It provides the leverage to overcome inertia and force a reply. The consequence of not replying in a reasonable time period is that the selection will arrive and have to be paid for or returned. Some writers have successfully presented this feature as a positive benefit, stressing its convenience and its contribution to self-discipline.

The purpose of negative option is emphatically not to ship unwanted merchandise, for that is to no one's benefit; it would result only in returns, no-pays, and cancellations. The objective is simply to overcome inertia and force a conscious, considered decision. Usually about 25 percent of club members will take the selection (if it is a desirable one) and another 25 to 50 percent will take an alternate. The figures vary widely from business to business and interval to interval, depending on the attractiveness of the product offered and the soundness of the presentation. Negative option can force a decision; it can't force a sale.

Note that I used the word "interval" rather than month or year. The original Book-of-the-Month Club concept has evolved into plans in which many book or record clubs offer fifteen, sixteen, or even eighteen different announcements per year. The innovative BookAmerica, conceived by Doubleday president Robin Smith, goes the other way; there are only four selections a year, but a purchase each quarter is required.

### Positive Option

To make this presentation complete, we must touch on the antithesis of negative option. Theoretically, a continuity plan might be constructed wherein the customer is sent preannouncements but need not reply. A commitment, discussed below, might apply and so the customer would have to buy something eventually. In principle, such a plan should have a higher initial response because it would attract people who don't want to be bothered with making a decision or sending a notice every month. In principle, the commitment should offset the loss-of-inertia reversal.

It's a nice theory, except for one problem: I have never seen it work. The closest thing to it being used on a large scale is the membership plan, discussed below.

### Commitments

A commitment is simply an obligation for the customer to buy a minimum number of units or a minimum dollar volume within a limited time period—traditionally a year or two. There have been clubs which tried to eliminate the commitment, just as some have tried to operate without negative option. While it might be possible to dispense with one, there is no way to do without both.

Why would customers accept the obligation of a commitment? For the same reason that they accept the negative option: an attractive inducement. A back-end obligation like "I agree to buy as few as four more tapes at regular club prices in the next three years" is the price the customer pays for a front-end reward like "seven tapes for 1 cent."

Note that the customer is as sensitive to the commitment as to the inducement. Large advertisers continuously test "three books for 98 cents" versus "four books for 10 cents" and similar offers. They also test whether the commitment on a given offer should be one item more or less, and whether the obligation should be fulfilled within one year, two years, an unlimited time period, or (as in BookAmerica) once every three months.

## Membership Plans

Most continuity plans offer the customer what Capitol Record Club called "Savings in Advance." Membership plans flip this concept around and, incredibly, offer the customer a pay-now, save-later option.

The way these usually work is that members are invited to join a plan, sometimes called a club, which will give them some immediate benefits or the right to future benefits in return for a fee paid at the onset. To the extent the fee is paid at the beginning, it is more like a subscription than any other type of continuity plan. There are several basic applications of this scheme, each of them with variations which may or may not be interchangeable.

*Discount Buying Service*   The customer is asked to pay a fee in advance. Membership then entitles the customer to buy from a catalog at presumably bargain prices not available to the public. Usually, the company counts on the membership fee to cover or at least defray advertising costs. The profit depends on the markup from subsequent sales.

*Catalog Subscription*   If a catalog has intrinsic value in itself, it can be the heart of a membership plan. Armstrong, the linoleum company, produces a "magalog"—a term coined by Maxwell Sroge Associates— which combines editorial content and product offers. The magalog creates interest in home decorating and provides the ideal medium for Armstrong offers of decorating items. The same approach has been tested in the gardening field, with O. M. Scott's *The Greenery*, and it has applications in many other fields.

*Customized Service*   Another membership approach is based on providing some type of personal service to the customer in return for the membership fee, leading into offers of related products. One dramatic example is the Sarah Coventry Personal Beauty Plan, which invites the customer to send $25, a photograph, and the answers to a questionnaire.

The photograph is enlarged and sent back with a professional face makeover, using real cosmetics on an acetate sheet. The colors recommended are available only in their own line of cosmetics. Modern computer technology makes it possible to produce personalized horoscopes, career plans, investment analyses, life expectancy predictions, and diet plans—all as part of related mail-order programs.

Most of the current membership plans have everything built in except some type of automatic shipment element. The real challenge for such companies is to find a way to combine the up-front appeal of their present propositions with the back-end profitability of some of the other continuity plans outlined here.

## TWO-STEP PROPOSITIONS

So far we have dealt with direct marketing offers which "ask for the order" at the initial contact with the prospect. This next section will deal with two-step propositions—leads, inquiries, qualifiers, listbuilders, samplers—which do not ask for the order until a later contact.

In general, most of the propositions we will cover now are ways of locating prospective customers for a more intensive, and necessarily more expensive, sales effort than would be affordable on a large-scale basis to marginal prospects. The later follow-up might be through a personal visit by a salesperson, an invitation to a showroom or sales event, a telephone call, or more direct mail—elaborate conversion packages and a series of selling letters.

This two-step technique is used by many of the largest corporations in the direct marketing business. Encyclopedia publishers offer a free booklet, which is delivered by a salesperson. Insurance companies offer a book of maps or a gardening guide, which is also brought by a sales representative.

Financial institutions offer free information or a prospectus, which is followed by an intensive series of mailings and telephone calls. Real estate developers invite prospects to make an appointment to see model homes; the sales effort begins at the site. Or a pipe tobacco may be offered in a 25-cent trial size, just to introduce the product, with the hope that its flavor will sell itself.

### Free Information

The simplest and most logical two-step plan is the offer of free information. It can be strengthened by further definition, such as "Send for free information about the amazing new XYZ device, including pictures, diagrams, detailed operating instructions, and our pay-as-you-go installment purchase plan."

## Free Booklet

When your advertising is aimed at an earlier horizontal positioning stage (see Chapter 11), it is often effective to offer a booklet about the generic subject instead of about the specific topic. North American Coin & Currency, for instance, offers the "Gold Guide" instead of asking for an investment right off. The guide, of course, sells not only the generic advantages of precious metal investments, but also the particular services offered by its publisher.

## Free Planning Kit

A further way to build on preceding offers is to make up a more complex "kit" of everything the client may need to plan a vacation or diagnose a lawn problem, for example. For Marriott Hotels, I developed a series of meeting and convention planning kits for particular cities where Marriott had hotels. The idea was to produce very hard leads, instead of the usual contest entries or booklet requests. Offers of these guides would only appeal to sales managers or other executives who were seriously planning a major meeting in a particular city.

## Free Book on Related Subject

Lanier, for instance, offers a copy of a book called *Time Management* along with information about their dictating equipment. The subject sets the stage for saving time by dictating, and the book has a perceived value of $2.50 or so, comparable to what the public expects to pay for paperback books.

## Free Gift

Here's the classic insurance offer again. "Just send us your birthdate and we'll send you a free book of maps"—or a tool kit, gardening guide, or some other popular item. The thinking here is that everyone is supposedly a prospect for insurance, it is not capable of being presold, and all you want is to get the salesperson in any door.

## Free Survey

"Let us survey your telephone costs." "Let us check your roof for leaks." "Let us inspect your car's tires." All of these offer a genuine service which should appeal only to people who have a suspicion that they have something to gain from such a survey. Hence, the leads should be good ones and the service profitable to offer.

## Free Sample

If your product lends itself to sampling, and if it is really good, so good that it sells itself, then consider giving it away in small units. Tobacco companies have handed out samples of new cigarette brands. Soap companies have placed samples on doorknob hangers. Why not offer a free sample and send it along with an effective selling message by mail or salesperson?

## Free Catalog

Some companies just send their catalogs to every logical mailing list. Where the catalog is costly or the lists are marginal, a two-step offer is sometimes preferable. Space advertising is an excellent way to get fresh names for a catalog business, just by offering the catalog. These catalog inquiry names are often better than buyer names from other catalog companies.

## Nominal Cost

All the above propositions can not only be made on a "free" basis, but they can also be offered for a quarter, a dollar, or more. Even the slightest charge qualifies the inquiry and makes it worth following up.

On one extreme, Film Corporation of America offered "free film" for the cost of postage and handling. On the other, International Silver offered low-priced silver-plated tablewear. The latter might not seem like a two-step offer, but it is—for these sales were intended to get qualified names for the company's catalog business.

## List-Building Offers

Some merchandisers, instead of offering a catalog or other information in their promotions, go right ahead and sell some product which is an example of their line and which represents an unusual value. You'll find clothing catalog merchandisers advertising in the *Wall Street Journal*, for instance. Often, these ads don't produce a profit over the cost of goods and advertising, but they do produce a list of qualified buyers for the company's full line of products at a lower cost per name than a straight "free-catalog" offer.

## LEAD SELLING

In a lead selling system, two-step initial transactions are completed by a dealer, agent, or salesperson rather than the company's own direct mail.

### Lead Flow Considerations

In supporting a sales organization, it is often necessary to maintain a steady supply of leads for all members of the sales force, in all seasons. This introduces a new consideration into media planning, as it is often necessary to mail or advertise in seasons that might be comparatively unresponsive. It is more important to keep the conversion rate high in most cases than to maximize the cost-per-lead figures.

Often leads come in geographically in a manner that brings in more leads in some parts of the country—perhaps the West or rural areas. Other areas need supplemental programs, sometimes using regional publications or local compiled lists in order to keep the sales force content. At LaSalle we called this a "local support program."

Too many leads sent to one salesperson will be "burnt off." The salesperson will prejudge them, and pick and choose the ones his or her hunches (almost always wrong) say are the easiest to sell. Too few leads sent to other salespeople will cause them to quit their jobs because they are not making enough money.

There is a chicken-and-egg dilemma in terms of planning for lead selling. Do you regulate your lead supply to satisfy your sales force? Or do you distribute your sales territories and dealerships to reflect the lead flow? This is usually a matter to be resolved between the sales force manager and the direct marketing manager, preferably without bloodshed.

### Lead Freshness

One question which everyone agrees on is that leads must be followed up promptly. Every day that passes before a prospect is contacted by a salesperson will noticeably reduce the conversion rate (see the discussion of conversion in Chapter 18). In some cases, I have advised companies to set up systems for telexing or telecopying leads to sales offices, to avoid the delay of postal transmission.

If a company's computer system takes too much time to get leads processed, it is often advisable to bypass the computer initially and send a manual lead to the sales force. This lead can be optically scannable so that a copy can economically get on the computer for later follow-up.

### Lead Distribution

Usually a lead is supplied on some type of computer form. The forms should obtain as much information as possible to help the salesperson relate to the prospect. Not only name, address, title (if a business lead), and phone number should be included, but the date of lead, the compnay's Standard Industrial Classifications (SIC) code or business classification, and the exact nature of the inquiry. The salesperson should know what ad or mailing piece the prospect responded to, in what publication.

The lead recipient should have one copy for filing and another to be transmitted back to the computer center for tabulation. The report form should indicate the date of contact and initial disposition, to be tabulated into sales reports.

A lead should be supplied, in my opinion, with some type of expiration date. Perhaps the lead can be exclusive for a given period and then become nonexclusive, with other dealers or the company's own mail conversion effort cutting in after a deadline. My experience has proved that salespeople will convert more if they have only a limited time to call on the prospect.

The computer should be programmed so that lead distribution is not automatic. Whether you are dealing with salespeople or dealers, the transmission of additional leads should be contingent on the prompt reporting and effective handling of leads previously sent. The computer should automatically cut off lead flow if the open lead ratio is too high or if subsequent confirmation questionnaires indicate that reporting wasn't accurate. Cutting off lead flow should not be left to the discretion of the sales manager, who should concentrate on getting the lead recipient to shape up or ship out. Unassignable leads should be sent to a dealer or salesperson in an adjoining area or converted by mail order rather than sent to an uncooperative or ineffective destination.

## Lead Reports

Reports should indicate, to both local and headquarters sales managers, exactly how many leads have been distributed, how many are "open" or uncontacted, and how many have been sold. If possible, the dollar volume of the sales should be related to the dollar cost of the leads. Such reports should be cross-tabulated by type of product, type of prospect, salesperson, or dealer, and by the initial promotion codes— mailing lists, media, etc.

The frequency of these reports—weekly, monthly, or quarterly—depends on the ability of management to find time to read and study the results. I prefer to reduce the frequency of reports and really work with them rather than have them come out frequently only to be stacked on a window sill.

These reports are not historical curiosities. They are blueprints for action, and it is essential that management respond by changing advertisements, schedules, products, or salespeople as necessary.

## QUALITY OF LEADS AND INQUIRIES

The quality of leads can be fine-tuned like a high-fidelity set. As the volume of leads goes up, the quality goes down, and vice versa. The slightest change in the advertisement or mailing piece can produce significant changes in lead quality, and so can changes in the type of publication, station, or mailing list used.

We refer to the relative "hardness" and "softness" of leads. A hard lead is super-qualified, ready to buy. A soft lead may be someone sending for a free gift. Usually we are operating between the two extremes and adjusting the lead flow and quality to meet immediate needs in the marketplace and to satisfy the concerns of the sales organization.

It is very useful to know how to harden leads or soften them as required.

### Lead Hardeners

If dealers or salespeople complain about the quality of leads, here's how to "harden" them:

- *Mention price.* Indicate what the product will cost.

- *Mention sales call.* Say someone will call.

- *Tell more.* Reveal more information about the product, including any potential negatives.

- *Ask for more information.* Get the telephone number and the best hours to call. Find out how many employees the company has.

- *Charge something.* Even a token amount for a booklet or sample will smoke out the real deadbeats.

- *Require a stamp.* Don't use a business reply card or envelope. Let the prospects buy the stamps—maybe even supply their own envelopes.

- *Narrow the offer.* Make it very relevant to the product or service you are selling.

**Lead Softeners.**

If more leads are needed, here's how you can loosen up the lead quality and permit more leads to come in from the same promotion expenditures.

- *Tell less.* Leave something to curiosity.

- *Computerize the response coupon.* Fill in the names and addresses of the prospects. Give them less to do.

- *Add convenience.* Supply the stamp, the envelope, and maybe even a pencil.

- *Give more.* Add a gift or premium—maybe one that is valuable independently of the product offered.

- *Charge less.* Make it free, free, free.

- *Ask less.* The fewer questions the better.

- *Add a prize.* A sweepstakes is the ultimate quality softener.

Don't forget that the medium will also have a material effect on lead quality. The low-cost-per-lead publication or list may be composed of teenagers or others who send for everything. Study the source data and change mailing and media schedules to improve quality. Fine tooling the media is just as important as fine tooling the coupon copy.

## CONTESTS AND SWEEPSTAKES

One sure booster to the number of responses is to try a contest or sweepstakes. A prize of as little as $10,000 has been known to boost response rates between 30 and 50 percent. Larger prizes, selected creatively, have done even better.

If you use a contest, consult a contest management company like Ventura Associates or D. L. Blair to help you select prizes, set up rules, and administer the contest. The legal restrictions are very exacting, and an independent management and judging organization will be well worth the small cost.

The cost of the prizes has to be taken into account when planning the costs of mailing. The larger the mailing, the less significant the sweepstakes cost. A mailing of 10 million pieces with a $100,000 contest costs only an additional $10 per thousand pieces and therefore needs only a slight lift over a nonsweepstakes package to be profitable.

The problem is not in initial cost but in quality. The added lift of a sweepstakes package represents a large number of people who are forced into a yes or no decision on the product offered with the sweepstakes, or who mistakenly believe that saying "yes" will help their chances of winning.

Sweepstakes produce a noticeable deterioration in the quality of business produced, not just in the initial acceptance, conversion or payment, but all the way along the line. In magazines, the payment rate, the initial conversion rate, and subsequent renewal rates are all reduced. The only remedy is to keep offering more sweepstakes, on the backend as well as with future new offers. To managers faced with maintaining sales levels originally set with sweepstakes offers, sweepstakes seem like an addiction.

Lately, sweepstakes have been losing their novelty and have needed larger and more interesting prizes in order to remain effective. Some variations have artificially hyped response by concealing the "yes" alternative in deliberately confusing formats. This is another form of self-deception that will cost its user a great deal in back-end performance.

The purpose of a sweepstakes is to get readership and generate a yes or no decision on the product offer, usually a trial subscription. It is a strategic anomaly of sweepstakes that adding more product sell, which might be expected to increase response, usually depresses it. That's why you see so many sweepstakes offers that seem to feature the contest to the exclusion of the product.

## REFERRAL OFFERS

Get-a-friend (GAF) or member-get-member (MGM) propositions are useful for almost any type of product or service. Their effectiveness depends heavily on the genuine satisfaction the customer derives from the product or service. There is no way to "bribe" a customer into recommending a proposition that has not been pleasing. However, if an offer is genuinely good, GAFs are a way of accelerating the word-of-mouth publicity that would ordinarily take place anyway. Whatever they are called, these offers come in several different forms discussed below.

### Name Requests

Simple requests for names and addresses of people who would be interested in the proposition can be very fruitful in building a mailing list, particularly if you also request permission to mention the referrer's name in your initial letter. Such a request can be a simple printed notice on the back of a statement or an inexpensive buckslip (see Chapter 15). Most advertisers do not offer an incentive for such names in order to avoid lessening their quality.

## Pass-Alongs

In the pass-along technique a simple brochure describing the basic proposition is included in a product shipment, along with a request to either mail it or give it to a friend. The offer might include a customer number or a place for the friend's name and address so a thank-you gift can be sent if the pass-along generates an order.

## Sales Brochures

In this case, customers are asked to function practically as sales agents, showing the product they have received to a friend or neighbor and soliciting orders in return for a commission, prize, or merchandise credits. Some companies have used this technique very effectively, creating an unofficial army of part-time salespeople.

This approach is most effective when the original customers have reason to feel smart about the purchase (maybe because it is well-priced) and can feel they are doing friends a favor. The feeling of passing along a good thing is an essential ingredient even more critical than the value of the incentive.

I don't know of anyone who has successfully sent out mailings devoted only to MGM offers. In most cases they are successful only to the extent they enjoy a "free ride" as a catalog page or package insert.

\*     \*     \*

The proposition is the heart of any direct marketing effort, and requires concentrated creativity independent of the more glamorous tasks of designing interesting new headlines or colorful mail pieces. Unfortunately, many companies seem to restrict their outside creative sources to implementing existing offers. Why bring in agencies or consultants to write fresh headlines when their talent may have much greater impact creating fresh offers?

Offers can be any combination of the offers outlined here, or any others. There is no limit. It is precisely the new offer that will have been created while this book is on press or after it is published that will be the most exciting news in the industry. Its very freshness will help it be effective.

The search for offers requires constant monitoring not only of your competitor's propositions, but of what's going on in the whole field of direct marketing—in the United States and all over the world. It requires your best talent, your most courageous thinking, and your most daring testing.

## CHAPTER FIVE

# MAILING LISTS

Direct mail is the world's largest advertising medium, and mailing lists are the key to its success. It is an industry axiom that a poor mailing to a good list can be profitable, but that no mailing—no matter how well conceived—will work if sent to the wrong list.

Those who know how to use this medium—how to select from over a billion names on 50,000 different mailing lists—have in their hands the most powerful and profitable tool in the world of marketing.

## THE WIDE WORLD OF MAILING LISTS

There are four broad categories of lists: response lists, compiled lists, business lists, and house lists. We'll review them one at a time.

### Response Lists

Other than a company's own house lists, response lists are the workhorse of consumer direct mail. Sometimes called "buyers' lists," or "mail-order lists," they include every classification related to a consumer's previous response to a direct marketing offer.

The names can be those of buyers, subscribers, inquirers, donors, members, or depositors. They can be new customers, active ones, or former ones. They can and do represent every conceivable area of human interest.

All have two things in common: one, they have identified themselves, by their own choice, as people with a specific interest, and two, they have demonstrated that they are willing, when properly motivated, to respond to a direct marketing offer.

Many list compilers publish books showing the kinds of lists they have available, but the definitive reference guide is the Standard Rate & Data Service (SRDS) *Guide to Consumer Mailing Lists* (Skokie, Illinois). This book contains over 1000 pages of small-type data about every consumer list that is generally available, with more than 400 pages devoted to response lists. However, no directory or listing can be completely up to date. Your list broker is the best source for the latest costs, quantities, and other data, as well as for expert advice.

When using SRDS, it helps to be aware of the broad classifications. Each classification describes dozens of mailing lists offered by a wide variety of list owners.

| | | | |
|---|---|---|---|
| 502 | Almanacs & Directories | 552 | General |
| 506 | Art & Antiques | 553 | General Merchandise Mail Order Buyers |
| 508 | Automotive | | |
| 510 | Aviation | 554 | Gifts—Gift Buyers |
| 512 | Babies | 556 | Health |
| 514 | Boating & Yachting | 558 | Home & Family Services |
| 516 | Brides | | |
| 518 | Business Leaders | 559 | Horses, Riding & Breeding |
| 520 | Children's | | |
| 520A | Collectibles | 560 | Insurance Buyers |
| 521 | College & Alumni | 561 | Investors |
| 522 | Contributors (Philanthropic) | 562 | Labor—Trade Unions |
| | | 563 | Land Investors |
| 524 | Crafts, Hobbies & Models | 564 | Literature & Book Buyers |
| 525 | Credit Card Holders | 566 | Mechanics & Science |
| 526 | Dancing | 568 | Men's |
| 528 | Dogs & Pets | 572 | Military, Naval & Veterans |
| 530 | Dressmaking & Needlework | | |
| | | 578 | Music & Record Buyers |
| 532 | Education & Self Improvement | 584 | Occult, Astrological & Metaphysical |
| 536 | Epicurean & Specialty Foods | 586 | Occupant & Resident |
| | | 588 | Opportunity Seekers |
| 538 | Ethnic | 590 | Photography |
| 544 | Fashions | 592 | Political & Social Topics |
| 546 | Fishing & Hunting | | |
| 548 | Fraternal, Professional Groups, Service Clubs & Associations | 593 | Premium & Catalog Buyers |
| | | 594 | Professional |
| 549 | Game Buyers, Contest & Puzzle Participants | 596 | Religious & Denominational |
| 550 | Gardening (Home) | 598 | Senior Citizens |

| 600 | Society | 606 | Travel |
|-----|---------|-----|--------|
| 602 | Sports | 612 | Women's |
| 604 | Teenagers | | |

Each mailing list is further described, with detailed information about quantities, sources, and various segmentation possibilities. Here's a sample:

COLUMBIA HOUSE
Media Code 3 578 2660 1.00
Member D.M.M.A.
Participant D.M.M.A. Mail Preference Service
Columbia House, a Div of CBS Inc., 1211 Ave. of the Americas,
New York, N.Y. 10036

1. *Personnel*
   List Manager—Margie Longo
   Director List Marketing Service—Evelyn Deitz
   Broker and/or Authorized Agent
   All recognized brokers

2. *Description*
   Active and former members. All names are credit checked. 14% are under 18; 61% are between 18 and 34; 25% are over 35; 51% female. Zip Coded in numerical sequence 100%.

3. *List Source*
   Space ads and direct mail.

4. *Quantity and Rental Rates*
   Rec'd January, 1980.

| | Total number | Price per thousand |
|---|---|---|
| Record Club: | | |
| Active members | 1,326,316 | 37.50 |
| Former members | 273,046 | 35.00 |
| Cartridge Club: | | |
| Active members | 1,336,706 | 37.50 |
| Former members | 375,722 | 35.00 |
| Cassette Club: | | |
| Active members | 525,875 | 37.50 |
| Former members | 74,817 | 35.00 |

|  | Total number | Price per thousand |
|---|---|---|
| Reel-to-Reel Club: | | |
| Active members | 13,676 | 37.50 |
| Former members | 3,894 | 35.00 |
| *Listening Preferences* | | |
| Classical: | | |
| Active members | 81,866 | 37.50 |
| Former members | 17,418 | 35.00 |
| Popular/Broadway: | | |
| Active members | 781,437 | 37.50 |
| Former members | 227,216 | 35.00 |
| Jazz: | | |
| Active members | 73,514 | 37.50 |
| Former members | 13,574 | 35.00 |
| Country & Western: | | |
| Active members | 440,790 | 37.50 |
| Former members | 118,985 | 35.00 |
| Young Sounds: | | |
| Active members | 1,824,969 | 37.50 |
| Former members | 350,286 | 35.00 |

Selections: club, listening preference, no extra charge; sex, multi-buyers, hotline, year, SCF, state, ZIP Code, 2.50/M extra: key coding, 1.00/M extra.

Minimum order 5,000

6. *Method of Addressing*
   4 or 5-up Chesire labels.
   Magnetic tape available.

8. *Restrictions*
   Sample mailing piece required.

As you can see, this listing includes the owner of the list and the name of the list manager—a company which has been retained to manage and promote the list on a commission basis. The list manager is the source of specialized information and the clearinghouse for rental availabilities. However, the customer need not contact the manager. Instead, you should work with a list broker—a company specializing in recommending and coordinating list rentals for customers. Such companies usually have all the data you need in their own files, plus experience on how the list has worked for their other clients. They will contact the manager when and if it is necessary to do so.

These listings include the rental price per thousand names for each of several subcategories, plus surcharges for additional segmentation. Usually there are also notations on minimum test quantities and on requirements for advance approval.

Many advertisers find it convenient to assemble their own file of list cards, usually 8- by 5½-inch horizontal cards with this same basic data. List brokers usually provide such cards as backup for their recommendations.

### Compiled Consumer Lists

People not familiar with direct marketing often think of compiled lists first. These might be names and addresses drawn from the telephone book, automobile registrations, association memberships, directories, warranty card registrations, or any similar source. The defining characteristic—what dramatically differentiates compiled lists from response lists—is that there is no indication of previous willingness to subscribe, buy, donate, or otherwise respond by mail.

Such lists provide expanded coverage of market areas, including certain psychographic and demographic characteristics as well as large quantities of names in precise definitions not available in response lists.

There is a theory in direct marketing that people who have recently made one key decision in their lives, or a basic change of any type, are more likely than most to make other changes. Consequently, very successful lists have been established identifying new parents (BIRTHS— FAMILIES WITH CHILDREN: 170,000 new names per month), newlyweds (COUPLES—NEWLY MARRIED: 150,000 names per month), and recently moved families (NEW MOVERS: 650,000 to 800,000 names per month). This type of psychographic characteristic can be successful for a wide range of products and services. Obviously, children's products do well with new-parents lists; but so do cameras, correspondence schools, and self-help publications. Evidently, the new addition to the family adds a new sense of ambition and responsibility as well.

Automobile-owner lists, in those states where compiling them is still permitted, are an extremely valuable means of selecting prospects by lifestyles. Number of cars, type of car, model (station wagon or sports car, for instance), and age of car can all be significant.

### Business Lists

The area of business-to-business selling is very different from consumer selling. As with consumer marketing, prospects on a list of people who have already responded to something related are much more likely to accept your offer than prospects on any compiled list. Unfortunately for most business propositions, there simply are not enough such lists.

Financial propositions can sell to the substantial subscriber lists of *Wall Street Journal* and *Boardroom Reports* readers, as well as to smaller but very responsive lists such as Kephart Communication's *Personal Finance*. There are lists of buyers of business equipment, inquirers about business services, subscribers to trade publications, and attendees at trade conferences. Lists of this type are handled in exactly the same way as consumer response lists.

Whereas such response lists are the keystone of consumer direct-mail efforts, they are usually a secondary consideration in business selling. Here the primary list sources are so-called compiled lists— those prepared by Dun & Bradstreet, National Business Lists, and others. The basic selector of such lists is type of business.

Also called vertical lists, they reach all types of executives in all sizes of businesses within a specific industry. The narrower the category, the more precise you can make the message, the offer, and the product offering.

Originally, such lists were compiled from the Yellow Pages issued by telephone companies, with all the obvious limitations and inaccuracies such a list would include. A look at Yellow Pages directories will show you that many categories are inconsistent, repetitive, and hard to define.

SIC codes were added to such lists as an attempt to narrow these business definitions even further. These four-digit classifications are published under the supervision of the U.S. Government Office of Statistical Standards and called Standard Industrial Classifications.

The first digit of the four-digit code defines a broad business category:

| | |
|---|---|
| 01-09 | Agriculture |
| 10-14 | Mining |
| 15-17 | Contracting |
| 20-39 | Manufacturing |
| 40-47 | Transportation |
| 48-49 | Communication and Utilities |
| 50-51 | Wholesaling |
| 52-59 | Retailing |
| 60-65 | Finance |
| 70-95 | Services |

Within these broad areas, over 100 separate business categories have been identified and coded with very finely detailed differentiation.

Here's a small sample, selected from the "Services" section, category 7. It is the "Business Services" subcategory, number 73:

| SIC | List | Quantity |
|---|---|---|
| 731X | ADVERTISING | 21,000 |
| 7311 | Advertising agencies | 15,730 |
|  | • Rated $10,000 & over | 15,510 |
|  | • Rated $20,000 & over | 2,070 |
|  | Firms that are secondarily SIC 7311 | 1,740 |
| 7312 | Outdoor advertising services | 2,280 |
| 7313 | Radio, TV & publishers advertising reps | 5,960 |
| 7319 | Misc. advertising services | 460 |
| 732X | CREDIT REPORTING & COLLECTION | 7,000 |
| 7321 | Collection agencies | 5,680 |
| 733X | MAILING, REPRODUCTION, STENOGRAPHIC | 32,000 |
| 7331 | Direct mail advertising services | 6,040 |
| 7332 | Blueprinting & photocopying services | 4,810 |
| 7333 | Comml. photography, art & graphics studios | 26,120 |
| 7339 | Stenographic & reproduction services not classified elsewhere | 12,260 |
| 734X | SERVICES TO BUILDINGS | 26,500 |
| 7341 | Window cleaning services | 5,190 |
| 7342 | Disinfecting & exterminating Services | 13,250 |
| 7349 | Misc. services to dwellings & bldgs | 16,670 |
| 7351 | News syndicates | 90 |
| 736X | EMPLOYMENT SERVICES | 10,500 |
| 7361 | Employment agencies, all types | 12,540 |
| 7362 | Temporary help supply services | 4,580 |
| 737X | COMPUTER & DATA PROCESSING SERVICES | 10,600 |
| 7372 | Computer programming & software services | 810 |
| 7374 | Data processing services | 9,800 |
| 739X | MISC. BUSINESS SERVICES | 64,500 |
| 7391 | Comm'l. research & development labs | 3,940 |
| 7392 | Management, consulting & public relations services | 30,840 |

| SIC | List | Quantity |
|-----|------|----------|
| 7393 | Detective agencies & protective services | 8,000 |
| 7394 | Equipment rental & leasing services | 12,160 |
| 7395 | Photo finishing labs | 3,140 |
| 7396 | Trading stamp redemption stores | 1,090 |
| 7397 | Comm'l testing labs | 3,420 |
| 7399 | Business services, not classified elsewhere | 61,670 |
| | • Rated $10,000 & over | 60,780 |
| | • Rated $20,000 & over | 59,570 |
| | • Rated $35,000 & over | 6,690 |

At least one list supplier, Ed Burnett, Inc., offers a further refinement—a fifth digit. Burnett breaks down 7313 into three segments:

| | | |
|---|---|---|
| 7313A | Newspaper advertising representatives | 2,340 |
| 7313B | Magazine advertising representatives | 1,130 |
| 7313C | Radio & TV advertising representatives | 2,770 |

### Primary and Secondary SIC Codes

As many firms are in more than one business, another variable exists in the designation of companies, usually by credit services, of the business they consider their primary one and others they may consider secondary.

An advertising agency, for instance, might be classified as 7311. If they consider themselves in the public relations and direct-mail business as well, they might carry secondary codes of 7392 and 7331.

Usually a business firm is looking to sell to everyone in a particular business, whether it be their primary or secondary business. Ordering a particular SIC code would get both. However, there are times when you may want only those firms which consider a business their primary one, or vice versa.

There are many refinements in working with SIC-categorized lists. Not the least important are the varying techniques for seeking out individuals you need within each corporate address, discussed later in this chapter.

### House Lists

No discussion of direct marketing would be complete without including the most obvious but most neglected list of all—a company's own house lists.

The *Reporter of Direct Marketing* points out, "Every transaction in the direct marketing field, whether it begins with direct mail, print, broadcast or telephone selling, always ends up on a list—of inquiries, of orders, of sales leads, of contest entrants, or whatever."

While building a list may not be the primary purpose of entrepreneurs running their first mail-order ad, it is the beginning of the process that makes the difference between a one-shot mail-order sale and a long-term direct marketing business. Even the smallest, newest company should begin, at the outset, to make the most of its mailing list.

First of all, a house list is the most profitable source of future resales. Second, list-rental income or the ability to exchange names can be very important. For these and other reasons, a house list can be a company's single greatest asset. Ways of protecting and utilizing this asset are discussed later in this chapter.

## HOW TO SELECT RESPONSE LISTS

The economic facts of life in using direct mail are that an advertiser will be spending 100 times what it would cost to reach a prospect compared to using print media, and even more when compared to broadcast.

This concentration of marketing effort on individual prospects is justified only by the concept of *selectivity*—the ability to pick out prospects much more efficiently than in mass media. Sometimes print and broadcast are called the "big guns" of marketing. Direct mail, then, is the medium of the sharpshooter. At the high cost of direct mail, you can't send your messages wildly into the night as in broadcast. You have to decide who your best target is and where to find that target, and you have to take careful aim.

In all direct marketing, the media is the market. In direct mail this applies doubly. The mailing list is not a way to reach a market; it is the market.

### The Principle of Affinity

In selecting mailing lists, the most important principle is the need for *affinity*, a logical connection between your offer and the prospects on a mailing list.

Some are easy. If you are selling gourmet cookware, you might try buyers of sophisticated cookbooks. If you are soliciting money for a charity, lists of donors to similar causes (health and religious organizations, the arts, etc.) are the first place to look.

If you are soliciting leads for an expensive, high-performance automobile like a Porsche, you might mail to owners of yachts and airplanes (who are affluent and love fine possessions); engineers (who would appreciate performance); readers of *Road & Track* and *Playboy* (whose self-image might include a Porsche); and top executives in advertising, entertainment, and other nonconservative fields (who could afford such a car and not be criticized for owning one).

Fortunately, direct-mail methods permit testing a wide variety of lists with some possibility for success. A list does not have to be a "sure thing" to be worth testing. It only has to have some logical affinity.

It's helpful to remind yourself, when picking lists to test, that not every person on a list has to be right for the offer. If you are looking for a 5 percent response, you can probably get it if 25 or 30 percent of the list consists of reasonable prospects. You can afford to build in a "waste factor" of people who are definitely not prospects, as long as there are enough people who are. The waste factor will be discussed below; it is one of the newer concepts in direct marketing list selection.

The total quantity of prospects in the list counts for less than the quality of the prospects. Better 20 very good prospects out of 100 than 40 so-so prospects.

## Recency, Frequency, and Unit Sale

When looking at SRDS or a list information card, some of the most valuable data is the buying history of the list being offered. The three factors of buying history, other than the type of product purchased, are *recency, frequency,* and *unit sale.* These should be compatible with the offer being made, independently of any other selection factor.

*Recency* is the time element between the date the list is rented and the date the people on the list sent in their order, inquiry, donation or subscription. The more recent, the better.

*Frequency* is the number of times a prospect has purchased from the company renting the name, or the length of the subscription, membership, or other association. The longer the better.

*Unit sale* is the amount of the highest transaction the customer has made through the mail. If your offer involves a substantial commitment, it is more likely to be accepted by people who have made other substantial purchases than by people who have not.

## List Sources

It's also important to look at the source of the mailing list. Direct-mail-sold lists will be most likely to work for other direct-mail offers. People who responded to telephone or television solicitations may not necessarily be accustomed to responding to mail offers. If the list has been built with sweepstakes offers, they are likely to not be responsive except to other sweepstakes offers.

## TESTING NEW LISTS

After consultation with a list broker and independent examination of list cards, SRDS, and directories issued by list brokers, every possible list worth testing should be sorted out into logical groups based on their common denominators. These categories can correspond to SRDS categories, or they can be arbitrary.

Lists should be grouped by the common denominator which makes them of interest to you, whether or not it is their basic identity. For instance, some groups could be purely affinity-based, grouping readers of magazines in related fields, buyers of similar products, buyers of books on the subject, buyers of items in a related price category, or any other segment.

*Pilot Lists*   Once the lists are sorted into categories, the next step in preparing a test mailing is to select one or more "pilot lists" in each category: the lists most likely to succeed. These pilot lists should be representative not only of the potential of the whole list but also of the entire group.

Quantities should be considered, of course. If you are using 10,000-name test cells, don't test a list of only 20,000 names, for there will be no place to roll out to if the list does succeed. The pilot lists should be larger lists or, at least, representative lists from a group of smaller lists with a substantial total.

## LIST SEGMENTATION

Once a mailing list has been chosen, there are still other alternatives available to the media manager. Mailing lists can be segmented in any way the list owner chooses and the computer can execute.

Some of the largest companies will make their lists available according to the type of merchandise purchased by their customers. Fingerhut offers these categories:

Automotive
Crafts, Hobbies & Models
Crafts, Hobbies & Models—Credit Card Holders
Education & Self Improvement

Fashions
General Merchandise Mail Order Buyers
Gifts—Gift Buyers
Home & Family Service
Insurance Buyers
Literature & Book Buyers
Men's
Music & Record Buyers
Opportunity Seekers
Women's

Doubleday Book Clubs sorts out their huge book club list according to the type of books selected by their members, with categories like this:

Change of Address
Doubleday Active Book Clubs
Children's Book Buyers
Cook Book Buyers
Cousteau—All clubs
Doubleday Book Club
Gardening Book Buyers
International Collectors Library
The Literary Guild
Merchandise Buyers from Doubleday
Military History Readers
Mystery Readers
Religious & Inspirational Book Buyers
Science Fiction Readers

Some owners sort their lists by size of purchase and whether or not the buyer has made more than one purchase. Almost all of them have a time frame built in, so you can start with the most recent names and work back to the older ones if results justify.

Lists can be selected by sex, by state, and by zip codes chosen for geographic or demographic criteria. Large mailers can identify clusters of zip codes where response rates and quality are exceptionally rewarding, and concentrate on those when sending out their mailings. Conversely, clubs or other credit propositions can screen out zip codes with historical bad-debt problems. Magazine publishers sometimes preselect zip codes in mail subscription solicitations in order to influence the demographic mix of their magazine's circulation.

*Hot-line names* are eagerly sought after. These are people who have recently bought, subscribed to, ordered, or inquired about the product of the company renting the list—usually within the last ninety days. The hottest of the hot-line names are those which are less than thirty days old. Such lists have been proved to do very well, and some advertisers contract for such names on a year-round basis.

One caution about hot-line names. Some list owners have included customers who eventually failed to pay for or returned their purchase, and thus are much poorer quality than names which stayed on the list long enough to become regular customers. One magazine rented out hot-line names which included complimentary-copy customers who had not yet paid their bills and converted to regular subscribers. Such names should not be on hot-line lists, and it is worth asking about them specifically if you do use this category.

Virtually every selection factor costs a bit more—maybe 10 to 15 percent—than the basic list, and many list owners charge a premium for sex or geographic selection. Considering that these charges are an even smaller percentage of the total mailing cost, and that selectivity is the essential ingredient of making the campaign work, such extra charges are a small price to pay.

There are different approaches to selecting segments for list testing. One school says that hot-line names and particularly favorable geographic areas or buyer classifications should be avoided, in order to make the test as "fair" as possible. This is true, if research is the objective. My approach is to put the best foot forward and give the list every chance of working by selecting the most favorable segments. If those are not successful, the list can be dropped anyway. If they are, testing can proceed with caution through the balance of the better names into older names and less affinitive segments.

The exception would be a campaign where, for competitive or other reasons, a major rollout must be conducted in the next season, with no time for extension testing. In that case, I would go with a list segment representative of the quantity that would be needed in the rollout.

The factor here is the total anticipated rollout quantity. If it's moderate, then the list program can be built gradually, beginning with the best segments, which should supply enough names without reaching into the bulk of the list. If the plan requires an ambitious rollout, then by all means test only large lists in typical segments.

## THE MAILING PLAN

The previous remarks deal with selecting lists for a test schedule. Actually, this process continues in one form or another throughout the life of a product.

An initial schedule would probably test 50,000 names for various pieces of copy. These names might be taken from one or two lists which appear to be very logical choices. Another 50,000 names might be divided among five or ten pilot tests representing substantial list categories.

An ongoing campaign would have three major groupings. The most important would be the *rollout* of lists which have been successful in previous testing. Then there would be *list extensions*—retests in larger quantities of lists which have proved successful in previous testing but where it is not yet considered safe to roll out the full quantity. Then there is *additional list testing,* which is divided into two areas. One area of list testing for an ongoing campaign would be the exploration of additional lists in categories where the pilot list was successful. The other is in searching for new list categories.

Let's say that ten lists (which we'll call A to J) were tested in an initial campaign, and five were successful. Those five would be rolled out or retested as extensions, depending on the quantities involved. Then additional lists in the successful categories would be tested, plus some new categories. The original unsuccessful test lists would be dropped, as would any other lists in the same categories.

Such a hypothetical schedule might look like this:

| List A | Rollout | 125,000, full list less previous tests |
| List C | Rollout | 87,000, full list less previous tests |
| List E | Extension | 50,000 of possible 1,250,000 |
| List G | Extension | 50,000 of possible 650,000 |
| List I | Extension | 50,000 of possible 325,000 |
| List K | List test | 10,000. Same category as A |
| List L | List test | 10,000. Same category as A |
| List M | List test | 10,000. Same category as A |
| List N | List test | 10,000. Same category as C |
| List O | List test | 10,000. Same category as E |
| List P | List test | 10,000. Same category as G |
| List Q | Category test | 10,000. New category pilot list |
| List S | Category test | 10,000. New category pilot list |

In this schedule, the original 100,000 mailing is now built up to 442,000, of which over 80 percent is rollout or extension. The percentage of testing is kept to less than 20 percent so that even if all the tests did only half as well as the rollouts and extensions, total results would only be depressed 10 percent. Even this is unlikely, as most of those tests are in categories that have already been proved successful.

This type of evolution, from highly subjective initial test to logical combination of tests, extensions, and rollouts, quickly converts the direct marketing manager from a chance-taking gambler into a statistician and scientist.

## USING COMPILED LISTS

The two major considerations in selecting direct-response lists are mail responsiveness and affinity. Neither of these is presumed when working with most mass compiled lists. Why, then, is this such a large industry, and how do these lists fit into the world of direct marketing?

Compiled lists offer two attributes ordinarily not available in the direct-response list field: saturation and precision segmentation. These attributes are interdependent. It is only the large quantity of compiled lists which makes precision segmentation economical, and it is only segmentation that makes it profitable for advertisers to use compiled lists.

There are two major types of segmentation: area selectivity and individual household selectivity. The nation's leading mass list compiler, Metromail, offers both these attributes in its national consumer household list—58 million names compiled from 3400 telephone directories.

### Area Selectivity

Local advertisers—retailers, banks, political candidates, charities—often need the geographic concentration of compiled lists. A compiled list such as Metromail's contains much smaller and sharper delineations than the usual zip code selection.

The United States Census Bureau, in every SMSA market of more than 50,000 population, divided each city into neighborhood units of about 1000 families, called census tracts. In about 2500 post offices (those serving more than 2500 population each) there is an even finer unit, sub-tracts, each consisting of about 250 families.

Metromail calls these units "Audience Cells" and "Subcells." For each "Audience Cell" and, where available, "Subcell," an incredible array of demographic information is available for analysis or selection. As people of like interests tend to live in like neighborhoods, this demographic data delivers an enormous degree of selectivity. The "Audience Cells" and "Subcells" are available in 260 SMSA markets which have been tracted. In addition, the same type of demographic information is available for the remaining post offices by zip code.

Virtually any census tract data can be used to select which cells, subcells, and untracted zip codes you wish mailed, in combination with geographic preference and with individual characteristics. The following is a list of twenty-nine primary demographic characteristics which can be selected easily from Metromail's "Audience Cell" file.

## AUDIENCE CELL AND SUB-CELL DEMOGRAPHICS

1. Household median income.

2. Percent households with income $25,000 and over.

3. Percent households with income $15,000 and over.

4. Percent households with income $10,000 and over.

5. Median value of owner occupied households.

6. Percent owner occupied households with value of $50,000 or more.

7. Percent owner occupied households with value of $35,000 or more.

8. Percent owner occupied households with value of $20,000 or more.

9. Median monthly contract rent for renter occupied units.

10. Percent renter occupied units with monthly contract rent of $200 or more.

11. Percent owner occupied households.

12. Median number of persons per household.

13. Median age of the male population 25 years old and over.

14. Percent married couples with husband under 45.

15. Percent households with children under 3 years old.

16. Percent households with children under 12 years old.

17. Percent households with children 13–19 years old.

18. Ratio of children 5 years old and under to households.

19. Ratio of children 6–13 years old to households.

20. Ratio of children 14–19 years old to households.

21. Percent males employed as white collar workers.

22. Median years of school completed (of population 25 years old and over).

23. Percent Negro households.

24. Percent households that are 1-unit structures (based on Metromail count).

25. Percent households that are 1-unit structures (based on census count).

26. Percent households that are 2 or more unit structures (based on Metromail count).

27. Percent households that are 3 or more unit structures (based on Metromail count).

28. Percent households that are 10 or more unit structures (based on Metromail count).

29. Percent households with 2 or more autos.

The 1980 Census has added extensively to the range of data that will be available by cell and subcell. Metromail and other suppliers will undoubtedly be adding to the sophistication and the diversity of their list segmentation.

## Individual Household Selectivity

Instead of, or in addition to, area selectivity, individual households can be selected based on characteristics deduced from telephone directory listings over a period of years. Metromail's data goes back over twenty years.

Each of these individual characteristics can be of value in itself or can be looked upon as a significant aid in increasing the probability of locating age, income, and family-size target groups.

- *Length of residence.* How long this family has lived (or at least had a telephone listing) at the present address. Long residence generally indicates an older head of household. A ten-year resident is likely to be twenty years older than a new resident.

- *Sex of household head.* Deduced from the first name of the person in whose name the phone is listed.

- *Type of dwelling unit.* Either single or multiple.

- *Surname ethnicity.* An imperfect, but sometimes valuable selector, used often in fund-raising and political campaigns.

Classifies last names according to their likelihood of being Catholic, Italian, Jewish, or Spanish.

- *Research-based preselections.* Based on correlations of research with individual and area characteristics, aimed at reaching a high proportion of older people (over 55 or over 65), affluent families (likely to have incomes over $25,000), and "influentials," based on educational and occupational characteristics and correlations.

## Specialized Consumer Lists

These very important and effective lists are based on psychographic characteristics rather than geographic or demographic factors, and there are many of them. While geographic and census tract data can be used as additional refinements, the appeal of the specialized lists is that they offer some indicator of the lifestyle of the prospective customer, and offer points of departure for specialized product, offer, or copy appeals.

1. *New parents.* Names of people who have had a child or who are expecting a child, selectable by number of months since birth and by number of other children (based on previous inclusion in the list).

2. *Newlyweds.* Couples who have just been married or who have indicated that they are about to be.

3. *New residents.* Changes of address, indicating a strong possibility that the residents have bought a house or are fixing up a rented home or apartment. These are good prospects for decorating offers.

4. *Families with children.* Children's Census prepared by Demographic Systems, Inc., offers a list of more than 7 million families with 10 million children. The selection factors are the age of the mother, the age and number of the children, and correlations with any census or individual telephone directory data.

5. *Automobile owners.* An interesting lifestyle indicator, based on common denominators of station wagon buyers, sports car buyers, new car versus used car buyers, luxury car versus economy car owners, etc. Offered by Polk for most of the United States.

## BUSINESS LISTS

The beginning of this chapter indicated that, while there are some business response and subscriber lists, the great bulk of business mailing activity involves compiled lists, usually sorted by SIC codes. The need for this selectivity is obvious for products that are usable by only one or two industries. However, if you are selling a general business product, such as imprinted business forms, small computers, typewriters, copiers, office furniture, or consulting services, then you have a different problem.

Often an advertiser will send out a sampling "across the board" to a typical cross section of SIC codes, company characteristics, and geographic areas, and will then set up a response analysis (Dun's offers this service to their list customers) analyzing the number of responses and the response rate percentage by every relevant factor. In this way, subsequent mailings can exclude SIC codes or other determinants which were not responsive. There can be a 400 to 500 percent difference, for example, depending on the company size and the SIC code.

Several segmentation factors can have a bearing on your list, and all of them are available.

- *Age of business.* When it was founded

- *Size of indicators.* Sales volume or number of employees

- *Type of business.* The primary or secondary SIC codes

- *Ownership.* Private or public

- *Headquarters or branch office.* Or the fact that this might be a single-location business

- *Credit.* The D&B credit rating and the general trend of the particular business

One particular advantage, especially where personalized letters are appropriate, is the large number of individual officer names and titles available through this supplier. They have already offered the names of presidents and chief financial officers, and have now added over 6 million additional names of various titles including vice president, secretary, manufacturing director, and purchasing agent, bringing the total to over 8½ million.

Unfortunately, no one supplier can give you the name of every manufacturing vice president in every type of company, and it will probably be necessary to deal with several list suppliers. Publishers of trade publications in specific fields often have very complete lists of the industries reached by their publications. Chilton, for instance, produces a very complete list of executives in the automotive field—one that is often used as a "credit-worthy" list by companies offering credit or banking services.

## HOUSE LISTS

The single most valuable list most advertisers will ever use is the house list. Tragically, it often is the most neglected. For most direct marketing companies, it is their single most precious asset—the one whose loss could put them out of business. It is usually the list most responsive to a company's additional offers.

There are several important ways in which this investment can be protected and maximized. The first is to set the list up right in the first place. Too many companies, when first starting out, simply copy a customer's name and address off a coupon the way it comes in, and preserve this name on labels, address systems, or a computer service.

Even the best computer service can be a mistake if it does not have specific experience in direct marketing list management. Companies like Polk, Metromail, LCS, and other specialists in list management should be considered. If you are publishing a periodical, by all means talk to Neodata in Boulder, Colorado, and similar magazine fulfillment specialists. Reinventing the wheel is not a good idea; there is just too much that can go wrong.

Your lists should be carefully edited to conform exactly with the *Direct Marketing Manual* (DMMA, Manual Release No. 200.2), which details exactly how to handle first names, titles, addresses, cities, and other information according to accepted industry standards.

Abbreviations, codes, and tape formats should be worked out so that they are compatible with other tapes used in this field, in order to enable you to use matching, updating, and suppressing techniques as discussed later in this chapter. Also, if you're going to rent the list, you don't want a reputation for having a "dirty" list. Such a reputation would lower your rental income substantially.

### Sales History

Another important factor to consider, right from the beginning, is the sales history or other activity that will help you fine-tool your own marketing efforts.

Your list should be identified with key information such as this:

- *Recency.* When did the customer make the first purchase— and the latest one?

- *Frequency.* How often has this customer ordered from you during the relationship or in the latest year?

- *Unit sale.* What is the average order size? The last order size? The highest order ever?

- *Source.* Where did this customer originate—from what ad, media, or copy appeal?

- *Credit.* If you are selling on credit, what is this customer's history? What is the largest credit limit you will permit?

- *Product line preference.* What does this customer buy from you?

This last item enables you to send offers only to those customers who are known buyers of a given type of product, making many mailings profitable that would not otherwise be. It is common to send out mailings to segmented lists such as this, appealing to known interests, before offering the same product to your own full list or to outside lists. If these buyers won't buy it, the chances are no one will.

### Protecting Your List

Anyone in the field will tell you at least one horror story about attempted list fraud. The value is just too great for some people to avoid temptation. I personally received a phone call, at one company, from the president of a competitor who had been offered my list for sale. It took a detective less than two days to track down the dishonest employee, with the help of the competitor, and to turn him over to the police. But don't let it come to this.

The first protections are obvious ones. The tape processing must be protected from theft as well as from fire or vandalism. Tapes should be stored in a locked room with tightly enforced access restrictions and a sign-in–sign-out system. Fire extinguishers should be built into the room, as well as alarms. Most important, a "grandfather system" should be instituted, in which original tapes and the latest updated tape are sent to a remote location for storage. Once a working tape is updated, it replaces the previous tape in storage. The idea is that there should always be, in another location, the basic data for reconstructing the current working tape.

"Seeding" names is another important step. Place some names and addresses on the list—your own name and that of several key employees and friends—with deliberate misspellings as codes. Whenever the list is used, you'll be able to spot the source of the list by the coded name. If an unauthorized mailing comes in with a misspelling, then you'll know that something is wrong.

## Postal Sorting

You'll probably want to maintain the list in zip code sequence, with postal carrier coding as it becomes available. Mail rates offer valuable incentives for presorting mail in zip sequence and by carrier route.

## List Cleaning

Every "nixie" should be removed from the file immediately. Nixies are mailings returned by the Postal Service with notations such as "No longer at this address." When new addresses are known, the listing can be updated and put back in the active file.

Address changes should also be promptly entered. This is vital, as bulk mail is never forwarded, and even first-class mail seems to have a mixed record for forwarding reliability.

There should also be a "match code" to enable you to spot new inquiries or orders from people who are already on the list, possibly under the name of another family member. The new order should supersede the previous file, but must be matched in order to avoid the expense of sending two mailings to the same household.

## List Rental

The list-rental business can be very profitable. There is no reason to worry about "protecting" your customers from other mail offers. They will be getting them anyway. The only question is who will be getting the list-rental income. You won't have to worry about directly competitive offers because you can refuse to rent to any offer you feel is competitive with you or offensive to your customers.

The first step is to set up your segmentation and pricing structure to make it appealing to other list-rental customers. The second step is to get a list management company to handle the promotion and administration of your list-rental business. A good list manager will have a good administrative operation and, more important, a strong sales organization to promote your list to likely users.

Some companies find the list-rental business so important that it contributes more profit than the sale of products. This can have a profound effect on marketing decisions.

## Using Your List

In addition to using your list for your own products or renting it out to others, you may find that your list will be so important that you will be looking for new ways to "mine" it.

One way is to use syndicated mailings—offers of products prepared and packaged by others for mailing to your list. It could be an insurance plan, a language course, or any other product. The letter goes out under your name to your customers, but all the expense and handling are the responsibility of the syndicator. All you do is handle the list and the orders. The syndicator will pay for the mailing, handle the product, and ship it out to your customers. You get your commission on each sale, and it can amount to a substantial sum if the product is the right one for your list.

The ultimate use of your list is to develop products that fit the reputation your company has built and the interests of the people on your list. As you are working toward a known customer base, it is relatively simple to work with researchers to arrange focus panels, questionnaires, or other forms of pretesting to help you develop an offer that will sell. The chances are that, if the offer appeals to your current list, it will also appeal to the media which you used to build your list.

## ORDERING AND PROCESSING MAILING LISTS

Selecting the right mailing lists may be a fine art, but ordering and processing them correctly is an exact science. As in every direct marketing activity, excellence requires the best of both.

Ordinarily, lists are rented through a list broker. A good list broker should be a willing and enthusiastic part of your marketing team. Select the best regardless of location. Convenience doesn't count.

Then you will need a list processor. This is sometimes subcontracted by your direct-mail letter shop or advertising agency. Many suppliers are tempted to increase their own profit margins by trying to do this type of work themselves, but often they do not have the computer capabilities or the depth of experience of the companies that specialize in list processing—companies like Magi, Wiland, Printronics, Marketing Electronics, and Creative Automation.

### Placing the List Order

List orders should be worked out with the list broker. There are many details to be worked out, and they often vary from list to list. Treat your list broker like a partner, not just a supplier.

*List Description*   For each list, you have to define exactly what you want. Include the name of the list and an exact specification of the segment you are ordering, such as "1980 Buyers" or "1979 Expires" or "Latest Hot Line."

*Quantity*   Usually, you want to test a fixed quantity or to utilize a previously ordered quantity of direct-mail packages. Often, though, you may want all available names in a geographic area, or hot-line names as available, or as many names as are available within recency parameters. In such a case, specify that instruction and be sure the list owner is told to provide an actual list count.

If you must estimate the amount of a mailing designated for a geographic area before the list is run, one handy way is to use state or SMSA counts published by the Census Bureau. Your list broker can supply this information.

This data includes the percentages of population, manufacturing, and retail sales for each state. Use the population figure for consumer lists, the manufacturing figure for business lists, and the retail sales figure for retail or professional lists. Just take the appropriate percentage and apply it to the total national list size.

Manufacturing and retail sales figures may not be available by individual SMSA market. To get these, take the state figure you need and then apply the "percentage-of-state" population figure to the manufacturing or retail figure. It's far from perfect, but it is usually close, with an error margin of 5 or 10 percent.

*Selectivity*   If you want a typical cross section for test purposes, the usual practice is to ask for an "Nth-name sample, to be taken from all reels." This means you want the total list size divided by your test quantity; a 300,000-name list used for a 10,000-name test would require that $N = 30$, or every thirtieth name.

I would avoid testing with what is called a fifth-digit zip select.

Arbitrarily taking a last number of a zip code and running those names does not give you 10 percent of the entire list. I have had this checked, and there is a dramatic difference in response by fifth-digit zip number.

The reason is that lower numbers, such as 0, 1, and 2, are often the downtown areas of major cities, while the higher numbers are more likely to be suburbs away from the city center. Also, many areas do not have the higher zips at all, and so a smaller postal area may have only the first few last digits.

On a test extension or rollout, you may want to specify certain geographic areas which you believe to be the most responsive to your offer, or you may designate a list of zip codes to be selected from or suppressed, as the case may be. You can also select by city size, seeking either urban or nonurban buyers.

You can designate sex by asking for "males only" or "females only." If your letter refers to the recipient by gender, you may want to avoid offending the opposite sex by adding this phrase: "Omit unidentified gender names." This will drop out those with only initials for first names.

Compiled and business lists can, of course, be selected by all the criteria indicated in the previous parts of this chapter, and such specifications should be clearly stated. Where names are not available individually, you may instruct the supplier to add a specific title, such as "purchasing agent" or "stationery buyer."

*Key Coding*   Your key numbers, by list, should be assigned at the very beginning, so that lists will be supplied to match your key numbers. You may request that the key number be printed on the label in a location you specify.

*Dates*   You must indicate the planned drop date and advise the list house if there are any substantial delays. Usually you will receive protection against competing use of a particular list one week before and one week after your scheduled mailing date. During this time another company should not have access to the same list. This should be indicated on the order. If a longer protection period is necessary, it will have to be negotiated in advance.

Your order should indicate both the scheduled drop date and the date you want the lists in order to begin processing.

*Telephone Numbers*   Some compiled lists can be supplied with telephone numbers, if so requested. This is a great convenience if you are using a list for telephone instead of, or in addition to, direct mail.

*Multiple Use*   If you are planning a second or third use of the same list, order them all at the same time. Most list owners will agree to a reduced rental rate (usually 50 percent) for repeat uses of the same tape as part of a series mailing.

If you are preparing a master prospect list, some list compilers will lease their list, at a higher price, for unlimited use during the contract period.

If your lists are going to be used for generating sales leads, for instance, you may want to order one set on labels for your mailing; another on 3- by 5-inch cards with telephone numbers for salespeople to use in making follow-up calls; and a third set in register form, by sales territory, for local managers to use in following up on sales efforts.

*Seed Names*   A list of seed names—names and addresses to be intermixed for checking mail delivery—should be included from the beginning and attached to each list order. These will be valuable in checking on the accuracy of the mailing house and the delivery time of the post office.

*Deliverability Guarantee*   Your printed list order form should include a standard line requesting a guarantee of deliverability by the list owner. A figure such as 95 percent should be acceptable, and the list owner should be willing to pay the minimum third-class or nonprofit postage rate on all returned mail over the 5 percent figure.

Such a guarantee should provide an incentive for the list owner to keep the list cleaned regularly, and to drop the names on returned mail from the list for future mailings.

*Mailing Identification*   The mailing order should clearly identify the product being offered and should be accompanied by a sample mailing piece. All orders are subject to the list owner's acceptance. Scrupulous honesty in regard to identifying mailings and barring reuse is expected not only by the list owner but by the entire direct marketing establishment.

## LIST FORMATS

*Cheshire Labels*   The standard way of supplying mailings is the Cheshire label, a continuous form containing four labels to a line, side by side (or "East to West"). These labels are 1 inch by slightly less than 3½ inches wide. Ungummed and unperforated, they can be affixed only by machine.

*Peel-off Labels*   At slightly higher cost, list owners can supply adhesive labels on a waxed-paper backing, each label being slightly smaller than a Cheshire label. These can be machine-affixed in the same manner, in situations where you want the customer to peel off the label and place it on an order form. They can also be hand-affixed very easily when labels are supplied to retailers or salespeople for local mailings.

*Sheet Listings*   A printout of data in listing form, this is usually fifty lines to a page. It is usable only for reference or checking, or for telephone selling operations.

*Card Files*   Each individual record can be printed on a 3- by 5-inch card, or on a form having one or more parts, for distribution to salesmen or for similar uses. Such formats often include additional information. Dun's sales prospecting cards include sales volume, number of employees, lines of business, telephone numbers, and the chief executive's name in a format intended for convenient use by field sales personnel.

*Magnetic Tape*   Larger mailers often prefer to order lists on magnetic tape, in a format specified by their list processor. These tapes can then be sent to a list processor for any of the services outlined in the following paragraphs, or they can be sent to mailing houses for the preparation of personalized computer letters using high-speed chain printers, laser printers, or Mead Digit ink-jet printing.

*Delivery Instructions*   The list broker should be told exactly where the lists are to be shipped and how they are to be marked. Usually you will have the lists or tapes not shipped to your office but sent directly to the mailing house or computer service that is to process them. The tapes should be clearly marked with key numbers, purchase order numbers, drop dates, and your company name, so that the lists will be properly routed when they arrive at the destination.

*Other Items*   Your list broker will also want to clarify such questions as how the lists are shipped, what the cost is with tax and all surcharges, and what payment terms are mutually acceptable. You may also be required to sign an agreement not to reuse the names except as specifically agreed upon.

## LIST PROCESSING

Most large mailers will eventually need the services of a list processor. These firms offer even the smallest advertisers the type of sophisticated computer equipment and advanced programming that otherwise only a handful of direct marketers would be able to afford.

The advantages of these processes are directly related to volume. Duplication may not be an important factor if you are only mailing 100,000 names nationally. But it can add up to a lot if you are sending out 10 or 20 million names a year.

## Duplicate Elimination

Duplicate elimination, or de-duplicating, is the most common list-processing service. Sometimes called "merge-purge," it basically consists of matching names and addresses from several lists against each other, searching for similarities (including family members at the same address), and consolidating duplications.

Magi's "Mailsave II" system uses different logic patterns for urban, suburban, and rural addresses to maximize overall de-duplication accuracy to better than 99 percent. Their system uses phonetic logic, which spots similar names although spellings are slightly different; transposition logic (which detects transposed characters); data entry error logic (for address keying errors); and zip code logic (to correct incorrect zip codes). This system, as well as others like it, works with magnetic tape input in any format supplied by list owners and sent directly to their facility.

The duplicate names are combined and merged into a separate multibuyer tape which can be mailed and tracked separately. Such names, because they appear on more than one logical list, usually have a higher response rate than the bulk of the lists which consist of de-duplicated names.

A duplication allocation system produces a report showing the duplication by list. This can be done on a priority basis, matching new names against a house list or other master list, or by the system Magi calls stratification allocation, which distributes duplication evenly.

Other by-products of the system are suppressions, if desired, of noncontinental United States, APO/FPO, military bases, prisons, and other unique zip code categories. Postal bag tags are computer-generated and printed to meet Postal Service requirements for various zip sorts. A report of "net counts by key" is also prepared, based on the final de-duplicated mailing.

## Merge-Purge Rate Adjustment

When ordering names from many lists to be "merged" into one file and "purged" of duplicates, how do you pay the list owner? What about when you are eliminating names that are already your customers?

In such cases you must ask your list broker to secure an "85 percent agreement" beforehand. This means that you agree to pay the list owner for no fewer than 85 percent of the names on the list mailed. Some also charge $3 per thousand deleted names, to cover computer costs. If the actual percentage after the merge-purge has been completed is higher, then you will have to pay the higher rate.

Such agreements are customarily granted only on orders of 50,000 or more names of a large list, or the full run of smaller lists. Without such an advance agreement, you will be expected to pay the full rate regardless of the number of unused names.

The computer house must submit proof of the number of names purged from the list. If 93 percent of the list is mailable, the renter has to pay for 93 percent of the names. But if only 65 percent of the names are mailable, the renter is still obliged to pay 85 percent, as per the agreement. This system protects the list owner and broker as well as providing some discount for the list user.

Large-scale mailers can sometimes negotiate a 75 percent agreement. On the other hand, some list owners permit no discount at all. The Metropolitan Opera House, for example, requires 100 percent payment for its subscriber list regardless of the net number of names used.

*List Cleaning*    If you have a large house list, you may want to have it cleaned by using the kind of system offered by Marketing Electronics. Called Data Match, it compares your customer file with two huge lists: a master file of 58 million households from telephone books and other sources, and a "nixie bank" of 34 million known movers, based on address deletions and returned mail from participating customers.

These lists are matched with your own to create four separate lists:

1. Cleaned names, confirmed by their presence on the master file.

2. Corrected addresses, movers whose new forwarding addresses are on file.

3. Confirmed nixies, which match the known movers file, saving you the expense of mailing these names yourself.

4. Possible nixies, names which did not match either the master file or the nixie file. These can be mailed, dropped, or mailed with an address-correction request, at your option.

Two valuable types of information can be added to the list as a by-product of the matching process. One add-on is carrier route codes, which can result in faster mail handling in the short term and probably postage savings later on. Another is Metromail-type demographic data by census tract or individual family characteristics, to be used in list suppression or data overlay processes.

The savings resulting from a "clean" list will pay for the address-correction process from the first large mailing, and it is certainly cheaper than current Postal Service charges for individual address correction.

The significance of this type of service lies in the fact that one out of five Americans moves each year, so that if your list is not updated, 20 percent of it becomes obsolete each year. Statistically, a one-year list is 80 percent accurate, a two-year list 64 percent, a three-year list 51 percent, and so on.

## List Suppression

Another process which has become standard for many large mailers is the suppression of selected names, performed by computer matching techniques. The names which might be suppressed from a mailing include:

1. The DMMA "Name Removal List"—people who have asked that they not be sent mail of any kind

2. Customer lists, to avoid sending introductory offers to persons who are already on your house list

3. Any other characteristic individually or by zip code, selected because of credit history, poor response records, or simple inappropriateness for the particular offer

4. People who have indicated that, while they wish to receive mail from a company they do business with, they prefer not to have their names rented to or exchanged with other companies. More and more companies are offering this option to their customers.

## Customer History Files

When list processors are used for maintenance of a company's own list of active customers, they can perform many valuable services in addition to list maintenance and the preparation of labels for mailing.

Business mailers can add to their customer lists any Dun & Bradstreet information, as discussed earlier, plus information on specific sales, sales commissions, purchases, and relative rankings.

Consumer catalog mailers can add a product-preference code, average and latest purchase amount, credit history, sex, birth date, ages of children, census tract data, and a profitability index taking into account the number of catalogs mailed.

Fund raisers can compile similar information for contributors, including interest groups, initial and subsequent contributions, date of last gift, and individual and census information.

Circulation promotion mailers can add subscription term, renewal information, income, advertising cost, additional purchases, and anything else that might be of value.

Reports can be compiled by source, by customer type, by product category, by month, by state or SMSA. Virtually any type of data can be produced providing it is in the system in some form in the first place.

## Special Systems

Some list processors and compilers have prepared total systems for list management, lead procurement, or direct marketing.

There are too many suppliers to try to mention all their services. At least one company supplies a business lead system integrated with mailings, reports, sales follow-up, and lead distribution. Another has a special program for the insurance industry, where local agents may select demographic specifications within their own areas and order mailings sent to their immediate neighborhood, with related lead follow-up systems.

Some companies have stock systems for continuity programs or card file mailings. Others have software ready to go for catalog operations, with or without credit sales. Your best bet is to talk to many potential suppliers and to find those who have learned how to handle your problem the hard way—by making their mistakes at some earlier clients's expense. It is much easier to adapt an existing computer program to meet your needs than to teach a company the basics of lead processing.

## SOME ADVANCED MAILING-LIST TECHNIQUES

Here are some of the list-buying and list-processing techniques used by some large advertisers. Most of these will only be necessary for companies who have exhausted conventional sources and who require very substantial mailing lists. In some cases, however, they may help a marginal company get bigger, if it has the time and patience to work out some of these sophisticated methods.

### Multibuyer Match

One way to pretest a mailing list is to match it against either your customer list or known profitable lists. The higher the match factor, the more likely it is that the total list will be successful. This is used to predict the likelihood that a list will work.

## Data Overlay

It is possible to match response lists against either the census tract or the individual characteristics of compiled lists, producing a list which combines both known response history and demographic factors. For instance, for a home repair book, you might overlay the factor of "individual residence" against known mail-order buyers, to produce a list of mail-order buyers who live in single-family homes. Or you might match a list of people who have responded to any book offer against other lists of families with children, to send out a mailing offering a set of children's books.

## Title Conformance

If you are looking for female mail-order buyers and have exhausted all known female names on your best lists, you can try arbitrarily adding a "Mrs." before the male names on the lists. The chances are that "Mrs. John Jones" will reach the woman of the household, even though a certain amount of such mail will be wasted on bachelors.

In neighborhoods with children, you can correct a title to read "To the children of Mrs. Smith" with a reasonable chance of successfully reaching your prospect. When you have the names of children, there's no problem in having the computer print out "To Amy Nash's Daddy" or something similar.

## Cluster Analysis

Companies like Claritas and consultants like Glen Cavender have perfected systems which enable you to analyze your customer data and determine which zip codes have the greatest chance of success for your mailings. Gross response, credit performance, buying patterns, and other factors are used to pick out which areas are worth mailing to and which are not. Cavender's unique analytical system is given credit for turning RCA Victor's record club from a $5 million loss into a like profit in just one year.

## Waste Calculation

Some advertisers back off from using lists because their message is too narrow. An example might be a special credit offer to college graduates.

Such lists are difficult to obtain in quantity, yet in some neighborhoods more than half the household heads are college graduates.

The waste calculation strategy deliberately ignores the off-target addresses and concentrates on the doughnut instead of the hole. Sure, some people will get mail with an offer that they will not be qualified for; but if the mailing produces an overall 2 percent response, and if that 2 percent is acceptable, then it is no longer important that a pure college graduate list might have produced twice the response. A half-efficient list is better than none.

### Skimming versus High-Penetration Strategies

"High penetration" is needed when you have few prospects and a high unit sale. Companies such as Avis Rent-A-Car and International Gold Corporation do well with a series of letters at a CPM over $1000. Many charities send inexpensive mailings to large lists, a technique called "skimming."

### Other Techniques

The more advanced techniques in this field are often carefully guarded secrets. Even some of the examples used here have been changed to respect confidences. We urge you to look at the techniques discussed here more as a way of thinking—of stretching your mind to the potential of what can be done with mailing lists—than as specific ideas for your company.

### PACKAGE INSERTS AND COOPERATIVE MAILINGS

Two mediums which are often lumped with mailing lists are cooperative mailings and package inserts. Like mailing lists, both are listed in SRDS Direct Mail, and like mailing lists, they are ordered through list brokers.

### Package Inserts

Several companies sell the right to insert an offer in their package mailings or their statement stuffers. Because they get a free ride with postage that would have had to be paid anyway, such stuffing opportunities can be available very inexpensively.

Here are some typical package inserts listed by SRDS, along with quantities and prices:

|  | Annual quantity | Price per thousand inserts |
|---|---|---|
| Lee Wards | 1,000,000 | $35 |
| Gurney Seed & Nursery Co. | 2,000,000 | $35 |
| Nora Nelson | 750,000 | $30 |
| Sessions Records | 1,100,000 | $25 |

These inserts have stringent weight and size limitations and so are most useful where a skimming strategy has proven effective. A disadvantage of these inserts is that it is difficult to coordinate them with other media or seasonal plans.

## Cooperative Mailings

Probably the best-known cooperative mailing is Carol Wright, which sends out some six mailings a year to over 20 million people. There are also many specialized cooperative mailings, including the Weight Watchers mailing to 5 million names, the Berkey Photo mailing to 6 million, and the United Equitable Life Insurance mailing to 1 million.

Costs range from $12 to $25 per thousand inserts, depending on the degree of selectivity, the amount of clutter (discussed below), and the number of inserts. Rates vary with the size and weight of the pieces inserted. Printing is extra. Some advertisers, especially those offering mass general magazines, recipe cards, or film processing, consider this medium very important and reserve choice dates and geographic areas years in advance.

Clutter is the number and type of other pieces inserted with yours in a cooperative mailing. Too many pieces will dilute attention and therefore response. More important is the professionalism of the other inserts and the perceived quality of the products offered. Both will rub off on yours.

Cooperative mailings are inexpensive to test. Direct marketers whose offers can be expressed in a small space should consider them.

*    *    *

This is easily the longest chapter in the book. No other medium is as important, varied, or complex. Working with mailing lists will never be as dramatic as designing a new mailing package, but it is more challenging. Suppressing or segmenting out the unproductive half of a mailing list is as valuable as doubling a response rate. It is just as profitable, just as feasible, and just as worthy of our time, attention, and talent.

## CHAPTER SIX

# PRINT-MEDIA PLANNING

The principles of planning newspaper and magazine schedules are not unlike those that apply to selecting direct-mail lists. The medium is the market, not just a way of reaching a market. There must be a logical affinity between product and audience. The quality of audience is more critical than the quantity. Divisibility permits segmentation and, therefore, both fine tooling of profitability and limitation of downside risk in test situations. The principles are the same, but the practice is significantly different.

## WHEN TO USE PUBLICATION MEDIA

Most businesses are launched in direct mail, and some giant firms use direct mail as their single most important way of reaching potential audiences. However, in every marketing situation some important role is played by other media. Some examples are given below.

### Extending Direct Mail

A frequent problem with successful direct-mail users is that they reach a point where the list universe is exhausted. Despite tailored appeals, segmentation refinement, and the testing of alternative direct-mail strategies, there simply are no more names to be tested.

At this point many advertisers, particularly magazine subscription managers, try to increase the frequency of mailing, but they find that lists that did well on an annual or biannual frequency roll over and die when mailed twice a year. The highest-affinity core list simply has only so many fresh names, and so many old names becoming ready to accept a product offer—and no more.

In such a situation, print media extends direct mail. If subscribers to a magazine are an effective list, for instance, then an advertisement in that magazine enables you to reach not only the subscribers, but also the newsstand buyers of the magazine. You'll also reach the publication's pass-along readership. According to some studies, this can be two or three times the circulation and up to six times the number of subscribers.

If a list such as World of Beauty is highly effective, then it is often possible to do well by going into the same magazines that World of Beauty did to build their list in the first place. This is another approach to extending mail.

Advertisers usually discover that, after house lists and a limited group of core lists, print media—and in some cases broadcast—are the most effective media sources. Noncore lists take up the next position in effectiveness and provide an opportunity to push sales volume ahead every year or two when the economic situation and the existence of a particularly effective direct-mail package permit.

### Alternative to Direct Mail

Some propositions work much better in print media than in direct mail. The reasons for this are (1) economics, (2) credibility, (3) buckshotting, and (4) the need to create new markets.

*Economics*    Print media reach a much larger number of people, at much lower cost, than direct mail, but possess much lower identified affinity levels with a given product. Chapter 5 discusses skimming as a strategic alternative to high penetration in direct mail. The skimming approach is carried to a greater extreme in print media, where a message can be presented to larger numbers of less motivated people at less expense.

Skimming is particularly appropriate for offers involving a low unit cost or for two-step propositions with initial free offers. There is simply not enough margin to support a 30-cents-per-unit ($300-per-thousand) mail contact on an offer that has no more likelihood of getting a response from any one prospect than a $3/_{10}$-cents-per-contact print-media message. In other words, unless there is 100 times the likelihood that a list addressee will respond—because of either list affinity or the added impact of a longer, more involving direct-mail message—then it will be more profitable to reach that prospect and others in a less involving, less expensive print-media message.

*Credibility*   Other direct marketing offers require the implied endorsement of a publication's pages to be successful, just as some direct-mail programs need the *imprimatur* of a well-known company. Readers presume, and rightly so, that a magazine or newspaper will stand behind the products advertised in their pages. Some publications, such as *Good Housekeeping* and the *New York Times*, are very strict about this, and so have greater credibility than publications which may not be as stringent in their requirements.

If your company is unknown, and especially if your product raises health or safety concerns on the part of the consumer, it may do much better in established magazines than in any direct mail other than that endorsed by a third party.

*Buckshotting*   Some companies have a product or service that can afford a highly targeted, high-penetration direct-mail effort, but simply do not have enough good lists. This is frequently the case in the business equipment and financial fields.

Mailing lists which identify key executives by name will do well for a maker of dictating or copying equipment, or a solicitor of investments in gold, gems, or money market funds. But there are just not enough of those names. Dun's Decision Makers, for instance, can provide the names of half a dozen top executives in a corporation, but hundreds more may have the authority to buy a dictating machine, reserve a car, or plan a plane trip. While direct mail may be much more effective on a cost-per-order basis, such products still require extensive print-media campaigns to reach all their potential prospects.

*Creating New Markets*   Starting something new often requires going into the widest possible marketplace and letting the product seek its own level or find its own market.

In some cases—such as prepaid health services, a magazine for tennis buffs, or a club for indoor gardeners—there are not enough mailing lists to build a business no matter what the strategy is. That's where print media can be extremely useful. In fact, I sometimes recommend using general publications for an initial round of ads followed by questionnaires to respondents to find unexpected list-affinity areas.

A valuable by-product of this approach is the building of a unique mailing list of buyers of your own product. This should have high value in the list-rental marketplace or as a foundation for additional product introductions.

Again, direct mail is a sharpshooter's medium, while print media and broadcast are shotguns. If your targets are few, worthwhile, and identified, nothing beats direct mail; but if they are hard to find, small in number, or hard to identify, then there's nothing like a shotgun to be sure to hit something.

## SOURCES OF INFORMATION

Before we go into selecting newspapers and magazines, the first step is to know where and how to get the information you need.

### Standard Rate and Data Service

As with direct mail, the basic tools are the directories published by Standard Rate and Data Service for consumer publications and other advertising media. International media are covered by special editions for England, Canada, Italy, Mexico, West Germany, Austria, and Switzerland.

The consumer magazine directory alone contains data on about 1500 magazines sorted into sixty-three classifications. The main classifications are worth noting:

| | | | |
|---|---|---|---|
| 1. | Airline Inflight | 14. | Dressmaking & Needlework |
| 1A. | Almanacs & Directories | 15. | Advertising |
| 2. | Art & Antiques | 16. | Education & Teacher |
| 3. | Automotive | | |
| 4. | Aviation | 17. | Entertainment Guides |
| 5. | Babies | | |
| 6. | Boating & Yachting | 17A. | Entertainment & Performing Arts |
| 7. | Brides, Bridal | | |
| 8. | Business & Finance | 18. | Epicurean |
| 8A. | Campers, Recreational Vehicles | 19. | Fishing & Hunting |
| | | 20. | Fraternal, Professional Groups |
| 8B. | Camping & Outdoor Recreation | 21. | Gardening |
| 9. | Children's | 21A. | Gay Publications |
| 9A. | Civic | 22. | General Editorial |
| 9B. | College & Alumni | 23. | Health |
| 10. | Comics & Comic Technique | 23A. | History |
| | | 24. | Home Service & Home |
| 11. | Crafts, Games, Hobbies, & Models | 25. | Horses, Riding & Breeding |
| 12. | Dancing | 26. | Humanities Topics |
| 13. | Dogs & Pets | 27. | Labor-Trade Unions |

| | | | |
|---|---|---|---|
| 27A. | Lifestyle/Service | 38. | Newspaper |
| 28. | Literary Reviews | | Distributed |
| 29. | Mechanics & | 39. | Photography |
| | Sciences | 42A. | Romance |
| 30. | Men's | 43. | Science |
| 30A | Metropolitan | 43A. | Senior Citizens |
| 31. | Military & Naval | 43B. | Sex |
| 33. | Music | 43C. | Snowmobiling |
| 34. | Mystery, Adventure | 44. | Society |
| | Fiction | 45. | Sports |
| 35. | Nature & Ecology | 46. | Travel |
| 36A. | News—Weeklies | 47. | TV, Radio & |
| 36B. | News—Biweeklies, | | Electronics |
| | Semimonthlies | 49. | Women's |
| 40. | Physical Sciences | 50. | Women's Fashions |
| 41. | Political & Social | | & Beauty |
| | Topics | 51. | Youth |
| 42. | Religious & | | |
| | Denominational | | |

Most people are surprised at the wide range of little-known and highly specialized magazines. The classification "General Editorial," for instance, is one that most advertisers might guess they would already be familiar with; but I doubt that anyone would be able to recall, unaided, all the following audited and nonaudited publications classified in the 1980 *Consumer Magazine SRDS* as "General Editorial."

| | | | |
|---|---|---|---|
| 1. | *Apartment Life* | 16. | *Hearst Magazines Corporate* |
| 2. | *Atlantic, The* | | *Buy* |
| 3. | *Attenzione* | 17. | *Leadership Network, The* |
| 4. | *Book Digest* | 18. | *Life* |
| 5. | *East-West Journal* | 19. | *Midnight Guide* |
| 6. | *Ebony* | 20. | *Money* |
| 7. | *Changing Times* | 21. | *Moneysworth* |
| 8. | *Energy Age* | 22. | *Mother Earth News, The* |
| 9. | *Futurist, The* | 23. | *Mother Jones* |
| 10. | *Geo* | 24. | *National Enquirer* |
| 11. | *Gourmet* | 25. | *National Geographic* |
| 12. | *Grit* | 26. | *Natural History* |
| 13. | *Harper's/Atlantic/Natural* | 27. | *New Harvest* |
| | *History* | 28. | *New Yorker, The* |
| 14. | *Harper's Magazine* | 29. | *New York Times Magazine* |
| 15. | *Harvard Magazine* | 30. | *Next* |

31. *Nuestro*
32. *Omni*
33. *People Weekly*
34. *Politics Today*
35. *Prevention*
36. *Prime Time*
37. *Psychology Today*
38. *Quest/80*
39. *Reader's Digest*
40. *Rolling Stone*

41. *Saturday Evening Post*
42. *Saturday Review*
43. *Scientific American*
44. *Sepia*
45. *Smithsonian*
46. *Star, The*
47. *Success Unlimited*
48. *Us*
49. *Wilson Quarterly, The*
50. *Yankee*

When we deal with less general publications, or with the 300 or so magazines in the classifications in *Business SRDS*, the challenge is even greater. Media buying cannot be done "off the top of your head." It is a rigorous and demanding science that demands the best tools of the trade.

Each listing of a single magazine incorporates, in a standardized format, all the objective data necessary to analyze potential media. Unlike rate cards supplied by the magazines themselves, SRDS listings are always comparable, point by point. Each listing includes all the following information.

*Introductory Material*
- Title of publication
- Media identification code
- Frequency of issue
- Name of publisher
- Address of publisher
- Telephone number
- TWX number
- Publisher's editorial profile

1. *Personnel*
   - Names and titles of those executives who have responsibility and authority relative to national advertising accounts

2. *Representatives and/or Branch Offices*
   - Representatives name only
   - Branch office
   - Name
   - Address
   - Telephone number

3. *Commission and Cash Discount*
   - Amount of commission allowed to agencies
   - Cash discount

4.  *General Rate Policy*
    • Contract cancellation clause
    • Policy on rate protection and rate revision
    • Conditions and/or regulations related to all advertising
      space contracts not given in Contract and Copy
      Regulations

5.  *Black/White Rates*
    • B/w discount structures

5a. *Combination Rates*
    • Rates when sold in combination

5b. *Discounts* (Gross Expenditures)
    • Discounts applicable to total dollars invested

6.  *Color Rates*
    • Color availability
    • Rates for standard colors
    • Rates for selected colors
    • Color discount structures

7.  *Covers*
    • Availability
    • Rates

8.  *Inserts*
    • Base rates
    • Special charges
    • Tip-ons

9.  *Bleed*
    • Space and color charge
    • Gutter bleed

10. *Special Position*
    • Availability
    • Rates
    • Spreads

11. *Classified and Reading Notices*
    • Classified rates
    • Reading notices
    • Display classifications
    • Mail order rates

12. *Split-Run*
    • Rates
    • Requirements
    • Circulation data and source

13.   *Special Issue Rates and Data*
- Rates and data pertaining to special or 13th issue (exclusive of regular issues)
- Issuance dates for special issues
- Circulation data and source

13a.  *Geographic and/or Demographic Editions*
- Rates
- Requirements
- Circulation data and source

14.   *Contract and Copy Regulations*
- Numbers shown here refer to standard regulations used by many publishers and summarized on a special page of the directory. Such terms refer to volume contracts, copy acceptability, payment terms, and various legal matters.

15.   *Mech. Requirements (Printing Process)*
- Trim size, number of columns to page
- Binding method
- Color available
- Mechanical requirements for Geographic/Demographic editions, where different from basic publication
- Dimensions—ad page (width and depth)
- Minimum depth R.O.P. for newspaper formats

16.   *Issue and Closing Dates*
- Frequency of publication
- Closing dates for:
- Black and white
- Color
- Inserts
- Set copy
- Special feature issues

17.   *Special Services*
- A.B.C. Supplemental Data Report
- Ad readership studies
- Advertising preparation services
- Direct mail services
- Direct-response services
- Merchandising services
- Reprints
- Reader service card
- Special stock printing

18.   *Circulation*
- Year established
- Single copy and annual prices
- Circulation data and source

- Territorial distribution
- Publisher guarantee or "rates based on"
  This discloses whether a publication is subscription or
  single copy. Direct marketers, looking for evidence that
  readers will respond to mail offers, usually prefer the
  subscription sold publications to newsstand ones.

19.  *Distribution*
   - Year established
   - Distribution data and source
     (Applicable to periodicals placing copies in distribution
     to specific places.)

20.  *Print Order*
   - Copies printed and offered for sale
     (Applicable to annuals, semiannuals, and magazines with
     less than quarterly frequency which are printed and
     offered for sale with definite "on sale" dates, and with
     established single copy or issue prices.)

A typical listing may help clarify the kind of data available. Figure
6-1, on the next pages, shows a typical magazine's listing in SRDS.
In addition to such listings, SRDS offers other specialized features
that are lesser known but can be helpful. Here are some:

*Magazine and Farm Publication Representatives*
Shows name, address, telephone number of home and branch offices
of firms representing consumer magazines and farm publications; in
alpha sequence.

*Promotional Dates*
Shows special days and weeks, such as National Baby Week, Law Day,
etc. Listed chronologically and updated monthly.

*Census Divisions Map*
Shows the states comprising each Geographical Division. Breakdown
under "Territorial Distribution."

*Magazine Group Buying Opportunities*
An alphabetical index of all group titles appearing in Consumer Magazine and Farm Publication Rates and Data, with reference to editorial
classifications in which listings have been assigned.

*Magazines with Geographic and/or Demographic Editions or Split Run
Advertising*
A two-section index, listed in alphabetical order.

*Magazines with Shopping Advertising Pages*

*International Consumer Magazines*

## POPULAR SCIENCE
### A Times Mirror Magazines, Inc. Publication
ABC                    MPA

Media Code 8 455 0500 7.00
Published monthly by Times Mirror Magazines, Inc.
  a Div. of Times Mirror Co., 380 Madison Ave.,
  New York, N. Y. 10017. Phone 212-687-3000
For shipping info., see Print Media Production Data.

#### PUBLISHER'S EDITORIAL PROFILE

POPULAR SCIENCE concentrates its editorial on new products that may be of special usefulness to men with strong interests in their homes, personal transportation needs and in recreation. Each month, the magazine reports on products still on industrial drawing boards. It also introduces products already in the marketplace, and provides "use" suggestions about products. Major articles and departmental features cover such product areas as automobiles; boats and engines; home workshop tools; garden and lawn equipment; electronic, TV, and photographic equipment; and recreational products. Rec'd 5/3/78.

1. *Personnel*
   President—John A. Scott.
   Editor-in-Chief—C. P. Gilmore.
   Vice-Pres. & Publisher—F. X. Wilkinson.
   Adv. Make-up & Production—Joe Clarke.

2. *Representatives and/or Branch Offices*
   Chicago 60611—Richard Moderhack, Western Adv.
   Mgr., 875 N. Michigan Ave. Phone 312-337-7717.
   Los Angeles 90010. K. M. Foss, Pacific Coast Mgr.,
   3550 Wilshire Blvd., Suite 908. Phone 213-380-1936.
   Southfield, Mich.—Sales Motivating Associates.

3. *Commission and Cash Discount*
   15% of gross to recognized agencies; 2% cash discount on bills paid within 10 days of billing date. Bills rendered on 15th of month preceding date of issue. Cash with copy except to those who have established credit. All remittances must be in United States exchange.

4. *General Rate Policy*
   Advertising rates guaranteed for one month following last issue closed. Short rates and rebates will apply if advertiser, within 12 consecutive month contract period, earns rate other than that which was billed.

#### ADVERTISING RATES

Rates effective January, 1980 issue. (Card No. 37.)
  Rates received October 9, 1979.
    Card received March 31, 1980.

5. *Black/White Rates*

| | |
|---|---:|
| 1 page (429 lines) | 15,625. |
| 2 column (286 lines) | 10,775. |
| 1/2 page | 8,280. |
| 1 column (143 lines) | 5,460. |
| 1/6 page (71 lines) | 3,130. |
| Column inch (14 lines) | 780. |
| Agate line | 56. |

#### VOLUME DISCOUNT

Advertisers who run these pages or equivalent space during their contract year earn the following discounts (apply against both regional and national ads):

**Figure 6-1.** *Source: SRDS Classification 29, Popular Science, a Times Mirror Magazines, Inc., Publication. Reprinted by permission.)*

| 3–5   pages | 3% | 24–29 pages | 20% |
| 6–11  pages | 7% | 30–35 pages | 25% |
| 12–17 pages | 10% | 36 pages or more | 30% |
| 18–23 pages | 15% | | |

Booklets, cards, full-page inserts and gatefolds (except cover gatefolds) do not earn, but contribute toward volume discounts.

5a.  *Combination Rates*

General display advertisers running a minimum of 4 pages (or equivalent) in 3 titles or 3 pages (or equivalent) in 4 titles can qualify for the following special combination discounts.

| | **3 titles** | **4 titles** | **Maximum** |
| --- | --- | --- | --- |
| *Popular Science* | 12% | 15% | 35% |
| *Outdoor Life* | 12% | 15% | 35% |
| *Golf* | 15% | 20% | 35% |
| *Ski* | 20% | 25% | 35% |

Network discounts apply to advertising placed by a single division, or subsidiary, by product category within a common contract period. These discounts are in addition to earned standard discounts shown on each magazine's individual rate card subject to the maximum discount off one-time rates. Equal network space must run in each title used. Minimum space unit 1/3 page. All credits due from network discounts must be used in space; no cash rebates. NRHA Spring and Fall Promotion Discount: May and October issues are tied-in with the National Retail Hardware Association's Spring and Fall Home Value Days. Special tie-in advertising discount opportunities available.

Maximum discount of 35% applies to all ROP advertisers including schools, publishers and clubs.

6.  *Color Rates*

| | **2 color** | **4 color** |
| --- | --- | --- |
| 1 page | 17,555. | 22,165. |
| 2 columns | 12,115. | 15,295. |
| 1/2 page | 9,310. | 11,755. |
| 1 column | 6,145. | |

7.  *Covers*

| | |
| --- | --- |
| 2nd cover (4 color) | 22,965. |
| 3rd cover (4 color) | 22,165. |
| 4th cover (4 color) | 29,120. |

8.  *Inserts*

Gatefolds, small size multiple page inserts, post card inserts, full page size inserts and many other types of special offers available. Rates available.

9.  *Bleed*

Extra                                                                                        10%

No charge for gutter bleed.

10.  *Special Position*

Orders specifying positions other than those known as preferred accepted but not guaranteed.

11.  *Classified and Reading Notices*

5.50 per word, per insertion. Minimum 10 words. Bold face, all capital letter words, 1.00 per word extra. Bold face headline or white space, 22.00 per line extra.

Per inch:

| | |
| --- | --- |
| 1–2 issues | 300. |
| 3–5 issues | 290. |

(continued)

6–11 issues                                                          280.

12 issues                                                          268.

Closing 8th of second month preceding issue.

*Display Classifications*

MAIL ORDER

Rates effective January, 1980. (Card No. 37M.)

Rates received October 31, 1979.

Card received March 31, 1980.

Available to advertisers of goods and services sold exclusively by mail. All ads positioned in the Shoppers' Showcase section.

| Frequency: | 1 pg | 2/3 pg | 1/2 pg | 1/3 pg |
|---|---|---|---|---|
| 1–2   times | 10,070. | 6,950. | 5,275. | 3,670. |
| 3–5   times | 9,820. | 6,775. | 5,145. | 3,580. |
| 6–8   times | 9,565. | 6,605. | 5,010. | 3,485. |
| 9–11 times | 9,315. | 6,430. | 4,880. | 3,395. |
| 12 times | 9,065. | 6,255. | 4,750. | 3,305. |

| | 1/6 pg | 1/12 pg | 1″ | Agate line |
|---|---|---|---|---|
| 1–2   times | 2,090. | 1,100. | 460. | 32.86 |
| 3–5   times | 2,040. | 1,075. | 449. | 32.08 |
| 6–8   times | 1,985. | 1,045. | 437. | 31.22 |
| 9–11 times | 1,935. | 1,020. | 426. | 30.43 |
| 12 times | 1,880. | 990. | 414. | 29.58 |

| Volume: | 1 pg | 2/3 pg | 1/2 pg | 1/3 pg |
|---|---|---|---|---|
| 3 pages | 9,770. | 6,745. | 5,115. | 3,560. |
| 6 pages | 9,365. | 6,470. | 4,905. | 3,410. |
| 9 pages | 8,965. | 6,190. | 4,695. | 3,265. |
| 12 pages | 8,505. | 5,870. | 4,455. | 3,095. |

| | 1/6 pg | 1/12 pg | 1″ | Agate line |
|---|---|---|---|---|
| 3 pages | 2,030. | 1,065. | 448. | 32.00 |
| 6 pages | 1,940. | 1,025. | 430. | 30.72 |
| 9 pages | 1,860. | 980. | 411. | 29.36 |
| 12 pages | 1,765. | 930. | 390. | 27.86 |

Black and 1 color (1/3 page or larger only),

extra                                                          10%

4 color (1/3 page or larger only), extra                                50%

Publishers, books, tape and record clubs 25% discount from display rates. All ads subject to copy screening and/or examination of product offered. Publisher reserves right to reject any ad which does not meet Popular Science acceptability standards. Advertiser must agree to handle mail orders promptly. Except for personalized services, advertiser agrees to refund full purchase price to dissatisfied readers who return merchandise within reasonable time.

12.   *Split-Run*

AB, numerical and geographical splits available.

13a.   *Geographic and/or Demographic Editions*

*Custom-Market Advertising Plan*

For less than national run ads, a Custom-Market Advertising Plan is offered whereby the advertiser may select any circulation combination from among the 50 states, Canada and/or the top three metro markets (New York, Chicago, Los Angeles).

**Figure 6-1.** *(continued)*

The Custom Market Advertising Plan is available in every issue subject to the following restrictions:
*(a)* Minimum space: full page; *(b)* Minimum circulation 400,000; *(c)* Closing date 1st day of 2nd month preceding date of issue.
Rates available on submission of advertiser's proposed specific Custom-Market Advertising Plan.

14. *Contract and Copy Regulations*
See Contents page for location-items 1, 2, 3, 8, 9, 10, 12, 14, 15, 16, 18, 19, 21, 24, 27, 30, 31, 32, 33, 34, 35, 36, 38.

15. *Mech. Requirements* Web Offset; (Classified and mail order Letterpress)
For complete, detailed production information, see SRDS Print Media Production Data.
Trim size: 8-1/8 × 10-7/8; No./Cols. 3.
Binding method: Perfect.
Colors available: AAAA/ABP; Matched; 4-Color
Process (AAAA/MPA); Simulated Metallic.
Cover colors available: 4-Color Process (AAAA/MPA): 5-Color Process; Simulated Metallic.

DIMENSIONS—AD PAGE

| | | | | |
|---|---|---|---|---|
| 1 | 7 | × 10 | 2 cols. | 4 5/8 × 10 |
| 1/2 | 4 5/8 | × 7 1/3 | 1 col. | 2 1/4 × 10 |
| 1/2 | 7 | × 5 | 1 col. | 4 5/8 × 5 |
| 1/6 | 2 1/4 | × 5 | | |

16. *Issue and Closing Dates*
Published monthly

| | | Closing | | |
|---|---|---|---|---|
| Issue | On Sale | (*) | (†) | (‡) |
| Jan/81 | 12/16 | 10/25 | 11/1 | 11/7 |

(*)4 color
(†)Black and white, black and 1 color.
(‡)Inserts and postcards.

17. *Special Services*
A.B.C. Supplemental Data Report released July 1978 issue.

18. *Circulation*
Established 1872. Single copy 1.50; per year 9.94.
Summary data—for detail see Publisher's Statement.
A.B.C. 6-30-80 (6 mos. aver.—Magazine Form)

| Tot. Pd. | (Subs.) | (Single) | (Assoc.) |
|---|---|---|---|
| 1,913,879 | 1,597,804 | 316,075 | |

Average Total Non-Pd Distribution (not incl. above):
Total 46,758

TERRITORIAL DISTRIBUTION 2/80—1,888,097

| N.Eng. | Mid.Atl. | E.N.Cen. | W.N.Cen. | S.Atl. | E.S.Cen. |
|---|---|---|---|---|---|
| 104,545 | 278,310 | 366,041 | 158,533 | 225,536 | 60,775 |
| W.S.Cen. | Mtn.St. | Pac.St. | Canada | Foreign | Other |
| 126,983 | 99,438 | 263,194 | 173,526 | 20,293 | 10,923 |

Publisher states: "Effective February, 1977 issue, rates based on annual average paid circulation of 1,800,000."

Similar types of features are included for *International and Farm Publications*, plus a listing of farm direct-response media, such as "Co-Op Dairy" and "Pig American" direct-response cards. Several of these specialized features are particularly helpful to direct marketers.

*Shopping Pages* lists magazines which accept small-space mail-order advertisements in special sections. Presumably, such sections are very effective because the rates are lower and the ads are grouped together near compatible editorial matter. This type of shopping-section ad has been the lifeblood of many small mail-order businesses.

*Demographic and Geographic Editions* lists magazines which can be segmented by type of reader or by area of the country—a valuable way to target expenditures to a specific market or to minimize downside risk on a test.

*Split Run Availability* shows magazines which will accept split-run advertising, facilitating copy testing with or without combination with geographic or demographic editions.

## Some Other Tools of the Trade

While SRDS is the indispensable tool of the media planner, other tools can sometimes be very useful.

*Audit Statements*    Audit statements began as a way of verifying circulation claims and providing an independent verification of publishers' sworn statements. The best-known individual magazine statements are those published by the Audit Bureau of Circulation. Today their most valuable function is their breakdown of circulation by source. An ABC statement will disclose whether a magazine is subscription-sold or newsstand-sold; whether it has been sold at cut rate, with premiums, or with a sweepstakes; and whether it has been sold by direct mail or through agents such as Publishers' Clearing House. All this data can be analyzed to indicate the quality of a publication's circulation. Direct-mail-sold readers, who have come in through full-price subscriptions, can be the most meaningful circulation if your own product is sold the same way. However, if you have a reduced-price introductory offer or are selling with a sweepstakes, it may be important to know that similar offers were successful in attracting the magazine's readers in the first place.

Usually, the data is helpful the other way around—in tailoring the offer. If a magazine ad has been marginal in response despite a logical affinity of editorial matter, it may be helpful to look at how it was sold in the first place. If the magazine was sold by sweepstakes, it might be worth trying your own sweepstakes offer there.

Another factor revealed by audit statements is the status of the circulation, as opposed to the source. If most readers are new, introductory readers, they may not be reading the magazine intensely if it is not what they expected. However, a large percentage of renewed renewals (RRs) indicates that the publication is being read thoroughly, giving your advertisement a better chance of being read as well. From a direct marketer's point of view, the quality of a magazine might be represented by this formula: MS% × RR% = QF, or percentage of direct-mail-sold times percentage of renewed renewals equals quality factor.

The quality factor can be applied to total percentages or to cost per thousand readers to produce a quality-adjusted circulation or cost per thousand. There should be a correlation between quality-adjusted cost figures and resulting cost-per-order data from actual insertions.

*PIB Reports*    Another tool is PIB reports, issued by Publishers Information Bureau. As discussed in Chapter 3, The Marketing Plan, the primary reason for reading PIB reports is to check on competition to see what publications they are using repeatedly.

*Simmons Reports*    Simmons reports, available in voluminous binders at great expense, are the most sophisticated application of research to publication-media buying. Simmons conducts extensive surveys, asking readers what magazines they read and what their hobbies and interests are, and draws valuable conclusions about magazine readership and reader interests.

Many agencies have this data on computer, and can quickly run through categories to produce media efficiency studies. For instance, if you wanted to run an ad selling golf clubs by mail, they would correlate readers who play golf and readers who buy by mail. They could then combine the results with income, education, age, family size, or any other factors to produce a media list based on cost per thousand targeted readers.

## THE MATHEMATICS OF MEDIA

For companies new to this field, a review of some of the basics will be helpful before going on to selection of magazine and newspaper media.

*CPM versus CPR*    The basic tool of media buying is cost per thousand, meaning advertising cost times one-thousandth of the circulation, producing cost per thousand circulation. This is a traditional index, and at one time SRDS used to quote CPM for a typical black-and-white page at the end of each listing. However, it is not the only index and certainly not the most important one.

The figure that counts, in the long run, is one that correlates results—or at least expected results—as cost per response (or order, or lead, or subscription). The CPR, the ultimate index for direct marketers, is simply advertising cost divided by number of responses.

Some advertisers and agencies also use a figure called orders per thousand to provide a constant figure for responsiveness of a given media space unit against all propositions and all advertisers whose data they can compare. OPM eliminates distortions due to volume discounts, remnant rates, or exchange space deals, and indexes the potential "life" of the magazine's audience without cost distortion. The value of the OPM factor becomes very clear if you presume that each publisher is reasonable and negotiable, as most are, and that—given the facts—they will bring their costs into line with other publications to make their magazine attractive to advertisers.

The OPM factor is also important when conducting tests in split-run or regional editions. Such smaller segments are always more expensive on a CPM basis. The use of the OPM factor evens out the premium cost and provides a consistent standard for comparing results.

*Mail-Order Rates*    Many magazines and newspapers offer special reduced rates for classifications of advertising which they consider particularly desirable or where competition with other publications is particularly severe. Philanthropic rates, cultural rates, publisher's rates, and retail rates are all common and can make a big difference in projected CPR.

I know of one mail-order book advertiser whose most important medium was the *New York Times*. The advertiser opened a retail store just to get that paper's retail rate. The retail store prospered unexpectedly and became the forerunner of half a dozen such stores.

*Volume and Frequency Discounts*    Many publications offer lower rates, called frequency discounts, for multiple insertions, either in a single issue of a publication or over a period of time. Publications also offer volume discounts, based on the total lines or dollar amount of space used during a fiscal or calendar year. Such discounts often allow large advertisers to support marginal propositions where other advertisers would not be able to make them work. In some cases, however, such discounts are not available if a mail-order discount is also being taken. Check with the publications.

At the end of a contract period, it sometimes pays to run some additional advertising that will help the entire schedule reach a lower rate breakpoint. CBS, for instance, is able to run advertising for its magazines and for specialty mail-order clubs in the same *TV Guide* issues as its Columbia House ads, making a much lower rate available to the smaller proposition than it would enjoy if it were independent.

One unfortunate by-product of such volume and frequency discounts is their tendency to accelerate the decline of individual, small direct marketers. Such rates make it possible for a giant advertiser to buy a smaller competitor or overwhelm their advertising. Volume discounts are attractive to big advertisers but, in my opinion, grossly unfair to smaller ones.

*Printing Costs*   In direct marketing media, advertisers often buy units with bound-in or tipped-on insert cards, multipage sections, or newspaper inserts. In such cases the printing cost should be considered part of the overall cost in all schedules, even though it is not billed by the magazine. A media schedule and subsequent analyses of results should always include printing costs as if they were part of the media cost.

*Premium Rates*   Almost all publications charge a higher CPM for regional or demographic editions than for full-run advertising. This is only fair, as a publication is segmented at great cost and difficulty, and only for the convenience of advertisers. However, the resulting CPR will be higher than if a full-run insertion were used. This should be kept in mind, and appropriate adjustments made, when determining whether regional or split-run advertisements can be rolled out on a full-run basis.

*Remnant Rates*   Many publications offer various kinds of remnant deals, particularly in the Sunday supplement field. The offer applies to units that remain unsold after premium regional edition buyers have made their pick. In some cases, publications will offer unsold space on a remnant deal subject to preemption if a full-price advertiser comes along. Even the prestigious *New York Times* has a half-price offer contingent on permitting the *Times* to select the date within a certain time frame. *Time* magazine offers flexible-date advertising at 35 percent less than the full rate.

*Surcharges*   Another rate consideration is the cost of surcharges. Most publications will charge extra for a premium position, such as a back cover, although few will charge for (or guarantee) positions such as the front of the magazine. Some newspapers charge different rates, or surcharges, for ads in a specific Sunday section, such as a magazine section.

One of the most common surcharges is for "bleed" pages—the right to run your advertisement over the entire page, right to the edge, rather than just to the margin. Many progressive publishers, recognizing that four-color bleed ads make their magazine more interesting and colorful for readers, are discontinuing this charge.

*Agency Commissions and Cash Discounts*     Most magazines and newspapers grant recognized advertising agencies a 15 percent agency commission. This is a practice that dates back to the days when agencies literally bought space in blocks and resold it to advertisers. Today agencies earn this commission by providing the creative services that used to be supplied by individual publications.

There was a time when any recognized member of the American Association of Advertising Agencies would be expected to work strictly on the commission system. Today that applies mostly to very large advertising accounts which require a full range of agency services. Some large clients who demand less than full service—perhaps excluding the agency from marketing planning or media buying—negotiate arrangements where the agency is paid only a partial commission. Or agencies may be paid on a fee or hourly basis, rebating all or part of the commission to the advertiser.

With smaller accounts this agency commission may be only part of the compensation paid by the advertiser to the agency for marketing, creative, media buying, and executional services. A minimum income guarantee or supplementary fee is often required in addition to earned commissions. Sometimes the commissions are credited against a guaranteed monthly income.

It is possible for an advertiser to set up a "house agency" to keep the commission, thus lowering advertising expense by 15 percent. This is generally a false economy, due to the cost of the staff required and the loss of the professionalism and objectivity provided by an outside agency. Any client who thinks a house agency is a good investment has probably never worked with a first-class advertising agency. In the direct marketing field particularly, any agency that can't lift its clients' results by much more than the 15 percent commission is not doing its job. The best solution in such cases is not a house agency but a different outside agency.

*Production Costs*     The costs of preparing artwork—type, photography, paste-up, etc.—can be substantial. Should these costs be figured in the media budget and in result analysis? My recommendation, and the general industry practice, is a negative answer.

If an ad runs only once, production costs will be substantial in relation to the overall budget. If it runs many times, in many publications, production costs may be insignificant. I have never seen a formula that anticipates this problem. The general practice is to treat production costs as a separate "above-the-line" budget against the total advertising appropriation—not against individual advertisements. The costs should be controlled, and economies should be related to the extent of intended use as a control on the production budget, not as a burden to individual media expenditures.

Whatever rates your company can earn, and whatever fees, surcharges, commissions, or discounts are involved, the bottom line remains the same: cost per response.

## SELECTING THE RIGHT PUBLICATIONS

How do you pick the best magazines or newspapers in which to place your first advertisements? If you have already proved that print media works for you, where do you run your next ads?

No matter what stage you're in, the selection process is the same, and the principles are very similar to those we explained for selecting direct-mail lists. If the media is the market, you want to know which media will pay off for you. The "affinity" approach is a logical place to start—with some exceptions.

### Mail Responsiveness

You might think that an art publication would be the right place to advertise art supplies or prints. It seems logical because of the affinity between audience and product; but you'd most likely be wrong.

When you're selecting from mail-order-buyers lists, the factor of mail responsiveness is already built in. That's where the list came from. But that's not necessarily the case with magazines.

Certainly look first at those publications where there is a clear relationship between their editorial subject and your product or service, but within that group of magazines, look for the factor of mail responsiveness. That's where you'll need either the ABC statement or a space salesperson who's willing to do more than take you to lunch.

Is the magazine sold by subscription or on the newsstand? Subscription buyers have at least responded to the subscription offer. Is the magazine sold by mail? That's good. Is it sold through association memberships or sweepstakes-based agents? That's bad. Whether you observe these factors empirically or calculate the quality factor discussed earlier, the quality factor has to be taken into account.

A simpler approach is to play follow the leader. Look at several issues of the magazine, and see if it carries a great deal of other direct marketing advertising. Then look up some of the advertisers in PIB and see if the ads are repeats, rather than first-time insertions. You might even talk to some advertisers that are not directly competitive with you and ask how the magazine pulled.

Ask whether the advertising is paid space. Don't be misled into going into a publication at full rate when the bulk of previous direct-response space has been there on an exchange or remnant basis.

If plenty of other advertisers have been repeating coupon advertising or if the publication has a high quality factor by observation or calculation, then it's worth a try—providing the audience is the right one.

## Editorial Affinity

How do you determine whether a magazine's audience is right for you? The key is editorial affinity, or an observation of the editorial environment—an observation which relies entirely on the subjective judgment of the person responsible for making the media recommendation or decision.

A vertical publication dealing directly with the field at which your product is aimed may not be right because the readership may be too advanced or too amateurish for your particular product. A general magazine with a strong mail-order advertising representation may be too down-scale or up-scale, or may exclude the audience or market segment you need. This is where judgment comes in, and is one of the ways direct marketing is still an art as well as a science.

There is no substitute for examining the actual magazines and getting a feel for the editorial content and the level of other direct marketing advertisements. The environment has to be right for your particular advertisement; or maybe you will have to prepare a special offer and advertising approach that will make this particular medium work for you.

## The Elusive Audience

The people you are trying to reach read many magazines and newspapers. They get direct mail. They listen to radio and watch television. There is no one way to reach them, but there is usually a best way.

It is essential to remember that we are usually only trying to get a response from less than one-half of 1 percent of a publication's readership. That means we are concerned with only 10 or 20 percent of the publication's circulation at best. Our target market segment does not have to be the majority of a magazine's readers; it just has to be there somewhere.

That somewhere doesn't have to be in the mainstream of the publication's circulation. They could be at the lower edge of an up-scale publication or the upper edge of a down-scale one. A mass-market mutual fund, for instance, can do equally well in *Barron's*, which is primarily directed at sophisticated investors, or in *Money*, which deals mostly with budget planning and shopping guidance rather than investments per se. Both may have attracted enough prospects to be successful for you. The only way to find out is to examine the magazine, use your own judgment, and—if you're not sure—take a chance and see what happens.

## Media Constellations

If the total potential media for a proposition is called a media universe, then the logical subcategories of that whole might be termed "constellations." Just as astronomers arbitrarily group stars into constellations, advertisers arbitrarily group publications into categories.

Once you've examined SRDS, considered the wide scope of possible magazines, and examined the data and the magazines themselves, you can sort the publications by any common attributes you desire. Your categories are as good as anyone else's.

Perhaps you'll have vertical publications, down-scale ones, prestige magazines, city or regional publications, newspaper Sunday supplements, foreign language papers, women's magazines. If your market is narrower, you might break down a category like women's magazines into even finer subconstellations like women's homemaking magazines, women's career magazines, women's cooking publications, and women's escapism magazines. With newspapers you might use categories like size of market, area of country, level of editorial, and political slant. Any category can be refined down to the ultimate subcategory: an individual publication.

The categories in SRDS are a handy place to start, but they are as subjective as the categories you would invent. That's why many magazines list themselves in more than one SRDS category, and that's why categories must be broken down into those that are relevant for you and your business.

## Pilot Publications

Once you've established the categories, you're ready for the next step—picking one representative magazine within each constellation to be your pilot publication. This is the magazine or newspaper that you want to advertise in that will enable you to make a decision about the entire grouping that it represents. As such, it must be typical of the constellation.

A pilot publication should not be the place to experiment on a single magazine that might be new or untried by others. You want to give this pilot every chance of succeeding and representing its group, and so it should be the publication in the group that appears to be most used by other direct marketers and most representative, editorially, of the group as a whole.

To minimize downside risk, a pilot publication does not have to be a full run of a given magazine or newspaper. It can be a region or a split run, providing that the publication will not double-handicap you—not only charge you a premium rate but also place your ad in a marginal back-of-the-book position.

Don't be concerned about picking a publication that is likely to do a bit better than most other publications in the constellation. If your group is news magazines, for instance, and you are looking for older, more serious readers, then by all means start with *U.S. News & World Report*. A *Time* regional buy might be more representative, but if your offer doesn't work in *U.S. News* it won't work in *Time* or *Newsweek*. So give yourself the edge by going with the stronger magazine and then rolling out cautiously after you see the results.

*TV Guide*    This single magazine is a media constellation in itself, and no discussion of media would be complete unless its unique attributes were reviewed. It is the key medium for some of the nation's largest direct marketers, and has been an important test medium for many others.

Because the magazine reaches an audience whose common denominator is simply ownership of television sets, it covers an almost universal audience. At the beginning of 1980 its total circulation exceeded 19 million households.

The magazine has over 100 editions, distributed according to TV markets, and offers a perfect A-B split in each of those markets. It is a weekly, which means you can get fast turnaround for testing. You can test a wide variety of copy appeals very quickly, sometimes in advance of a general national campaign.

This publication's readers have many interests—the outdoors, decorating, shopping, entertainment. It is a unique place to use the skimming strategy and let a proposition seek its own audience.

Part of the success of the magazine is due to its low cost per page, a product of its small page size. Actually, on the basis of cost per square inch per thousand circulation, it is quite expensive, but an offer that doesn't need much space to fully explain and sell it can do very nicely.

Inserts and foldout units are eagerly sought after, but they are very sensitive to position, timing, and competitive factors. With printing costs, a typical book club or encyclopedia insertion can cost over $300,000 an insertion—and there's usually a waiting list.

### Letting the Consumer Make the Decisions

In direct marketing, we don't try to figure out the consumer. We just try to set up opportunities for consumers to tell us what they want.

In general advertising, expert opinion and statistical data lead to a high budget for scheduling each magazine for several insertions, to build frequency. In direct marketing, on the other hand, where each ad has to stand alone, a small budget is appropriated for pilot publication testing with one insertion per publication. Then the direct marketer waits to read the results. The balance of the appropriation is held in reserve for a campaign to run during a good season after getting the results of the pilot tests. In an ongoing campaign these tests might alternate with rollouts. Summer tests, for instance, are intended to influence the following summer schedules, not the winter campaign. Turnaround time becomes very important in integrating tests and roll-outs.

Fast closing dates might influence the selection of a pilot publication. Weekly rather than monthly publications are also a plus in testing. Weekly magazines are readable a full month sooner, after the sale date, than monthlies, and usually have faster closing dates as well.

General advertisers often have difficulty in accepting the constant change and step-by-step decision making of direct marketing media plans. They are accustomed to taking $100,000 and committing it all at once. A direct marketing schedule might commit half that to testing, put the other half in reserve, and then ask for an additional half-million dollars if results justify it.

## MAGAZINE CONSIDERATIONS

Circulation numbers and characteristics are only one consideration in planning a magazine schedule. You also have to know what kind of space unit to use, what position to ask for, and whether or not to use some type of segmentation.

### Space Units

Let's look at the space unit first. Should it be large or small? One page or two? What about those spectacular units like multiple-page inserts or heavy stock preprinted bind-ins, perhaps with a reply-card flap?

The traditional rule is to use as little space as possible to get your message across and to avoid wasting money on white space and irrel-evant illustrations. That's a good starting place, but its not a rule without exceptions.

On one end of the spectrum, a small 3- or 4-inch, one-column advertisement in a shopping section can be the safest and most profitable insertion you can make, on a return-on-investment basis. After this unit is placed in every applicable publication as often as results hold up, what's the next step?

Running larger ads seems to be the obvious solution, but often the larger ad produces little more response than the original ad. That's because space alone is not an attention getter. As I'll explain in Chapter 14, Advertising Layout, the perceived size of an ad is not the size of the space unit, but the size of the largest single element in the advertisement. Just blowing up an ad to a larger size gives you a larger element, but not necessarily more selling power or more impact.

A larger ad should be redesigned and conceptually thought through from the beginning. If the ad is to have proportionately greater result-getting appeal than the original ad, it must use the space better. Perhaps the larger version can add testimonials, or dramatize a guarantee or product feature that there wasn't room for before. Or perhaps the main attention-getting element—a headline or illustration—can be made even more dramatic to multiply the stopping power of the ad even more than the increase in the size of the space.

For some types of products or services, a standard fractional unit like a half page or page can be important because of the credibility it adds, by itself, to the advertisement. This is the only case where sheer size can add results. An "exciting announcement" is much more exciting in a full-page ad, as a message from a company which purports to be large and important. This theory is most important with companies that are not well known. A major institution that already has a widely established name can get away with smaller space units than a newcomer to the field.

Once a space unit reaches its optimum level of responsiveness, increasing the space unit to a larger size is still sometimes worthwhile. For example, a philanthropic advertiser soliciting contributions uses double-page spreads in its best magazines, rather than pages. The cost per donor is slightly higher, but the incremental return for the second page is still greater than if the same money were spent on a marginal medium or greater frequency.

## Spectacular Units

So-called spectacular units are very substantial investments which produce equally substantial improvements in results. The old rule of thumb is that a simple insert card costs 2½ times the cost of a page but produces four times the results.

There are several kinds of spectacular units. The simplest is the bound-in reply card. The greatest importance of this unit is the ease of reply which it offers the reader interested in your proposition, but it also "indexes" the magazine, causing it to open at that page while being thumbed through.

Full-page inserts, with your ad printed on both sides, also offer the same advantages, plus even more impact due to the sheer weight of the inserted page.

Four-, six-, or eight-page inserts, or even longer ones, can also be bound in, where it is necessary to offer a large choice or a long presentation of copy points. Such units are often on coated stock, card stock, or standard magazine coated paper. They may or may not include a reply card; some advertisers deliberately omit the business reply card as a way of trading response rate for quality improvement.

Such units are often hard to schedule, as publications have relatively few such positions available in each issue. Advertisers who have used them before generally have an option to continue to use the same unit on the same date in subsequent years.

### Color or Black and White?

There's no hard-and-fast rule to this question either. Color is particularly valuable if used well—especially to illustrate a colorful product. The only test I know of color versus black and white showed that color paid for itself, although it did not lower the cost per order. The rule is to use color only if it adds to the visual appeal of the product or the impact of the advertisement—both highly subjective evaluations.

One alternative that is always wrong is two or three colors. If your message isn't appealing in black and white, a color headline or background isn't going to make a difference. And certainly it's not worth the money just to put your company trademark in a second color. Either go with black and white, or go all the way to four-color with lifelike illustrations.

### Magazine Positions

Virtually all advertisers agree on the relative ranks of various positions in most magazines, although they disagree on the exact percentage difference between them. However, everyone agrees that position is an important influence on results.

In magazines, insert card positions are the most effective, with the first better than the second and so on. Pulling power declines until just before the back of the magazine, where the last insert card does only

10 percent less than the first. This is a general rule, and results vary depending on the type of magazine. Fashion publications, handicraft magazines, and financial publications seem to hold up better throughout the magazine than other types of publications.

In general space, right-hand pages pull better than left-hand, with the first right-hand page the very best and others declining at 3 or 4 percent for each subsequent right-hand page.

Back covers are particularly desirable, and will do as well as a first right-hand page, if the publication does not impose a punitive surcharge for the position. The inside back cover will do as well as a first right-hand page, with the page facing it producing as well as a second right-hand page. These unique back-of-book positions are more likely to be available than first right-hand pages, and should always be considered when negotiating with a space representative.

One of the errors general advertising agencies and direct marketing beginners make is presuming that the magazine will give them the best possible position, or that nothing can be done to influence the choice of position. It may be easy to mail out an insertion order reading "Far forward right-hand position requested," but this is not doing everything you can. Talk to the ad sales representative for the publication and stress the importance of position, particularly in terms of potential repeat insertions. Specific pages should be negotiated for and an understanding reached, even if they cannot be guaranteed. One insertion order clause which is sometimes accepted by magazines is "Page xx or better right-hand position urgently requested, or notify agency prior to cancellation date."

## Segmented Editions

As discussed above, it is not necessary to buy a full national circulation of a magazine, and there are many times when it will be desirable to pay a higher rate per thousand circulation in order to target a specific area or demographic group, or to limit downside risk.

A wide variety of options is offered by magazines. Here are some examples of the alternatives available.

*Better Homes and Gardens* is a good example. With 8 million circulation, it offers the following choices:

- 51 regional marketing editions, generally states, with circulations ranging from as little as 14,000 to almost half a million, with any combination available.

- 56 top markets, generally metropolitan areas, with circulations as little as 29,000 (Providence, RI) or as much as 478,000 (New York).

- Metro/Suburban. A single edition covering the metro marketing area surrounding and including every A county in the U.S.—25 top marketing areas sold in one 4,000,000 copy edition.

- Travel sections. State circulations grouped for the convenience of the travel industry, each comprising more than one million people in travel origination areas such as East, Great Lakes, and West.

- Alternate copy. One half of the circulation, sold on an every other copy basis evenly distributed throughout the publication's circulation.

*Time* has been particularly innovative in segmentation and offers over 150 different markets in editions of as little as 25,000 copies. They also offer some unique demographic editions:

- *Time* Student/Educator Edition     550,000

- *Time* Doctor's Edition     165,000

- *Time* B     1,550,000     business executives

- *Time* T     300,000     subscribers in top management

- *Time* Z     1,200,000     subscribers living in 1414 top income quintile zip code areas

- *Time* A+     600,000     ultrahigh income professional/managerial households

Not to be outdone, *Newsweek* has several similar editions, plus two unique ones:

- *Newsweek* Woman     500,000     female subscribers

- *Newsweek* Hometown     1,000,000     non-urban subscribers

These examples give an idea of the opportunities available in special editions. Over 160 magazines offer segmentation opportunities for advertisers.

## NEWSPAPERS—ROP, SUPPLEMENTS, AND PREPRINTS

In general advertising the most important attributes of the newspaper medium are its ability to achieve a very high penetration of each market, its high credibility, and its immediacy.

These same attributes are of interest to direct marketers, but overall, they are offset by the medium's lack of "mail responsiveness." Very few newspapers are sold by mail, and few carry significant amounts of direct marketing advertising in relation to other advertising. This trend is changing, as home-delivered papers use direct mail and telephone calls to solicit subscriptions, but it still generally prevails.

## ROP Newspaper Advertising

There are very few national direct marketers who advertise in daily or Sunday newspapers in preference to national magazines or other forms of newspaper advertising. When such ads are not specified for a specific section, such as the financial section, they are "run of paper" (ROP).

Gerber's life insurance division has been running full- and double-page spreads offering term policies for many years, and other insurance companies seem to be following suit. However, this field seems to be the exception.

In addition, newspapers are used when the product or service is local, or when a specific newspaper editorial section targets a needed audience.

In direct marketing, schools and seminars advertise in newspapers to build enrollments for their classes. In such advertising, location and starting date should be prominently featured, as in "Fayetteville Classes Start October First." This makes the ad a news item in itself, with its own elements of localness, immediacy, and newsiness. In effect, this adapts the ad style to the media environment.

Many advertisers use newspapers to tie in with local dealers, particularly where the product must be sold through a dealer. This is not strictly a direct marketing application but more of a sales promotion scheme, although direct marketing agencies work with such projects frequently.

The most effective use of local newspapers by national direct marketers appears to involve "reader notice" advertising, where 50- or 100-line ads are designed to resemble newspaper items. (There are 14 agate lines to an inch; this is a standard way of expressing newspaper sizes. A 100-line ad can be 100 by 1 or 50 by 2, the second figure indicating the number of columns.)

Successful newspaper "reader notice" ads include many self-improvement subjects, in areas such as memory, vocabulary, and conversation. An interesting new application is Bradford Exchange's large schedule of advertisements with testimonial headlines like "Claremont woman buys dish in garage sale for $1—worth $1100."

Newspaper advertising rates are covered in a *Newspaper SRDS* that is very similar to the one previously described for magazines. Newspapers are listed by market area, with rates generally in cost per agate line. Most newspaper advertising is sold ROP. Your ad can be placed anywhere. Specific classifications or sections of the paper, such as "Food Editorial," "Main News Section," "Sports Section," "Financial Pages," and "Business News," usually have a separate higher rate, or require a position surcharge. There are also surcharges for specific positions such as "top of column."

Newspaper positions can and should be negotiated in the same manner as magazine positions. A prominent, far-forward position is often worth any extra surcharge. In buying newspaper ads, caution should be taken before automatically placing advertisements in "appropriate" classifications. The education section is often not the best place for a school ad, just as the stamp and coin page would not be the best place for an ad selling coins to investors—especially if you were seeking to bring new people into the market.

Both placement (location in the newspaper) and position (location on the page) should always be tested.

### Sunday Supplements

The two principal newspaper supplements, *Parade* and *Family Weekly*, together deliver over 30 million households in 480 newspapers. This is a big medium and one that is often used by direct marketers.

Sunday supplements are published on a large scale, usually in a magazine format, sometimes as comics. They are distributed in newspapers around the country. The larger ones can be broken down into regions or "target groups." Because Sunday supplements are usually printed on calendered stock, the four-color reproduction rivals that offered by magazines.

Back covers are particularly effective but are hard to get. National advertisers such as Doubleday and CBS have tied up many of them, and they are also sought eagerly by cigarette and other general advertisers. Some of the national supplements are shown in Table 6-1.

**TABLE 6-1**

| Supplement | No. of Papers | Circulation |
| --- | --- | --- |
| *Family Weekly* | 353 | 12,000,000 |
| *Greenleaves* | 35 | 1,600,000 |
| *Metro Comics* | 89 | 23,200,000 |
| *Midwest* | 140 | 650,000 |
| *Parade* | 130 | 21,000,000 |
| *Puck Comics* | 160 | 17,687,000 |
| *Sunday* | 51 | 14,000 |

In addition, there are excellent individual magazines published by newspapers in many large cities. The magazine sections of the *New York Times, New York News, Chicago Tribune,* and *Los Angeles Times* are excellent editorial vehicles and have been successful for a wide variety of direct marketing advertising. Some specialized publications, such as the *Los Angeles Times Home Section* and the *New York Times Book Review,* are recognized and important media in their own right.

Sunday supplements have a very different readership pattern from newspapers in general. The supplement is likely to be treated as a magazine and kept around the house for several days until it can be read leisurely.

Consequently, many ads work in supplements which do not work in newspapers. Small-space shopping-section ads often do well, as do major units. Many advertisers place half- and full-page ads on a standby or remnant basis. In return for a substantially reduced rate, they accept date flexibility or editions left over from other advertisers' regional buys.

## Newspaper Preprints

Sometimes called free-falls or freestanding inserts, newpaper preprints are the big guns of modern direct marketing. They offer all the impact of the most spectacular magazine or direct-mail unit, complete with envelopes, reply cards, or pop-up membership cards, with the saturation effect of Sunday newspaper circulation.

Preprints are exactly what the name implies. The advertising unit is printed by the advertiser, generally in large quantities, and shipped to individual newspapers for insertion with the Sunday paper. It is like a separate "section" of the Sunday paper and most likely tumbles out when the paper is opened, just as a blow-in card falls out of a magazine. The reader has to handle the preprint even if only to throw it away— and if it is handled, it is likely to be looked at.

The range of propositions that work in preprints is truly amazing, from the most general of book club, insurance, or magazine propositions to highly selective invitations for ballet subscriptions or mutual funds.

The cost of preprints is high. Including space costs, printing, and freight, a preprint campaign can cost $50 to $75 per thousand circulation, depending on the format. However, the results are higher still.

Preprints offer the opportunity to use a reply device and to have enough space to tell the entire story and ask for the order. There are booklet formats, gatefold formats, and envelope formats. The choice is so versatile that the medium is sometimes considered closer to direct mail than to print advertising. The main difference is that the newspaper, rather than the post office, delivers the message to the customer.

There is another advantage as well. Many newspapers can permit preprints to be distributed to specific geographic areas within the newspaper market. You can often specify the kind of neighborhoods you need. An investment product might go into higher-income areas only. A home repair or gardening product might be advertised only in suburbs rather than in apartment building areas. A bank or real estate proposition might select only their own trading area rather than have to buy the entire city's circulation.

The Starrett City apartment complex in New York utilized newspaper preprints by concentrating on the most likely target areas. The same budget that had been spread over the whole metropolitan area in routine ads was reallocated to preprints to be disseminated in select neighborhoods. There was no increase in budget, only a redistribution of it.

One caveat before designing a preprint: Particularly in Illinois, have your lawyer look into what has been called the Cleary Patent claim. This is a patent on one type of preprint that has been supported in one state. Many advertisers have paid a royalty rather than contest the claim. Although the patent is expiring in a few years, and although the application may be limited or the claim disputed, this is a matter for your lawyer to advise you on. You would not want to get a letter claiming a substantial royalty after you have inserted millions of preprints into newspapers.

Preprints also are an ideal medium for television support advertising, which is discussed in Chapter 7, Broadcast Media.

## BUSINESS MEDIA

The same principles apply to business magazines and business newspapers as to general publications. General business magazines like *Business Week* and the *Wall Street Journal* can be very responsive; others are not.

There are two basic kinds of business publications. "Horizontal" ones cut across industry lines and address themselves to job titles or management levels, financial officers, engineers, purchasing agents, and marketing specialists. "Vertical" publications like *Hardware Age* and *Modern Plastics* talk to everyone within a specific industry.

Most specialized magazines do not do well for direct marketing offers, at least not as compared to renting the lists of the same publications and addressing the readers by mail.

The *Wall Street Journal* and *Business Week* straddle the fence between being general business publications and business-oriented consumer magazines. They are listed in both editions of SRDS. Segmentation is offered for both, and they can be tested by using a regional edition first and projecting what the results would have been on a national basis.

If you do use specialized business publications, I suggest that you ask the publication not to list your product in their "bingo" card—the reply card which the magazine provides to readers so they can easily request information about products. The ease of reply is so great, and the temptation to circle a few more numbers while filling it out so inviting, that such bingo leads have a reputation for very poor quality. This doesn't mean that all the responses are bad; only that the good ones are lost among the curiosity seekers. This applies to any type of publication, but the cards are much more common in business publications.

## WHAT'S THE BEST SEASON FOR ADVERTISING?

After you pick the right magazines for your direct marketing program, you still have to decide what time of the year would be the best for your advertising campaign. Seasonal influences can cause substantial differences in results.

Many advertisers have tested direct-mail seasons and have been able to precisely plot the best times of the year for mailings. However, testing is not as easily done in print advertising. If the same ad runs month after month, a fatigue factor sets in, automatically making the first months look better than the later ones.

However, here's the "state of the art" agreed to by most major advertisers:

1.  The best month is January, meaning January magazines with on-sale dates just after Christmas, or January weeklies or newspapers.

2.  February and October tie for the number 2 position, about 10 percent behind January.

3.  July and September are also acceptable, with only another 10 percent decline behind February and October.

4.  March and November are possibilities, especially if you can't find an open date anywhere else. Another 10 percent drop.

5.  The second quarter—April, May, and June—is the worst part of the year, along with December and August. Drop these 10 percent, and avoid these months if you can.

To translate these comments into a scale would produce an index like this:

| | |
|---|---|
| January | 100 |
| February | 90 |
| March | 70 |
| April | 60 |
| May | 60 |
| June | 60 |
| July | 80 |
| August | 60 |
| September | 80 |
| October | 90 |
| November | 70 |
| December | 60 |

Theories about why certain months do better than others are plentiful. Prevalent is the "change-of-season" theory, which says the second quarter is when people are looking forward to summer, and October is when they are finally "back to work" in the new fall season. Everyone agrees on the reason for January—another "back-to-work" feeling after the hectic Christmas season, plus a sense of affluence from Christmas bonuses and the feeling that the New Year is the time to start new projects or fulfill newly adopted self-improvement resolutions.

There are many other factors as well. Weather can play a big role in results, particularly in newspaper schedules. Bad weather is good, as people will stay in and read the paper—providing the weather is not so bad that they can't get the paper at all. Good weather is bad, for people may go out on a Sunday drive instead of staying home to read your advertisement. Broadcast is even more sensitive to weather factors. Newspapers are sometimes saved to be read another day, and magazines always are, but a missed radio or television announcement is missed forever.

Elections can have an influence. Just after a hotly contested presidential election, about half the country will feel a letdown because their candidate lost, and this can show up in ad results. Before an election, there may be too many interesting items to read in a newspaper. In fact, anything worth reading can depress ad results. A major news event of any kind that's worth reading leaves your prospect less time to look at ads. Fortunately for advertising (and unfortunately for the state of today's journalism), this is not a frequent occurrence.

*       *       *

Now that we've covered the science of media planning, let's conclude with a word about the art. There's no way to plug in a computer and produce an ideal media schedule. There's still a great need for subjective judgment in evaluating editorial environment, selecting audience targets, and picking the best publication and the best season—particularly when the ones you really want have already been reserved by some other advertiser.

There's still a place for instinct in media buying—for the hunch based on years of experience that is too complex to recall and explain but is right more often than not.

## CHAPTER SEVEN

# BROADCAST MEDIA

One of the most significant developments in direct marketing is the emergence of radio and television as direct-response media. Not only are broadcast media an important added market for products proved effective in more traditional media, but also they have made possible entirely new types of direct marketing successes.

### BROADCAST IS UNIQUE

Radio and television require a very different approach from direct mail or print. On the one hand, they lack a "hard-order" device; there's no card to fill out, and not even a coupon. On the other, they offer incredible impact, coverage, and credibility.

Broadcast is perishable. It can't be torn out and read carefully at a more convenient time. It's now or never.

Broadcast is impatient. You have seconds to tell your whole story—to attract attention, offer a benefit, demonstrate your product, and motivate a desired action. Then you still must communicate an address or telephone number in a way that will make it memorable. In broadcast, you have to say it quickly, say it simply, say it effectively—or save your money.

However, the opportunities are fantastic. Broadcast goes into the home and talks to your prospect. It finds a viewer. It doesn't wait for a page to be turned or an envelope opened.

Because it offers sight, sound, and motion, broadcast communicates 100 percent, not 10 percent. The body language and tone of voice which must be simulated in copy style and graphics in other media are available to support your message with appropriate degrees of sincerity, enthusiasm, conviction, or urgency.

Broadcast has credibility. In focus panel research, the most often repeated objection to buying by mail order is the wish to see the product. On television it can be seen from every angle. Consumers can see it working. They can see what it does, what makes it tick, and how to operate it. Television is the ultimate illustration, and it does its work at the lowest cost per thousand of any medium.

## TWO KINDS OF BROADCAST

There are two basically different kinds of broadcast direct marketing—and I don't mean radio and television. There is another, more fundamental dichotomy: *direct response* and *direct support*. They are as different as night and day. They require different formats, different copy treatments, different media strategies. And they have entirely different purposes.

*Direct response* applies to advertising designed to produce an immediate inquiry, order, or donation. By definition, it must offer an address and/or a telephone number. By necessity, it must be lengthy enough to accomplish several creative objectives—usually 120 seconds in length, compared to the 30- or 60-second ads used by conventional advertisers.

*Direct support*, on the other hand, is exactly the opposite. It needs no address or telephone number. It can be effective in very short units, even 10 seconds or 30 seconds. It is bought in the same way, and usually at the same rates, as conventional advertising commercials.

The purpose of direct support is not to get inquiries or orders but to increase the effectiveness of other media. I've called direct support a media extender, the "Hamburger Helper" of direct marketing. It is always used in conjunction with direct-mail or print campaigns which would still be effective without broadcast. It makes a good medium larger, not necessarily better.

## DIRECT-RESPONSE BROADCAST

Direct-response broadcast is not for every product. It requires products or services that either appeal to very general audiences or to audiences segmentable by program adjacencies. A kitchen knife or a set of pots may work because everyone who cooks is a prospect for it.

A set of books on World War II may work best when it is adjacent to a war movie, a violent sports program, or another form of violence—in some cities, the local news. Although detailed programming is not usually available in quantity, special-interest propositions can still be very successful on general programming, providing the allowable margin is adequate.

Television stations use "day parts" as newspapers use different editorial sections. Daytime shows are often soap operas and game shows appealing to homemakers, who are responsive to offers of household products. News and sports shows deliver predominantly male viewers. Tennis and golf deliver smaller but more up-scale audiences than baseball or boxing. Children's shows and family-appeal movies attract their own unique audiences. Usually selectivity in direct response is limited mostly by the day part that is available.

Radio stations have adopted single-format programming. Each station generally has a reputation for a type of news or programming, rather than the original concept of balanced programming with a little of everything. Rock stations reach teenagers, easy-listening stations find older adults, country and western selects blue-collar workers, and news programs reach more general audiences. In radio you reach specific audiences by selecting the station that aims at your audience.

It is sometimes possible to reach specific audiences on radio by sponsoring a specific show, such as farm or stock news, if the programming is relevant to your product.

As in all other direct-response media, the medium is the market, and your offer will be successful in broadcast only if the market is the right one for your product.

## Broadcast Offers

Just as different products do well on broadcast rather than in print or direct mail, so do different offers. If your conventional offer requires a great deal of explanation or legal copy, it won't fit on a radio or television spot. If it requires a signed agreement, you won't have a form to give out. If you usually give people a choice of fifty records or fifteen sizes and colors, it will be too complicated.

Credit quality is another problem. If your offer involves a free magazine or other premium, the percentage of people taking the gift and electing not to buy or pay for the rest of the offer will usually be greater than with any other medium. Broadcast, as the name itself indicates, casts a broad net over a wide variety of people and personalities. It will pull in the deadbeats along with the good customers, unless your offer is designed to be selective.

More often than not, successful offers in print or direct mail have to be changed in order to be successful in radio or television. Choices have to be eliminated or reduced. Credit has to be simplified. Offers have to be attractive and easy to understand. Here are some examples:

- A magazine that generally sells a full-year subscription in print media offers a short-term introductory offer on television.

- A book club which usually offers a wide choice of gift books for new members offers a preselected library.

- An appliance which is usually sold "off the page" is featured in a two-step offer, offering a free information kit.

- Another special interest club offers a single book at a nominal price—a straight deal which does not require explanation or legal copy. The buyers are then converted with a letter which suggests they "tear up the bill" and take the book free as part of a standard club offer, which is explained in full in the letter.

- A major catalog merchandiser, who usually sells only on a prepaid basis, makes an exception and accepts credit card orders on television in order to get qualified prospects.

Many advertisers who would not accept credit card telephone orders or token cash payments in other media do accept them in broadcast. The point is to be flexible and to accommodate the offer to the requirements of the medium.

## Direct-Response Media Principles

In buying direct-response radio or television time, you must forget anything you think you know about the conventional way of buying these media.

In order to make direct-response broadcast profitable, the key is to get the most gross rating points (GRPs) for your money. Gross rating points are the sum of the percentage of homes viewing each commercial in a series in a given market. Ten spots with a 7 percent AA (average audience) have 70 GRPs. This is sometimes expressed mathematically as $R \times F = GRPs$, which means reach (the average audience coverage in percentage for each commercial) times frequency (the number of times it is aired in the market) equals gross rating points.

Gross rating points are the currency, so to speak, of the broadcast industry. GRPs are what stations have to sell in the same way as magazines sell circulation. (The equivalent magazine formula would be circulation times frequency equals impressions.)

The objective is to get as many gross rating points—in the right day parts—as you can for your money. The challenge is availabilities.

If you were buying time for a conventional advertiser you would call in the local station representative and work out the best combination of available time slots for your commercial. But in direct marketing, you have to pay at least 75 percent less than the amount paid by the general advertiser. In order to accomplish this, you purchase preemptible availabilities.

The trade-off in preemptible availabilities is that the station will give you a very low rate providing they can use your spot as a standby for unsold time. Time is a perishable commodity for stations. Magazines can cut back on the number of pages, but each commercial broadcast second will never exist again.

Because of the low rates, local station representatives are usually not involved in these arrangements. Advertisers and their agencies try to deal directly with the station manager, putting together packages of commercials to help fill unsold time slots in slow seasons. One hand washes the other, and the advertiser with the best package gets the best rates and availabilities.

Advertising agencies maintaining media-buying departments cultivate personal relationships with station managers. Media buyers are assigned to groups of stations and keep in touch with them every week, putting together mutually advantageous deals. Buyers tour the stations and attend conventions of station managers to reinforce these contacts.

Officially, the deals are for run-of-the-station spots, with day parts requested but seldom guaranteed. Unofficially, not only day parts but even particular adjacencies are often verbally agreed upon.

The catch is that they are always preemptible. If a general advertiser comes along and offers full rate for the direct-response spot, it is moved to another time slot or bumped altogether. During busy seasons it is necessary to order 120 or 150 percent more time than is really needed in order to buy the desired coverage.

The personal contact between media buyer and station manager continues after the spots are run. Each week, and sometimes on a daily basis, the buyer checks the results and calculates the cost per order. The commercials are continued as long as the order cost is satisfactory. If the response is inadequate, the buyer "pulls" the schedule. Sometimes an effective buyer can get the manager of a marginal station to throw in "bonus spots," in order to bring the station to a profitable level so the campaign can continue. These are de facto result guarantees when arranged in advance.

The bottom line is the only consideration. The media buyer must have the responsibility and authority to spend a given budget as effectively as possible, in any stations in that buyer's area of responsibility. Neither the client nor the account group can be consulted on every decision. The buyers must make decisions on the spot, while talking on the phone, to increase schedules or pull them. This is fine as long as they achieve cost-per-response goals. Effective buyers are given bonuses, trips, and awards. Ineffective ones find other employment.

Usually a commercial needs two or three weeks to build to a level of awareness that is indicative of its effectiveness. Three-week flights are generally scheduled, with the third week pulled on stations where initial results are disappointing. The buyers then transfer that money to the better stations for a fourth or fifth week. Usually, the client agrees to keep providing additional advertising funds as long as the CPR is holding up.

For direct-response commercials, the usual length is 120 seconds. There are exceptions to this rule: Some well-known advertisers, including *Newsweek* and Save the Children, have made 60-second commercials work.

Another practice is double spotting, in which a 120-second ad is followed by a repeat of the 120 or by a 60 within the same hour. The idea is to give the consumer a reminder while the first impression is still fresh. This practice is effective but difficult to arrange.

## Setting Up a Broadcast Schedule

As little as $30,000 to $50,000 can get an initial reading on the possibilities of broadcast direct response for a direct marketing proposition. This includes not only the cost of the time purchased but also the production of the commercial and a fee for professional marketing and creative counsel.

The place to begin is with the areas of direct-response broadcast most likely to succeed. This generally means starting with television, not radio, and with 120-second commercials, not more or less.

The choice of cities and stations should be made on the same basis. A new-offer viability test is not the place to experiment or succumb to "deals" offered by untried stations. It should be made with tried and proven stations which have worked well for other direct marketing propositions. Day parts and adjacencies are a different matter. There can be very dramatic differences in response by day part, including weekday versus weekend, and testing several day parts within the selected stations will be necessary.

Awareness of television builds, and a two- or three-week flight is necessary in order to read the potential of the station. Unlike direct mail and print, there is no statistical curve by which you can forecast early results. The building of response rates is erratic, but once it reaches the full response level it usually holds at that level as the flight is extended for several more weeks. After a while, a noticeable downward curve develops, and the spots are continued only as long as they are still profitable.

A typical campaign in a medium-size market might build like this:

| Week | 1 | 2 | 3 | 4 | 5 | 6 | 7 | 8 | 9 |
|------|---|---|---|---|---|---|---|---|---|
| Responses | 11 | 19 | 37 | 39 | 41 | 38 | 40 | 27 | 13 |

If twenty-five orders per week were needed to make the station pay, it would have been a mistake to pull the campaign after only two weeks. This is the most common error made by companies using broadcast media for the first time. They pull out too soon and draw the sweeping conclusion "Broadcast doesn't work."

In the example above, the campaign should have been pulled at the end of week 8, demonstrating the need for prompt result reporting and continuous decision making. Once pulled, the proposition can be taken to other markets or "rested" for a year or so.

As test results come in, day-part selection should be adjusted and adjacencies revised in consultation with the station management. Good station managers will understand the needs of a direct marketer and the value to their stations of having this use for unsold time. The broadcast buyer should get full cooperation of station managers.

Weak cities are dropped. Trends are identified for the successful stations and day parts. A pattern soon emerges for the best size of city, type of programming, and relationships to other direct marketing results. Once the first results come in, the schedule can build rapidly as fast as cash flow permits, and a $50,000 test schedule can become a $1 million campaign in a matter of weeks.

In direct-response broadcast some typical errors seem to come up frequently. One is imposing personal taste on scheduling. It happens that the top-rated or intellectual shows are often not the best place for direct-response broadcast. We cannot sneer at schedules which include *Bowling for Dollars* or *The Flintstones* or *The Midnight Movie*, because such schedules are often exactly what works the best.

Mike Fabian, chairman of March Advertising, believes that there is a relationship between responsiveness and interest. The lower-rated the show, the better. People won't leave the room to make a phone call in response to your commercial when *Archie Bunker* or *Sunday Football* is on. Direct response works best when the programming is less interesting than the commercial.

## Response Options

Every direct marketing message ends with a request for some type of action. But what kind of action do we ask for on radio and television? There are only two choices: mail and telephone.

Mail is desirable when you're trying to screen out unqualified respondents or asking for a token payment to ensure quality. Also, older people are more likely to respond by mail. If you use mail, you may have to prepare a slide for each station, including the product name, the address, the price, and a key number. The station will add this at the end of your commercial. If the address or U.S. Postal Service box number is complicated, the chance of errors is increased. Usually, you'll also have to reveal the actual name of the sponsoring company and state some type of guarantee in order to satisfy station requirements. Slides with key codes are necessary because mail responses come in slowly and would otherwise be diffcult to track against particular stations or day parts.

Many such companies use Postal Service box numbers, but I feel that they should be avoided unless the sponsoring company is well known. Boxes have a suggestion of impermanence and don't inspire consumer confidence. I'd rather include a real address, where people can walk in if they have a mind to, even if that address is a bit more complicated.

Telephone response has become the most important reply device of mass direct marketers, and will probably continue to grow in importance. Despite some problems, telephone numbers are now used with the great majority of direct marketing commercials.

The greatest problem is the busy signal customers get when hundreds call the same number immediately after a commercial has run. The impulse factor vanishes quickly, especially if the program gets exciting and lures your customers back to the television set. Jammed telephone lines are a major problem and are the most important consideration in setting up a means to handle telephone orders or inquiries.

Considering that the phones must be fully covered day and night because a commercial might be aired at any time anywhere in the country, it is usually out of the question to try to set up your own organization for incoming telephone calls.

## Inbound Telephone Services

Many organizations, including Avis in Tulsa, TEAM in Omaha, and NICE in Ogden, provide this type of incoming telephone service. Avis Rent-a-Car's Telecommunications division is able to use their huge reservation facility in Tulsa for handling direct marketing calls because direct marketing calls peak at times when automobile reservations are slow. Other companies with large reservation phone systems might consider this business as well.

For the buyer of telephone service, the key considerations are the number of phones available, how many of them are staffed, and what their load factors are. Before selecting a telephone service, get a list of the company's clients and check references. Also, call in on a broadcast offer for one of their clients to see how long it takes to get through and how courteously and efficiently the telephone is answered. If you have a bad experience, go elsewhere. Don't let anyone argue that you reached the one exception. There shouldn't be any exceptions if the staff has been properly selected and trained before being placed on line.

Because jammed telephone lines can cost you an estimated one-half to two-thirds of your potential response, selection of a telephone service is serious business. Take the time to pick the right telephone supplier for your needs and to check out every detail in person.

Most advertisers today select a company with incoming 800 service located in a remote state so fewer people will have to note WATS exceptions like "In Oklahoma, call. . . ." The available numbers should be easy to remember and unique to the particular advertiser if at all possible.

Phone answering companies should have efficient systems—manual or computerized—for indicating all necessary information about the offer and the order. The best systems are those where the operator has a cathode-ray tube (CRT) computer terminal and can display information on the product and a list of questions on the screen. The operator says exactly what is on the screen, giving information or asking for it as necessary. Questions to be asked appear on the screen. If there is information to be checked, such as available inventory for a particular item being ordered or the validity of a credit card number, it is done automatically and simultaneously while the customer is still on the phone. The customer's answers are punched right into the computer, displayed on the screen, and stored in memory.

Really professional telephone suppliers can do more than just answer the telephone and capture name, address, and item ordered. They can train their telephone answerers to be salespeople as well.

Telephone trade-ups are a growing trend, but they require trained salespeople. Some magazines offer short-term subscriptions on the air and then offer "added savings" on the telephone to try to convert the respondent to a longer subscription. Some companies invite COD or to-be-billed orders on television and then have the telephone operator offer a premium if the customer pays by giving a credit card number on the telephone. Some advertisers invite viewers to mail cash to a certain address but suggest that credit card holders only may call and order by phone.

Whatever system or supplier you select, I strongly urge that you have a backup or a second supplier lined up before you start to shoot your commercial (see Chapter 16). Otherwise, if your telephone service goes broke or gives you bad service, you'll have to go to the expense of reshooting the phone number portion of the commercial. Also, if the commercial is a big success, it's a good idea to use more than one supplier when running on several stations at one time, to reduce the busy signal ratio.

*    *    *

Direct-response television is big, colorful, and exciting. The potential is enormous for the right product and offer, but the chances are against any particular product's succeeding in this or any other media. While the rewards may be greater in this medium than in most other direct marketing media, the risks are also greater. If you decide to go on the air, do it with your eyes open.

## BROADCAST SUPPORT

Broadcast support is not a medium in itself but only an adjunct to other media. As such, it must always be planned in terms of its effect on the media it supports.

### When to Use Broadcast Support

With few exceptions, support does not lower cost per order. What it does do is increase the number of orders that can be obtained from other media.

If a $100,000 preprint insertion would ordinarily produce 20,000 responses at $5 each, the addition of support cannot be counted on to lower the cost to $4. What it can do is increase the number of $5 orders from that insertion in proportion to its own added cost. If the preprint in this example is supported by a $50,000 television support campaign, the objective should be to garner 30,000 responses from the insertion.

In order for such an investment to be effective, the coverage of the supported media within the television market must be substantial. Unless you are deliberately spending out of proportion for testing purposes, a proposed support program must be measured in terms of broadcast support cost per thousand prospects (BSC/M). But what is a prospect in this case? Not every television viewer reached by the station is a prospect, for the commercial is only relevant to people who receive your ad, preprint, or direct-mail piece.

If your newspaper preprint reached 250,000 households in a city of 500,000, you would have 50 percent market coverage in that medium. If you supported this with broadcast which produced an average rating of 25 percent, you would be reaching 25 percent of homes using television (HUTV).

If the HUTV is 80 percent, for example, then 80 percent, or 400,000 homes, are watching TV, and 25 percent of them see your commercial. That's 100,000 homes. Expressed another way, this means a "reach" of 20 percent. This 20 percent reach applied to the 50 percent preprint coverage gives you a "support penetration" of 10 percent. Fifty thousand homes in this market will see both the preprint and the TV commercials supporting it.

Let's say the preprint costs $12,500 and the purchase of 300 GRPs in this market, to give you 20 percent reach, costs $5000. The $5000 is effectively reaching only the 50,000 homes that are getting both. The BSC/M is $100. If the supported preprints cost $50 per thousand, the combined cost is $150 per thousand—200 percent more than the preprints alone. Therefore a 200 percent lift is required—usually an impractical objective for support advertising.

Putting it another way, if the support cost is applied to the total preprint cost, the investment is 250,000 × $50/M, or $12,500, for the preprints, plus $5000 for the support. Divide 5000 by 12,500, move the decimal point two places to the right, and you get 40 percent—the overall lift required to make the support investment pay.

This is the way the total campaign will be measured, but the BSC/M method is the best way to test the reasonableness of expecting a particular support investment to achieve a desired lift. A 200 percent lift on the BSC/M method is unreasonable, an indication you would not get from the 40 percent overall lift requirement.

We have an entirely different picture if we use direct mail instead of preprints in the same hypothetical market. If direct mail costs $400 per thousand, reaching the same 250,000 households would require $100,000. The same 300 GRPs still cost $5000, and the broadcast reach is still 20 percent, producing a support penetration of 10 percent.

The BSC/M is still $100 for the 50,000 households, but this is now only 25 percent more than the cost of the mailing alone to the supported households, and only a 25 percent lift factor is required. Compare the 200 percent lift required in the previous example. On an overall basis, the $5000 support investment is just 5 percent of the $100,000 mail cost, so only a 5 percent overall lift is required to justify the expenditure. The likelihood of success is much greater here.

One major advertiser buys as many as 3000 GRPs in prime seasons—ten times this example. This advertiser aims for a 50 percent overall lift and usually gets it. Increasing the GRPs, the reach, and subsequently the penetration level is effective, providing there is a sensible relationship to the media being supported.

One rule of thumb is that the mailing or other supported media must reach one of three homes in a television area for support TV to be cost-effective. Often a combination of media is used to accomplish this. I'm told *Reader's Digest* mails to as much as 50 percent of some markets, combining several product offerings under the same support umbrella.

Theoretically, that means that, if we can invest 25 or 50 percent in support dollars instead of 10 percent, we should be able to get 25 or 50 percent more orders. This presumes the additional support dollars are spent effectively to get increased reach and penetration. But how do we spend effectively? Read on.

## Support Media Buying

As indicated in the previous section, all support schedules must be in relation to the media being supported. The more media that can be concentrated under one support umbrella, the more effective the support program will be.

One advertiser uses a common sweepstakes to send out various product offerings to different people in the same market and thus widen the coverage. This enables the support program to cover all the products by referring to the sweepstakes instead of the product. I have proposed similar tactics for multiple-product book club groups, using a copy theme or response device as a common supportable theme.

The examples given here had a penetration factor (supported media coverage times support media reach) of no more than 10 percent. A good media buyer should be able to achieve between a 30 percent and a 50 percent penetration factor by making a comparable investment in the support media. Some advertisers believe this is a minimum range for support to be worthwhile.

The budget for support is developed by working backward from the media coverage and expenditure, and calculating how much penetration is available in various TV markets for a given level of expenditure.

Let's say a market has $75,000 in all supported media, and a decision has been made to aim for a 33 percent lift for a comparable expenditure. The media buyer then determines what can be bought for 33 percent of the $75,000, or $25,000.

The budgeted sum is then spread over a variety of targeted day parts in a precise pattern over a period of three days adjoining the expected on-sale date of the publication or the expected delivery date of a mailing. The objective is to see how many GRPs (gross rating points, obtained by multiplying reach times frequency) can be purchased in the particular market. Estimates are prepared indicating the number of individual households reached by the number of GRPs obtained, and calculations quickly indicate whether the penetration of households receiving the supported media justifies the expenditure.

In some markets this may not be feasible. In others, it may be relatively simple. No matter which comes first—GRP level, penetration level, or support budget as a percentage cost of media supported—all the factors must interact before final recommendations are assembled.

In direct response, a campaign can be run a few weeks later or in a different market, but support schedules must be precisely timed. To be effective, the campaign must run as scheduled. This means that at least the foundation of the schedule usually has to be placed at negotiated but nonpreemptible rates. This is closer to 80 percent of the rate card—the station's published schedule of rates—instead of the 20 percent paid for direct-response campaigns.

Direct-response campaigns flourish on marginal programming and midnight movies, but support must produce raw audience counts in the same manner as general advertisers. Thus prime-time day parts and top-rated shows must be part of the schedule.

One trick of the trade is to set up a minimum schedule, say at the 30 percent budget level, with orders placed at negotiated card rates, and then arrange a campaign in direct-response programming, usually at 60-second length, to supplement the minimum schedule. The full-rate minimum schedule guarantees the required penetration, while the preemptible direct-response schedule adds additional exposure at bargain rates if time is available.

Does this all sound complicated? It is. It's very time-consuming as well, which is why agencies and time-buying services seldom will handle broadcast campaigns of any kind, support or direct response, without getting a full commission and sometimes even supplementary fees or incentive arrangements.

Another complication involves direct-mail support. When a campaign is being supported, it is critical that the mail arrive on time. This requires close coordination and special arrangements with Postal Service customer representatives. If the mail is delayed, the support campaign must be delayed too. One of the very largest users of TV support had a major snafu in timing, with their multimillion-dollar support campaign appearing just when a competitor's mailing was arriving instead of theirs. A major management shake-up took place soon afterward.

Support commercials are closer to general advertising than any other area of direct marketing. As in general advertising, shorter commercials—30- or even 10-second ads—are used to put together the most economical combinations of reach and frequency. Again as in general advertising, the creative theme must be single-purpose, chosen to be easily dramatized and remembered. There is only one action request: Look for this message in your newspaper or mailbox.

### The Transfer Device

One creative innovation, credited to Lester Wunderman, founder of Young & Rubicam's Wunderman, Ricotta & Kline direct marketing operation, is the transfer device. Now widely used, it involves offering an extra premium to those viewers who indicate in some way that they have seen the commercial when they are filling out the card or coupon in the supported media.

Columbia Record Club invites new members to get an extra free record by writing a number in a "secret" gold box. Other viewers are invited to turn an S into a dollar sign and get a free handyman's apron in connection with a home repair set. Consumer Reports subscribers are invited to draw a circle around a picture of the magazine and get an extra issue free with their subscription. Transfer devices may have started out as a testing method, but today they are an involvement factor with lift effects of their own.

### OTHER BROADCAST FACTORS

When testing both direct support and direct response, we often use matched markets—pairs of like markets selected according to station and supported media characteristics, population demographics, and the client's own experience in the markets. Perhaps six markets are selected, half of them supported and the other half not. Two different commercial treatments or offers can also be tested in this way.

The techniques of support advertising are equally applicable to coupon programs. I expect general advertisers to begin supporting product coupons with television spots saying "Look for this coupon in your paper." This technique would be a natural application of direct marketing techniques to general advertising.

Sometimes direct marketing broadcast applications are used in retail marketing. The Eicoff agency, a pioneer in this field, uses the same general theories outlined here to force distribution of mail-order products through retail drug chains and discount houses instead of through mail order. They reportedly have achieved some incredible sales successes for products distributed in this manner.

*     *     *

Direct-response and support television are multi-million-dollar media, but they are still in their infancy technologically. They are somewhat like baby elephants—big, strong, but not yet housebroken.

Part of the problem is that the initial users of television were often those with the least regard for the public. In some cases product quality left something to be desired. In others, there was simply contempt for the taste level of the viewing audience.

"In New Jersey call. . . . That number again is . . ." should not be the public's only impression of direct marketing on television. There is room for creativity and imagination, for adding entertainment values that not only attract and hold an audience but also make selling points subtly, memorably, and effectively. Chapter 16, Producing TV Commercials, will offer some ideas on how to accomplish this.

# CHAPTER EIGHT

# THE TELEPHONE

There is nothing new about using the telephone as an advertising medium. The "boiler room" filled with telephones has been a sales institution as far back as anyone can remember. Insurance agents have called newlyweds, compiling their lists from the wedding announcements in the local newspaper. Stockbrokers have called newly promoted executives, scanning trade papers for names of prospects. The most aggressive users of all have been politicians, whose paid and volunteer workers canvass voters, raise funds, and get supporters to the polls on election day.

What's new is that telephone selling is now big-time, that its techniques have become highly refined, and that large-scale telephone canvassing organizations have become important tools of the direct marketing planner.

## ATTRIBUTES OF TELEPHONE SELLING

Like direct mail, telephone selling is highly selective. Like direct mail, it is expensive, even with WATS lines and independent long-distance networks, and its high cost is only justified by utilizing maximum selectivity. Like broadcast, it reaches out to its customer with ultimate immediacy and ultimate ease of responding.

All the customer has to do to get the entire message is not hang up. A muttered "OK" will replace filling out a coupon, finding a stamp, and going out to the mailbox. A recited charge card number will prepay the order.

However, unlike all other media, the telephone call is involuntary for the prospective customer, who cannot simply turn the page, look away from the TV set, or toss a letter into a wastepaper basket. Prospects are contacted—one-on-one with another human being—in their own home, at a time when they might have been enjoying a nap or eating dinner. The prospect gets out of a chair or bed and walks over to the telephone, where a commercial message is the last thing expected. Once in conversation, most people feel the obligation to be courteous. Few people just hang up.

The power to capture and hold the attention of the prospect is the strength of telephoning—and its weakness as well. Nothing will irritate a consumer quite as much as a poorly timed, poorly conceived, or poorly executed telephone call. Nothing will terminate a long-term customer or donor relationship quite as quickly, or generate quite as angry a letter to a congressional resspresentative.

For this reason, the telephone must be used with caution and with good taste. Late calls should be avoided, as well as Sunday calls, with particular attention to local custom. Farmers should not be called after nine o'clock in the evening, as they retire early so they can attend to farm chores in the morning. Jews and Seventh Day Adventists, if their identity is known, should not be called on Saturday. Business people should not be called early in the morning when they are scrambling to leave for work, nor should they be bothered at the office regarding personal matters. Maintaining the goodwill of the consumer is the responsibility of everyone in direct marketing who uses the telephone.

## USES OF THE TELEPHONE

The best uses of this medium involve preexisting relationships. A phone call from a company to its customers may be positioned and perceived as a service. The same call to a stranger may be an intrusion. Though there have been very successful mass telephone campaigns (Ford Motor Company once made 20 million phone calls to produce leads for automobile salesmen), I recommend utilizing this medium with caution except where there is some prior relationship. Also, because of its cost, it should generally be used after less expensive media, such as direct mail, have been utilized. In fact, the combination of direct mail followed by telephone may be the most profitable way to use this medium.

*Service Calls* "To approve your credit application." "Your order has been delayed." "The color you wanted isn't available, may we substitute another?" (Note that delayed orders must still be confirmed in writing as well, according to FTC procedures which, for some reason unknown to anyone in business, do not recognize this superior form of customer communication.)

*Trading Up and Cross Selling* "We have your order, but wanted to let you know it's now available in a deluxe format." "There's a new accessory for your . . . we thought you'd like to know about." "We're having a special sale, three for . . . , and thought you might like to increase your order." "The item you bought once is now on sale, and we thought you might like to purchase another at this low price." "We're having a private sale for our credit card customers. We wanted to give our present customers first chance to. . . ." "If you're happy with the present service you buy from us, we invite you to try another. . . ."

*Direct-Mail Follow-Up* "We haven't received your reservation yet for our hummingbird collector's plate, and before we close out the edition. . . ." "We have been saving a place in the next excursion bus to our resort development for you and before we release it. . . ." "There is still time to take advantage of the introductory offer we wrote you about. . . ."

*Business Contacts* Personal sales calls are costing over $130 each, according to a McGraw-Hill survey. Telephone contacts may cost about $5, and produce fast and substantial results. Purposes can range from sales calls positioned as restocking to old-fashioned collection calls. Help is available in the form of "phone power" training courses and brochures from most telephone companies, or companies like Campaign Communications Institute of America, Inc. (CCI), will train your staff for you. Sales calls positioned as service calls are very effective.

"Summer is coming, and you might want to check your stock on our. . . ." "We've had reports that our . . . is selling out, and we wanted to see if you need more." "Our ad campaign is about to break, and we thought you might need some of our. . . ." "We know you like to be among the first to stock new items, and so I wanted to tell you about. . . ." Calls to dealers, sales agents, and franchises are the most effective way of exchanging information—getting it out fast and getting a fast reply. Sometimes a simple, "I'm not calling to sell you anything, just to thank you for last year's business" can be one of the best long-range investments a company can make.

*Renewals and Reactivation* Telephone selling is uniformly recommended as part of a magazine's renewal series. After a series of letters has gone out, another label is generated and sent to a telephone center instead of a mailing house. "Your subscription is expiring, and we wanted to give you a last chance to. . . ." Reactivation of inactive customers is another use: "We've enjoyed having you as a customer, and wonder why you haven't bought from our catalog lately."

*"Immediacy" Situations*   The telephone offers a very believable sense of immediacy, and fits well with efforts like these: "Have you read about the plight of the children in Thailand? Well, we're raising a special fund to help, and we thought you, as one of our past donors. . . ." "The election looks very close, and if we can just raise another $100 from each contributor for a last-minute TV campaign. . . ." "We only have a limited supply of this product, and wanted to give you a chance to place your order. . . ." "The price is about to go up, but if you get your order in now. . . ."

*The Telephone for Prospecting*   In both consumer and business selling, telephone lead solicitation is a widespread application which has proved very effective. In some cases, the telephone is used to ask for the order, usually for a low-unit sale—newspaper or milk delivery, a magazine subscription, or a trial examination of the first volume in a set of books.

Another common telephone use is "bird-dogging." The term refers to hound dogs trained to "point" at birds or game. Cold-canvass field salespeople used to have trainees set up their appointments for visits later in the evening, and the trainees were called "bird dogs." Today the term applies to telephone lead prospecting.

The end product of a bird-dogging call is not a sale but an appointment. The mailing list uses every appropriate type of list selection, as described in Chapter 5, Mailing Lists. The offer can be any of the lead-generation approaches described in Chapter 4, The Proposition. The caller can offer information, a free booklet, a valuable gift, a discount—anything that proves to be effective.

Insurance salesmen now offer financial planning. Encyclopedia salesmen offer booklets. Real estate agents call owners of desirable homes and offer free appraisals or tell of a buyer who has expressed interest in their home. Coincidentally, the same offers that work on broadcast are likely to work over the telephone.

## ECONOMICS OF THE TELEPHONE

The telephone is a direct marketing medium in that its cost can be measured in relation to its results. The concepts of CPR (cost per response), conversion rates, and allowable margin, as well as every aspect of mail-order math, apply in exactly the same way.

If you deal with one of the established suppliers of telephone contact services, you will know your costs exactly. They can give you an all-inclusive estimate based on your own particular needs and taking advantage of their own established systems, telephone automation, and trained personnel.

If you plan your own telephone campaign, you will have to anticipate a variety of costs, including:

- Renting and processing of mailing lists
- Phone number acquisition, from a list supplier or by looking up numbers in the telephone book
- Telephone operator costs, including time, overhead, supervision, and any incentive bonuses
- Phone company equipment and toll charges
- Management, creative preparation, forms, scripts, operator training, meetings, and results analysis

In determining costs, a great deal will depend on the selectivity of the list, the percentage of valid telephone numbers that can be obtained, and the efficiency of the telephone operators. The operators must be trained to dial quickly, terminate unproductive conversations, and stick to a proven script.

Telephone number look-up costs are an important consideration. Few mailing lists are available with the numbers already provided, and those that are charge extra. For most mailing lists you'll have to rent your list from one source and then have the numbers provided by another. Metromail and Army Times have a service which computer-matches phone numbers to lists with an average 60 percent match-up rate. Additional names can then be obtained from other look-up services at a cost between 7 cents and 10 cents a name.

Wide Area Telephone Service (WATS) is most efficient when calls are made in rapid sequence, with little downtime. Independent long-distance networks can be less expensive than WATS lines under certain conditions. Some large telephone services maintain computer switchboards that automatically select the most economical calling route, depending on time of day, utilization of phone lines, and other factors.

As a general rule of thumb, telephone responsiveness can average ten times that of direct mail—as high as 25 or 35 percent of all calls made. This, of course, is for a successful campaign. At the same time the cost of making calls (depending on the length of the call, the distance, and the cost of lists, among other things) can average between $2 and $5 a call. Considering the cost of small-quantity direct mail, this is usually less than ten times direct-mail cost, and the cost efficiencies become obvious. However, as always, there is no such thing as an average proposition. Yours will do better or worse depending on its applicability to telephone selling. This medium, like any medium, requires its own evaluation.

## THE TELEPHONE SCRIPT

The presentation of a telephone message has become a unique and highly creative art form. The script must never be clever, tricky, or gimmicky, as it must sound sincere and courteous. This is no place for dramatics.

A phone message generally begins with a simple introduction, including the name of the caller and the company being represented, followed by a request for or confirmation of the identity of the person called. The next statement is a qualifier or screener—giving enough information to get a reaction as to whether this call is worth continuing.

There has to be room for the person to respond if the call is not going to sound like a one-sided lecture. Once the qualification response is obtained, the basic message is delivered. Campaign Communications Institute has developed a highly effective way to handle this part of the presentation. Often, after getting the consent of the called party, they play a short recording of a message by an authority figure or a celebrity. Then the payoff begins: An offer is presented and an acceptance requested.

The script is not simple. Depending on answers at various points in the conversation, the script must provide for various alternative messages. In some cases, it moves to "Thanks anyway. Goodbye." In other situations, it asks other questions or provides more information. Questions have to be answered and objections overcome. The operator cannot improvise; everything has to be provided for in the script.

Below is an example of a typical telephone script, copyrighted in 1978 by Campaign Communications Institute of America, Inc. Variables are eliminated for simplification. The purpose of the script was to invite families with precise characteristics (such as car ownership) to make an appointment to visit Starrett City, a large nearby housing development. Note that, in this case, the taped message used not a celebrity but a resident of the development whom it was believed the caller would identify with. Several different testimonial inserts were used, depending on who was called.

CAMPAIGN COMMUNICATIONS INSTITUTE
OF AMERICA, INC.
Delmar Management—Starrett City
Appointment Generation Program
Communicator Script

CARD ONE: INTRODUCTION TO HOUSEHOLD

Hello, may I speak to (NAME ON CARD) please?

IF ASKS WHO IS CALLING, SAY: This is (YOUR NAME) is Mr(s) _____ available?

IF ASKS WHAT CALL IS ABOUT, SAY: I'm calling on behalf of Starrett City because I have a special message for Mr(s) _____ from Joan Mandelion, Director of Community Relations. Is Mr(s) _____ available please?

IF NOT AVAILABLE, SAY: When might I be able to reach Mr(s) _____ please? (RECORD DATE AND TIME OF RE-CALL AND POLITELY TERMINATE)

CARD TWO: INTRODUCTION TO PROSPECT

Hello, Mr(s) _____, this is _____ calling on behalf of Starrett City and Joan Mandelion, the Director of Tenant and Community Relations. Mr(s) _____, are you familiar with Starrett City? (NOTE ON CARD)

I'm calling (TODAY/TONIGHT) because many former residents of your area have moved to Starrett City, and . . . (CONTINUE WITH INTRODUCE TAPE)

CARD THREE: INTRODUCE TAPE

Joan Mandelion, a resident of Starrett City and the Director of Tenant and Community Relations, has prepared a brief message on tape we thought you would be interested in hearing. It's about 2 minutes long, and I'd like to play it for you now and get your questions and reactions afterwards. May I do that, Mr(s) _____?

IF YES: PLAY TAPE—GO TO AFTER TAPE

IF NO/HESITANT: GO TO IF HESITANT ABOUT TAPE

CARD FOUR: IF HESITANT ABOUT TAPE

Mr(s) _____, because many former residents from your area have moved to Starrett City, we thought you might be interested in knowing more about this unique community, and the very low rents, large rooms, excellent security, fine schools and the many other benefits of living at Starrett City.

But, Mrs. Mandelion explains it much better than I do, and her message is only about 2 minutes long—may I play it for you, Mr(s) _____?

> IF YES, SAY: Fine, here's Mrs. Mandelion, and I'll be back on afterwards to get your reaction . . . (PLAY TAPE—GO TO AFTER TAPE)

> IF NO, SAY: May I ask why Mr(s)_____? (NOTE ON CARD) If you'd like, we can call back at a more convenient time . . . (NOTE CALL BACK TIME OR GO TO RESPONSES TO QUESTIONS/OBJECTIONS IF APPROPRIATE. OTHERWISE: POLITELY TERMINATE)

#### TAPE FOR TENANT RELATIONS DIRECTOR

Hello, I'm Joan Mandelion, Director of Tenant and Community Relations at Starrett City. I'm using this special way to reach you because I want to tell you personally how *proud* we residents are of New York's newest neighborhood.

We're lucky in this day and age, to be part of a community that offers us the unique benefits of a small town, in the *heart* of New York! Starrett City is a totally self-contained community, with almost 6,000 apartments in 46 buildings, situated on 153 beautifully landscaped acres overlooking Jamaica Bay. We have over 16,000 trees, bike paths, a new 8 million dollar recreation center with 2 swimming pools, and 10 tennis courts!! Waldbaums and *20* other stores make up our *own* shopping center. Fine elementary and intermediate schools are here too—P.S. 346 ranks near the top in New York City, and our children have a median reading score *2 years* above the national average!

*And* it's all incredibly safe here—we have our own security force of over 60 men; most are former New York City policemen—we hired them when the city had to cut back on the force because of financial problems. You know, we have the *lowest* crime rate in *all* of New York City!

I've been giving you some of the facts and figures, but now I'd like to introduce Judy Moskowitz a resident who will tell you what it all means to her. Judy . . . ?

#### TAPE FOR TESTIMONIAL

Thank you, Joan—I'm Judy Moskowitz. My husband and I have been living in Starrett City with our 4 children for 2 years now. The first day we walked in and *saw* it, that was it! Our apartment has *much* larger rooms and a lot more closet space that we had in Bensonhurst—and our rent is actually *less* than we *used* to pay and our utilities are *included* . . . so we can keep our air conditioners on *all* summer for free!

Everything we want is right here: shopping . . . a new recreation center, lots of grass and open areas. Our kids go to excellent schools

2 blocks away and my husband rides his bicycle to work. We feel so *safe* going out at night, and I *never* have to worry about my children.

Our friends are amazed when they visit and some have already moved here too! You know, you can look at blueprints . . . but you really have to come to Starrett City *yourself* to see the community we have.

---

END TESTIMONIAL—JOAN MANDELION RESUMES

Thank you Judy.

Starrett City is already 80% occupied. But there's still time to join us. If you'd *like* to know more about our special community, our representative, who's coming back on the line, will be happy to schedule a visit for you at your convenience. As Judy said, you have to see Starrett City to believe that something this good is so close by!

Thank you for listening—I hope you'll visit with us. Now here's our representative.

END TAPE

---

CARD FIVE: AFTER TAPE

Mr(s)_____? (PAUSE) Thank you for listening— did you hear that all right? (ACKNOWLEDGE)

As Mrs. Mandelion and (TESTIMONIAL) mentioned, there's only one way to really appreciate what Starrett City has to offer you and your family . . . and that's to make an appointment—for whenever it's most convenient for you—to come out and look at the completely furnished model apartments. There's no obligation and I think you'll be very pleasantly surprised, Mr(s)_____. What day and time is most convenient for you and your family?

IF YES: GO TO ACCEPTS APPOINTMENT

IF NO/HESITANT: GO TO IF HESITANT ABOUT APPOINTMENT

---

CARD SIX: IF HESITANT ABOUT APPOINTMENT

As Mrs. Mandelion and (TESTIMONIAL) mentioned, we have excellent security for you and your entire family, a shopping center and the elementary and junior high schools that are right on the site are the best in all of New York City. There is a magnificent new pool and tennis club available to all tenants, outdoor recreation of all kinds. As many tenants have said, you could live your entire life if you wanted to, without leaving Starrett City!

You know Mr(s)_____, in making an appointment to see a model Starrett City apartment and to look around the entire 153-acre site, you're not commiting yourself in any way at all. We just think that, when you *see* it for yourself, you'll fall in love with Starrett City like so many thousands of others since it first opened in 1974. May I make an appointment for you now Mr(s) _____?

IF YES: GO TO ACCEPTS APPOINTMENT

IF NO: GO TO NOT INTERESTED

---

CARD SEVEN: ACCEPTS APPOINTMENT

COMMUNICATOR NOTE: APPOINTMENTS MUST BE SCHEDULED 7–10 DAYS FROM THE DATE OF YOUR CALL, DURING THE FOLLOWING HOURS:
MONDAY–SATURDAY   10:15–12 NOON OR 1:30–4:30
SUNDAY   11AM–5PM
THURSDAY EVENINGS   6–8PM

Thank you very much Mr(s)_____, I've scheduled your appointment for (DAY/DATE/TIME). One of our representatives from the rental office will be calling you within the next few days to confirm. Have a good (DAY/EVENING). Goodbye.

---

CARD EIGHT: NOT INTERESTED

May I ask why, Mr(s)_____? (NOTE ON CARD) IF POSSIBLE GO TO RESPONSES TO QUESTIONS/OBJECTIONS, OTHERWISE: POLITELY TERMINATE.

---

The remainder to the script contained an additional eleven cards with responses to anticipated questions or objections that could arise. Note that this script provides alternatives depending on prospect responses.

⋆    ⋆    ⋆

Telephone marketing has become a highly specialized subcategory of direct marketing, and I have presented only highlights here. For further information about this aspect of direct marketing, I recommend the book *Telephone Marketing* by Murray Roman (McGraw-Hill, New York, 1976). This book, with a foreword by Professor Theodore Levitt of Harvard Business School, is the definitive work on using the telephone as a marketing tool.

## CHAPTER NINE

# RESEARCH

It was not that long ago that direct marketing pros looked down their noses at research techniques, as if they were some kind of "sissy stuff" used only by general advertisers. After all, direct marketers knew what worked. We set up split runs, counted coupons, and consequently knew all the answers.

Looking back on those days, it was as if the old-timers were the "mountaineers" of direct marketing. They read the moss on the trees and the shadows on the ground, and needed none of those newfangled compasses.

All this has changed today, and while split runs and statistical methods are the mainstay of direct marketing decision making, we have found valuable—even essential—uses for modern research methods. The methods we use today are more analogous to radar, infrared photography, and gyrocompasses than to the compasses that once amazed mountaineers.

## WHY RESEARCH? WHEN?

The merging of conventional advertising techniques and the experience of direct marketers led to three major areas for applications of research: (1) creative guidance, (2) pretest screening, and (3) posttest qualitative analysis. Each of these areas supplements conventional direct marketing testing and has something of value to offer the direct marketer.

### Creative Guidance

In the classic creative approach one or more direct marketing executives draw upon their own experience, judgment, and knowledge of the marketplace to produce advertising. Usually there is an exchange of opinions, and those belonging to the most authoritative or most assertive person prevail. Unfortunately, no one's judgment is that good, and no one person's depth of experience is all-encompassing.

Focus panels, field interviews, and questionnaires can give advertisers a chance to get a current reading on the thinking of the marketplace. Advertisers can check on whether their messages are understood, determine the jargon used by readers and viewers, and uncover objections that would otherwise go unanswered. Most important, research can identify opportunities that might otherwise be missed.

Today's creative directors must be objective enough to realize they are not omniscient and make full use of modern research. But research directors must recognize that their methods are a source of creative inspiration, not a substitute for it.

## Pretest Screening

Even the largest advertisers cannot afford unlimited split-run testing. Sample sizes and the number of cells in direct mail should have some relationship to a total budget. Print advertising is limited by the flexibility of the print media being tested. Where color ads or brochures are involved, production costs can quickly become prohibitive if several four-color executions are being tested against each other.

On the other hand, as discussed in Chapter 4, The Proposition, Chapter 11, Positioning, and Chapter 12, Creative Tactics, the number of possible advertising concepts for a given product is virtually unlimited.

Pretest techniques range from simple screening methods to complex physiological methods involving voice pitch, eye movement, and even brain waves. A Doyle Dane Bernbach review of advertising testing services lists more than fifty different approaches to copy testing.

Pretest techniques, in my experience, cannot pick a winner; they are no substitute for split-run testing. What they do is identify the losers. If there are a dozen possible concepts for a campaign and only four can be tested, pretesting can eliminate the half-dozen least likely to succeed. Then, with only six left to choose from, the odds that the combined subjective judgment of client and agency will pick the best four are greatly improved.

## Posttest Analysis

An axiom of direct marketers is that we always know what went wrong, or right, after the results of a split-run test are in. Theories abound to account for breakthrough results or to explain away the concepts at the bottom of the response rankings. It appears that hindsight is a gift possessed by all practitioners in this field.

Too many advertisers are too willing to settle for "Which ad did best?" without knowing *why* it did best. Research methods exist that enable us to get to the "why." Once we know who responded to our offer and who didn't, telephone surveys and in-depth interviews can uncover the motivations and perceptions of our customers. The one thing research can't do is determine who would really order the product. However, once we know the who, the why is relatively simple to find out.

## FOCUS PANELS

Focus panels are the antithesis of direct marketing's scientific testing methods. They are not subject to measurement at all. Individual panel members may be atypical of the market as a whole, and there is almost never a definitive resolution of any question. Yet their value is immense.

Basically, a focus panel is like a group therapy session. Its basic structure involves between six and twelve people who are engaged in an open discussion. A moderator, who must be more of a psychologist than a researcher, guides the group into areas of interest to the advertiser. The whole proceeding is watched, through a two-way mirror or on closed-circuit television, by clients who are in a position to influence the direction of the meeting and direct further exploration into topics of special interest.

### Planning for Focus Research

The first step in using focus panels is to consult with a research specialist and prepare a plan. This plan must include several vital subjects: objectives, geography, composition, screening criteria, and a discussion guide.

The objectives may be open-ended, and must recognize the limitations of this technique. A focus panel objective cannot be quantifiable, as in "Determine percentage of market familiar with client's trademark." A realistic objective, however, can be "Obtain consumer reactions to client trademark." It cannot be selective, as in "Select which advertisement to run." It can be subjective, as in "Determine understanding of advertising concepts as expressed in various treatments."

Some of the most productive panels have the most open-ended objectives. One asked how people opened a direct-mail package—and how they felt about it. Others sought attitudes toward new book clubs or other direct marketing ventures.

Geography is another consideration. Most focus panel researchers are affiliated with testing services around the country and are in a position to obtain screeners, panels, and focus group rooms in any city in the country.

It is usually possible to assemble panels representing different lifestyles and demographics within almost any city. Sometimes a researcher will recommend a suburban location, if that is where the market is. More often it is necessary to sample groups in a variety of areas—perhaps the East, Midwest, South, and West—to get a good cross section of opinion.

One group of six panels was held in New York, Charlotte, and Kansas City, with younger and older age groups in each. It turned out that geography produced little variation in attitudes, but age or prior product usage produced very different reactions.

Composition refers to the makeup of the groups. Groups can be selected within any age, income, education, or lifestyle parameters. There are often very significant reactions depending upon age, sex, or education. Career women and housewives may have severely different reactions to a product.

The standard I recommend for all research is *usability*. Education or income standards may do very little good because it is usually impractical to select lists or media by education or income, but other categories are very useful. For one financial product I separated *Wall Street Journal* readers, our core group, into separate panels from the general audience of savings account depositors. The different insights could be addressed differently in the two media categories—financial and general.

Sometimes product attitudes can be important. A magazine may want to explore the attitudes of groups who logically should read the magazine but never have, of newsstand buyers who have never subscribed, and of former subscribers who failed to renew. Obviously each of these groups should reveal very different attitudes.

How many groups should one have, then? Some arbitrary choices have to be made, especially as professionally done focus groups can cost between $1500 and $2500 each, not counting the travel expenses of the moderator and marketing personnel. Two different panels in each of three cities can run between $10,000 and $15,000. It is preferable to limit the number of panels and reserve some money for quantitative research. Additional panels can always be scheduled after the first reports are studied. The additional panels can then concentrate on target groups or focus topics that require further exploration.

*Screening Criteria*   Once location and composition have been established, it is necessary to establish screening criteria, the key determinant of a panel's usefulness. A necessary requirement for direct marketing focus groups is that they be composed of people who have bought by mail. People who are hostile to mail order will be useless, and their opinions and attitudes will color the comments of the rest of the panel. Only people who have bought by mail in the past have opinions that are relevant for our purposes.

Other criteria include employment, media readership, and history of purchasing similar products, as dictated by the researcher and client. Your criteria should also be designed to eliminate competitors, people in related fields, or people in news media who might compromise the trade information exposed to the focus panel.

"Screeners" employed by the research firm telephone lists of people supplied by the client or assembled from local directories. They telephone hundreds of people until they can get the handful needed for each product—people who are qualified according to the criteria established and who are willing to participate in a panel in return for a nominal payment. The more restrictive the screening criteria, the more people must be called in order to assemble the panel.

Below is an example of a telephone screening questionnaire, as used in an actual direct marketing focus panel, reprinted with the permission of Sidney Furst, president of Furst Analytic Center in New York, a direct marketing focus panel specialist, and Doubleday Book Clubs. In this case, the book club was seeking people who were not previous buyers to test a new concept designed to reach such prospects.

## NON-MEMBERS
## SCREENING QUESTIONNAIRE

Hello, I am _____ from _____, and we are conducting a survey on attitudes toward leisure time reading, and would like to ask the adult FEMALE HEAD OF HOUSEHOLD a few questions. . . .

1.  Are you or any member of your immediate or extended family associated with Book Publishing, Editorial or Manufacturing, Book Distribution, Book Retail, Public Relations, Advertising, Media or any form of Market Research?

    Yes                              (  )    TERMINATE
    No                               (  )    CONTINUE

2.  What age range are you? Are you . . .

    Under 18                         (  )    TERMINATE

    18–25                            (  )    GROUP 1
    26–35                            (  )    GROUP 1

|  |  |  |
|---|---|---|
| 35–40 | ( ) | GROUP 2 |
| 41–45 | ( ) | GROUP 2 |
| 46–50 | ( ) | GROUP 2 |
| Over 50 | ( ) | TERMINATE |

3.  Are you employed . . .

| | |
|---|---|
| Part-time | ( ) |
| Full-time | ( ) |
| Not at all | ( ) |

RECRUITER: AT LEAST 4 RESPONDENTS IN THE EVENING GROUP SHOULD
       BE EMPLOYED FULL-TIME.

4.  What was the last grade of school you completed?

| | | |
|---|---|---|
| Attended High School or less | ( ) | CONTINUE |
| Completed High School | ( ) | CONTINUE |
| Attended College | ( ) | CONTINUE |
| Completed College (Bachelor's) | ( ) | TERMINATE |
| Attended Graduate School | ( ) | TERMINATE |
| Completed Graduate School | ( ) | TERMINATE |

5.  Do you have children under 18 living at home?

| | | |
|---|---|---|
| Yes | ( ) | CONTINUE |
| No | ( ) | CONTINUE |

RECRUITER: AT LEAST 50% OF THE GROUP MUST HAVE CHILDREN
       UNDER 18 YEARS OF AGE LIVING AT HOME.

6.  Which of the following Sunday Supplements or Magazines do
you read *regularly*—(read 6 of the last 12 issues)?

| | | |
|---|---|---|
| *Family Weekly* | ( ) | CONTINUE |
| *Parade* | ( ) | CONTINUE |
| *Reader's Digest* | ( ) | CONTINUE |
| Do Not Read Any of Above | ( ) | CONTINUE |

7.  Do you have a subscription to *Reader's Digest* at present?

| | |
|---|---|
| Yes | ( ) |
| No | ( ) |

RECRUITER: IF "YES": PREFERRED RESPONDENT.
       IF "NO": STILL ELIGIBLE—CONTINUE.

8.  How many hardcover books do you own—not including
encyclopedias?

| | | |
|---|---|---|
| Less than ten | ( ) | TERMINATE |
| Ten or more | ( ) | CONTINUE |
| Don't know | ( ) | TERMINATE |

9. How many books have you read in the last year?

| | | |
|---|---|---|
| Less than three | ( ) | TERMINATE |
| Three-five | ( ) | CONTINUE |
| Over five | ( ) | CONTINUE |
| Don't know | ( ) | TERMINATE |

10. Have you *ever* belonged to a Book Club—such as Doubleday Book Club, Book-Of-The Month Club, Literary Guild, or the like?

| | | |
|---|---|---|
| Yes | ( ) | TERMINATE |
| No | ( ) | CONTINUE |

RECRUITER: RESPONDENT MUST NOT NOW, OR IN THE PAST, EVER BELONGED TO A BOOK CLUB.

11. How often do you purchase items, other than books, by Mail Order?

| | | |
|---|---|---|
| Very often (several times a year) | ( ) | ELIGIBLE—INVITE |
| Somewhat (1 or 2 times a year) | ( ) | ELIGIBLE—INVITE |
| Seldom (less than once a year) | ( ) | TERMINATE |
| Never | ( ) | TERMINATE |

( ) GROUP 1: Friday—3:00 P.M.
( ) GROUP 2: Friday—6:00 P.M.

RECRUITER: INFORM RESPONDENT THAT DISCUSSION WILL LAST APPROXIMATELY 2 HOURS, AND SHE WILL RECEIVE $20 AS A GRATUITY FOR HER PARTICIPATION. INFORM HER OF DATE/TIME/LOCATION, AND DIRECTIONS.

## Discussion Guide

The final item is the discussion guide which is often omitted in early stages of a proposal. This is the step which requires the most work, and researchers will usually not prepare the guide until they have been awarded the contract.

The discussion guide is basically an agenda—a step-by-step guide to the various discussion topics as they are to be exposed to the audience, including a list of the samples or promotional materials to be shown to the groups.

There is no one right way to prepare a guide. Moderators develop styles which fit their own personalities. No two are alike. Some are analytical. Some are flamboyant. Yet most of them have some elements in common. The following composite of many panels I have observed is basically an attempt to abstract common denominators.

*The Opening Remarks*    The first objective is to relax the participants and to set the ground rules for the next couple of hours. Most moderators encourage the members of the group to say whatever is on their minds— to be honest in their opinions and feelings. A casual environment is established, with refreshments and light conversation. A joking comment or two doesn't hurt.

Introductions are made for two reasons. One is to help the participants to feel comfortable with one another. The other is to be able to relate their backgrounds to the comments made when audio or video tapes are later reviewed.

Some moderators disclose the presence of observers on the other side of the mirror; most do not. Almost all of them advise participants that the discussions that are to take place are not being judged nor rated, nor will there be any resolution of the topics. They are told that one person's opinion is as good as any other's, and there is no pressure to obtain agreement.

*Attitudinal Exploration*    The next step is to inquire about general attitudes toward the product category, buying by mail order, or other relevant topics. Questions are open-ended and tend to further provide background for the more specific comments that will come later.

During this stage analytic methods are often used to encourage amplification. "Mmm hmmm." "I see." "Why do you feel this way?" "Can you tell us more about that?" "Who else feels this way?" All these are appropriate comments which serve to draw out the group's feelings and attitudes.

*Development Stages*    The question at hand is brought up in a variety of ways. If the subject is a magazine, the panel might be asked where they get information about a certain topic or how they have learned certain things. They will be led into mentioning magazines, and the magazine in question, in a way that conceals that it is the magazine that is the central interest of the moderator. The reason for this is to forestall any bias, and to solicit comments which might be withheld out of courtesy if the sponsor were known right away.

Often competing advertisements or products are shown, sometimes with the advertiser's name blacked out. This is to obtain comments about the product or advertisement uncolored by positive or negative attitudes that have developed toward the brand name.

One excellent focus panel explored attitudes toward conventional mail-order propositions and identified positive and negative reactions. The sponsor's proposition, which overcame many of the objections to conventional propositions, was then introduced. The features of the new product would not have been as evident without the contrast with the previous ones.

*Subject Exploration*   Finally, about halfway through the session, the subject at hand is unveiled, with the same casualness as the previous queries. By now the group should be warmed up and comments should come freely.

One technique is to show a commercial or read the headlines of an ad or mailing piece and then, at a signal, ask the participants to quickly jot down the points they recall which were important to them. Comments are solicited later about what those points were and why they were important. If there were no written notes, the panel would tend to echo the first comments made rather than expose each person's own honest reactions.

Where several ads are shown, the panelists may be asked to rate the likelihood that they would buy the product on a zero-to-ten scale in the same manner. They are then asked for their scores and their reasons for the scores.

*The Redirect*   Up to now the moderator has been in complete charge, pursuing a line of questioning previously worked out with the client. Then, thirty minutes or so from the end, the moderator makes an excuse to leave the room, invites the group to have some refreshments, and proceeds to the room where the clients have been watching. In hurried conference, the moderator and clients exchange ideas on how the next segment should be handled.

Clients may ask that a particular person's viewpoints be explored further, that a point be stressed, or that a major change be introduced. "Stress the guarantee and see if that changes anyone's mind." "Tell them who is behind this new product and see if it adds credibility." "Would they join this club if they didn't have to pay anything up front?"

The moderator rejoins the group and finishes the session with the suggested revisions. After each panel, the client, agency, and research people discuss their observations on the spot. They often revise the discussion guide before the next session. Sometimes new layouts or package designs are created between one session and the next, in response to comments.

*The Write-Up*   When everyone is back home, the researcher's work begins anew with a comprehensive written summary of the various focus panels, objectives, and conclusions. Correlations are made with the backgrounds of the focus panel members, and patterns and differences are observed from one group to the next. These written reports are extremely valuable and are usually circulated to all interested parties. Such reports are notoriously unable to predict the success of a direct marketing idea, but they do provide valuable insight into idea comprehension and often lead to modified plans, products, and promotions.

## PHYSIOLOGICAL RESEARCH METHODS

Some of the major breakthroughs in applying modern research methods to direct marketing have been in the field of physiological research. In general, these methods measure uncontrolled emotional response, free of the bias and pretension which distort simple verbal exchanges.

Few interviewees will admit that they are "turned on" by advertising themes appealing to lust, power, or greed, or responding to fears of poor health, job loss, or even death. They elevate their answers on questionnaires or in interviews, but they can't fool a physiological test. The reactions are, in effect, involuntary and completely honest replies. Still, there are serious limitations.

Probably the most severe limitation is the one that these methods have in common with all other kinds of research: the typicality of the people tested, interviewed, or questioned. In general advertising, a very large percentage of people encountered on the street or in the phone book might be likely to buy a new product available through conventional outlets—a food item sold in supermarkets, for example. In mail order, however, a proposition can be considered a success if only a tiny fraction of an audience respond affirmatively. Unless samples are very large, the few potential customers can be overlooked and the research can be meaningless to direct marketers.

In physiological research, all the various known techniques share the limitation of the choice of subjects, and all of them have perfectly valid ways of measuring reactions to copy statements.

Experience has shown that when these techniques are used, they do not pick winners; they only eliminate losers. An intense reaction to copy may be a positive or a negative one, a meaningful one or a feeling based on an irrelevant emotional response. The only sure thing is that no reaction means no interest, and no interest means no sale.

### Types of Physiological Research

*Brain Wave Measurement*   The Neurocommunications Research Laboratory in Danbury, Connecticut, utilizes an electroencephalograph (EEG) to record the brain's spontaneous electrical activity. Between 50 and 200 subjects are recruited for these tests. Electrodes are taped to their heads, and the individuals are each shown a series of advertising messages and other stimuli.

A pattern of cortical evoked potentials (CEP) brain waves is recorded and measured. The pattern appears to be an accurate indicator of attention and arousal and may, through a study of CEP patterns, also indicate whether the subject's response is favorable or unfavorable.

*Eye-Movement Tracking*   One of the most interesting physiological techniques is the one offered by Perception Research Services of Englewood Cliffs, New Jersey, to measure print advertising and direct mail. This involves use of an eye-movement recorder to indicate exactly where a subject is looking, how long the eye rests at a particular point, and the sequence in which the message is perceived.

Groups of 50 to 100 subjects are each shown ten ads in this manner— five test ads and five control ads for comparison. After each measurement, recall interviewing and additional testing takes place, including specific queries about likes and dislikes, a checklist of adjectives, and a determination of interest in purchasing the product.

The test purports to indicate the subject's relative attention, involvement, and memory in relation to the various test ads, as well as detailed indications of what elements of each ad or mailing piece had the most impact.

*Galvanic Skin Response*   This is the physiological method I happen to have had the most experience with. Despite an initial skepticism about the entire field of physiological research, I have found this method to correlate with actual split-run tests in general, if not specific, response-rate ranking.

Offered by the Walt Wesley Company of Sierra Madre, California, this technique utilizes panels of about twenty-five individuals selected according to predetermined criteria. Each has psychogalvanometer electrodes attached to the fingertips, and is shown a series of ads, mailing pieces, or television commercials. Reactions are involuntary, as with a lie detector, and the rate of sweating is recorded every 2½ seconds. Initial arousal, salient arousal, and sustained arousal are measured by the sweat rate, indicating the intensity and frequency of a subject's feelings about the advertisement or commercial.

## SIMULATED MEDIA SITUATIONS

Researchers have sought ways to develop research techniques that can simulate the reality of split-run testing, without the expense and complications to be discussed in Chapter 10. A particular consideration is the need to conduct low-profile testing—making experimental offers to a few thousand people instead of exposing them in the media at large.

## Pseudopublications

One technique which, as far as I know, was developed by DDB Research for its general advertising clients, is particulary suitable for direct marketers.

The researchers produce a simulated local newspaper, using human-interest articles picked up from real newspapers. This publication, which resembles a newspaper in its first pages, contains many legitimate ads plus a full-page insertion of the test ad. The paper is distributed door to door, without charge, in selected neighborhoods. Different versions might contain different ads, or the newspaper may be distributed for several consecutive weeks to gain the impact of frequency for the test campaign.

Some orders may be produced from the limited circulation of the publication, but the number of responses is usually not statistically significant. What is meaningful is a telephone canvass conducted later, asking families if they saw the paper, remember the ad, and what they recall about the sales message.

The telephone canvassers can ask not only about ad recall but also for a buying decision on the tested ad product, increasing response factors to a level which may be statistically valuable.

## Interactive Television

The first installation of two-way, or interactive, television took place in Columbus, Ohio, in 1977. Station QUBE, operated by Warner Brothers on a cable hookup, provided its 30,000 subscribers with a five-button unit with which they could send signals back to the television station.

The implications for research were immediately apparent. The audience of QUBE became a huge research panel with instant response capability. Viewer responses were processed by a computer, which could not only count responses and produce a tabulation in a matter of seconds but also—because the characteristics of the viewing households were previously identified—segment likes and dislikes by types of audience.

The system was used to test new shows, new products, and new general advertising campaigns. Direct marketers cautiously subscribed, at a typical cost of $500 for a two- or three-minute test to expose different ads or commercials to the audience. My company was one of them.

The surprise was that it didn't work. When four ads were shown and the audience signaled the ad they liked best, the answers didn't correlate with previous split-run testing. The same thing happened when we offered a free book. Responses were all too high, out of proportion to the percentage that would respond in a real-life test, and the differences between copy appeals or product featured were not in line with actual experience.

Evidently, everyone is a prospect when the offer is "free," and everyone has an opinion on which ad they like best. Teenagers and senior citizens, stay-at-homes and the unemployed, outnumbered more typical audiences in offering their opinions. Worse yet, audience segments which never buy by mail were skewing the results.

If we had offered the product at full price, the number of responses would have been too small to be significant. So we compromised. We varied the offer by selling a book, which ordinarily sold for $7.95, for only $1. The income wasn't the point. What we wanted was to qualify the respondents.

An old mail-order theory states that the true deadbeat won't pay anything, almost as a matter of honor. Even a nominal charge like 99 cents for ten records will smoke out the unscrupulous respondent who has no intention of fulfilling the purchase committment. The theory worked here: The $1 respondents were typical of demographic profiles from conventional offers, and the number of respondents was sufficient to produce a valid and statistically meaningful response. Using this system we were able to demonstrate the viability of a new product positioning which resulted in a whole series of breakthroughs for an important continuity advertiser.

Today QUBE is being expanded, with installations in Houston, Texas, and other cities. What started as a research tool may one day be a major medium in itself.

## MAIL, TELEPHONE, AND FIELD SURVEYS

In the world of conventional advertising, various kinds of questionnaires—sent by mail or presented to people while shopping or at their doorsteps—are to the army of researchers what bullets are to soldiers. For some general advertisers, a questionnaire is the first and most logical step for virtually any common research task. For direct marketers, it is more often the exception than the rule.

As in screening for focus panel participants, it is possible to ask about age, sex, previous mail-order history, or key attitudes. The percentage of prospects who fit all the qualifications is usually low, as is the incidence in the population of people who fit all the specified criteria. It is usually not economically feasible to reach enough typical prospects to make such a survey worthwhile for a direct marketer.

## Uses of Field Surveys

The most common uses, therefore, are in after-the-fact research—surveys directed at people who have already identified themselves as significant by voluntarily responding to an advertisement or mailing piece.

Costs rapidly come into line when you can supply the researcher with a list of prospects whose opinions are of value to you. Then the only falloff factor is the number who can be reached by phone or in person and are willing to cooperate, or the number who will reply to a mailed questionnaire.

There are three broad areas in which research can be used to reach such lists. One might be to find out why someone became a customer and to identify the positive motivations which are important. Another is to find out why a former customer no longer buys. A third is to discover where the selling process broke down—why a club member never fulfilled, a trial subscriber opted to cancel, or an inquirer didn't convert to a buyer.

When used to test new mail-order products, field surveys can measure concept comprehension and the relative appeal of different approaches. However, they cannot indicate whether the proposition will be successful.

## The Tracking Study and Direct Marketing

The problem with most research is that it is applied too late. Too many advertisers wait until their operating statistics show that a large percentage of their customers have suddenly gone inactive, and then the advertisers wonder what went wrong. Others pooh-pooh a competitor's entry into their own field, without finding out whether the consumer may perceive the competitor as offering a better deal.

The solution is an application of what general marketers call a "tracking study." In its normal application, an advertiser will retain a national research firm to conduct an annual survey of awareness of its product, the attitudes and perceptions of various market segments toward the product, and reports of recent purchases or intentions to buy. Trademarks are shown and customers are asked whether they know what it represents—not only for the client's own symbols but also those used by competitors. (The startlingly low unaided recall of most trademarks and even company names—particularly names using initials—is usually a shock to advertisers.)

At first glance, it might seem academic to note that 18 percent of the marketplace associates attributes like "quality" or "long-lasting " or "easy-to-use" with your product. Such associations become important when you discover that a higher or lower percentage relates the same terms to your competition.

The greatest significance occurs when you relate one year's figures to the next and track the awareness, attitude, and intent levels of the marketplace. Often there is a direct relationship between changes in these levels and the advertising budget.

In direct marketing, the principle is identical. It might not be practical to track attitudes of the country at large (except for the largest advertisers), but it is possible to measure the attitudes of our own customers. Their perception of our catalogs or promotion materials, their evaluation of the company as reliable or prompt, and the credibility they accord our copy claims and guarantees are the equivalent of general attitudes and intentions for general advertisers.

However, tracking studies are only effective if they are the result of advance planning. They should be set up in the good years in order to get important information in the bad ones. It is too late to apply this technique if you wait until the need for research is desperate.

## Preparing Mail Questionnaires

I believe the most accurate questionnaires are those using personal interviews of preidentified subjects at home or office, in person or by telephone. However, the most economical and convenient type of survey is the mailed questionnaire.

There are two dangers in such surveys. One is that they seem simple to prepare, and therefore too many advertisers fail to retain professional researchers to handle them. The other is that they are too difficult to answer, resulting in skewed responses—a disproportionate ratio from people with nothing better to do, who may not be typical prospects.

The solution to the first problem is obvious. Work with a professional. The second is more difficult. I recommend that questionnaire results not be acted upon until it has been validated that the questionnaire respondents are typical of the prospect list as a whole. This can be done by following up a mail questionnaire with a telephone survey to nonrespondents, attempting to determine—even if just on a spot basis—whether nonrespondents are substantially similar to respondents. Once this has been established, mail questionnaires can be used freely.

Obviously, the larger the percentage of response, the greater the chance that the questionnaire will be typical of the group at large. Here are some ways to improve questionnaire response.

*Make It Easy*   The ease of filling out the form is a critical factor. Except for unaided recall questions, where you should ask for a one-word reply, everything else should be answerable by making a simple check mark or circling a number. Don't ask for complicated rankings. Put touchy queries like age into groups rather than asking for specific data.

*Make It Interesting*   Begin with the "meat" of the survey, and use any illustrations, trademarks, headlines, or product packages in the earlier questions. Ask the dry (and sometimes too personal) questions like age and education at the very end. Also, include some questions that the respondent will enjoy even if they are not very important to you.

*Make It Personal*   Wherever possible, include a letter addressed to the individual, and make it clear that only a small number of people are being sent this form and that every answer represents tens of thousands of consumers.

*Make It Important*   Explain, if it is true, that a major corporation is holding up a multi-million-dollar new-product launch until the person's opinions are received, or that it is the practice of the company to act on this type of information in the name of good consumerism. The questionnaire should also look important. This is not the place to skimp on paper quality or typesetting.

*Make It Profitable*   Most researchers use some type of premium—a small gift either promised in return for the questionnaire or enclosed with the quiz. The future gift is difficult because it requires disclosure of the name and address of the respondent. I prefer a small cash gift— perhaps a $2 bill, which is an interesting oddity in itself, or a check for $5 or $10. When sending questionnaires to business prospects, you can suggest that they may want to donate the gift to their favorite charity if there is a policy prohibiting the acceptance of such incentives.

*   *   *

Previous books on direct marketing didn't include the subject of research at all. Its applications are still being discovered, its methods still being perfected. The point is that, today, research is *usable* to direct marketers, and research professionals should be an important part of any company's direct marketing management team.

## CHAPTER TEN

# TESTING

The measurability of direct marketing is such an integral part of this business that the word "testing" is used very lightly. Direct marketers talk of testing media, testing copy, and testing an offer. We run test campaigns, dry tests, split-run tests, element tests, and concept tests.

In its simplest form the word can be used as a synonym for "try," as in running an advertisement in a publication or using a mailing list for the first time and then seeing if the results are satisfactory. In its most complex form, two- and three-dimensional grid tests can be constructed to simultaneously read media, offer, and copy variables on a new business proposition.

## DIRECT-MAIL TESTING

If a mailing list has 1 million names and you mail to the entire list the first time you try it, you aren't testing, you're gambling. The pragmatic defining characteristic of "testing" in direct mail is the desire to minimize downside financial risk.

Because direct mail is believed to be subject to the rules of statistical projectability, you should be able to mail as few as 3000 or 5000 pieces and determine a range of response rates that might be expected from the entire list.

### Sample Size

How many pieces of mail do you have to send out in order to rely on the test results? Most books on direct marketing include a table which can be referred to for this answer. These tables are based on game theory, the laws of chance, and algebraic interpretations of sampling practice and the principles of statistical probability. Unfortunately, they are all different, and there is no universal agreement about which table to use or whether in fact any of them are at all meaningful.

The tables which I often refer to are included in this chapter. They were prepared by Prof. Robert C. Blattberg of the Graduate School of Business, University of Chicago, and are included in detail in the *Direct Marketing Manual*. Other charts appear in other widely used books, or are distributed by well-known direct-mail list brokers.

Walter Marshall, who is an accomplished mathematician as well as a prominent direct marketing executive, points out that direct marketing is not a matter of chance but a business which involves a series of separate factors that are virtually impossible to quantify. If you send out 1000 pieces, how many will be addressed correctly, how many may get lost in the post office, how many will be opened, how many will be seen? How many people will be interested, how many will want to respond affirmatively or negatively, and how many will overcome inertia and respond at all? Each step may involve its own random, and unquantifiable, element of chance.

Also, in theory, if a 5 percent response to a sample would not produce a valid sample, but a 95 percent response would, then wouldn't it be fair to say that the fact that 95 percent of the sample ignored your offer is as significant as the fact that 5 percent accepted it? Yet direct marketers generally base their decisions only on the probability factors relating to the affirmative decision.

Marshall's most telling argument is the empirical one relating to actual business practice. If you test 20,000 pieces and get what is supposed to be a statistically valid answer, would you then risk your money to send out a mailing of 10 million pieces using the same package? I know of no direct marketers who would answer in the affirmative. We would schedule test extensions: first 250,000 names, then a few million, and finally the balance of the names. Yet testing theory *should* give us the confidence to go right to the 10 million.

Perhaps the statistical theories are incorrect. Perhaps the problem is not the theory but our industry's collective lack of confidence. More likely, the root of the dilemma may lie in the fact that we are dealing in a fluid environment. A mailing sent out even a few months after a test might encounter changed attitudes, economic circumstances, or competitive activity, not to mention weather, news events, and other influences on direct marketing results.

At any rate, direct marketing practitioners should be familiar with the most widely accepted ways of selecting sample sizes and determining the validity of tests—if for no other reason than to draw their own conclusions.

*Confidence Level*    The laws of chance are admittedly imperfect. The chance events which occur nine times may not be applicable to the tenth. Each roll of the dice, random flipping of a coin, or arrival of a direct-mail package is a unique event. Therefore certainty is attainable only within certain limits of error and at certain confidence levels.

What we can say is that if a given mailing piece produced a certain response rate, we are 90 percent (or some other figure) confident that a subsequent mailing which is identical will produce approximately the same rate. The width of the "approximately" is a matter of "error limit," discussed below. A 90 percent confidence level is a way of saying that 90 out of 100 times the result would be within an indicated range. Different confidence levels, factored into algebraic equations for probability, produce entirely different mathematical tables.

*Limit of Error*    At any given response level a margin of error will be needed in order to project what would happen in the future. For instance, if your expected response rate is 2 percent and the error margin is 0.5 percent, this means that the next time you send out the same mailing to other similar names on the list, the rate might be 2 percent, but it could also be anywhere from 1½ to 2½ percent. This is the actual limit of error, at a 95 percent confidence level, if you only mail out at least 4243 pieces in a test cell.

If a 1½ percent rate of return would not be acceptable in a rollout, then a larger sample must be mailed to narrow the error margin. At the same 2 percent response rate and 95 percent confidence level, a mailing of about 12,000 pieces will project to a range of between 1.7 and 2.3 percent—an error limit of 0.3 percent. If you wanted to go to a 0.1 percent error limit, for a projection range of between 1.9 and 2.1 percent, you would have to mail a sample size of 106,000 pieces. At a 90 percent instead of 95 percent confidence level, the comparable figure for the last example is 64,000 at a 0.1 percent factor, 7000 at a 0.3 percent factor.

At the 95 percent confidence level, a 1.5 percent response rate would require 3199 pieces at a 0.5 percent error limit. However, the percentage limits are absolute, not relative, and the impact of error is much greater at the lower response rates. A 0.5 percent range is a one-third margin at this rate and anywhere between 2 and 3 percent. To get the same proportional error margin as 0.5 percent at 2 to 2.5 percent, you would only need an error margin of between 1.875 and 1.125 percent. This 0.375 percent error limit is between 3.5 and 4.0 percent on the chart

**SAMPLE SIZES FOR VARIOUS PERCENTAGES OF EXPECTED RESPONSE —
COMPARING TWO MAILINGS**

CONFIDENCE LEVEL = 90.0%

ACCEPTABLE % DIFFERENCES

| EXPECTED RESPONSE % | 0.01 | 0.02 | 0.03 | 0.04 | 0.05 | 0.06 | 0.07 | 0.08 | 0.09 | 0.10 |
|---|---|---|---|---|---|---|---|---|---|---|
| 0.10 | 328376 | 82094 | 36486 | 20523 | 13135 | 9122 | 6702 | 5131 | 4054 | 3284 |
| 0.20 | 656095 | 164024 | 72899 | 41006 | 26244 | 18225 | 13390 | 10251 | 8100 | 6561 |
| 0.30 | 983156 | 245789 | 109240 | 61447 | 39326 | 27310 | 20064 | 15362 | 12138 | 9832 |
| 0.40 | 1309559 | 327390 | 145507 | 81847 | 52382 | 36377 | 26726 | 20462 | 16167 | 13096 |
| 0.50 | 1635306 | 408826 | 181701 | 102207 | 65412 | 45425 | 33374 | 25552 | 20189 | 16353 |
| 0.60 | 1960395 | 490099 | 217822 | 122525 | 78416 | 54455 | 40008 | 30631 | 24202 | 19604 |
| 0.70 | 2284826 | 571207 | 253870 | 142802 | 91393 | 63467 | 46629 | 35700 | 28208 | 22848 |
| 0.80 | 2608601 | 652150 | 289845 | 163038 | 104344 | 72461 | 53237 | 40759 | 32205 | 26086 |
| 0.90 | 2931717 | 732929 | 325746 | 183232 | 117269 | 81437 | 59831 | 45808 | 36194 | 29317 |
| 1.00 | 3254176 | 813544 | 361575 | 203386 | 130167 | 90394 | 66412 | 50846 | 40175 | 32542 |

**Figure 10-1.** (Source: Robert C. Blattberg, "Decision Rule and Sample Size Selection for Direct Mail Testing," Direct Marketing Manual, Direct Mail Marketing Association, New York, Manual Release No. 610.1, October 1979.)

CONFIDENCE LEVEL = 90.0%

ACCEPTABLE % DIFFERENCES

| EXPECTED RESPONSE % | 0.05 | 0.10 | 0.15 | 0.20 | 0.25 | 0.30 | 0.35 | 0.40 | 0.45 | 0.50 |
|---|---|---|---|---|---|---|---|---|---|---|
| 1.10 | 143039 | 35760 | 15893 | 8940 | 5722 | 3973 | 2919 | 2235 | 1766 | 1430 |
| 1.20 | 155885 | 38971 | 17321 | 9743 | 6235 | 4330 | 3181 | 2436 | 1925 | 1559 |
| 1.30 | 168704 | 42176 | 18745 | 10544 | 6748 | 4686 | 3443 | 2636 | 2083 | 1687 |
| 1.40 | 181498 | 45374 | 20166 | 11344 | 7260 | 5042 | 3704 | 2836 | 2241 | 1815 |
| 1.50 | 194264 | 48566 | 21585 | 12142 | 7771 | 5396 | 3965 | 3035 | 2398 | 1943 |
| 1.60 | 207005 | 51751 | 23001 | 12938 | 8280 | 5750 | 4225 | 3234 | 2556 | 2070 |
| 1.70 | 219719 | 54930 | 24413 | 13732 | 8789 | 6103 | 4484 | 3433 | 2713 | 2197 |
| 1.80 | 232407 | 58102 | 25823 | 14525 | 9296 | 6456 | 4743 | 3631 | 2869 | 2324 |
| 1.90 | 245069 | 61767 | 27230 | 15317 | 9803 | 6807 | 5001 | 3829 | 3026 | 2451 |
| 2.00 | 257704 | 64426 | 28634 | 16107 | 10308 | 7158 | 5259 | 4027 | 3182 | 2577 |
| 2.10 | 270314 | 67578 | 30035 | 16895 | 10813 | 7509 | 5517 | 4224 | 3337 | 2703 |
| 2.20 | 282896 | 70724 | 31433 | 17681 | 11316 | 7858 | 5773 | 4420 | 3493 | 2829 |
| 2.30 | 295453 | 73863 | 32828 | 18466 | 11818 | 8207 | 6030 | 4616 | 3648 | 2955 |
| 2.40 | 307983 | 76996 | 34220 | 19249 | 12319 | 8555 | 6285 | 4812 | 3802 | 3080 |
| 2.50 | 320487 | 80122 | 35610 | 20030 | 12819 | 8902 | 6541 | 5008 | 3957 | 3205 |
| 2.60 | 332965 | 83241 | 36996 | 20810 | 13319 | 9249 | 6795 | 5203 | 4111 | 3330 |
| 2.70 | 345416 | 86354 | 38380 | 21588 | 13817 | 9595 | 7049 | 5397 | 4264 | 3454 |
| 2.80 | 357841 | 89460 | 39760 | 22365 | 14314 | 9940 | 7303 | 5591 | 4418 | 3578 |
| 2.90 | 370240 | 92560 | 41138 | 23140 | 14810 | 10284 | 7556 | 5785 | 4571 | 3702 |
| 3.00 | 382612 | 95653 | 42512 | 23913 | 15304 | 10628 | 7808 | 5978 | 4724 | 3826 |
| 3.10 | 394958 | 98740 | 43884 | 24685 | 15798 | 10971 | 8060 | 6171 | 4876 | 3950 |
| 3.20 | 407278 | 101820 | 45253 | 25455 | 16291 | 11313 | 8312 | 6364 | 5028 | 4073 |
| 3.30 | 419572 | 104893 | 46619 | 26223 | 16783 | 11655 | 8563 | 6556 | 5180 | 4196 |
| 3.40 | 431839 | 107960 | 47982 | 26990 | 17274 | 11996 | 8813 | 6747 | 5331 | 4318 |
| 3.50 | 444080 | 111020 | 49342 | 27755 | 17763 | 12336 | 9063 | 6939 | 5482 | 4441 |
| 3.60 | 456295 | 114074 | 50699 | 28518 | 18252 | 12675 | 9312 | 7130 | 5633 | 4563 |
| 3.70 | 468483 | 117121 | 52054 | 29280 | 18739 | 13013 | 9561 | 7320 | 5784 | 4685 |
| 3.80 | 480645 | 120161 | 53405 | 30040 | 19226 | 13351 | 9809 | 7510 | 5934 | 4806 |
| 3.90 | 492781 | 123195 | 54753 | 30799 | 19711 | 13688 | 10057 | 7700 | 6084 | 4928 |
| 4.00 | 504890 | 126223 | 56099 | 31556 | 20196 | 14025 | 10304 | 7889 | 6233 | 5049 |

**Figure 10-2.** (Source: Robert C. Blattberg, "Decision Rule and Sample Size Selection for Direct Mail Testing," Direct Marketing Manual, Direct Mail Marketing Association, New York, Manual Release No. 610.1, October 1979.)

CONFIDENCE LEVEL = 90.0%

ACCEPTABLE % DIFFERENCES

EXPECTED
RESPONSE
| % | 0.50 | 0.60 | 0.70 | 0.80 | 0.90 | 1.00 | 1.10 | 1.20 | 1.30 | 1.40 |
|---|---|---|---|---|---|---|---|---|---|---|
| 4.20 | 5290 | 3674 | 2699 | 2067 | 1633 | 1323 | 1093 | 918 | 783 | 675 |
| 4.40 | 5531 | 3841 | 2822 | 2160 | 1707 | 1383 | 1143 | 960 | 818 | 705 |
| 4.60 | 5770 | 4007 | 2944 | 2254 | 1781 | 1442 | 1192 | 1002 | 854 | 736 |
| 4.80 | 6008 | 4172 | 3065 | 2347 | 1854 | 1502 | 1241 | 1043 | 889 | 766 |
| 5.00 | 6245 | 4337 | 3186 | 2440 | 1928 | 1561 | 1290 | 1084 | 924 | 797 |
| 5.20 | 6482 | 4501 | 3307 | 2532 | 2000 | 1620 | 1339 | 1125 | 959 | 827 |
| 5.40 | 6717 | 4664 | 3427 | 2624 | 2073 | 1679 | 1388 | 1166 | 994 | 857 |
| 5.60 | 6951 | 4827 | 3546 | 2715 | 2145 | 1738 | 1436 | 1207 | 1028 | 887 |
| 5.80 | 7184 | 4989 | 3665 | 2806 | 2217 | 1796 | 1484 | 1247 | 1063 | 916 |
| 6.00 | 7416 | 5150 | 3783 | 2897 | 2289 | 1854 | 1532 | 1287 | 1097 | 946 |
| 6.20 | 7646 | 5310 | 3901 | 2987 | 2360 | 1912 | 1580 | 1328 | 1131 | 975 |
| 6.40 | 7876 | 5470 | 4019 | 3077 | 2431 | 1969 | 1627 | 1367 | 1165 | 1005 |
| 6.60 | 8105 | 5629 | 4135 | 3166 | 2502 | 2026 | 1675 | 1407 | 1199 | 1034 |
| 6.80 | 8333 | 5787 | 4251 | 3255 | 2572 | 2083 | 1722 | 1447 | 1233 | 1063 |
| 7.00 | 8559 | 5944 | 4367 | 3344 | 2642 | 2140 | 1768 | 1486 | 1266 | 1092 |
| 7.20 | 8785 | 6101 | 4482 | 3432 | 2711 | 2196 | 1815 | 1525 | 1300 | 1121 |
| 7.40 | 9010 | 6257 | 4597 | 3519 | 2781 | 2252 | 1862 | 1564 | 1333 | 1149 |
| 7.60 | 9233 | 6412 | 4711 | 3607 | 2850 | 2308 | 1908 | 1603 | 1366 | 1178 |
| 7.80 | 9456 | 6566 | 4824 | 3694 | 2918 | 2364 | 1954 | 1642 | 1399 | 1206 |
| 8.00 | 9677 | 6720 | 4937 | 3780 | 2987 | 2419 | 1999 | 1680 | 1432 | 1234 |
| 8.20 | 9897 | 6873 | 5050 | 3866 | 3055 | 2474 | 2045 | 1718 | 1464 | 1262 |
| 8.40 | 10117 | 7026 | 5162 | 3952 | 3122 | 2529 | 2090 | 1756 | 1497 | 1290 |
| 8.60 | 10335 | 7177 | 5273 | 4037 | 3190 | 2584 | 2135 | 1794 | 1529 | 1318 |
| 8.80 | 10552 | 7328 | 5384 | 4122 | 3257 | 2638 | 2180 | 1832 | 1561 | 1346 |
| 9.00 | 10768 | 7478 | 5494 | 4206 | 3324 | 2692 | 2225 | 1870 | 1593 | 1374 |
| 9.20 | 10983 | 7627 | 5604 | 4290 | 3390 | 2746 | 2269 | 1907 | 1625 | 1401 |
| 9.40 | 11198 | 7776 | 5713 | 4374 | 3456 | 2799 | 2314 | 1944 | 1656 | 1428 |
| 9.60 | 11411 | 7924 | 5822 | 4457 | 3522 | 2853 | 2358 | 1981 | 1688 | 1455 |
| 9.80 | 11622 | 8071 | 5930 | 4540 | 3587 | 2906 | 2401 | 2018 | 1719 | 1482 |
| 10.00 | 11833 | 8218 | 6037 | 4622 | 3652 | 2958 | 2445 | 2054 | 1750 | 1509 |

**Figure 10-3.**   (Source: Robert C. Blattberg, University of Chicago.)

CONFIDENCE LEVEL = 90%

ACCEPTABLE % DIFFERENCES

EXPECTED
RESPONSE
| % | 0.50 | 1.00 | 1.50 | 2.00 | 2.50 | 3.00 | 3.50 | 4.00 | 4.50 | 5.00 |
|---|---|---|---|---|---|---|---|---|---|---|
| 11.00 | 12872 | 3218 | 1430 | 805 | 515 | 358 | 263 | 201 | 159 | 129 |
| 12.00 | 13884 | 3471 | 1543 | 868 | 555 | 386 | 283 | 217 | 171 | 139 |
| 13.00 | 14871 | 3718 | 1652 | 929 | 595 | 413 | 303 | 232 | 184 | 149 |
| 14.00 | 15830 | 3958 | 1759 | 989 | 633 | 440 | 323 | 247 | 195 | 158 |
| 15.00 | 16764 | 4191 | 1863 | 1048 | 671 | 466 | 342 | 262 | 207 | 168 |
| 16.00 | 17671 | 4418 | 1963 | 1104 | 707 | 491 | 361 | 276 | 218 | 177 |
| 17.00 | 18552 | 4638 | 2061 | 1160 | 742 | 515 | 379 | 290 | 229 | 186 |
| 18.00 | 19407 | 4852 | 2156 | 1213 | 776 | 539 | 396 | 303 | 240 | 194 |
| 19.00 | 20235 | 5059 | 2248 | 1265 | 809 | 562 | 413 | 316 | 250 | 202 |
| 20.00 | 21037 | 5259 | 2337 | 1315 | 841 | 584 | 429 | 329 | 260 | 210 |

**Figure 10-4.**   (Source: Robert C. Blattberg, University of Chicago.)

CONFIDENCE LEVEL = 95.0%

ACCEPTABLE % DIFFERENCES

| EXPECTED RESPONSE % | 0.01 | 0.02 | 0.03 | 0.04 | 0.05 | 0.06 | 0.07 | 0.08 | 0.09 | 0.10 |
|---|---|---|---|---|---|---|---|---|---|---|
| 0.10 | 540664 | 135166 | 60074 | 33791 | 21627 | 15018 | 11034 | 8448 | 6675 | 5407 |
| 0.20 | 1080245 | 270061 | 120027 | 67515 | 43210 | 30007 | 22046 | 16879 | 13336 | 10802 |
| 0.30 | 1618744 | 404686 | 179860 | 101172 | 64750 | 44965 | 33036 | 25293 | 19984 | 16187 |
| 0.40 | 2156161 | 539040 | 239573 | 134760 | 86246 | 59893 | 44003 | 33690 | 26619 | 21562 |
| 0.50 | 2692494 | 673124 | 299166 | 168281 | 107700 | 74792 | 54949 | 42070 | 33241 | 26925 |
| 0.60 | 3227746 | 806937 | 358639 | 201734 | 129110 | 89660 | 65872 | 50434 | 39849 | 32277 |
| 0.70 | 3761916 | 940479 | 417991 | 235120 | 150477 | 104498 | 76774 | 58780 | 46443 | 37619 |
| 0.80 | 4295002 | 1073751 | 477223 | 268438 | 171800 | 119306 | 87653 | 67109 | 53025 | 42950 |
| 0.90 | 4827006 | 1206752 | 536334 | 301688 | 193080 | 134084 | 98510 | 75422 | 59593 | 48270 |
| 1.00 | 5357928 | 1339482 | 595325 | 334871 | 214317 | 148831 | 109345 | 83718 | 66147 | 53579 |

**Figure 10-5.** (Source: Robert C. Blattberg, "Decision Rule and Sample Size Selection for Direct Mail Testing," Direct Marketing Manual, Direct Mail Marketing Association, New York, Manual Release No. 610.1, October 1979.)

CONFIDENCE LEVEL = 95%

ACCEPTABLE % DIFFERENCES

| EXPECTED RESPONSE % | 0.05 | 0.10 | 0.15 | 0.20 | 0.25 | 0.30 | 0.35 | 0.40 | 0.45 | 0.50 |
|---|---|---|---|---|---|---|---|---|---|---|
| 1.10 | 235511 | 58878 | 26168 | 14719 | 9420 | 6542 | 4806 | 3680 | 2908 | 2355 |
| 1.20 | 256661 | 64165 | 28518 | 16041 | 10266 | 7129 | 5238 | 4010 | 3169 | 2567 |
| 1.30 | 277768 | 69442 | 30863 | 17361 | 11111 | 7716 | 5669 | 4340 | 3429 | 2778 |
| 1.40 | 298832 | 74708 | 33204 | 18677 | 11953 | 8301 | 6099 | 4669 | 3689 | 2988 |
| 1.50 | 319852 | 79963 | 35539 | 19991 | 12794 | 8885 | 6528 | 4998 | 3949 | 3199 |
| 1.60 | 340829 | 85207 | 37870 | 21302 | 13633 | 9467 | 6956 | 5325 | 4208 | 3408 |
| 1.70 | 361763 | 90441 | 40196 | 22610 | 14471 | 10049 | 7383 | 5653 | 4466 | 3618 |
| 1.80 | 382654 | 95663 | 42517 | 23916 | 15306 | 10629 | 7809 | 5979 | 4724 | 3827 |
| 1.90 | 403501 | 100875 | 44833 | 25219 | 16140 | 11208 | 8235 | 6305 | 4981 | 4035 |
| 2.00 | 424305 | 106076 | 47145 | 26519 | 16972 | 11786 | 8659 | 6630 | 5238 | 4243 |
| 2.10 | 445065 | 111266 | 49452 | 27817 | 17803 | 12363 | 9083 | 6954 | 5495 | 4451 |
| 2.20 | 465783 | 116446 | 51754 | 29111 | 18631 | 12938 | 9506 | 7278 | 5750 | 4658 |
| 2.30 | 486457 | 121614 | 54051 | 30404 | 19458 | 13513 | 9928 | 7601 | 6006 | 4865 |
| 2.40 | 507087 | 126772 | 56343 | 31693 | 20284 | 14086 | 10349 | 7923 | 6260 | 5071 |
| 2.50 | 527675 | 131919 | 58631 | 32980 | 21107 | 14658 | 10769 | 8245 | 6515 | 5277 |
| 2.60 | 548219 | 137055 | 60913 | 34264 | 21929 | 15228 | 11188 | 8566 | 6768 | 5482 |
| 2.70 | 568720 | 142180 | 63191 | 35545 | 22749 | 15798 | 11607 | 8886 | 7021 | 5687 |
| 2.80 | 589177 | 147294 | 65464 | 36824 | 23567 | 16366 | 12024 | 9206 | 7274 | 5892 |
| 2.90 | 609592 | 152398 | 67732 | 38099 | 24384 | 16933 | 12441 | 9525 | 7526 | 6096 |
| 3.00 | 629963 | 157491 | 69996 | 39373 | 25199 | 17499 | 12856 | 9843 | 7777 | 6300 |
| 3.10 | 650290 | 162573 | 72254 | 40643 | 26012 | 18064 | 13271 | 10161 | 8028 | 6503 |
| 3.20 | 670575 | 167644 | 74508 | 41911 | 26823 | 18627 | 13685 | 10478 | 8279 | 6706 |
| 3.30 | 690816 | 172704 | 76757 | 43176 | 27633 | 19189 | 14098 | 10794 | 8529 | 6908 |
| 3.40 | 711013 | 177753 | 79001 | 44438 | 28441 | 19750 | 14510 | 11110 | 8778 | 7110 |
| 3.50 | 731168 | 182792 | 81241 | 45698 | 29247 | 20310 | 14922 | 11424 | 9027 | 7312 |
| 3.60 | 751279 | 187820 | 83475 | 46955 | 30051 | 20869 | 15332 | 11739 | 9275 | 7513 |
| 3.70 | 771347 | 192837 | 85705 | 48209 | 30854 | 21426 | 15742 | 12052 | 9523 | 7713 |
| 3.80 | 791371 | 197843 | 87930 | 49461 | 31655 | 21983 | 16150 | 12365 | 9770 | 7914 |
| 3.90 | 811353 | 202838 | 90150 | 50710 | 32454 | 22538 | 16558 | 12677 | 10017 | 8114 |
| 4.00 | 831291 | 207823 | 92366 | 51956 | 33252 | 23091 | 16965 | 12989 | 10263 | 8313 |

**Figure 10-6.** (Source: Robert C. Blattberg, "Decision Rule and Sample Size Selection for Direct Mail Testing," Direct Marketing Manual, Direct Mail Marketing Association, New York, Manual Release No. 610.1, October 1979.)

CONFIDENCE LEVEL = 95.0%

ACCEPTABLE % DIFFERENCES

| EXPECTED RESPONSE % | 0.50 | 0.60 | 0.70 | 0.80 | 0.90 | 1.00 | 1.10 | 1.20 | 1.30 | 1.40 |
|---|---|---|---|---|---|---|---|---|---|---|
| 4.20 | 8710 | 6049 | 4444 | 3402 | 2688 | 2178 | 1800 | 1512 | 1289 | 1111 |
| 4.40 | 9106 | 6324 | 4646 | 3557 | 2811 | 2277 | 1881 | 1581 | 1347 | 1161 |
| 4.60 | 9500 | 6597 | 4847 | 3711 | 2932 | 2375 | 1963 | 1649 | 1405 | 1212 |
| 4.80 | 9892 | 6870 | 5047 | 3864 | 3053 | 2473 | 2044 | 1717 | 1463 | 1262 |
| 5.00 | 10283 | 7141 | 5246 | 4017 | 3174 | 2571 | 2125 | 1785 | 1521 | 1312 |
| 5.20 | 10672 | 7411 | 5445 | 4169 | 3294 | 2668 | 2205 | 1853 | 1579 | 1361 |
| 5.40 | 11059 | 7680 | 5642 | 4320 | 3413 | 2765 | 2285 | 1920 | 1636 | 1411 |
| 5.60 | 11444 | 7947 | 5839 | 4470 | 3532 | 2861 | 2364 | 1987 | 1693 | 1460 |
| 5.80 | 11828 | 8214 | 6035 | 4620 | 3651 | 2957 | 2444 | 2053 | 1750 | 1509 |
| 6.00 | 12210 | 8479 | 6229 | 4769 | 3768 | 3052 | 2523 | 2120 | 1806 | 1557 |
| 6.20 | 12590 | 8743 | 6423 | 4918 | 3886 | 3147 | 2601 | 2186 | 1862 | 1606 |
| 6.40 | 12968 | 9006 | 6616 | 5066 | 4003 | 3242 | 2679 | 2251 | 1918 | 1654 |
| 6.60 | 13345 | 9267 | 6809 | 5213 | 4119 | 3336 | 2757 | 2317 | 1974 | 1702 |
| 6.80 | 13720 | 9528 | 7000 | 5359 | 4234 | 3430 | 2835 | 2382 | 2030 | 1750 |
| 7.00 | 14093 | 9787 | 7190 | 5505 | 4350 | 3523 | 2912 | 2447 | 2085 | 1798 |
| 7.20 | 14464 | 10045 | 7380 | 5650 | 4464 | 3616 | 2989 | 2511 | 2140 | 1845 |
| 7.40 | 14834 | 10302 | 7568 | 5795 | 4578 | 3709 | 3065 | 2575 | 2194 | 1892 |
| 7.60 | 15202 | 10557 | 7756 | 5938 | 4692 | 3801 | 3141 | 2639 | 2249 | 1939 |
| 7.80 | 15569 | 10811 | 7943 | 6081 | 4805 | 3892 | 3217 | 2703 | 2303 | 1986 |
| 8.00 | 15933 | 11065 | 8129 | 6224 | 4918 | 3983 | 3292 | 2766 | 2357 | 2032 |
| 8.20 | 16296 | 11317 | 8314 | 6366 | 5030 | 4074 | 3367 | 2829 | 2411 | 2079 |
| 8.40 | 16657 | 11567 | 8498 | 6507 | 5141 | 4164 | 3442 | 2892 | 2464 | 2125 |
| 8.60 | 17016 | 11817 | 8682 | 6647 | 5252 | 4254 | 3516 | 2954 | 2517 | 2170 |
| 8.80 | 17374 | 12065 | 8864 | 6787 | 5362 | 4343 | 3590 | 3016 | 2570 | 2216 |
| 9.00 | 17730 | 12312 | 9046 | 6926 | 5472 | 4432 | 3663 | 3078 | 2623 | 2261 |
| 9.20 | 18084 | 12558 | 9227 | 7064 | 5581 | 4521 | 3736 | 3140 | 2675 | 2307 |
| 9.40 | 18436 | 12803 | 9406 | 7202 | 5690 | 4609 | 3809 | 3201 | 2727 | 2352 |
| 9.60 | 18787 | 13047 | 9585 | 7339 | 5799 | 4697 | 3882 | 3262 | 2779 | 2396 |
| 9.80 | 19136 | 13289 | 9763 | 7475 | 5906 | 4784 | 3954 | 3322 | 2831 | 2441 |
| 10.00 | 19483 | 13530 | 9941 | 7611 | 6013 | 4871 | 4025 | 3383 | 2882 | 2485 |

**Figure 10-7.** (Source: Robert C. Blattberg, "Decision Rule and Sample Size Selection for Direct Mail Testing," Direct Marketing Manual, Direct Mail Marketing Association, Manual Release No. 610.1, October 1979.)

CONFIDENCE LEVEL = 95%

ACCEPTABLE % DIFFERENCES

| EXPECTED RESPONSE % | 0.50 | 1.00 | 1.50 | 2.00 | 2.50 | 3.00 | 3.50 | 4.00 | 4.50 | 5.00 |
|---|---|---|---|---|---|---|---|---|---|---|
| 11.00 | 21194 | 5298 | 2355 | 1325 | 848 | 589 | 433 | 331 | 262 | 212 |
| 12.00 | 22860 | 5715 | 2540 | 1429 | 914 | 635 | 467 | 357 | 282 | 229 |
| 13.00 | 24484 | 6121 | 2720 | 1530 | 979 | 680 | 500 | 383 | 302 | 245 |
| 14.00 | 26064 | 6516 | 2896 | 1629 | 1043 | 724 | 532 | 407 | 322 | 261 |
| 15.00 | 27601 | 6900 | 3067 | 1725 | 1104 | 767 | 563 | 431 | 341 | 276 |
| 16.00 | 29095 | 7274 | 3233 | 1818 | 1164 | 808 | 594 | 455 | 359 | 291 |
| 17.00 | 30546 | 7636 | 3394 | 1909 | 1222 | 848 | 623 | 477 | 377 | 305 |
| 18.00 | 31953 | 7988 | 3550 | 1997 | 1278 | 888 | 652 | 499 | 394 | 320 |
| 19.00 | 33317 | 8329 | 3702 | 2082 | 1333 | 925 | 680 | 521 | 411 | 333 |
| 20.00 | 34637 | 8659 | 3849 | 2165 | 1385 | 962 | 707 | 541 | 428 | 346 |

**Figure 10-8.** (Source: Robert C. Blattberg, "Decision Rule and Sample Size Selection for Direct Mail Testing," Direct Marketing Manual, Direct Mail Marketing Association, New York, Manual Release No. 610.1, October 1979.)

and so would require a sample of about 6000 pieces, more than the 3199 that a 0.5 percent error factor would require.

This concept of proportional error margin seems to have been overlooked in other books on direct marketing, leading to some unnecessarily large test samples for some propositions.

The first step in determining sample size is to work backward from your overall profit and loss (P&L) and determine the minimum acceptable response rate (MINARR). This will be a function of allowable margin and the cost of the mailing, as explained in Chapter 20, Mail-Order Math.

The MINARR figure is the indicator of the bottom figure at any acceptable projection range. If the anticipated response rate is known from comparable experience, then the MINARR can be used to determine the permissible error limit. If it isn't known, then a combination of this MINARR figure and the error limit is used to select the acceptable test quantity.

## Grid Testing

The quantity used for each test being conducted, whether of copy or lists, is called a "test cell," and each test cell is assigned its own key number. If five new lists were being tested, you would have five test cells. If other mail were being sent to previously tested groups of names, each separately keyed group would be called a "rollout cell" or an "extension cell."

Often a variety of tests are being conducted simultaneously—perhaps new concepts, offer variations, and new lists. If the combination of anticipated response rate and required error limit produces large mailing samples, and if there are many variables to be tested, the test quantities can be enormous. In the interest of minimizing downside risk, an alternative method is needed, and that alternative is grid testing.

Under the grid method, each test cell is still the minimum quantity indicated in the discussion of sample size earlier in this chapter. The difference is that each cell may represent more than one variable, as long as the total number of cells for each variable meets the minimum-sample-size test.

Let's say we have three copy tests and three list tests, and a sample size of 60,000 was required for statistical validity. That would ordinarily require a mailing quantity of 300,000 pieces. Instead, structure the test as shown in Table 10-1.

Note the total mailing required is only 180,000 instead of 300,000. Yet there is a 60,000 quantity against each variable being tested, the

**TABLE 10-1**

| Lists copy | A | B | C | Total |
|---|---|---|---|---|
| X | 20,000 | 20,000 | 20,000 | 60,000 |
| Y | 20,000 | 20,000 | 20,000 | 60,000 |
| Z | 20,000 | 20,000 | 20,000 | 60,000 |
| Total | 60,000 | 60,000 | 60,000 | 180,000 |

minimum in this example. The results are read against the totals for each variable, not against each cell. Any observation of results against each individual cell would be futile because of the wide error limit for the smaller quantity; only the totals can be read.

### Economies in Direct-Mail Testing

The grid test is one way to lower the investment in testing. There are others which depend on what is being tested.

List tests require only changes in the key number. Offer tests should require only changes in those areas where the offer appears. Substantial production economies can be effected by omitting the offer, if it isn't absolutely necessary, from the four-color brochure or other printed elements. A premium versus no-premium test can be accomplished by keeping the entire package the same and only adding a buck slip (a slip of paper stating the offer; see Chapter 15), changing the reply device, and adding a paragraph to the letter. It isn't necessary to do an entire new package for every variation.

When CBS Publishing introduced a new gardening magazine, there were several fundamental approaches that had to be tried: a conventional announcement package, a how-to positioning for beginners, and an "exotic-plants" positioning for advanced gardeners. This was accomplished very inexpensively by designing an envelope with a full-back cellophane window and a circular in which each appeal was centered on a different section. The brochure was designed so it could be folded with a different appeal facing out, visible through the window. Only one press run of the brochure was required, effecting substantial economies; only the folding had to be varied.

For Weight Watchers, I developed a package that varied only in the response card, part of which showed through a window of the outer envelope face, and in one insert. Everything else remained the same, except for the opening paragraph of the letter. Two very different appeals were tested—one dramatizing the social aspect of weight-reduction groups, the other the eating pleasure of the varied menus.

## List Sampling

In testing a mailing list, it is essential that the names tested be representative of the entire list. In Chapter 5, Mailing Lists, there is a discussion of why Nth-name samples are the most accurate way of doing this. This system will provide a true cross section of the entire list, if it is supplied correctly by the list owner. Any short cuts, such as taking a single geographic area or a fifth zip-code digit, add a considerable measure of risk.

Also read the discussion in Chapter 5 of the relative merits of hotline names, active customers versus expires, and other factors, all of which must be taken into account when testing lists.

## PRINT-MEDIA TESTING

Where direct-mail testing opportunities are limited only by imagination and economics, newspaper and magazine testing is limited by the production capabilities of the publications themselves.

There are two principal objectives of testing in magazine space. One is to test a magazine as a medium; the other is to test alternate copy, offers, or products.

## Testing a New Magazine

In Chapter 6, Print-Media Planning, there is a lengthy discussion of the pilot testing theory applied to magazines. It deals with grouping magazines in constellations, and testing the most representative magazine in each group.

Often downside risk can be minimized further by using only one portion of a magazine instead of the entire publication. Some magazines permit you to buy one-half of the circulation, across the board on a national basis. Many magazines will permit you to buy one or more sections of the country. Either plan will enable you to run an advertisement and discover a magazine's response rate without having to buy the entire circulation. Adjustments must be made, in such tests, for seasonal or position variations. Often regional insertions are placed in the back of a magazine, where response would be marterially less than the same ad placed nationally.

As little as $5000 can test full-page ads in the largest magazines, like *Time* and *TV Guide*, in small regional or city editions. As little as a few hundred dollars can test small-space advertisements in any of hundreds of magazines.

The small-budget advertiser can start with a fractional unit and work up, little by little, to larger sizes and even spectacular units. Some of the largest firms in the direct marketing business started in just this way. The only difference between them and advertisers with more substantial budgets and wider-reaching test programs is the element of time. The larger firms compress the testing experience and step-by-step building of smaller advertisers into one season, enabling them to quickly establish a multi-million-dollar business instead of building it slowly.

## A-B Split-Run Testing

There is no more accurate way to determine which magazine advertisement is the best than split-run testing. Whether you are testing an offer, a copy approach, or one product or business against another, this testing approach will always give you a clear and meaningful basis for decision making.

SRDS defines split run this way: "A technique to measure the relative strength of different copy approaches . . . for example, by means of coupon returns from equally divided portions of a specific edition or issue of a publication's circulation, each identical except for the varying copy approaches." There are more than fifty magazines which offer split-run testing. Some require that a full page be purchased for the test; others offer A-B split runs on fractional units. The SRDS listing is as follows:

| | |
|---|---|
| Aero | Horse, Of Course! |
| American Business | House & Garden |
| American Hunter, The | Industry Week |
| Architectural Digest | McCall's Magazine |
| Argosy | Modern Romances |
| Athletic Journal | Modern Screen |
| Better Homes and Gardens | Moneysworth |
| Boat Builder | Moody Monthly |
| Brides | National Enquirer |
| Capper's Weekly | National 4-H News |
| Christian Herald | National Observer, The |
| Dun's Review | 1,001 Decorating Ideas |
| Esquire | Organic Gardening |
| Family Circle | Our Sunday Visitor |
| Family Handyman, The | Parents |
| Family Health | Penthouse |
| Fortune | Popular Photography |
| Glamour | Prevention |
| Golf Magazine | Reader's Digest |
| Good Housekeeping | Redbook Magazine |
| Grit | Redbook's Young Mother |

| | |
|---|---|
| *Science News* | *TV Guide* |
| *Sport* | *Weight Watcher's Magazine* |
| *Sports Illustrated* | *Westways* |
| *Star, The* | *Woman's Day* |
| *Time* | *Workbasket* |
| *Travel/Holiday* | *Yankee* |

To run a test, you simply prepare two different versions of your advertisement, each with a different key number, and place both of them in the publication as a split insertion on the same date. Usually some small extra fee is charged.

The publication is probably printed "two-up" (a process in which two copies of the same publication come off the same press and bindery equipment side by side) on one or more enormous web or rotogravure presses. The magazines are either bound separately and the streams of finished magazines merged, or a double magazine comes off the press and is sheared in half after binding.

In either case, every second magazine has a different advertisement. Usually, looking through a pile of magazines on a newsstand, you can see ad A in one magazine, B in the next, A in the next, and so forth. As these magazines are distributed throughout the country to magazine distributors or mailed out to subscribers, there is an absolutely perfect sampling of the whole—50 percent for one, 50 percent for the other. The validity of this type of test is virtually unchallenged, providing the difference between test results is large enough.

What result size is "large enough" to be meaningful is a controversial question. One commonly used guide for determining statistical significance in split-run print advertising involves varying significance factors based on the percentage difference between two alternatives at varying total number of responses. Although some major companies rely on this type of table, at least some statisticians appear to be at a loss to identify the underlying mathematical formula.

The chart in Table 10-2 is widely used and simple. Combine the total response to the two versions of your ad, usually the control and the variation, to get the total response figure. Then divide the numbers for each split to produce the percentage of the total response (not the response rate). Look up the total response figure in the left-hand column, and refer to the significance figure in the right column.

If your test result, expressed as a percentage of total response, is greater than the figure listed, then you have a significant improvement. The test ad should become your control ad in the future. If the test result is less, and if the control figure is also not greater than the significance figure, then you have a "tie," and you can use the new ad-

TABLE 10-2
SIGNIFICANCE FACTOR IN SPLIT-RUN ADVERTISING
(95 PERCENT CONFIDENCE LEVEL)

| Total (Both Sides) | Factor |
|---|---|
| 50 | 64.24 |
| 100 | 60.00 |
| 200 | 57.07 |
| 300 | 55.77 |
| 400 | 55.00 |
| 500 | 54.47 |
| 1,000 | 53.16 |
| 1,500 | 52.56 |
| 2,000 | 52.23 |
| 3,000 | 51.83 |
| 4,000 | 51.58 |
| 5,000 | 51.41 |
| 10,000 | 51.00 |
| 20,000 | 50.71 |
| 30,000 | 50.58 |
| 40,000 | 50.50 |
| 50,000 | 50.45 |
| 100,000 | 50.31 |

vertisement or not based on nonstatistical considerations, such as its effect on the long-term image of your product and company. Some companies with extensive schedules will elect to use such "tie" ads to alternate with other ads and thus avoid the "fatigue" factor.

## Multiple Split-Run Testing

The A-B split provides a reliable comparison of one advertisement against another in a given publication. But what happens when there are a half-dozen valid concepts to be tested in magazines?

Multiple split-run testing, sometimes called "telescopic testing," is designed to solve this problem. It combines the A-B split, just described, with the availability of regional editions of magazines. If a magazine has four regional editions, as House & Garden does, you can test four different ads against your control ad. For example, see Table 10-3.

The results of such a test might be as shown in Table 10-4. The helter-skelter of result figures can be quickly made meaningful by either (1) calculating the "lift factor" for each insertion, independently of the results of the control ad A; or (2) by adjusting the ad A results to a national average, calculating the adjustment against all of the other numbers, and restating the figures accordingly.

TABLE 10-3
HOUSE & GARDEN GEOGRAPHIC EDITIONS

| West | Ad A versus ad B |
|------|------------------|
| South | Ad A versus ad C |
| Northeast corridor | Ad A versus ad D |
| Midwest | Ad A versus ad E |

Either of these techniques compensates for geographic or distribution variations and enables you to read the results correctly. Similarly, the various advertisements can be indexed, with the control ad designated 100. Table 10-5 shows an example of an adjusted result report including all the preceding factors and with the figures adjusted against the control. Note that the greatest lift resulted from ad C, although ads B and E had lower CPR figures because of regional variation.

Referring to the significance chart in Table 10-2, we see that at this level of total response we need only a 54 percent factor for the new ad to be declared a valid winner. Ads B, C, and E all are valid winners. Statistically, ad D is also equivalent to ad A, though it did not beat it.

Some magazines have so many editions—*TV Guide* with 110 local editions or *Time* with 34 metropolitan editions, for instance— that it is possible for the sample sizes to get too small to be meaningful. In such cases the practice has been to cluster the editions by regional demographics, with each cluster containing a mix of urban, rural, eastern, and western areas of the country.

## Flip-Flop Testing

Unfortunately, many magazines don't have split-run testing facilities, particularly those whose circulation is not large enough to enable them to be printed two-up. Very few newspapers offer this service, although most magazine sections of Sunday papers do.

The best available technique is "flip-flop testing," and even this requires geographic editions. The *Wall Street Journal* is sold in four editions but offers seventeen different plants, and each plant can carry separate copy. A local newspaper might have a city and a suburban edition.

TABLE 10-4
HOUSE & GARDEN TEST RESULTS

| Edition | Control | Response | Variation | Response |
|---------|---------|----------|-----------|----------|
| West | Ad A | 351 | Ad B | 416 |
| South | Ad A | 297 | Ad C | 376 |
| Northeast corridor | Ad A | 328 | Ad D | 302 |
| Midwest | Ad A | 345 | Ad E | 420 |

**TABLE 10-5**
**HYPOTHETICAL *HOUSE & GARDEN* SPLIT-RUN TEST**

| Edition | Adjusted cost* | Control | Number | CPR | Test | Number | CPR | Lift (%) |
|---|---|---|---|---|---|---|---|---|
| West | $ 1,836 | A | 351 | $2.62 | B | 416 | $2.21 | 18 |
| South | 2,856 | A | 297 | 4.81 | C | 376 | 3.80 | 26 |
| Northeast corridor | 3,060 | A | 328 | 4.66 | D | 302 | 5.07 | (7) |
| Midwest | 2,448 | A | 345 | 3.55 | E | 420 | 2.91 | 21 |
| Total | $10,228 | | 1,321 | $3.86 | | 1,514 | $3.37 | |

*Excluding $1800 split-run charge.*

In this kind of testing you run ad A in one edition and ad B in the other, on the same day. Then, a week or two later, you reverse the ads, running B where A ran and vice versa. By running two ads and reading the combined total response rates instead of individual ones, you cause the distortion factors to offset each other. One edition or region might be stronger than another. The ad that runs the first time will probably do better than the second ad in each section because it has "creamed" the market somewhat. However, this qualification applies to both ads and both editions. The total response rate of ad A compared with ad B should be valid.

## Full-Page Bind-Ins

At times the best testing medium may be full-page bind-in cards (too costly for most advertisers), which are preprinted by the advertiser and supplied to the publication for insertion. Usually the cards are "perfect-bound" rather than saddle-stitched. They can include perforated reply cards, areas for tokens or stamps, sweepstakes numbers, pop-ups, or other devices not possible with conventional soft-space units (ads using ordinary coupons or asking for a phone response, as opposed to ads with mailable cards, called hard-space units).

As the cards are preprinted and premixed by your own printer, virtually any number of variations can be tested simultaneously. This is an excellent technique for major advertisers whose potential investments are so large that six, eight, or twelve concepts must be tested before a major campaign is launched.

The unit is atypical in that the ad must be designed to utilize both sides of the bound-in card. Some advertisers have gotten around this requirement by placing a separate advertisement for a different product on the reverse side of the page. When this is done, one side of the reply card for one ad appears on the other side. This could be confusing, but my experience indicates that the format is successful.

If you are selecting a publication for this type of testing, you'll want to pick one that is sold mostly by subscription rather than newsstand. Though your space rates are based on actual circulation, you still have to print enough card units for the magazine's total press run, including unsold newsstand copies. Newsstand-sold magazines have a much greater waste factor than those sold mostly by subscription.

### Bound-In Reply Cards

A more common format for major advertisers is the combination of a single- or double-page advertisement with a bound-in reply card, usu- ally called an "insert card." While this is a very successful unit, pro- ducing four times the result of a page alone at an average cost increase only two or three times higher, it does have limitations as a test vehicle.

With few exceptions, there is no way to match cards to an alternative A-B split. If the card is to match the page, it is impossible to be sure that the cards are inserted in synchronization with the page. One error and the entire test can be ruined.

One solution is to confine the test to the card alone, without changing the advertisement for the page. This is really only suitable for testing offers or minor proposition variations. If it does not appear on the page, several different offers can be featured on the card itself. For instance, it is easy to test one card with a premium featured and another with no premium at all, to determine the lift factor of the premium. Or you can try coupon wording modifications on the reply card: simplified commitment copy, postage and handling costs included in the price, the availability of a trade-up option, or quality-improvement tests such as requiring respondents to an inquiry ad to provide their own stamp as opposed to a business reply card paid by the advertiser.

Another way to do split testing when insert cards are involved is to use a transfer code, first developed by Walter Marshall in space ad- vertising for Capitol Record Club and Time-Life Books. This is a useful device when several basic concepts are being tested for a proposition which is usually only successful when an insert card is used. In this case, the insert card is constant and the ads change, with as many variations as A-B splitting and regional editions permit.

One version of the transfer code is to offer a choice of book bindings or other options, asking respondents to use a designated letter for one color and a different letter for the other. The customer is asked to place the letter in a designated space on the insert card to indicate the choice. Better still, if you have product order numbers, put an A after each number on ad A, a B after those in ad B, and so on. These letters are later translated into key numbers, and the results are analyzed as with any other split run.

Where a choice is not available, a premium can be used instead. The respondent can be asked to place a designated letter on the card for a free poster, for example.

The most direct and straightforward approach of all seems to work as well as the others, but it might depend on the type of product being offered. This is a simple statement on the printed page which says "To help us evaluate our advertising, please put this letter in the space indicated on the reply card."

## Deliberate Underspacing

If a proposition usually works in a page but as a half-page doesn't do well, we say it is "underspaced." The same consideration applies to format as well as space size. If a proposition works best with an insert card or a bound-in multipage unit, and we run a simple black-and-white page instead, we have also "underspaced" the ad.

Deliberate underspacing is one way that an advertiser with a modest budget can enjoy the benefits of multiple testing. All that is needed is to use regional editions and A-B splits for a smaller unit than would otherwise be profitable, knowing in advance that the overall results will be disappointing. If the primary objective is to test various copy appeals, for instance, and the basic proposition has already been proved, it may be less expensive to use soft-space black-and-white pages than to make the space, printing, and production investment of card testing. The reduced responses may be less of a price to pay than the multiple testing costs, but the relative pulling power of the different appeals will still be meaningful. One caution, though: Don't expect black-and-white ads to demonstrate the relative effectiveness of advertising appeals where the visual element is critical and must be in color. This approach will only work where the concept is not dependent on color.

One example of this technique is to use the listing pages of *TV Guide* in clusters of local editions to reduce regional distortion. This approach is far less costly and more readily available than a multipage center insert or a wraparound position, which can cost a quarter of a million dollars, when you can get it.

Another technique is the use of half-page black-and-white ads in Sunday supplements of newspapers in a few regions before investing in a full-page, full-run, full-color advertisement. The trick with all of these underspacing approaches is to keep your focus on the original objective and the original expectations.


## NEWSPAPER PREPRINTS

The possibilities for copy testing in preprints are infinite. You can arrange with your own printer to produce as many different versions of your advertisement as cost and statistical validity permit, and to deliver them, premixed, to newspapers for insertion in their Sunday editions. The only limitation would involve trying to mix formats, as the insertion equipment can only be set to handle one size and thickness of your preprint and they can't be interspersed.

The problems with preprint copy testing don't come at the publication; they come at your printer. It is essential that someone visually check the shipment of inserts after they are mixed and before they are sent out to the newspapers.

Some printers don't have the presses to automatically "stream" the different versions together on press, and they rely on something they call "hand spanning." This means that they pack the inserts from different stacks or skids, one handful from this stack, another from that stack, and so on. This is adequate for a test, if it's really done. Unfortunately, there are too many temptations for the individual supervisor to take shortcuts and invalidate your test. For instance, in a four-way split, if the press is only doing two versions at a time, the printer has to store the entire run of the first two versions before packing anything, to wait for the beginning of the production of the second two versions. Unless the printer has adequate floor space, this may not happen—and no one is going to tell you. There are many scrupulous and careful printers who would never permit this to happen, but caution still requires that your own inspector check the skids before they are shipped.

Another caution might be to include a pure key test if possible, with no changes other than the code number itself. The results should be identical, within statistical error limits. If they're not, you'll know that something is wrong. However, it will be too late to do anything about it other than change printers in the future. The on-site inspection is still the preferred choice.

Statistical validity is always a consideration, as with any other test factor. Use the same statistical validity chart as with direct mail, except that the response rates may be too low for the chart. It is reasonably accurate, as a rule of thumb, to adjust decimal points; that is, if you expect a 0.05 percent response, use the quantity indicated for 0.5 percent and multiply it by 10. For instance, at a 0.1 percent error limit you would need 191,000 circulation for each split.

## Picking Test Markets

With the exception of a few large cities with more than one newspaper, print media provide a very broad range of demographics—rich and poor, educated and not, mail-order buyer and retail buyer—representing the entire scope of the area covered by the newspaper.

Geographic characteristics, such as median income and buying power, are the key variable, and so they are the prime consideration in selecting which newspapers to use in conducting a preprint test. Size of market is generally the most influential characteristic. For a test, pick a variety of papers in different-size markets: one or two large cities, several medium ones, and a handful of smaller towns.

In all cases the newspapers should be those whose sales representatives can demonstrate a large number of repeat insertions by other mail-order advertisers, with rate structures which are not punitive.

Within these broad parameters, availability will be the prime consideration. On key dates you may find that your competition has already reserved space, or there may be too many other advertisers scheduling preprints on the dates you want. You will have to check availabilities and weigh the trade-offs of preferred dates versus preferred markets in making your selections.

## BROADCAST

As discussed in Chapter 7, there are two very different kinds of broadcast—support and direct response. They are very different in their purpose and methodology, and just as different in the ways of testing their usefulness or refining scheduling.

## Direct-Response Testing

This is the place to use the "best-foot-forward" approach. The place to test is not the stations expected to be most typical of the broadcast media at large. Testing should begin on those stations most likely to succeed, where experience shows that your own propositions or those of other direct marketers have been successful.

There can be substantial differences in response by type of market, and so a variety of stations should be included in a test schedule: urban, rural, East, West, South, Midwest, independent stations, and network affiliates. Often there are patterns showing one type of station working better than others. More often the key variable is the willingness of stations, regardless of type of market or programming, to establish a rate structure and make available time slots that will be cost-efficient.

*Day Parts*    The time of day is usually the most constant and controllable variable other than the station itself. The time of day is the most effective selector of audience segments. Weekend mornings reach parents whose children are watching children's shows. Afternoons reach women at home, enjoying the never-ending stream of soap operas. News programs and adventure shows reach a higher number of men. Late-night programming seems to find older people, or at least restless ones. Programming adjacencies, to the extent they are available for direct responses, offer even finer selection, for certain shows seem to attract audiences of predictable affinities.

*Other Testing*    Other than the stations or type and time of programming, there are often times when it is necessary to test other factors, such as frequency, length, or content of the commercial.

The technique most used is a variation of flip-flop testing, discussed earlier in this chapter in the section on print media. A different phone number is assigned to the new campaign, and it is run in alternate weeks on several stations, beginning with the new campaign on half the stations and the old one on the other half. Half the stations are running A-B-A-B-A while the others are playing B-A-B-A-B. This tends to offset differences by station and by whether a commercial is played earlier or later in a flight.

This test method is generally used to test entirely new commercials or frequency. It would not be possible to test prices or other offer variations this way. Such testing requires a "paired-market" test—the selection of market areas with similar demographic patterns and previous response experience.

## Support Broadcast

The choice of markets in support broadcast is dictated by the media to be supported. Within each market, however, there are usually several stations to choose from, and within each station, there is a choice of day parts and frequency.

Often it is necessary to use every station in a market in order to reach the 300 or so gross rating points most direct marketers feel is a minimum for effective media support. As support spots must be aired in a precise pattern during three or four days adjoining the appearance of the ad being supported, it may be difficult to line up enough good availabilities.

The first objective is usually to test the effectiveness of support broadcast itself. The usual technique is to select between six and ten similar markets, supporting some of them at one frequency level, others at a higher level, and some not at all.

The costs of the broadcast are added to the costs of the preprints or direct mail being supported. The total advertising cost is divided by the number of responses received and—*voila!*—we have cost-per-response figures for each market and a conclusion about whether support costs are justified and at which GRP level.

Similarly, an ongoing campaign can test various day-part concentrations, commercial lengths, or even different creative appeals.

I suggest that readers considering any type of broadcast testing reread Chapter 7 and keep in mind the objective of a broadcast support test. Support advertising cannot be expected to lower CPR, although it sometimes does. A more reasonable expectation is to extend the media being supported—a higher level of orders at the same CPR, or at a CPR that is less costly than other media alternatives.

## TESTING STRATEGY

Now that we've covered how to test in each media, let's look at the basic philosophy which applies to any and all kinds of testing. The first consideration is what to test—how many tests to run, what kinds are the most important, and how to use the information you get from testing. And the approach to this depends on the personality of your company.

Continuing the military analogy of Chapter 2, General Patton and Field Marshall Montgomery became archetypal examples of two different military strategies. Patton was aggressive—a man who seized every opportunity, took risks, bent the rules of warfare, and swept across miles of enemy terrain without bothering to mop up pockets of resistance. Montgomery was cautious. He planned carefully, regrouped slowly, and moved his forces ahead step by step, with due care to logistics and supply lines.

While I regard myself as a Patton fan, I will not say that the Montgomery approach isn't right for some companies. One of my banking clients is a Patton-type company. They will test one or two fundamental approaches and, if successful, roll out a major national campaign so fast the competition is unable to copy the concept. Another corporation is a Montgomery-type company, with each direct-mail program studied and planned and poked at for such a long time that, by the time the smallest test gets in the mail, the competition may have already tested, rolled out, and reaped the profits from similar programs.

## What to Test

What you can test depends on your budget, mailing size, objectives, and willingness to assume risk. It is easy to test a wide variety of mailing lists, or a simple direct-mail variation. Each split costs very little to execute. It is more costly to test different TV commercials, color magazine ads, and total mailing concepts. The cost of testing should be in relation to the size of the expected benefits.

The greatest difference in results can be expected from changes which affect the product being offered or the way the product is positioned. Offer changes run a close second, with very dramatic changes resulting from changes in price, premium, commitment, term, etc.

Creative changes are next, with very broad differences sometimes created by a change in headline or illustration, or in print and direct-mail formats. Layout revisions or different copy treatments of the same theme usually show very little difference, presuming they were professionally executed in the first place.

The big differences—200 and 300 percent lift factors—almost always come from product positioning, offer changes, or the selection of different lists or publications.

As you can't afford to test everything, the selection of what to test has to be done methodically. First, list test opportunities within your basic mailing or media schedule—publications you are using anyway which make testing feasible. Then list the things you would like to test, in the order of expected result improvement.

In a recent mail-order product introduction I still had twelve possible ad variations even after focus panel reviews and predictive research. There were eight testing opportunities, between direct mail and a Sunday supplement regional–A-B split. When the opportunities were reviewed, all the copy alternatives were set aside in favor of testing product and offer variations.

## Evolutionists versus Fundamentalists

Another issue is how boldly to test. One school, which I'll call the evolutionists, advocates strictly "readable" testing, with all elements in an ad or mailing piece identical except the single factor being tested. If you are testing a headline, they will tell you, don't change the layout anywhere and leave every element of type size and color exactly the same. The question to ask in this approach is "When the results come in, what conclusions will I be able to reach?" If more than one element changes, the ability to make a final pronouncement on what works or doesn't work is muddied. Barry Mark is a brilliant advocate of this approach, and his company, Doubleday, does enough testing to make it work for them.

The fundamentalists, on the other hand, are looking for the big break-through, the dramatic result, regardless of whether or not they ever know why one approach works and another one doesn't. Publishing consultant Dick Benson has long advocated supplier versus supplier testing—a Bill Jayme direct-mail package versus a Linda Wells package, a Sol Blumenfeld package versus a Richard Jordan package. His advice is not to try to work out an overall testing plan that leads to definitive knowledge, but to pit one supplier against another and see which approach does the best.

I personally lean to the evolution approach, as I find that even the best free-lancers, like those named above, are pressured by the fundamentalist system into looking for creative gimmicks and major departures, sometimes overlooking the creatively less exciting but more profitable breakthroughs that often occur with a simple coupon revision or offer change.

I think the best approach depends on "What do you have to lose?" If you are running a successful business, then changes should be evolutionary, building upon existing success in a manner which identifies principles that can be used on other mailings and for other products. On the other hand, if you're in trouble, go for broke with completely fresh, way-out approaches.

## Which Medium to Test In

Each medium has its unique advantages. Direct mail offers great flexibility if you are testing a wide variety of offers, and great economy if the basic color circular can remain the same with only the letter and reply card changing. It also offers a very low profile, if you don't want your testing activity to be spotted by your competition.

Print media, on the other hand, let you test broad creative concepts very dramatically and inexpensively in black-and-white magazine or supplement splits. Such basic design differences cost less to execute in art, type, and platemaking for print media than for direct mail.

Broadcast is expensive to test, with each commercial variation costing thousands of dollars. Even the slightest variation requires payment of added session fees and residuals under Screen Actors Guild (SAG) and American Federation of Television and Radio Artists (AFTRA) regulations.

It is possible to do broad testing in media units other than those which will eventually be the most profitable. Larger units like bind-in cards, or smaller ones like black-and-white fractional units, may give a reading that will project accurately to color pages with bind-ins or other units which will be the mainstay of the basic campaign. The added CPR, because of the less efficient unit, is a cost to be charged against your testing budget.

In direct mail, for instance, tests are sometimes sent out as first-class mail, with a small panel of bulk mail sent at the same time. The faster-arriving first-class mail gets responses to you fast and gives a quick reading of which mailing approach does best. The bulk-mail panel determines which class of postage to pay in the subsequent rollout—a decision that can be made after everything is printed. This permits a much faster turnaround than would be possible if testing were done by bulk mail.

An interesting advantage of print advertising is its virtually certain transferability into other media, including direct mail. A print-tested concept almost always proves out in direct mail and broadcast. A direct-mail concept, on the other hand, hardly ever translates into a successful print ad.

## When to Break Out the Champagne

In introducing a new product or improving an old one, it's only human to be impatient for results. Impatience arises from desire to use the knowledge quickly, and also from plain curiosity.

For many years "doubling points" was a convenient way to read results. "Half-life" points, a concept taken from nuclear physics, showed when half the output had been received. A Sunday newspaper ad would reach a half-life point on the first Thursday, a *TV Guide* insert twelve days after orders started arriving.

However, use of doubling today would be misleading, unless you can establish your own half-life points. The standard tool today is *response curve forecasting*. Table 10-6, a composite of several companies' experiences, shows the cumulative percentage of total orders received by the end of each week after mail drop, air date, or on-sale date of a publication.

For example, if at the end of the third week of a bulk mailing, you have received 500 orders, Table 10-6 shows that this represents 41 percent of the total orders to be received based on average experience. You can reasonably expect a total of 1200 orders.

The figures used in compiling Table 10-6 differed as much as 15 percent from company to company. Error in interpolation may also

**TABLE 10-6**
**RESPONSE FORECASTING**

| Cumulative percentage for: | Full weeks after mailing or ad on-sale date | | | | | | | | | |
|---|---|---|---|---|---|---|---|---|---|---|
| | 1 | 2 | 3 | 4 | 5 | 6 | 7 | 8 | 9 | 10 |
| Bulk mailing | 3 | 12 | 41 | 67 | 80 | 85 | 90 | 93 | 95 | 97 |
| First-class mailing | 14 | 75 | 87 | 91 | 93 | 95 | 96 | 97 | 98 | 99 |
| Broadcast (phone orders) | 95 | 98 | 99 | 100 | 100 | 100 | 100 | 100 | 100 | 100 |
| Newspaper preprint | 26 | 73 | 85 | 89 | 92 | 94 | 95 | 96 | 97 | 98 |
| Weekly magazine ad | 10 | 36 | 61 | 70 | 76 | 81 | 84 | 87 | 88 | 89 |
| Monthly magazine ad | 7 | 28 | 43 | 55 | 64 | 71 | 76 | 82 | 85 | 87 |
| Catalog | 3 | 17 | 31 | 40 | 47 | 53 | 59 | 64 | 69 | 73 |

Source: Confidential data from the Marketing Council, DMMA.

occur because some companies measure from date of first response instead of drop date or on-sale date.

Response curves vary by type of product, publication or list, proposition, and local postal efficiency. Each company should record day-by-day responses and develop its own response curves.

### Response Variations.

Your own response experience may not only differ from Table 10-6 but also be inconsistent from one promotion to the next. Phone orders arrive faster than mail, and postpaid responses come in faster than those requiring a stamp, envelope, or check. Local mailings or ads have a faster response curve than national efforts.

*Mail delivery* varies according to season and postal area. Business reply mail is sometimes accumulated and delivered in batches for the convenience of the postal worker. Carrier presorted mail is supposed to travel faster. First-class mail which doesn't "look" first-class may travel slowly.

In *magazine insertions,* "hard space" with business reply cards comes in faster than coupon ads. Responses from subscription-sold magazines come in perhaps a week faster than those from newsstand-sold magazines. Orders may start arriving before the supposed on-sale date. Magazine distributors ship out magazines as soon as they get them.

Editorial content also influences response curves. A home decorating magazine may be saved, while a news magazine is usually read immediately.

*Broadcast* orders have practically no curve. Phone orders come in within hours or not at all, mail offers in a week or two.

*Outbound telephone selling* results are instantaneous. Knowing each day's results allows you to modify the list and the script as needed.

*Catalog offers* have the longest curve. Major catalogs mailed in early September pull orders strongly until mid-December. Also, response curves can vary as much as a week depending on whether the catalogs are mailed from one post office or trucked to major bulk mail centers around the country.

## Rollout Strategies

Once the results are in, there is usually little time to analyze the results and make decisions. New publication closing dates demand decisions on whether to place orders and run more ads or print more mail. Competitors are already speculating about the effect of your test program on their campaigns. Good mail-order seasons must be exploited or passed up.

Some cautions should be observed. A new approach may work because it is fresh and new, not because it is better. It might work the first time it is run or mailed, but not again. Some ads tire more quickly than others. An approach may not work because of some unusual coincidence. Whenever results seem illogical, always check the medium in which the ad ran. Perhaps a competitive ad ran in the same issue, diluting your responses. Maybe a major news event kept readers from getting into the ads, or a weather aberration kept them from reading the paper or watching television at all.

Whether to act on projected figures or wait until final results are in and back-end experience is gained is another decision which will depend on corporate personality.

Usually the best decision is somewhere in between. Unrepeatable opportunities—a key season, a difficult-to-get insert card or back-cover position—should be reserved at an early date because the opportunity is perishable. On the basis of projected figures, lists can be reused with increased quantities but not with the whole list. With broadcast you can drop the weak stations and add a larger number of new stations in order to gradually build up the schedule.

My own observations are that the risk takers do better in the long run and that a winning proposition should complete its rollout within a year. Taking longer to complete the rollout means marketing circumstances might change, mitigating the success of the early results. Remember, timing is a factor in the original test results as well, and next year may not be as good as this year. The maxim about making hay while the sun shines applies very much to the field of direct marketing.

# POSITIONING

The single most important creative decision in the making of a successful ad or mailing piece is positioning. This concept can apply to basic marketing strategy or to the writing of a single mailing piece. It can be constant—the same for all products created by a company and for all media and offers—or it can vary from campaign to campaign and from mailing to mailing.

First developed as an aspect of packaged goods marketing and popularized by Rosser Reeves, it has become a basic part of advertising jargon. It has become like the weather: Everyone talks about it, but few people do anything to change it.

In direct marketing, we have the ability to refine our positioning very precisely, to measure the results, and to make dramatic changes from one advertisement to another. We can, in effect, be all things to all people, just not at the same time.

The difference between direct marketing and traditional advertising is that direct marketers do not have a history of awareness and associations. Each ad stands alone, adopts its own position, and seeks out and sells the portion of the market segment attracted to that position.

## VERTICAL POSITIONING

The classic approach to positioning is based on the dictionary definition of the term: the portrayal of a product in its proper status vis à vis other products. A hierarchy is presumed: the most obvious categories are price and quality. The products are classified as good, better, best or cheap, cheaper, cheapest.

All the conventional uses of this discipline involve some type of relative placement over or under others. Thus I call this kind of positioning "vertical positioning" to differentiate it from horizontal positioning, described below.

## Perception as the Standard

Before going into the various kinds of positioning, I first want to point out that positioning is not necessarily related to reality. It is, instead, a function of perception.

From a pure marketing standpoint, it is *not* important whether your product is the best of its kind. What *is* important is whether people think it is the best. Positioning in the marketplace means positioning in the mind. Though it is easier and more ethical to place a product where it should be placed on the basis of merits, its position in the marketplace is not necessarily dictated by considerations of merit. The ratings in *Consumer Reports* magazine often shoot down our previous conceptions of which products were the best, while pointing out little-known products that really are the best.

## Product Placement

Within the sphere of vertical positioning, product placement is a more common consideration than its companions, offer placement, audience placement, and media placement.

Product placement is a function of how the product is presented in relation to competing products. It involves choice—choice about what real attributes are selected for prominent attention, or choice about the images, associations, and conventions which are to be attached to the product's public presentation.

A product can be "New!" or it can be "A Tradition since 1829." It can be "Solid," built to last, or it can be "Lightweight and Portable." It can be "Bigger" or "Compact."

A camera can be super-simple—"Just point it and shoot"—or it can offer the ultimate in dials, knobs, gadgets, and other controls for maximum flexibility.

None of these positions are necessarily right or wrong, but all of them are different, and all of them give you something to say about your product that differentiates it from competition. The position that is almost always wrong is "right in the middle," with a committee-designed concept that tries to be all things to all people at the same time.

## Offer Placement

Book clubs constantly maneuver against each other with offers such as six for $1 or three for 49 cents, and magazines present their introductory subscription prices in countless variations. (See Chapter 4, The Proposition.)

The offer is a positioning consideration as well. The examples above are attempts to offer the lowest price—or at least to appear to. This is the most common direction, but it is not the only one and certainly not always the best one.

A full-price offer sets your product apart. So does "A little more expensive, but worth it." There is a subtle difference, with not so subtle results, between "Regular price 50 cents" and "$1 but for you, half price." The first is just cheap; the second is a bargain. It may not be logical, but neither is human psychology.

The offer is another way of placing your product. A high price is presumed to represent conservative quality. Too low a price is presumed to be cheap. A price slightly higher or lower than the competition can be fine, providing the placement is justified. A price dramatically higher is a way of appealing to snobbery. A price dramatically lower is often unbelievable. This applies not only to pricing but to introductory or trial offers which result in de facto new prices.

Personally, I prefer to go after the "slightly higher" position in most cases, with a good-quality story to justify the added cost and some premium or discount for immediate action. It is easier to point out the better features in a high-priced product than to explain why the cheaper product is low-priced.

## Audience Placement

The classic audience positioning is related to age, income, education, occupation, and other demographic or geographic characteristics.

A product may be salable to many audiences, but a given advertisement in a given medium usually has to choose one audience segment as its primary objective. Within any given medium—magazine or newspaper, direct mail or television—there are a wide variety of audiences. How else can you explain the success, within one publication, of many widely varied promotions? Which audience you reach is a function of both copy and art, and both of these crafts can be adapted to attract whichever audience segment is desired.

Some headline styles and type faces connote elegance; others imply newness, news, or bargain images. Some appeal to most women, and others to most men.

Older people are more willing than younger to read long copy messages, providing the type is legible. Color makes a difference, and so does the choice of illustrations. The age and apparent lifestyle of a model, for instance, will attract similar readers and repel dissimilar ones.

Psychographic considerations are, in my opinion, a more important aspect of audience placement than demographic ones. The lifestyle and life stage of the prospect is a more sensitive positioning selector for direct marketers than any categories related to age and income only.

For example, more dramatic result differences occur from aiming a message at newlyweds, new parents, homeowners, and retirees than from any demographic selectors. On a finer level, positioning a product as one for people who value independence, macho sex appeal, culture, or other psychological delineators is the most dramatic difference of all.

Such emotional placement is the ultimate audience selector. Conventional market segmentation would never lead you to write an ad with this headline: "Lonely?" Yet "lonely people" who are precisely targeted by such a lead may be just the right audience for self-confidence courses, dating services, dance lessons, or even bowling shoes.

Media selection is another way of implementing overall market planning. What we do within the media is a matter of positioning. Usually we are positioning not just against other products, but against every other direct-response advertisement in the magazine or mailbox.

## Size

Size is the exposition of media positioning. You say a lot about what you are selling by the space unit you select and by the location in the publication.

A double-page spread or a full-page newspaper ad tells the reader, before a word is read, that this message is big! It's important! It also says that the advertiser is substantial (or they couldn't afford such a large space unit.)

A philanthropy, on the other hand, might prefer a smaller, half-page unit, to convey a humbler, more appropriately frugal image.

In direct mail, this effect is infinitely more flexible, as described in Chapter 15, Direct-Mail Formats. Relative placement against other mailing pieces can be accomplished with infinite creative combinations, but the choice of positioning is relatively simple.

A personal message is conveyed in one group of techniques, an ethical or financial message in another. A bargain catalog is presented one way, an expensive collectible another. A sweepstakes offer aimed at young mothers calls for styling in copy, art, and format selection very different from a proposition addressed to presidents of corporations.

The size aspect of positioning is the choice of how you want the communications vehicle, as a medium, perceived by your prospect.

## HORIZONTAL POSITIONING

Horizontal positioning is the new dimension in positioning—one which I identified while preparing marketing recommendations for Rapp & Collins clients and of which I have become the principal exponent. Horizontal positioning adds a new perspective: *time.*

Horizontal positioning refers to the point in the consumer's decision-making process chosen as a starting point for an advertising message. It can deal with any of the four basic parameters—product, media, offer, and audience. It is a supplement to conventional positioning, not a substitute for it. This leads to a positioning grid, such as that illustrated in Figure 11-1, offering a matrix of placement opportunities rather than one dimension or another.

The spectrum of horizontal positioning begins, at the left side of Figure 11-1 with "create desire." At the right is "overcome inertia." In between are "fulfill a need," "sell competitively," and "motivate by price." Each of these are primary appeals which should be chosen as creative starting points as carefully as other positioning factors are chosen. Let's review them one at a time, in the order of their evolution in the mind of the consumer.

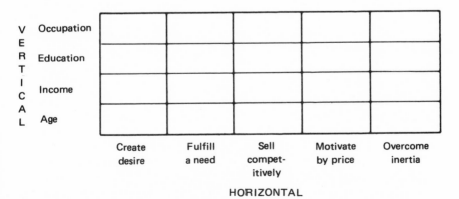

Figure 11-1. The positioning grid. Both vertical and horizontal positions should be considered in planning direct marketing strategy.

## Create Desire

Does anyone remember carbon paper? Not too many years ago, that was how we made duplicate copies of letters. Today xerography is the standard, and most manufacturers sell competitively against other copiers. When copiers first came out, however, specific product features, pricing, and other approaches would not have been as relevant as the merits of the product generically.

But what if you now can offer a new, lightweight copying machine with an unusually low price? The expected strategy would be to dramatize the price or the features and compete with the established copiers, but there is another strategy which may do much, much better and is certainly worth testing: creating desire.

Take the same copier and instead of featuring product benefits or pricing, aim your message at the "new-user" market. Imagine an ad headlined "Why every home should have a copier" and describing general uses: keeping tax records, preparing shopping lists, making copies of valuable papers. Imagine a targeted version in a school newspaper: "How a copier can help your grades."

Such an ad doesn't begin with the product at all, except as a general product category. It stops the reader who hasn't been considering such a purchase and says, in effect, "Hey, you! You need one of these."

Once that point is established, the role of this particular copier and its suitability for home use become very relevant. It then becomes a simple matter to be the particular product which just happens to be in the right place at the right time. A lead procurement version might, in fact, simply offer a booklet about the use of copiers in the home. The sales call and follow-up literature would, of course, promote the particular product.

At any given time, and in any given marketplace, there are always some market segments in each stage of the decision-making process. Which one should be selected will depend on just how many segments are at each stage.

For instance, home computers are a very new product, and most advertising for such products should be (but amazingly isn't) selling by creating desire. Obviously, at this point, the bulk of the marketing possibilities lie in the creation of desire.

However, there are some people who have already decided that they must own a home computer and are looking for one with the right features, comparing different brands, or waiting for the price to come down—or simply have to be pushed into buying now. All these segments represent stages of horizontal positioning, and all exist side by side.

For an investment product, I wrote a headline, "Just what are money market accounts anyway? And why should I keep my savings in one?" This is the create-desire position and, according to research with beginning investors, was the headline which was most appealing and would most generate interest and readership.

To create desire, a smoking deterrent should sell readers on quitting smoking, rather than addressing itself "To people who want to stop smoking." A pocket calculator ad should sell parents on the merits of giving one to their child, rather than announcing the latest price reduction or the addition of an exotic mathematical function. A typewriter manufacturer should sell college students on "How typed papers get better grades" rather than pointing up a new feature or a reduced price.

In each of these examples, the choice is not either/or. It is "Which comes first?" The choice of positioning, properly executed, will demand very different copy, art, and even media choices, even if every possible copy point appears in every possible version.

### Fulfill a Need

In the previous position, a need has to be created. In this position, the need already exists, the consumer is aware of it, and advertising need only announce that there is now a way to satisfy that need.

Using the copier example, this position leads to advertising which says "Looking for a lightweight home photocopier? Here it is."

Fulfilling a need is probably the most common position for most advertising, and it appears to be the starting place for those advertisers who do not employ strategic planning generally or positioning in particular. The presumption, and it is one, is that the world knows it needs what you have to sell.

"Motor's Auto Manual Helps You Fix Any Car Fast" is such a presumption, even though it also states a benefit. This classic ad runs in publications where large audience segments want to fix their own or others' cars and believe they can do it. For that segment, the ad offers help.

For a more general, less handy portion of the population, the need might have to be created in the first place, with something like "Make Money, Have Fun—Now Anyone Can Fix Cars." Here the theme is the generic one, and the desire is being created rather than fulfilled.

One difference in fulfillment ads is that the customer knows there is a need prior to reading the ad. Time-Life begins an ad for its American Wilderness library with a glorious mountain scene and the word "Escape!"—fulfilling a psychological need. *Bon Appetit* tempts you with a close-up photo of a scrumptious chocolate cake, appealing to a sensual need to enjoy the food one eats. The Dreyfus Tax Exempt Bond Fund appeals to a universal need with its headline "Zero Tax." All these examples are proven winners, having been the subjects of split-run testing.

## Sell Competitively

This middle position is probably the second most used direct marketing position but the single most common general advertising position.

Most advertising presumes that a portion of the media audience already knows it has a need (say transportation), wants to fulfill that need (by buying a car), and has only to choose (which car to buy). For automobiles, that is probably correct. But it would be interesting to see someone do a direct-mail campaign to non-car owners on why they should own a car, or to one-car families on why they need a second. The very successful direct-mail and phone campaigns used by Ford, Mercedes, and Chrysler aimed at motivating owners of two-, three-, four-, and five-year-old cars are creating a desire to own a new car rather than an old one.

Most advertisers generally presume that a product is needed and wanted and that the only consideration is which brand to buy. Using the copier example, such ads might have the theme "Why the XYZ copier is the one you need for home use because of this unique feature."

Competitive selling can be very competitive and may, in fact, be most powerful when it takes on competitors by name. You've seen car ads do this, but very few direct marketers seem willing to meet the competition head on. Those who do are often very successful.

Equitable's Money Market Account was introduced as "the new alternative" to certificates of deposit, while savings banks were countering with ads attacking mutual funds. Discount stockbrokers such as Kingsley Boye Southwood compare their rates openly, not only with the general brokers like Merrill Lynch but with other discounters, by publishing charts listing examples of actual commissions for each firm.

Probably one of the best examples of this technique in the direct marketing field is the campaign developed for Newsweek: "Take the Newsweek challenge. Try Newsweek for 3 weeks without cost. If you don't like it, we'll ask Time to send you their best offer." The mailing showed a speaker holding both magazines. Ads showed Time and Newsweek covers with boxing gloves slugging it out. The effect, of course, was to equate the smaller-circulation Newsweek with Time, and to imply parity of editorial content by the simple willingness to make such a challenge.

## Pricing Motivation

Price emphasis is another distinctly separate aspect of horizontal positioning—the aspect most common to advertising by retail establishments. It is the easiest, least imaginative, and usually least profitable form of advertising, saying in effect, "Buy now because we're cheap."

In direct marketing, pricing motivation is usually manifested by announcements that you can now get thirteen records for 1 cent from the RCA Victor Record Club, six books for 99 cents from a Doubleday Book Club, or a JS&A closeout on a travel alarm for only $14.99.

The limitations of price emphasis are obvious. For one thing, it is only effective if the pricing is genuinely attractive. For another, attractive pricing may cut into allowable margin so severely as to make the offer unprofitable.

It is far preferable, and a much greater challenge, to find motivations, positions, and appeals which will sell a product without resorting to price emphasis. Good marketing and advertising are capable of doing this. Price emphasis should be a last resort after all conventional positioning options have been fully explored.

Notwithstanding this admittedly utopian goal, pricing and offers will produce a dramatic variation in response rate and CPR, virtually without exception. This is why major advertisers always give price testing a high priority in the selection of ads or mailing pieces to be tested.

Capitol Record Club, in an early split run in a *TV Guide* centerspread position, tested thirty offers, including "Take 8 Free," "Take 9 Free," "Take 10 Free," "Take 12 Free," and "7 for $1.00."

Fotomat, in its testing of the mail-order film processing market, began with an eight-way offer split in newspaper-inserted envelopes. These offer tests included: "This certificate good for ONE DOLLAR off our already low prices." "1¢ Sale. Pay for processing your first roll at our regular low price. Pay only 1¢ for processing your second roll." "HALF PRICE. Yes—take 50% off our already low regular prices for film processing."

Our first entertainment subscription client, the Paul Taylor Dance Company, launched its professional use of direct marketing with a six-way split of different offers, including: "The Incredible $50.00 Dance Discount Certificate (Good as Cash)." "A most intriguing dance offer. (Only in New York!)" "The Incredible $25 Dance Discount Certificate (Good as Cash)." The winner of this last test, incidentally, was an unusual simplified offer, without the usual variations for seat selection or day of week, of $99 for two subscriptions, with the headline "The amazing $99 subscription for two (still another reason to love New York!)."

The position based on price, discount, premium, or introductory offer may be the least imaginative from the creative viewpoint and the most obvious from the strategic planning standpoint, but it is still the easiest and fastest way to produce a dramatic change in advertising response.

## Overcome Inertia

The middle positions—fulfilling need, competitive selling, and price competition—are already used extensively, if not scientifically. I advocate testing all five positions in split-run testing when research indicates they may be appropriate.

The middle three positions are already used often and effectively. The forgotten positions are at the two extremes. The create-desire position is discussed above. The other extreme is overcoming inertia, or to put it another way, basing the fundamental theme of the advertisement on immediacy. This is not the same as adding an immediacy element to an ad based on another position, which is one of the fundamental tactics discussed in Chapter 12.

In retail advertising, the immediacy concept is based most frequently on a sale, a closeout, a discount, or a cents-off coupon good for a limited time only.

In direct marketing, when immediacy is the position, then the offer, the copy, and the layout must all be developed with the dramatization of immediacy as a primary objective.

This position is driven by the inertia theory. In brief, it presumes that at any given time in the life cycle of an established product, there are people who have never heard of the product, others who have tried and rejected it, and still others who have bought or are about to buy it. In addition, another large, very significant market segment has heard of it, likes it, intends to buy it someday, and just hasn't gotten around to it yet. This last segment is the prime target of this position. Its intent, in very simple language, is to flag these people down, grab them by the shoulders, and yell, "Do it now! Don't put it off a minute longer!"

Save the Children advertising is a clear example of this. After years of exposure to their advertisements and those of other child-sponsorship philanthropies, a large audience was ready and waiting, according to a Yankelovich survey. All that had to be done was to overcome inertia.

These ads presumed prior knowledge and went right for the order—now—with headlines like, "Fill out this coupon now and save a child." This simple position change, first tested in split runs, turned Save the Children around completely and helped produce one of the lowest-percentage fund-raising expenditures of any philanthropic advertiser.

**Split-run copy testing for Save the Children Federation tests dramatically different positioning. The winner was the full-page coupon (top center).** (*Source:* © *Save the Children Federation, Inc., Westport, Connecticut.*)

A letter I wrote for Hearst's *Motor Book Manual* began, "You're a busy man, so we'll get to the point in a hurry. We want to save you hundreds of dollars in car repairs."

Telegram approaches, with their abbreviated sentence structure and implied urgency, communicate immediacy in style, but so do hand-written messages and other devices described in Chapter 12, Creative Tactics. The difference is that they are dominant instead of supportive themes.

Knapp Publishing's *Architectural Digest* magazine was positioned differently in split run magazine advertisements. The winner was the testimonial approach (bottom left).   (Source: Knapp Communications Corporation, Los Angeles, California.)

Deadlines are, of course, one of the most effective methods of all, whether real, as with a limited quantity or special offer, or implied, as in "Please reply by date indicated."

Many magazines, for example, promote their subscriptions once or twice a year, when their replacement or growth needs require it. Often

these offers promise savings of between one-third and one-half off the newsstand price.

Imagine how much more effective such offers might be if, instead of relying solely on price, they moved the position to that of immediacy by making the reduced-rate offers true special offers, good only for the sixty days or so of the promotion, with a meaningful and legitimate deadline for responding at that price.

Thinking in terms of positioning forces the issue: How do we take the normal half-price offer (a price motivation) and move it to the overcome-inertia position. The answer is simple but usually overlooked: Add a deadline for acting on the offer.

## ESTABLISHING A POSITION

How do you determine which position is right for your advertising campaign? How do you revise a position which has been firmly established in the consumer's mind?

### Locating the Correct Positioning

First, when do you do it? Some advertisers go through the positioning exercise only at the inception of a new-product launch. Others consider positioning only when a basic ad program starts to fail. Of course, positioning is one of the considerations that should be raised at such times, even though most advertisers will, instead, concentrate on revising lists and media. It is incorrect to presume that an entire publication or list no longer works when, in fact, what is really happening is that the relatively small portion of each media which has been responding is no longer doing so to the same extent as before.

A different position may "talk to" a different segment of the same media universe. It may hit an emotional "hot button" with a larger percentage of the original audience segment than before. More likely, the number of prospects who were reached by the original horizontal position has declined. Advertising must then address itself to those who have moved to a later point or to those just entering the market who must be addressed at an earlier position placement.

Relocating either the horizontal or the vertical positioning can radically alter your entire marketing picture, significantly increasing response rates and substantially increasing the size of the total media universe.

### Vertical Alteration

Advertising can be adjusted vertically in very subtle ways not immediately discernible to previous users or to competitors. An important requirement is that present audiences not be lost in the search for a slightly higher or lower demographic profile.

As discussed in more detail in Chapter 13, The Art of Copywriting, and Chapter 14, Advertising Layout, vertical positioning can be altered by simply revising copy style and graphic appearance.

You can move a product up-scale or down-scale by changing typefaces, copy vocabulary, graphic image, and the selection of models or actors used in the advertising. For multiproduct companies, of course, the selection of which product is featured will make a material difference in the type of customers produced for later promotions.

Beer and cigarette advertising have adopted the concept of vertical positioning in dramatic ways. There is the "Marlboro man," attaching a masculine image to a previously "sissy-image" cigarette. On the other hand, Virginia Slims appealed to an emerging feminist market with "You've come a long way, baby."

Some brands of beer—Michelob and Lowenbrau, especially—position themselves for the white-collar suburbanite entertaining in the home. Others aim for the larger blue-collar beer market, with scenes set at ball games, bowling alleys, and bars, showing macho spokesmen implying that viewers could be as tough as truckdrivers or construction workers if they would just drink more of this particular brand of fermented hops.

Direct marketing has, until recently, not taken advantage of the science of vertical positioning, and even less of horizontal positioning. The acquisition of direct marketing agencies by giant generalists like Young & Rubicam and Doyle Dane Bernbach has accelerated this consciousness. Ads for Columbia Record Club and Time-Life's *Wild West* series and direct mail for Weight Watchers and Doubleday Book Clubs now routinely reflect carefully thought out audience positioning.

*Bon Appetit* presents an interesting example. Research showed that, when it was at 655,000 circulation, it was perceived as a "poor person's *Gourmet*." A new campaign, one of several tested, repositioned *Bon Appetit* as a publication to be used. Ads showed a suburban kitchen in which a 35-year-old woman was cooking for her family, with the headline "Clip it! Mark it! Use it!" The implication was that the competitive magazine was one to look at; this was the one to use. Two years later the magazine's circulation was at 1,145,000, or almost double.

### Horizontal Alteration

Changing horizontal positions almost always requires a fundamental change in advertising concept. At times it is possible to broaden an existing advertisement by adding appeals to another horizontal placement, but usually an entirely new ad, mailing piece, or commercial is required.

An early ad for Black's Classic Club offered works by Aristotle and Bacon as a premium for joining the Classics Club, presuming there was already a desire to know the classics—fulfilling a need.

Later ads changed the picture considerably. At one time, I added a theme creating a desire for such books as "furniture," showing a shelf of classics with the line "Start now to build this fine home library." Later ads by the brilliant Len Reiss created a different image, and sold readers on the educational and cultural satisfaction of reading such great classics. I don't know the relative results, but these approaches are both examples of moving the proposition back to an earlier position to appeal to new audience segments.

Let's look at another example, the simple calculator. When calculators first came out they could be sold by creating a desire for them among non-calculator users or by fulfilling the need of office calculator users for a small portable model. One ad would sell their usefulness, the other would presume knowledge of what a calculator does and stress size, weight, and portability.

Eventually, many calculators came into the market, and smart advertisers abandoned their earlier ad themes and moved into competitive selling (if they had a superior product) or into the pricing position (if price was a viable appeal). Even while new and sophisticated calculators at unbelievably low prices were flooding the retail market, direct marketers still reaped huge sales. Older, higher-priced models took the route of overcoming inertia, placing attractive reasons to "act now" in prospects' hands via space ads and direct mail.

At any given time, even today, each and every horizontal position is the best position to be used by some manufacturer. The desire to utilize such marketing appeals impels research and development (R&D) departments to find ways to make their products better or cheaper in some way, to some market. Examples are children's educational calculators, game calculators, race handicapping calculators, programmable calculators, and miniature calculators the size of a business card.

Let me make clear that, in direct marketing, you are not limited to a single position for all of your marketing efforts. A position can be adopted for a specific medium or list, as the best position for the particular target audience. The marketing director of Consumers Union, Joel Feldman, uses a food-oriented product position for women's lists and magazines, an automobile-related position for male lists and publications, and a home repair emphasis for lists of homeowners.

As new products are developed, marketers are called on to find new ways to appeal to new audiences. In return, manufacturers are called on to innovate, improve, and economize in order to please the consumer. This free, competitive interplay of marketer and manufacturer is the strength of America's capitalist economy, and the search for better advertising is its catalyst.

## CHAPTER TWELVE

# CREATIVE TACTICS

The artist William de Kooning, in a *New York Times* interview, said "I see the canvas and I begin!" His results are bold, spontaneous brush-strokes acclaimed as masterpieces by advocates of nonobjective art—a result that would be absurd in advertising.

The late Victor Schwab, cofounder of Schwab & Beatty, used to quote Corey Ford's story about the rider who jumped on his horse and rode off in all directions—an allusion to copywriters who sit down at their typewriters and write subjective copy without adequate planning.

One of the greatest copywriters of all time, Tom Collins of Rapp & Collins, took the pro-planning position a step further, with fewer words. His credo: "Advertising is hard!"

Brilliant ideas and sudden inspirations come to people who have done their homework, who have done the basic *conceptual* thinking that is essential before trying to write copy or design layouts.

The largest ad agencies require their account staffs and writers to prepare "creative strategy statements" or "creative workups" as one of the first steps in the ad-making process—*after* the marketing plans are written, *after* the product and its positioning are selected, *after* the offers are finalized, and *after* the media or list schedule is determined. Preparing the creative workup is the step that comes before the fun starts—the exciting, challenging, stimulating, fulfilling process of creating the advertisement or mailing piece to meet prescribed positioning and tactics.

A large advertiser may want a formal copy platform reviewed in meetings with several supervisors. A smaller advertiser may write a list of copy points on a pad, talk it over with a coworker, and sleep on it before selecting creative priorities. The process in the two cases is identical: (1) develop alternative concepts, and (2) select and prioritize.

Chapter 11 discussed positioning, the single most critical aspect of the creative process. In later chapters we will go into the actual processes of copywriting and graphic design. Here we will limit ourselves to the principles which precede the conceptualizing of headlines and the writing of copy. In essence, this chapter deals with the creative planning, other than positioning, that any writer needs to do in order to deliver an on-target assignment.

## SEVEN ELEMENTS OF CREATIVE SUCCESS

The preparation of an effective copy platform requires the selection of creative tactics in each of seven basic areas. These are: (1) audience targeting, (2) product presentation, (3) involvement devices, (4) convenience factors, (5) immediacy incentives, (6) credibility, and (7) style.

Once the basic marketing plan has been completed, including the positioning decisions, it is necessary that these seven factors be considered for each individual mailing or advertisement that is to be tested or rolled out at each stage of a program. Not only the front-end solicitation of orders or inquiries is involved, but also the back-end follow-through to obtain payment, renewals, and reorders.

These steps do not have to change with each separate test or each letter in a sequence. Within a fixed combination of the seven factors there is room for dozens of different copy and layout executions. In my experience, however, fundamental conceptual differences will produce a greater difference in results than will different creative executions of the same concept.

In some organizations the selection of these concepts is left to the copywriter or copy-art creative team. In others it is selected by the account person or product manager and included as part of the specifications for a creative execution. In either case, it should be a separate and distinct process, participated in or at least reviewed by both marketing and creative personnel. Agreement should be reached before anyone jumps on a typewriter and rides off in all directions.

## AUDIENCE TARGETING

Once you select your audience, you have to figure out how to get to them. Presuming you have picked your lists and media correctly, you know you are reaching them, but you don't know whether they are seeing your message.

The classic AIDA—attention, interest, desire, action—formula begins with the concepts of attention and interest. Another way of saying this is, "How do you get the right people to stop and read your advertisement or open your letter, in the midst of dozens of competing advertisements or mailing pieces?"

## Attention Appeals

The obvious way to target an audience is to simply announce who your message is for. A money market fund begins its ad, "A new alternative for people who have $2500 in a savings account or certificate of deposit." You can't get much more specific than that.

A book club directed at new market entrants begins, "If you've never joined a book club before, maybe its because you never knew about. . . ."

Here are some other, less wordy applications of this type of headline: "Hard of hearing?" "Good news for denture wearers!" "Women with narrow feet."

## Appeals to Needs

If your product or service appeals to too broad an audience, you won't have much luck applying this principle. "Readers!" or "To people who like to dress well" may be too general. In most cases you'll do better getting the attention of your audience by addressing their needs, physical and psychological ones alike.

Such needs include the entire range of human desires and emotions: independence; importance; self-image; the respect of others; energy and health; wealth and security; pride and satisfaction; adventure and excitement, or tranquility and escape; eating well; dressing well; having a good job, a nice home, a healthy family; finding love and affection, sex and romance; being amused, excited, and entertained; being smarter, or at least appearing smarter; being happy, or at least happier; doing good, feeling good, looking good, and maybe even being good.

Select any of these needs and see how they fit the product or service you have to sell. A book club can appeal to any of these needs through one book or another. Even a specialized product can appeal to many of them.

Take, for example, a product or plan that helps readers stop smoking. The broad "attention" approach would be simply "For people who want to stop smoking"; but let's say you want to talk to smokers who have not yet made that decision. You could write a headline about health or long life, or you could state that food tastes better to nonsmokers. You could say that the reader will look better without nicotine stains or smell better without smoky hair and clothing, and point out how this improvement could lead to new friends, a better job, or a new romance.

Try this exercise with any product, and you'll be amazed at how many needs your product can fulfill. Then make a deliberate choice before you start to write a headline.

## The Floating Audience Appeal

Sometimes, with an unusual product, it is important to let a product find its own audience by appealing to curiosity, snobbery, or independence. Some examples: "Why is *Rolling Stone* the most misunderstood magazine in America?" "What is *Ms.* magazine, and why is it saying all those terrible things?" Any ad which says "X—it's not for everyone."

## PRODUCT PRESENTATION

Chapter 3, The Marketing Plan, suggested describing your product or service from every possible viewpoint, and gave the example of how as simple a product as a pencil could be described from physical, historical, scientific, emotional, and psychological perspectives. When you are ready to present your product is the time to make that exercise pay off for you.

Once the product is described, you can then select certain attributes or appeals around which to build your advertising. The choices may depend on the positioning decision made for a specific ad or mailing piece, as discussed in Chapter 11. They may depend on your understanding of the nature and needs of the target audience. They may vary depending on the available media and format you have to work with. (Decorator colors, for example, would not be as demonstrable in a black-and-white ad as in a color one; an impressive action or motion would come over better on television than in print.)

## Feature Dramatization

One creative tactic is to find a way to dramatize one or more attributes of the product or service. This can be done as a logical presentation, as in "Seventeen reasons why you should read *U.S. News & World Report*," or a dramatic one, such as "See how this wonder knife cuts through solid steel."

Dramatization often involves exaggeration—giving an example or case history that is accurate but atypical. Demonstrating that your glue can hold a suspended elephant or pull a freight train has nothing to do with your prospect's intended use but serves to dramatize the attribute of strength. The case history of a homeowner who built a whole new wing with the help of a do-it-yourself book may not echo the prospect's intention, but it will serve to dramatize the attribute of usefulness.

While working on the introduction of a money market fund, I discovered the importance of dramatizing liquidity in the form of the check-writing feature of such funds. This appeal proved to be indispensable, even though operating data indicated that very few such investors ever took advantage of the feature. They just wanted to know it was there in case of a sudden emergency or opportunity.

## Unique Selling Proposition

The concept of the unique selling proposition (USP) is most important in general advertising where a single association is needed to aid recall and association, but it is also useful to direct marketers. It is most relevant at two levels of horizontal positioning (discussed in Chapter 11): (1) creating a need and (2) competitive selling.

In creating a need, the USP is often a generic concept for an entire category of products. In such instances the ad must point out the desirability of your product as compared with the product in prevailing use.

When television was first introduced, its USP, a visual image, was sufficient to sell a great many sets by companies that are no longer factors in the business. Today, in order to sell competitively, electronic manufacturers constantly search for new USPs, such as color correction signals, room light adjustment devices, remote control units, and built-in accommodation for cables, recorders, game controls, computer attachments, and phone hookups.

## Selling Benefits

Most important, every product attribute must be interpreted in terms of benefits, whether it is generically unique, competitively unique, or not unique at all.

Never assume that a customer knows why a certain feature is important. No matter what you're selling, look for interpretations of product attributes as potential planks for your copy platform. For example, a Krugerrand contains exactly 1 ounce of pure gold—an attribute. Because the price of an ounce of gold can be found in the daily paper, it is easy to determine the value of a Krugerrand—a benefit. An appliance may have a plastic body for lightness, a metal body for sturdiness, or a glass body so you can see how it works or keep it clean easily. No matter what the attribute, thinking in terms of benefits can lead to important and effective selling points.

## Building an Edge

In direct marketing, we presume that the market and its needs are the given, and any product can be adapted to fit. Therefore, where there isn't a unique selling proposition or a feature whose benefits can be dramatized, we can always invent one.

Even with a going business, there is always some way to give it an edge to help sales. Add a guarantee, a service, an updating method. Invent an accessory, an attractive display case, or some element that will make the product a bit easier or more effective to use.

The power of marketing can and should be used as a two-way street— not only to sell consumers on using new products but also to motivate manufacturers to improve products to meet consumer needs and desires.

## Getting to the Point

The specifics of a copy platform are governed by the attitudes of the consumer. These attitudes have changed over the years and will continue to change.

If you look at the typical buyer scenario suggested in your marketing plan, it will probably be evident that this prospect is very different from the prospect who was enticed into reading such long copy messages of yesteryear as "They laughed when I sat down to play the piano. . . ." Today's consumer is distinguished, in the eyes of direct marketing copywriters, by laziness, impatience, and procrastination.

Consumers are reluctant to seek out information on different brands and analyze which is best. You must bring the facts to them. They don't want to wade through long copy messages to find reasons why your product is one they should buy. You must make your message interesting and rewarding to read. Furthermore, when presented with the facts, consumers don't want to interpret them. You must make an interpretation for them.

Most consumers not only don't want to read long copy messages in advertising and direct mail, they don't want to read your ad or direct mail at all—no matter how short the message. Ads such as "Forty-nine reasons why you should buy . . ." usually are not as successful today as they once were, precisely because your prospects won't keep reading until they find the one reason that would really be convincing. If you've got something to say, you'd better say it up front, simply and clearly.

A classic philanthropic ad read, "For $16 a month you can help Rosario Torres. Or you can turn the page." The motivations were buried in the body copy. Most readers just turned the page. It was later discovered, in split-run testing, that this ad did only one-third as well as a new advertisement built on the concept of *involvement*. To quote from Victor Schwab's poetic interpretation of a consumer's advice to writers, "Tell me quick, and tell me true, or else my love, to hell with you."

## INVOLVEMENT DEVICES

Presuming your prospect has been stopped and has enough interest in your product to hesitate on the way to turning the page or tossing the letter in the wastepaper basket, how do you hold that interest long enough to get your whole message across? The key need here is some way to "involve" your prospect. Here are some ideas.

### Quizzes

"Do you make these mistakes in English?" is an old classic that ran for years. Another is "Should you invest in a tax-exempt bond fund?" Both ads ask a question and offer information which involve the reader's desire to learn the answer.

Checklists are a variation, such as, "Which of these important stories have you missed because you haven't been subscribing to . . . ?" Another variation is a headline with a simple "yes or no" request.

### Fascination

Every once in a while a copywriter has an opportunity to hold the reader's interest through the sheer eloquence of the story being presented. Often such a message is an entertaining narrative, an intriguing case history, or step-by-step instructions on building a craft project or cooking a sumptuous recipe. A message that is rewarding in itself, because it entertains or informs, can be one of the best ways to hold a prospect. Alas, writers who can do this kind of copy are rare today.

### Value

A coupon which, graphically, appears to have value in itself will involve the reader of an ad or mailing piece. While "checks" must be used carefully in a way that will not deceive the reader, any item which in fact can save the reader money does have value and should look valuable. No one wants to throw away an envelope which contains a valuable certificate. Fewer still will toss out one which has a coin showing through a window, contains a bona fide check (even for a token amount like 10 cents), or has a real postage stamp on the reply envelope.

I have received mailings containing a $2 bill (from *Money* magazine), commemorative stamps, packets of seeds, and good-luck charms—all attempts to get me to pay attention to a message by offering obvious and immediate value.

## Personalization

Nothing is as fascinating as a person's own name, and evidently the more frequently and prominently it appears, the better many mailings will do.

Even more effective is evidence that the advertiser is addressing not just a name but a person made "special" by an address, past buying, political affiliation, or other data. Good personalization involves not only using the name often but using it well, with as much customization as computer technology and available data permit.

## Play

Tom Collins quotes the saying, "Within every person there is a child, and that child likes to play." This is the underlying reason why stamps, stickers, and tokens of all kinds more often than not lift response. *U.S. News & World Report* achieved a major breakthrough by using a West-vaco-patented reply card which told the addressee, "Press here to subscribe." A trick fold popped out a picture of a handshake indicating that the prospect was accepting the offer.

Other mailings ask readers to scrape off a coating, lift a flap, scratch a surface which will release a scent, pull a strip which will reveal a message in a window, look for a lucky number, examine a photograph through a colored filter, or moisten a surface to reveal an invisible ink message. Corny? Sure. But like everything else in direct marketing, these kinds of play devices are used because they work.

## Completion

The brilliant direct-mail innovator Sol Blumenfeld identified the concept of "completion" as a factor in direct-mail response devices.

This is the true magic of stamps, peel-off labels, and tokens, used particularly in direct mail. The "yes" or "no" stamp is not just a "toy"; it is a tool for fulfilling the compulsive need to finish an apparently incomplete design.

Imagine a response card which shows a picture of a man looking into empty space with his arm outstretched and—yipes!—a hand missing! How can you resist pasting in the stamp which (1) adds the hand, (2) places the magazine being held by the hand in a position where the man appears to be reading it, and (3) coincidentally, indicates your acceptance of the publisher's proposition?

Try this experiment to see for yourself the power of completion. Draw a circle or a square on a blackboard, with one segment omitted. Leave a piece of chalk nearby and watch how visitors to your office feel a need to finish the shape.

Here's a simpler method. Start telling a story on an envelope, and leave it in midthought. The completion urge will get your reader inside faster than any plea to "see inside." For the same reason, I always insist that direct-mail letters be typed with the last paragraph on each page interrupted in midthought, as a powerful way to get people to turn the page and keep reading.

### Choice

Perhaps one of the most successful involvement devices is the simplest: choice. "Which records do you want for only . . . ?" "How many weeks of this magazine shall we send you for . . . ?" "Do you want the red or green display case for your recipe card file?" "Do you want your contribution to help a needy boy or a girl?" Or simply "Yes or no?"

## CONVENIENCE FACTORS

"Make it easy to respond" has always been a fundamental requirement for direct marketing advertising. In fact, convenience is one of the cardinal reasons for the growth of direct marketing as an industry.

After all, shopping by mail means you don't have to use your precious time and even more precious gasoline to drive downtown. You don't have to look for a parking space, push through crowds, fumble through shelves and racks, and reason with a salesperson who knows nothing about sales and sometimes less about courtesy.

You see what you want in an ad or a catalog. You fill out a coupon or make a phone call. In a matter of days, someone from the Postal Service or UPS brings it to your door. If you don't like it, you just pop it back in the mail.

The concept of convenience must be extended into every type of response advertising, and there are several ways that responding to such advertising can be made even easier.

## Coupon Readability

Not only copy but especially coupons and commitment or guarantee information should be crystal-clear in style, meaning, and typography.

Some art directors seem to think that a coupon is a necessary evil to be kept to a minimum size regardless of how much copy is to be included. Not so. As explained in Chapter 13, The Art of Copywriting, the coupon is the place to start writing, and the place to summarize your selling theme. It deserves as much space as it needs to be clear and easily readable. Some very successful ads I've been involved with have used an entire page as one giant coupon.

Just as important, the coupon should be easy to fill out. Lines should be long enough, and spaces high enough, so the consumers can write their names, addresses, cities, states, and zip codes comfortably, without abbreviating or printing in tiny letters. If someone writes illegibly, you're out an order. If another prospect gets frustrated trying to write in a cramped space, you're out another order. And if a third consumer has to look for a pair of eyeglasses in order to read the small type in the coupon, you're out a third order.

What a shame! Why put the right offer in the right medium, present it so you stop the right people and hold their attention through the copy and into the coupon, and then lose them because of lack of simple readability?

## Ease of Response

Most sales are impulse sales to some extent, and every second of delay minimizes your chance of getting a reply.

Format has a lot to do with ease of response. Soft-space ad coupons should be easy to tear out—not buried in the gutter of a magazine or the middle of a page.

Where budgets permit, bind-in cards, flaps, and tip-ons all are more than worth their added expense in increased response, not because they attract attention but because they make it easy to respond.

In direct mail you can make response even easier by providing an envelope or a reply card, ready to mail back. Computerization will let you fill out a reply form so your prospect doesn't even have to write in a name and address, and business reply mail will even save a trip to the post office or the stamp box.

Some successful mailings have included a small pen or pencil. Where a choice is involved, stamps, tokens, labels, and other devices can be used to make selection and ordering simple.

## Avoiding Calculations

It is safe to assume that most of your prospects don't really like to do math. I'll grant that veteran mail-order buyers can tackle a Sears catalog and calculate a maze of shipping costs and sales tax rates depending on the items ordered, shipping weights, and varying routes. However, I can't help wondering how much more business even Sears might do if the costs were all calculated in advance and included in parentheses next to each item.

If you're expecting multiple orders, don't confront your reader with a need for multiplication and postage calculations. Instead, make it simple with predetermined totals as much as possible.

Consider a typical ordering phrase: "Send me ____widgets at $1.49 each plus 50¢ postage and handling (additional widgets add 35¢ postage and handling); Ohio residents add 5% sales tax." Instead, try this:

( ) SEND ONE WIDGET FOR $1.49, plus 50¢ shipping. Total $1.99

( ) SEND THREE WIDGETS FOR $3.99 (A 10% SAVING!) plus $1.20 shipping. Total $5.19

( ) SEND FIVE WIDGETS FOR $5.99 (A 20% SAVING!) plus $1.90 shipping. Total $7.89.

Ohio residents please add 5% sales tax—7¢ for one, 20¢ for three, 30¢ for five.

Note that this example limits choice of quantity but encourages larger unit sales through both simplification and the discount. We have calculated shipping costs, multiple-order prices, and totals except for the Ohio residents, and for them the percentage sales tax has been calculated.

## Ease of Payment

The easier it is to order, the greater the likelihood of impulse purchases. In many cases, selling on credit and including on the coupon the option "Bill me later" is worth the risk. On high-cost goods, of course, the risk can be excessive.

Credit cards are a godsend to the direct marketing business. They make it not only easy to pay but also easy to order. Most people find credit cards more convenient to use than checkbooks. They can pull out the cards, copy in the numbers, and send their orders on the way.

Even more significant, credit cards have enabled the majority of mail-order buyers to pay by telephone, opening up the airwaves to direct-response radio and TV offers that previously could only ask for COD or prepaid orders.

## The Magnificent Telephone

Permitting a customer to inquire or order by telephone is the ultimate convenience. A phone is always handy, and dialing ten or eleven digits of a toll-free number takes far less effort than mailing most reply cards.

Phone services can be open twenty-four hours, seven days a week, just as mailboxes are. Your phone operator can also answer simple questions, do calculations, advise whether an item is in stock, and take credit card payments over the phone.

Ironically, the anonymous telephone operator, trained to be courteous, knowledgeable, and quick, is rapidly replacing the personal service that most retail salespeople used to provide on a face-to-face basis.

## The Need for Convenience

Our audiences have become less literate and less legible than they used to be. Most people coming out of government-run school systems either have not been taught to write or, just as deadly, don't like to write. If they can put sentences together, the chances are that any attempts at legible penmanship were abandoned in the third grade.

We have come a long way from the exchange of neat, handwritten letters transacting business between sellers and buyers who treated each other with respect for literacy. Today, in the age of the computer, we are well advised to make our messages easy to read, easy to understand, and easy to respond to.

## IMMEDIACY INCENTIVES

One evangelical fund raiser sent its past supporters an imitation telegram with this short message: "Urgent. Please send $20 by return mail. Will explain later."

This may be the purest and shortest known implementation of the immediacy criterion in direct mail. It contains all the basic elements: urgency, copy, command terminology, graphic expression, and deadline. All these conceptual elements should be included in direct marketing copy whenever there is any justification for them.

### Urgency Copy

Ideally the immediacy concept should be an intrinsic part of the basic proposition, as discussed in Chapter 4. Even if immediacy is not intrinsic, however, there are many ways to convey a sense of urgency. The telegraph style in the example above is a style approach. News headlines or words like "now," "new," and "introducing" do the same.

The need for prompt action can be related to the proposition, if justified with reminders about limited quantity or possible price increases. In such cases it pays to dramatize the result of inaction, as in "Why pay more later?"

Try dramatizing the imminent savings, comfort, or other advantages of the product or service offered, as well as the costs, discomfort, and disadvantages of putting off a decision. Examples are: "Winter is coming sooner than you think. Order this coat now so you'll be ready for the first frosty day." "Send your contribution today. A child's hunger has no patience."

The emotional level can be tapped as well. "Imagine how much fun it will be when you receive this wonderful novelty in the mail . . . taking it out of the carton and watching it perform its amusing movements . . . sharing the excitement with your friends. Why put off this moment a day longer than you have to?"

### Command Terminology

One copy approach which seems to be consistently effective is what I have called "command terminology." This is the simple second-person declarative sentence: "Do it today," "Send it now," or simply "Mail this coupon." Somewhere, before a copy message is completed, it is important to answer the unspoken question "So what do you want from me?" The answer is a command—a statement of exactly what you want the person to do. In the AIDA formula, "action" is the payoff. The request for action should be as much like a command as good taste permits.

### Graphic Expression

How do you make a layout look like it has news value? The key is "recency." An old message doesn't demand immediate attention or action. A message that is hot off the presses conveys the impression that it is worth reading and acting on immediately.

Imagine that you are driving your car, looking for a parking space, and suddenly you see one near what appears to be a little-used driveway. Stenciled in faded letters is the warning "Do not park here." It looks as if it has been there for a long time. Many people would ignore it. However, as you pull into the space, someone appears and hands you a note with the same message. Suddenly it's immediate. You are likely to pay immediate attention to it.

Some media have immediacy built in. Radio and television are prime examples, particularly because of the possibility of positioning commercials near news programs. Newspapers are more immediate than magazines, weekly magazines more immediate than monthly ones.

In direct mail, a telegram format is the ultimate immediacy. "Air mail" seems more urgent than other classes of mail. Even though all first-class mail now goes for the same rate, a simple red-and-blue diagonal border around an envelope or reply card still conveys the idea of speed, promptness, and importance.

Handwritten notes appear more recent, and thus more immediate, than printed letters. Rubber stamps or facsimile stickers also convey urgency. An interesting direct-mail technique is to put part of the text, the postscript, and some marginal annotations in facsimile handwriting, to suggest that they are afterthoughts.

In print advertising, immediacy can be conveyed by setting the ad in a typewriter face or the headlines in crayoned hand lettering. One retailer ran sales ads with hand-printed or typed copy and photos with visible cut marks—a concept called "calculated crudity."

The more finished the ad, the more permanent it looks—and therefore the less immediate. The trick is to strike a balance between the graphic respectability you want to convey and the need for immediacy. It isn't easy, but it is possible.

## Deadline

The most important of all immediacy elements is the deadline. If the proposition permits, you can say "Offer expires on November 8." This is the strongest deadline of all.

"Offer expires in ten days" is good but not quite as strong as a specific date. I often recommend an undated deadline where there is risk that the mailing may not get out on time. Otherwise a dated mailing that is delayed could be a costly loss.

Where there is no genuine offer deadline, there are ways to suggest it. For instance, in a market where prices are rapidly increasing, you might say, "This price not guaranteed unless reply is received before _____" or more simply, "Please reply by _____."

Other deadlines can be related to supply rather than date, for example, "Only 5000 plants available at this price." Sweepstakes often include a bonus for early entry—a proven stimulus to the total response. Some propositions offer a premium or discount only to the first few thousand people who reply.

The common denominator is the same in all these examples. Set a deadline or give a reason for action now. In direct marketing, it is now or never.


## CREDIBILITY

The consumer today has probably never been more distrustful. Automobiles are recalled. Favorite foods turn out to have dangerous ingredients. Why should consumers trust a product they have never seen but have only read about in an ad or mailing piece that is transient by its very nature?

The element of credibility is a must item on any copy checklist. Fortunately, there are many ways to provide it.


### Advertiser Reputation

Nothing is quite as effective as sponsorship by a company which has built a good reputation over the years. If your company is well known, then make it clear that you stand behind the product being offered, and put your name in a prominent place. If your company is owned by or affiliated with a well-known substantial company, be sure to feature that company name. Split-run testing indicated a 25 percent lift for a new magazine introduction that featured the name of the broadcast network which owned the magazine over an identical ad which did not. When Conde Nast introduced *Self*, they felt their other magazines were better known than the publishing name, and so the opening campaign showed covers of *Vogue*, *Glamour*, and *Mademoiselle*.

If your company isn't well known but is large or reputable, has won awards, or is licensed by the government, then by all means say so. If you are just starting out, then make something of that; say your president reads every letter or the item is your only product.


### The Bandwagon

People flock to see why a store or restaurant is crowded. If your product is selling well, then say so. Tell them that your direct marketing business is prospering, that so many thousand people have used your product, that certain big companies or such famous personalities as so and so have bought it. Everyone loves a winner.

## Endorsers

If your company isn't well known, or even if it is, then consider finding an endorser, a well-known spokesperson who offers instant identity and therefore believability for your message. Where would National Liberty be today without Art Linkletter's endorsements?

## Corporate Personalization

Your spokesperson doesn't have to be a movie star or national celebrity. It can be your own chief executive officer (CEO). A CEO who looks and sounds sincere might provide an ideal image in your advertising. Look at the famous mail-order fruit marketers Harry & David, or Gloria Steinem's *Ms.* ads. A personal message from the founder or the publisher can have a very nice ring—in copy style and at the cash register.

## Testimonials

Testimonials were once the mainstay of mail-order advertising, and it is surprising how few advertisers make good use of them today. They are still very effective. There is nothing quite like an honest face and the signature of someone in a nearby part of the country to add believability.

The problem is that testimonials are difficult to come by. In our lazy, nonliterate age, unsolicited testimonials are few and far between. When you do get one, you may not be able to get a release to use it in advertising.

Today, you have to ask for testimonials. Send out a questionnaire soliciting opinions and comments, including a section with prewritten statements and the introduction, "Which of the following statements would you subscribe to?" Respondents who check appropriate statements or add desirable statements in their own words can then be contacted by telephone and asked for a release. If the respondent agrees, a local photographer may be commissioned to take a photograph and secure the signed release.

## Outside Guarantors

A guarantee is always helpful, and is more helpful if the guarantor is well known. If your company isn't well known, consider getting an outside source to back up the guarantee and ensure that money will be refunded if the customer is not satisfied. Perhaps an insurance company, such as Lloyds of London, or a local bank can endorse the guarantee. Perhaps an independent testing laboratory can vouch for the product claims. A newspaper clipping might be quoted, citing the effectiveness of your product's principal ingredient. An industry association may grant you its "seal of approval."

### "Why Are You Being So Good to Me?"

To the extent that your offer sounds "too good," it may be perceived as unbelievable. Don't blame today's consumer for asking "What's the catch?" when the word "free" shows up.

Offer qualifications should be clearly stated up front, not just where required by law but as a matter of good business. Split-run ads have confirmed that the various rules requiring that club commitment and return policies be spelled out actually help response rather than hurt it.

## THE TACTICAL PROCESS

The general strategy is established in the marketing plan. The creative task is to implement that strategy with maximum effectiveness, and the tactics will change for each individual mailing piece, ad, or commercial.

Often a writer is charged with the problem of developing several alternative concepts to be tested—some of them implementations of specific offer strategies and some pure, creative variations on a theme.

The process of developing these tactics is a transitional area between strategy and copywriting. These processes can also be used in developing the initial strategies or in working out headline, illustration, or other creative problems.

There are two directions from which one can approach this process: the logical and the fantastic. Both work, and the two work well together.

### Logical Approaches

The logical, traditional approach to problem solving is one of forming concepts from the ground up. The sum of knowledge about the product and the audience in the marketing environment is considered and digested, and connections are identified. In fact, the ability to make abstractions—to build logical bridges from one idea to another—is the quantified element of "intelligence." Some people do it better than others, not necessarily because they have more brainpower but because they have learned to use more of their brain and to put in more effort.

Forming a logical approach is exercising the obvious, and the obvious solution is often the best solution. Such solutions may not be clever and may win no Gold Mailbox Awards for innovation, but they work. The elements here are concentration, stimulation, and evaluation.

*Concentration* is a matter of studying everything that might in any way be pertinent. This is best done individually.

*Stimulation* can be the internal use of free-association methods to generate alternatives, but it is more often done in conversation with others who are also knowledgeable and also motivated to identify the best tactical solution. The group size can vary, from two people to a dozen, and it can include fellow workers, friends, agency people, clients, or suppliers. The exercise must be open, positive, and solution-seeking, and participants must share the common goal of finding answers rather than impressing or finding fault with one another.

*Evaluation* processes vary. The simplest is to sleep on it and look at your notes objectively the next day. More complex processes involve establishing criteria charts and checking off each and every requirement. Another approach is to try to build an ad out of the idea and see if it makes sense.

My approach is to develop the idea before sharing it with anyone else; to find a way to make it work before the whole idea gets shot down because one detail hasn't been worked out. Once the idea is all worked out, I write it up and submit it to others for discussion. A well-thought-out proposal will get serious attention and is likely to get suggestions for revision rather than a flat, general rejection.

### Fantastic Approaches

Henry David Thoreau advised his readers, "If you have built castles in the air, your work need not be lost; there is where these should be. Now put foundations under them."

The fantastic approach begins by building castles in the sky—by generating ideas that are far from obvious and may, at first glance, even seem ridiculous.

*Brainstorming* was an early version of this approach. In its simplest form, a group of concerned people attack a problem by generating ideas without allowing for criticism, negative reactions, or evaluation during the idea-generating process. Anything can be said, added to, or developed, but nothing can be criticized. The more ideas generated, the better for the process. The wilder the ideas, the more likely it is that a truly innovative thought will be uncovered.

*Forced field* is another creative process used to "force" thinking into predetermined categories. For instance, a publisher may list magazine articles down one side of a chart and audience needs across the top, and then try to force-fit article-based headlines into each resulting box.

A manufacturer might list product features down one side and market segments across the top, and then try to find ways to make the features seem useful to each segment. Most of the ideas would not be usable, but the probability is that some would occur that would not be generated in a conventional approach.

*Guided fantasy* is another, more advanced type of creative mind stretching. The basic principle involves helping participants break out of the limitations of negative thinking and leap over the barriers to imagination that inhibit so many middle managers in business.

There are many ways to stimulate fantasy by guiding a group to find associations with visual or verbal images, or by creating exercises that give permission to conceive the inconceivable in a way many have not done since childhood.

One technique widely used in the direct marketing field is Effective Problem Solving, an approach to creative thinking developed by Stan Rapp and Liz Forrest. Innovation Labs of Stamford, Connecticut, utilizes these techniques in idea-generating and problem-solving meetings for such clients as Doubleday, Donnelley, Litton, and the Direct Mail Marketing Association.

The technique begins by defining problem roles. The person with the power to act in the situation is designated the problem owner. The "traffic cop," or the person setting the structure of the meeting, is the facilitator, and the remaining members of the group are the participants who offer ideas.

The trained facilitator then guides the participants on an exciting, mind-expanding journey that first explodes the problem with wishful thinking and then slowly narrows down to trouble-free new ideas that relate directly to the needs of the problem owner. The goal is to come away from the meeting with actionable steps the problem owner can take to solve the problem. The system has led to many important ideas that have produced profitable results for direct marketers.

Which process to use is, to some extent, a matter of personal preference and ability. For some propositions, the obvious solution is sufficient if it meets your criteria for taking action in the situation. For others, only a major departure from the obvious will produce the big idea that will launch a new proposition or save an old one.

## CHAPTER THIRTEEN

# THE ART OF COPYWRITING

Up to now we have dealt mostly with the science of advertising—the planning, the research, and the strategic and tactical considerations that precede writing the first word of copy.

It is as if the navigators have now set the course and the pilot is ready to take over the highly skilled responsibility of getting the plane into the air. Or the architect and engineers have completed the plans for a new office building, and the artisans of many crafts are now ready to break ground.

Copywriting is the original "art" of advertising, and especially of mail-order writing. All the historic greats of the field started as copywriters, and all the early classics are essentially expressions of the copywriter's art.

An old-timer in the field once told me, "Copy is king." This is an exaggeration today, but copy is still the fountainhead of great innovations in direct marketing. The experience of copywriting is extremely valuable, perhaps indispensable, to those whose creativity would extend to the whole process of direct marketing management.

## "ADVERTISING IS HARD" AND OTHER APPROACHES

Vic Schwab emphasized the importance of relating product benefits to human needs. In his classic *How to Write a Good Advertisement* (Harper & Row, New York, 1962), he listed several basic needs: better health, more money, greater popularity, improved appearance, more comfort, more leisure, pride of accomplishment, business advancement, social advancement, and increased enjoyment.

David Ogilvy added story value, with text and illustration, subheads and captions, all telling a story that bridges the common interests between the producer of a product and its potential consumer. The Ogilvy style, with booklike typefaces, sentence or title headlines, highly readable layouts, and dramatic illustrations, has become instantly recognizable. Above all, Ogilvy ads have been literate, showing proper respect for the English language, its structure, and its punctuation. I believe these ads are unusually effective because they treat the consumer with respect and invite the reader to respond in kind to the message and product.

Bill Bernbach was the first to adapt advertising style to its media context. Recognizing that advertising almost always appears in an entertainment medium, whether in the pages of a magazine or adjoining a television show, he added the dimension of entertainment to advertising itself. As a result, Doyle Dane Bernbach advertising for clients such as Polaroid, Volkswagen, and American Airlines often includes touches of humor, suspense, pathos, conflict, or contradiction, to make them at least as appealing as the editorial or programming content they adjoin. It's a lot easier to get your point across if people *want* to read or watch your message.

Tom Collins summed it up with an aphorism reminiscent of Will Rogers: "Advertising is hard!" This classic understatement says it all. There's no easy route to successful advertising. The stroke of creative inspiration is a rare phenomenon that comes only to those who have been immersed in research, planning, strategy, and tactics.

The hard work of marketing scientist and creative artist pays off in successful advertising. The quickie tossed off by a free-lancer or an inexperienced in-house ad department may be an ad technically, but it will never realize the true potential of direct marketing done the hard way, the slow way, the sure way.

## GET READY, GET SET . . .

Regardless of what other role you might play in your client or agency organization, for the purposes of this chapter *you* are now a copywriter. Even those company presidents who occasionally exercise their right to toss off an ad of their own are, at the time and place of writing, copywriters and only copywriters.

Whether your starting point is your own inspiration, an informal discussion, or a carefully prepared "project assignment" with marketing plans, briefings, and spelled-out creative specifications, the copywriter's first steps are the same.

*Define the Assignment*  Are you doing concepts for discussion or finished copy for a concept that has already been agreed upon? What are the medium and the space unit? Is there a formal marketing plan for the entire product line? Have creative tactics and positioning been worked out for this particular project, or are you expected to propose them? (If the latter, get agreement on them before you submit headlines or copy; you'll save yourself a lot of false starts and wasted time.) Also, what's the history of this project? Why is a new ad needed? What is different about the audience, medium, positioning, or strategy from previous ads? What is the result history of those ads?

The more you can learn, the more you can contribute. If it helps, quote me as recommending that no data be held back from the copywriter. If there is a need for secrecy about actual CPRs and margins, than ask for some type of target or index figures that can be shared with everyone on the creative team.

*Abstract All Information*  Restate everything for yourself, in your own words, in your own notes, and for your eyes only. Ignore the repetitious instructions and information you already know about, but spell out the key points you must add to your knowledge and the key criteria expected of you for this assignment.

It is important that the elements of strategy and tactics, as well as all relevant product and market information, be digested and restated in your own words. This process is necessary to integrate the data into your own mental processes, and to be sure you understand and can explain it.

### Beat the Winner

Often a writer has a broad assignment: to find a way to improve results— either up-front or with better-quality responses—as compared to either a previous winning effort or a competitor's ad.

You know that your ad or mailing will be put up against a control package which may have beaten dozens of tests before. The medium is fixed. The offer is fixed. You must overcome the winner with pure creative superiority.

The first step is to take the other package apart creatively. This too must be done in writing as a way of helping you to fully identify what is important about it. The best approach is what I call a "reverse outline"—a list of copy points used in the piece being studied. Paragraph by paragraph, read the competing copy and draw conclusions like these: What is the writer trying to say? What need is being appealed to? What position is being taken? How is it good?

You know the winning ad works, and so you can't dismiss it just because you wouldn't have written it that way. When a point is repeated, check it against your original list. Give the headline appeal ten checks, appeals in subheads three, and the main points in the coupon two or three. Add up the checks to see where the emphasis is.

Then take the list and regroup it. What are the constants that you would have in your package anyway? Isolate the main themes. What does this package have that other tested packages did not have? Identify the variables—the optional appeals which you can retain or drop as you see fit.

Once you've done this you will be in a position to take the plunge; to gamble on what you think the strong points are and where you think the copy can be improved. Rather than trying an alternate approach or trying to please the client by being clever, begin with the basics and write out your own copy platform for the new effort.

The copy platform is your choice, as a writer, of which appeals you want to put your chips on. Take the ones you think are strong, and see how you can make them stronger. Take the weak ones and drop them or turn them around into positives. Then, as your edge, find the new copy points that you think will strengthen the previous effort and make yours the winner.

Check your benefits list, and see what you can add. Look at your positioning options, if they haven't been spelled out in advance. Even if they have been spelled out, feel free to contest the client's or marketing planner's selection. Just don't ignore it.

### Three Secrets of Great Ad Writing

In real estate, the three most important considerations in selecting a property are location, location, and location. Similarly, the three great secrets of copywriting are research, research, and research.

Sure, any writer can fill up a page. The Blarney stone blesses all Irish and all ad writers with equal fervor. Consequently, it is no trick for any of us to spontaneously sound forth for as many pages as you'd like on any subject you want. Politicians and debaters have been doing it for years, on whatever side of a subject is required. Making something out of nothing is a clever trick; it is not an art.

One common denominator of really fine copy is that it is "meaty"— filled with details, choice examples, and clever anecdotes, all of which make points with examples rather than with broad and empty claims.

I have had to write copy on electronic capacitors, automotive additives, books on bridge (which I had never played), and religious rituals which were unfamiliar to me. I knew nothing about these subjects before I wrote about them, and nothing soon afterward. While I was writing, however, I was steeped in each subject and knew enough to talk intelligently with experts.

Let's face it. If you can't talk about a subject in your own words, how can you write about it? If you haven't found enough about it to interest you, how can you make it sound interesting to others? If you can't explain it to your spouse or best friend, how can you explain it to the person whom you want to read your mailing piece?

Someone asked me how I wrote this book. I answered, "One word at a time." Actors in commercials sometimes look at the cameras and freeze at the thought of the millions of people who might soon be watching them. They have to be reminded to think about and talk to just one person at a time. Copywriters too should heed this advice. If you can't talk to one person, you'll never talk to tens of thousands successfully. This means you must master each new subject with research, research, and more research.

First, get answers to every question which occurred to you when you read the briefing material or sat in on an orientation session. Don't be proud and stupid; be humble and smart. Let someone know what you didn't understand so you can get explanations of every point that isn't clear. No one is judging you in any way except by counting the coupons that will come in as a result of your efforts.

Study the product. If it is a magazine, go back two years or more to find articles with a wide range of appeals, and write out a catchy summary of each one. If it is a book, even an encyclopedia, go ahead and read it—or at least try to. As you read, make notes in copywriting form, as if you were writing a list of contents to be included in a mailing piece. (Maybe you'll use it this way, maybe not; but it's a great way to get examples for points you intend to make in your main copy message.)

One hint: Do note the page numbers and source of each such item you write out. Sooner or later a client or a lawyer is going to ask you for your sources, and it's a lot easier to make marginal notes as you go along.

After you study the product, head for the reference books. Go to the library, and look in the card files and in the *Reader's Guide to Periodical Literature* to get all the information you need on the subject. Call associations or technical groups and see what they can offer you. One such inquiry led me to spend three days at the library of the Society of Automotive Engineering just to get one key point for an advertisement for an automotive product.

Don't just talk to the product manager or ad director. Ask to speak with—in fact, insist on speaking with—the engineers, editors, technicians, or other specialists who really know what's happening. The more you know, the more you can write. Ideally, all the facts should be in the marketing plan, but it's more likely that the writer will be helping to write this section of the plan. In a small company without formal planning, you may be going through the processes on your own without benefit of a formal strategy.

## The Creative Workup

You've defined the assignment. You've done your homework. Now, you're ready to write—almost. Just one more thing: Make a list.

This list is a simple one. Put down all the copy points you want to make, based on your selection of positioning. Include the creative tactics you've selected and how you'll dramatize the offer and product attributes, interpreting everything in benefits. Perhaps you'll have twenty or thirty basic points. Even if you know them all, write them down, so you can use the list later to help you sell the ad to whoever has to approve it.

Then put numbers or letters next to each point, indicating the relative importance of each. Which are major points, which minor? Which is the single most vital point to be worked into the headline? Which points should be clear even if the prospect reads only captions and subheads? Which ones are optional—to be left out if space limitations demand it?

## Harnessing Your Subconscious

Now put away your research. Put away your notes. Tape your list to a wall, and get away from it all. Take a nap. Take a walk. Take a drink. Take whatever you need to let your mind digest all the research, strategy, and creative specification. Sleeping on it works for some people. A walk around the block is my technique. The point is to let your subconscious mind digest all the information you have acquired.

Your brain will, in effect, switch to "automatic" and integrate all this knowledge with everything else you've ever heard, seen, read, or been taught—making connections with the whole of your life experience much as a "method" actor interprets a role.

If your thinking has been logical and scientific; if you've been a sensitive observer of the human process; if you've allowed yourself to think, feel, and communicate on both an emotional and an intellectual level; if you have managed not to block out your experiences as an adult or as a child—then you will be able to draw upon the sum total of your entire life to help you understand, create, and express the ideas you need to do your job.

Your job is infinitely challenging: to make the complicated simple,

the dull fascinating, and the mundane marvelous; to bridge the communications gap between a lifeless product and a living consumer. The
power to meet this challenge is already within you.

## ... AND GO!

Now you face the legendary blank sheet: the drawing pad or typing
paper whose stark whiteness has, at one time or another, intimidated
not only ad writers but novelists, poets, and playwrights as well.

Presumably you have done your homework. You know the subject.
You understand the assignment. You have a picture in your mind of
whom you are talking to. You know what you want to say. Now, where
do you start?

### The Mental "Dump" Process

Computer technicians use the phrase "dump" to mean emptying the
data stored in memory. It's a process I recommend for copywriters as
well.

The first attempt at writing should be not to write at all but to pour
out everything that is on your mind about the subject at hand. It's a
freeing process if it is done right and honestly. You type, write, or
doodle whatever comes to mind, including "What the hell am I trying
to say here?" or "I hate this job" or "I'd better wax my skis before I leave
this weekend."

By getting random, irrelevant, and sometimes irreverent thoughts
out on paper, you are freeing your mind to get to the task at hand. This
dump process is for your eyes only and is only a way of getting warmed
up.

After a page or two of nonsense, resentment, or corn, the juices start
to flow and random ideas show up on the page. The first few are often
terrible. They are the clichés, the slogans that someone else has done
before, or obscene plays on words making fun of your task.

Some "pump-priming" phrases that have worked for other writers
might be helpful. "The point I am trying to make is. . . . " "Imagine
yourself. . . . " "Please buy my product because. . . . " "Here's how I'm
going to change your life. . . . "

I find that this process not only gets rid of the blocks; it gets rid of
the obvious. After a few pages of stream-of-consciousness writing, the
ideas start to concentrate on the selling job you have to do. The checklists start coming to life, played back by your subconscious mind, and
sooner or later some really choice ideas start showing up. The good

ideas generate other good ideas, and soon the writer is on a creative "high," with choice ideas filling the pages. A genuine enthusiasm wells up. There is an anticipation, a sense of excitement. "Hey," you tell yourself, "this is going to be one of the best things I've ever written!"

Now you are ready. The hours or days of research, study, and planning pay off in a few hours of frenzied, productive writing.

If you build logically from the facts and begin to write, you will lack enthusiasm and that will show in your writing. If you jump in excitedly without having done your homework, the style will be there but not the substance. The process I recommend is certainly not the only approach, but it does offer one way for the direct marketing copywriter to set the mood for advertising copy that will be more than just satisfactory and may be great. One thing is certain. Your copy will be no better than the standards you set for yourself.

### Begin at the End

This advice may seem strange, but it is sincere. The first thing to write is the coupon. Most writers save it for last and treat it as a necessary nuisance along with copyright notices. They are missing a bet.

Most people, when reading an ad, don't act on it immediately. Some do tear out the ad and act on it at once. Most, however, tear out just the coupon and put it in a pile of bills to be paid or in a notebook, or just pin it to a calendar or bulletin board.

Later, when the time comes to write out the envelope and perhaps a check, the coupon itself is the only reminder of the reasons behind why they tore it out in the first place. The headline is gone. The pictures are gone. All that remains is the reply card or coupon.

At that point, which do you think would get a greater response? "Send me____widgets at $4.95 each," or "Yes. I want to double my car's gasoline mileage without sacrificing speed or power, with your new Widget Wonder-plugs (only $4.95 each) developed by the U.S. Government for the space shuttle program. I understand that if I'm not completely satisified I will get my money back by just. . . . "

Writing the coupon first not only assures that it will get the important attention it deserves but also will help you crystallize the main point of your advertising copy. Both ways, you win.

### The First Draft

Some writers prefer to visualize the entire ad, jotting down a headline and subheads in sort of a skeleton concept. This is a fast shortcut to presenting a finished idea and is handy when several different conceptual treatments must be visualized for presentation. Unfortunately, many advertisements which begin in this manner don't hold up in the finished version; the copy execution simply lacks the spark of the original idea.

My recommendation is to write the first draft of the advertisement before working out a detailed visualization and, in some cases, even before perfecting a headline or subheadlines. More often than not, good copy will suggest its own subheads, and any of them should be adaptable to main headlines.

There are as many approaches to the craft of copywriting as there are products to write about. My suggestion is to write the coupon first and the copy next, and then to extract the subcaptions and headlines from the body of the copy. If the copy is good, they'll be there. If they're not there, write new copy.

The first draft of a selling message should begin where the reader is; bridge the gap between attention and interest; create desire; fulfill need; provide positive benefits linked to product attributes; dramatize the offer; and provide proof, assurance, guarantee, and a reason to act now. In short, it should include all the selling motivations that have been determined to be appropriate for the particular proposition, even though only one of them is emphasized as the basic positioning for the advertisement or mailing piece.

The first draft is for content and should be worked on until every selling point is included in the most logical sequence and in the most persuasive manner. Then some basic decisions have to be made.

*Style*   Ninety percent of all communication is supposed to be nonverbal. How you say something has far greater impact than what you are saying. The same is true in advertising.

Copy style is like tone of voice. Layout is like body language. The tone of voice of your message has to be chosen as carefully as the elements of the copy platform. Style can support your message or contradict it. The choice of style and its appropriate use is one of the finer points of the copywriting art.

*Flow*   Once you've gotten readers into your message with the right headline and illustration, how can you keep them reading? If it's a mail piece, the prospect has other letters to glance at. In a magazine or newspaper ad, a hand is poised to turn the page at the slightest loss of interest. In a TV or radio commercial, there are snacks to be gone after, washrooms to visit, channels to change the moment your message ceases to be appealing.

Tricks of the trade can help create interest. Using numbers is one trick. "Fourteen reasons why . . . ," with numbered paragraphs, should keep people going. Subheads breaking up blocks of copy into readable eyefuls is another trick. Still a third is a narrative style in which the message unfolds in sequence as if you were describing the product to a friend.

These tricks are helpful, but they are no substitute for copy that is genuinely interesting, smoothly written, and easy to understand.

*Level*   The level of copy should also be chosen deliberately. Related to vertical positioning, copy level should reflect the self-image of potential purchasers by not being too simplistic, while recognizing that their self-image is probably well above their actual reading comprehension. The writer has to walk a tightrope in order to appear literate on the one hand and to assume a minimal vocabulary on the other. The safe bet is to keep the vocabulary simple and the style colorful, to presume nothing and explain everything.

## Making It Sing

The first draft is done. The content is complete, readable, right on target. Well done. But you're still not finished.

Of course, many writers polish up the first draft and call it an ad, and many such ads are successful. However, what makes the difference between a good writer and a great one is professionalism.

The pursuit of professionalism calls for another important step. Put the first draft aside until the next day, and forget about it. Go to a movie. Read a potboiler. Have fun. Then come back the next morning and look over the first draft as if you've never seen it before.

This time, look at it solely from the standpoint of style. Sit down and rewrite it completely, keeping the content but adding story value, entertainment, and fascination. Take the words you wrote yesterday, set them to music, and make them sing.

In the musical *My Fair Lady*, Liza Doolittle sings "Don't talk of love, show me!" Copywriters should heed this advice, especially in the final draft.

Don't say a book is entertaining. Give a sample of the humor or other satisfaction. Don't say a product will save you time in the kitchen. Describe exactly what you can make in how many minutes. Don't talk of something being informative. Start informing! Support your copy claims with specific examples, interesting examples, pertinent examples, and more examples. Examples are what's interesting to your prospective buyer, and *that's* why you did all that research when you started.

### Stopping Power

Once the selling message has been worked out for both content and style, it's time to concern yourself with stopping power—the appeals you'll use to get the envelope opened, the ad noted, the TV viewer riveted to your commercial.

This final step in producing a really effective advertisement is the moment of truth in the craft of writing copy. The selling message may be superb, but if no one stops to read it, you've wasted your time and your client's money.

The headline must instantly flag down prospective buyers and intrigue them with an offer, a broad benefit or need fulfillment, or a curiosity-provoking specific selected from the body of the advertisement. The range of headline opportunities will have widened considerably once the copy is written.

My suggestion is to put off writing the headline. Instead, go paragraph by paragraph and write pithy subheadlines with story value, curiosity, powerful benefits, and gripping emotional involvement. Then write captions for every illustration and try to come up with additional illustration ideas to dramatize every major point. Each caption should translate the interest value of an illustration into a powerful selling point. All the subheads and captions, taken together, should add up to a convincing communication which will bring in the order even if the prospect doesn't read a word of the precious copy which spawned all these ideas.

If the copy, research, and planning are done right, the copy will be excellent. If the copy is right, the subheads and captions will be superb. The problem now should not be "coming up with a headline." It should be selecting which of several very fine, very persuasive subheads or captions to use as the main headline.

Of course you can write a headline as the first step, putting down on that blank sheet of paper the first thing that pops into your head after you study the assignment. However, more often than not, such headlines are either clichés or concept statements without benefit of the subjective integration, content assembly, style rewrite, and stopping-power processes recommended here. As always, the hard way is the sure way. That's why advertising *is* hard and why it's right that it should be.

## SOME GENERAL COPY CONSIDERATIONS

No discussion of the craft of copywriting is complete without answering some questions that have been raised over the last decade and will continue to be raised in the future. To those of us in the field, some of these questions have become downright boring. I address them here only in the hope of minimizing the number of times I will have to address them in the future.

## How Long Should a Letter Be?
## An Ad? A Brochure?

The answer: long enough to do the job. There is a story of a boy who asked the unusually tall Abe Lincoln how long he thought a man's legs should be. Lincoln's now-legendary answer was, "Long enough to reach the ground."

If you are giving away something free, with no strings attached, you don't need a long letter to make your offer. If you are selling something that a prospect has never seen before, you have to show it, explain it, tell how it works, and dramatize the benefits. If your readers know you, just give your name and a tag line. If they don't, you might have to put in your whole corporate history and financial statement.

Don't be afraid of long letters—or short ones.

The thing to remember is that it is not length in itself that gives effectiveness, it is content. If you can cut a four-page letter down to two without losing a major selling point, the chances are that the two-page letter will pull just as well with a slight reduction in CPR because of the printing costs saved. The same applies to a speech, a book, or a presentation. Length is not significant; content is.

## Which Comes First, Format or Copy?

In the previous section, I advocated writing the copy before the head-line, an admittedly "backward" approach which also involved doing the rough draft before sketching out a copywriter's rough of how the ad might look in the magazine, on the air, or in the mailbox.

In print ads or television the format is usually fixed. Writers are told they have a page or 120 seconds to work with—and that's that. The format is usually dictated by media economics, and there is little ability to accommodate copy innovations.

Direct mail, however, is another matter. I am constantly amazed at clients or account people who specify, to the writer, that a mailing piece should consist of "Four-page letter, 11- by 17-inch brochure, outer envelope, reply card, lift memo." There is nothing intrinsically wrong with such a format, but there is no reason to tie the writer's hands by dictating *any* format.

The format should grow out of the copy concept. The choice of brochure or booklet depends on copy flow and illustration requirement. Whether a mailing should be "all-in-one" or a group of small pieces— an invitation, a guarantee slip, a choice dramatization folder, a die-cut product representation—is a creative consideration which should await the writer's thinking process. Chapter 15, Direct-Mail Formats, details the infinite variety of possibilities. For now, accept the idea that, in direct mail at least, the choice of formats should be a product of the creative process, not a specification.

## Handling Rush Jobs

"All this is very nice," a writer might ask, "but where do you find the time to do this step-by-step process when half the jobs you get call for 'rush' schedules?" The question is fair, and the problem is typical.

The first approach to rush jobs is to avoid them. Any account executive or product manager can appease a client or boss by saying "yes" to every request. The real professional will know when to say "no" and will insist on giving creative sources adequate time to do their job correctly.

The chances that something will go wrong in the execution increase dramatically with rush projects, and it is safer to risk offending a boss or client by saying "no" to an unreasonable request once than to risk ending up with a job that no one is happy with. If the ad doesn't work, no one will remember the time allotted, and the failure will be your fault.

Accept a rush project only when you really want to and when you are already so interested in the project and enthusiastic about the prospects of it working out well that you really want to do it. If that is the case, you'll find the time to go through each and every step listed above, taking less time for each.

Don't cut out research. Instead, have an apprentice do the research while you do your other planning. Don't eliminate the sleep-on-it phase. Just condense it into a quick nap or a fast walk around the block. If you have a rush job, don't take shortcuts. That's where trouble lies. Travel the tried and true route, but walk a lot faster.

## The Curse of Cleverness

Just as all of us fall in love with our own corny jokes, copywriters are especially prone to falling in love with their own pet phrases. That's why we can't begin with headline ideas and try to justify them with postnatal copy platforms. The planning must come first, the creativity later. That's also why copywriters cannot judge their own writing. Some element of objectivity is essential, from supervisor, account person, or client ad manager.

The greatest temptation to be "clever" instead of "craftsmanlike" is peer group pressure. Every art has its critics, and artisans tend to try to impress their critics instead of their customers. You've seen it in novels or poetry with eccentric but unreadable styles, in plays with obscure plots, in paintings whose themes were conceived in marijuana and interpretable only under opium.

In art and literature, people sometimes gain national attention and critical acclaim just by being different, and this approach might also work in some fields of general advertising. In direct marketing, however, such acclaim—if it comes at all—will last only until the coupons come in. In this field the only real critics are the thousands of potential customers west of the Hudson River who won't give 2 cents if your concept is cute or your execution different but will give $20 or more if you can convince them that your client's product is one they need and want.

Sure, a clever ad or mailing might look good in your "book" when you apply for your next job, but consider that perhaps you'd be better off with fewer clever samples and the reputation for results that makes it unnecessary for you to keep a book at all or to apply for another job ever.

## Repetition: Right or Wrong?

Another area where battle lines are frequently drawn is repetition. I don't mean the kind of repetition used by general advertisers, who find it desirable to repeat ad themes and brand names to reinforce awareness.

I do mean the key point that's flagged in the headline, mentioned in the subhead, illustrated and described in a photo caption, referred to in a brochure and lift letter, and then summarized in the body copy and on the response card.

"Reiteration" is a better word than "repetition" for what I am advocating, for there is no need to say the same thing again in the same way. There is a need to put your best copy claim forward in every part of your message, in any medium, that might be read by your prospect.

You have no way of knowing what part of your message is going to be read first. Some research shows that a postscript is the most-read and often the first-read part of a sales letter. In some cases, depending on format and graphics, the brochure may be read before the letter, or a supplementary flyer may be the first thing out of the envelope.

In an ad, people attracted by the illustration may read the caption before they read the headline. Others may read the coupon before the body copy. If you have a principal selling point, get it out front in every part of your message which might conceivably turn out to be the first part read.

Newspaper preprints offer a clear illustration. Writers often put a great headline on page 1 of a four-page insert and use the back page for miscellaneous points. When the insert falls out of the newspaper, however, the back is just as likely to be seen first as the front. Thus the principal selling theme must be evident on page 4, perhaps worded differently.

Though repetition is desirable, there is no reason to present a selling point the same way over and over again. To avoid boring the reader who comes across the point a second or third time, reword it. Give a different example or a different analogy, and at the very least, use a fresh choice of words.

Presume that your first expression of the main theme is what stopped the prospects and got them to read your message in the first place. You know the message has appeal, or they wouldn't be reading, so keep it in front of the readers' minds by reinserting it in each and every main segment of the ad, mailing, or TV commercial. Be sure to make the message fresh at the moment of truth when you are asking the readers to fill out the coupon.

## EVALUATING ADVERTISING COPY

In evaluating your own or someone else's advertising copy, here are some simple tests that will separate the children from the grown-ups.

*The Tightness Test*   Try to cut the copy. Sit down with a blue pencil and see how much shorter you can make it without deleting a material selling point. If it's easy, the copy is soft, mushy, fatty, or whatever pejorative fits your style. If the copy is hard to cut without breaking up the flow or omitting an important point, then you've got tight, meaty, hard copy—the real thing.

*Interchangeability*   Take out the name of your product and see if you can use the same copy for a competitor or another product. Your ad should be uniquely appropriate to your proposition. If it fits others just as easily, the marketing plan lacks a unique selling proposition.

*The Glance Test*   Give yourself five seconds to look quickly at the headlines, subheads, and captions. Is there enough meat to convince you that you want to read the rest of the ad? If not, then move your project back to "Go," and don't collect $200.

Then give yourself ten to fifteen seconds to read all the heads and subheads that call out to you in large, boldface type. Do they do a selling job in their own right? For instance, is a "contents" listing headlined "Table of contents" or "The secret of eternal life and 88 other things you must know"? Every head, subhead, and caption should be a selling message in itself, and the whole should make the sale even if the reader does not read one single word of body copy.

*Intelligibility*    Ask your secretary, the receptionist, and the elevator operator to read the ad. They don't have to be prospects and the ad doesn't have to interest them, but they should be able to understand what in the world you are talking about.

I have been amazed to discover that points I thought were obvious and clear were completely misunderstood by exactly the people who should have followed them without difficulty. So, let people who have had nothing to do with the creation of the ad or mailing piece read it, and have them play back what they think you said. If the playback is way off base, you may want to do a more professional job of seeing whether the copy is clear by running it through a focus panel or two.

I have heard writers defend their work by elaborating on copy points. My answer is, "If you promise to accompany each and every copy of this ad or mailing and offer the same explanation, I'll approve it. Otherwise, make the ad stand on its own."

*Actionability*    Now ask people to respond to the ad. Do they know exactly what to do, or do they start asking unnecessary questions? Is the coupon easy to fill out? Are the prices and any extra charges clearly understood? Is the phone number clear and legible, and is the fact that it's toll-free easily discernible?

You should be able to hand the ad to anyone in your office and say "Order this for me" with no further explanation. If an explanation is necessary, check through the response devices all over again.

## A TRIBUTE TO COPYWRITERS

Maybe because I started as a copywriter, I expect writers to be the miracle workers of the advertising business. All the marketing planning, all the steps developing strategy and inventing tactics, have one basic presumption: that copywriters can do anything.

Like the debating society member who can argue any side of the question, the copywriter must be prepared to sell any product to any audience with any positioning. For anyone who thinks writing copy is easy, let me offer a challenge:

First, take a product, any product—preferably one that you see being handled poorly—or take fund raising for a worthy charity.

Describe the product on every level—practical, scientific, and emotional—as discussed in the pencil example in Chapter 3. Imagine that you are the audience. Prepare a copy platform and write some ad concepts.

Then adjust the style up-scale or down. Vary the horizontal positioning, and rewrite the ad for an earlier position.

Then change the size unit. What would you do differently in a small-space ad? In a double-page spread?

Then change the medium. Rewrite the ad for television or radio. Or change the style so it is appropriate for direct mail.

Then dramatize a benefit, feature the offer, do an audience-selection ad, or lead with a premium.

The copywriter doesn't have to do all these things with every assignment, of course. Writers do have to have the inner conviction that their skills are ready and waiting and that they can produce winning direct marketing communications for any product in any medium at any positioning. Versatility is the mark of a truly professional writer. To paraphrase Star Wars, "May the skill be with you!"

## CHAPTER FOURTEEN

# ADVERTISING LAYOUT

Too commonly the art department is considered a mere implementer of creative strategies developed by marketers and writers. Art directors are capable of making profound contributions to the overall creative process. Exceptional art directors should be part of the team that develops overall strategic plans, and good ones should make a recognizable contribution to a finished ad or mailing piece, rather than simply implementing the thinking of others.

The really fine art directors who know and appreciate the challenge of direct marketing are skilled practitioners whose talents could produce any kind of advertising.

As such talent is hard to find or to recruit, I am outlining some principles and rules which, if followed, can help less skilled artists produce superb, thoughtful executions, as well as helping advertising managers and account executives understand and discuss layouts in consistent terms.

The examples in this chapter are all for print advertising. The more flexible applications available for direct mail and broadcast will be discussed in subsequent chapters.

## SELECTIVITY

It is the art director who must bring to life the ideas in the marketing plan and the words in the copy. Subtle changes in type face, size, location, and format can convey different images and stress different aspects of the final message.

Copy style is tone of voice in nonverbal communication, and layout is the equivalent of body language. The art director should be capable of taking the same copy and adapting it to any positioning, any image, any emphasis, any media, any audience.

The same message can be laid out to stress the headline, the illustration, the copy, the coupon, the offer, the lead item, the end product, the endorser, the guarantee. It is up to the art director to make the selections necessary to convey entirely different moods—elegance, bargain price, stability, excitement—all with identical copy.

An interesting exercise for art directors is to lay out a common ad several times to stress different elements, and then lay it out for a different medium or turn it into a TV commercial. This exercise will remind art directors of their immense influence on the finished product, as well as the immense flexibility with which they can approach their work.

## FIVE BASIC PRINCIPLES

My work with art directors has led to the identification of five basic principles which all well-executed layouts have in common. These five Cs of advertising layout are concentration, cohesion, convention, contrast, and convection.

### The Principle of Concentration

*Attention-getting ability is proportional to the size of the largest single element, not to the total size of the ad.* A small space unit with a single large element—a word, a headline, an illustration—will get more attention than a unit the same size or even larger, with smaller elements.

To understand this, look at newspapers. The article perceived to be the most important is not the longest one but the one with the biggest, boldest headline.

In any advertising layout, or in any art form for that matter, balance is dull. Everything can't be equal. An artist or the creator of an ad must make a deliberate choice about which visual element should be the most important.

I have seen full-page ads so cluttered with conflicting subheads competing for attention that the reader must be confused and bewildered. At the other extreme, I have done a successful ad that was only 2 inches on one column, with a 1-inch-high black, bold headline: "Opium!" This small advertisement for Evergreen's reprint of the Jean Cocteau classic achieved very acceptable order costs.

Some ads are built around a dominant illustration, perhaps a square halftone photograph taking 60 percent of the page. Others have a clean, dominant headline which is obviously the place to start reading, and which does not have to compete for attention with other elements of the same ad.

Imagine, for a moment, two billboards along a highway. One is 50 feet high and has a 5-foot-high message. The other is 25 feet high and has a 10-foot-high message. It is obvious that the size of the message, not the size of the billboard, will determine how far away motorists see it and how many it will attract.

Whether your unit is large or small, and whether your medium is print or broadcast or direct mail, it must attract attention by the inherent strength of the lead element, not by the total size of the page or printed piece or by the total length of the message.

### The Principle of Cohesion

*The space in any direction between elements of a graphic presentation should not exceed the space between the message and the border of the layout.* This rule sounds simple and obvious, but it is constantly ignored in direct-response advertising. The violations usually take place in the art studio, where a fine layout is turned over to unmotivated production artists for type specification and mechanical paste-up.

Cohesion is most frequently absent where it is most needed: in newspaper advertising. An ad "breaks up" if the space between the headline and the body copy is greater than that between the headline and the adjoining advertisement, or if the headline or closing copy is isolated by white space from the main selling paragraphs. Some advertisements might have been more effective if the agency had simply purchased less space, instead of a standard unit, and closed up all the elements.

Does this mean that "white space" doesn't belong in direct-response advertising? No. But white space, like any other styling, selling, or attention-getting element, has to be used in conjunction with all the other elements and not as an end in itself. For instance, I prefer to distribute leading throughout the body copy rather than have extra space between paragraphs.

What should the art director do when divisive space appears on the mechanical paste-up? Here are some idea starters: (1) Enlarge the most important element, probably the headline or key illustration, and tighten up the remaining elements. (2) Reset the body copy in a larger or more leaded type. (3) Move all the elements toward the center of the advertisement or mailing piece, and let the white space add to the margin around the message.

The principle of cohesion is vital in fractional-unit advertising. Layouts for such ads should always be pasted in the newspaper or magazine to see how the ad will look on a busy page. Don't cheat! Pick the busiest page, not the one you would most like the ad to appear on. There should never be more space between elements of your layout than there is between your layout and the next ad.

## The Principle of Convention

There is a principle in fine art called "convention," which refers to the perceptor's past experience and associations as an influence on how new perceptions are evaluated.

For instance, imagine for a moment that an artist has taken a canvas and painted the bottom half green and the top half blue. Most viewers, when asked to guess what is being portrayed, would call it a landscape, with the green bottom representing grass and the blue top the sky. Add some white blobs in the top area and, depending on their size and the color blue used, they will be perceived as clouds or stars. A yellow blob might be seen as a sun or moon, depending on the total coloring.

Typeface studies have shown that the eye reads reflected light, not darkness, and that theoretically white type on a green or dark blue background should be the most readable. Yet, because people are not used to reading books or newspapers in this way, reverse type is difficult to read.

*Quality Perceptions*    Perceptions of quality, cheapness, bargain price, and elegance are all influenced by past experiences. If you look at department store windows, for instance, you'll see that a cluttered window is used to convey the feeling of a sale. A stark, relatively empty window, with only one or two mannikins displaying the new season's fashions, is used when the garments are exclusive and expensive.

*Type Associations*    Typography is also associated with past experiences and conveys its own form of nonverbal communication as the "body language" of an advertising message.

A sans-serif typeface such as Univers or Helvetica is associated with modernity. A traditional book face such as Garamond, Caslon, or Times Roman is the classic kind of face associated with books, magazines, and newspapers, and so implies reliability, authority, and credibility.

Type at an angle, or noncursive italic, gives the impression of speed or imminence. Bold faces convey importance or loudness, thin faces quiet or restraint. Gothics and other historic faces are associated with tradition, the old, perhaps the tried and true.

A bold Franklin Gothic face implies "Headline!" in most parts of the country, and the presumption is that its message is an important announcement. Century Schoolbook, a standard textbook face, seems right for an educational message. Bauer Bodoni is a modernized serif face, with a good combination of readability and a contemporary look. Various pseudoengraving faces are reminiscent of invitations and wedding announcements, and suggest elegance and exclusivity.

*Pictorial associations*   Both the choice of illustrations and their style constitute another form of body language. Luxury settings imply a luxury product, which is why expert photographers spend as much time finding the right props as worrying about lighting. A picture of a spokesperson suggests sincerity and straightforwardness but also hard selling. A diagram or blueprint suggests that the product is well made.

All these illustration and typography associations, as you can see, do convey images and messages independently of the words and subjects involved. These layout considerations should be planned in accordance with the basic strategy and tactics, so that the visual communication supports the copy theme rather than conflicting with it.

## The Principle of Contrast

The chameleon, which survives by blending into its environment, should be the mascot of any art department, not as an inspiration but as a reminder of the deadliest sin of advertising art.

The first law of layout is to be noticed. In any medium, to be noticed your message must look different from its environment.

If a newspaper ad blends into the newspaper's editorial content or looks like just another advertisement, if a magazine ad looks like every other ad in the publication, if a radio or television commercial blends into the program or into preceding commercials, you are throwing your money away.

Your advertisement must stand out. Your mailing must look fresh and different from the others in the day's mail. Your commercial must make people stop and take notice.

Boutique layouts which give a particular art studio or agency's work a distinctive look is good business for the supplier but not for the client whose money is being spent. The last thing in the world you want the prospect to say is, "Oh, isn't that clever. It's just like the ads for. . . ."

The artistic expression should not call attention to itself at the expense of the message. The object is not to cause people to say "What a clever (or pretty) ad!" or (even worse) "What a clever artist (or agency)!" The object is to catch the reader's eye, to present the sales message clearly, and to use graphics to visually support that message, all leading to an immediate positive action in response to the proposition.

A corporate style is just as damaging. A corporate quality image or trade logotype may be desirable, to establish identity and authority once a message is being read, but it should not stand in the way of getting attention in the first place.

If people think they know what your ad is going to say, they won't read it. If a bank, for example, sends out all its promotions in envelopes which look identical (perhaps to falsely economize on printing costs), prospects will presume that the mailing is making the same offer as previous ones. The envelope will go unopened, the letter unread, and the proposition unconsidered.

Copycatting is self-defeating in a dozen ways, not the least of which is that the advertiser being copied is probably moving on to another format just as you are copying the old one. *Newsweek* came to us at a time when almost everyone in the field was planning to imitate their Mead-Digit subscription package which featured the prospect's name, for the first time, in large bold type. Every week brought an announcement from another supplier who was putting in that equipment or a request from a client who wanted to try the *Newsweek* approach. What *Newsweek* knew was that the technique was already fatiguing, which is why they were looking for fresh approaches.

Cycles seem to exist in advertising layout. Sam Sugar of Sussman & Sugar, Inc., the leading book-promotion agency, once observed that the first step for an art director was to review the publication an ad was going to run in and to determine what the current fad was so you could go the opposite way. Sure enough, for two years I saw other book advertisers follow each other back and forth like sheep, with borders, white space, dark backgrounds.

The same thing happens in typography. Every typeface has had its fad. I have seen our industry overdose in Optima, Helvetica, Caledonia with descenders, and Century Schoolbook. It's as if some secret newsletters, like the ones in the fashion world, forecast the type of the month and so made the prediction come true. The smart move is to watch what everyone else is doing and find a way to make your own ads look distinctively different.

## The Principle of Convection

Once you've managed, through concept, copy, and layout treatment, to attract the right readers and get them into your message, the job that remains is to keep them there long enough to get enough copy read to make the sale.

This is a matter of "flow" or "convection," the art of designing the message in a manner that carries the reader along in a logical fashion from one element to the other, right to the coupon.

In an ad you want to stop readers with a headline or illustration, and then pay off the promise or curiosity in a subhead or in the first paragraph of copy. You then want the main copy to read in a manner that takes the reader to the point of action, the coupon or phone.

Support elements, the readership of which is optional, should be placed in a way that doesn't disrupt the primary copy flow. Items such as feature listings, testimonial panels, credentials, or detailed specifications should be there for those who want them but should be out of the mainstream.

If you are pulling for inquiries for an automobile, for example, the inclusion of technical specifications is necessary for some readers, but for others it would be a distraction—a turnoff that would get them to stop reading altogether. Therefore, optional elements must be handled so they are optional reading as well.

Draw a line down the main copy story to indicate how you think the reader will follow the message. Then ask someone else, an uninvolved writer or artist, to look at another copy of the same ad and draw a similar flow line. If the two lines are different, then perhaps the flow is not as obvious as you think it is.

In a mailing piece the flow should be just as well defined. The first thing prospects look at is their own names on the outer envelope, and then they look again wherever their names appear. Nothing is as fascinating as our own image, signature, photograph, or other personalization.

The back of the envelope is less critical than the copy and image portrayed on the front. You cannot count on the reader to turn to the back, so there should be enough incentive to get the envelope opened even if the back is never seen.

The rest of the elements should then be collated in a logical manner. If you don't want the price to be the first thing seen, cover it with a fold or flap.

If you want the letter to be the first thing read, address the letter and let that be the envelope show-through, and let it be the first thing seen when the envelope is opened. The element seen through the window of an envelope will be the first thing seen inside, and everything else will be viewed after that.

If you want a color broadside to be the next thing read, then be sure it is the next thing viewed. Supplementary inserts should be smaller, or less colorful, so they don't cover up or distract from the main pieces. If everything is equally important, or equally interesting, then you have no control over the flow of the message.

One trick of the trade that applies to both letters and long copy advertisements is to recognize that curiosity is a more powerful drive than a plea such as "see next column" or "see other side." Paragraphs should never be completed at the bottom of a column or a page, even though every secretarial school trains typists to strive for this. Instead, interrupt the last line in midsentence and, better yet, in midthought. Use the natural desire to complete things as a force to encourage readership of your sales message.

Don't build barriers within your ads. Subheads that are larger size than the body copy will actually interrupt readership of the copy instead of encourage it. You may want only the subheads read, if you believe they tell the whole story and the copy is purely optional, in which case their size should be exaggerated. Do this only when the copy is weak and you want it passed by.

Bold borders that break up copy elements into panels will force the reader to "jump" from one to the other and leave half of them unread. It is better to use borders to separate optional reading elements or to separate your ad from others.

A photo can be a barrier also. Don't expect readers to continue reading a column of type if, in the middle, you distract them with a photo and caption. Such photos can break up the look of an ad to make it appear more attractive to read, but place them alongside the main theme rather than in its path. Illustrations should be supportive—pleasant additions to a copy point made on the way to the coupon payoff—rather than competitive.

The five principles of concentration, cohesion, convention, contrast, and convection apply to all advertising, but their violation shows up faster and more directly in the measurable world of direct marketing than in general advertising.

## SOME SPECIFICS

### Illustrations

The first question is, almost always, whether to use a photograph or to use a painting or drawing. There is no doubt about the answer; it has been the subject of split-run testing. Photography, with all its realism, is clearly the winner, particularly with product illustrations.

That is not to say that there aren't times when drawings or diagrams will be superior to make a point or to illustrate something that doesn't lend itself to photographs. Good artwork can often contribute to a unique style, set a mood, or dramatize a benefit better than photos.

When taking a photograph, you should strive for action, motion, and dimension. Even a straight product shot can be given a sense of action by surrounding it with props that make it appear to be in use or about to be used.

Motion is difficult to capture, but showing it makes the difference between "posed-looking" shots and candid news photographs. A good model doesn't look like a model.

Dimension, a matter of lighting and camera angles, is essential if a photograph is going to "come alive" and do more than lie flat on the page. The standard is realism.

Working with a photographer, the art director should be involved with every basic decision. Most important is the choice of models. This should never be left up to the photographer. Instead, go through the submissions of the model agencies yourself. When you find one you like, check with the modeling agency to be sure the photograph is current.

The standard for selecting models is not whether you find them attractive but whether your prospects will relate to them. The ages and styles of models determine whether they are people the prospect can identify with or people who can be perceived as authority figures. The choice depends on the theme of the advertisement.

Once the model is hired, talk with him or her in person to explain the nature of the shot and the kind of clothing and hairstyle that will be needed. It is amazing how little information is given to models by agents and photographers unless you take the time to do it yourself.

Then be at the session. See the shot through the camera as the photographer does (even though it may be upside down.) You may see something that other people overlook—subtleties like scratches on your product or too suggestive a pose. Also, of course, you and the art director should see the contact prints and select which shot should be blown up for final retouching.

Working with an illustrator is very similar, except that you see sketches instead of a photography session. The illustrator will most likely work with a "swipe file" of photos and other ads. Get agreement on the subject, the style, and the dress. I once had to reject an illustration because an artist dressed a character in a tuxedo in an ad for a mass-market book club. In another rejected illustration, retirees who were supposed to be pleased that they had invested in gold coins were drawn with insipid grins.

Cost control is always a problem. Negotiating art costs should never be left solely up to the art director, who is likely to be too sympathetic to the needs of peers in the art world. The art budget should always be approved by a product manager or account executive who has the total project budget in mind.

Costs have to be kept in perspective, related to the value of the medium the illustrations are being used in and the total promotion budget. While I am usually the first to raise an eyebrow over the photography session that "must" be shot in the Caribbean or the commercial that can "only" be filmed in California, I will admit that there are times when such expenditures are justified.

## Typography

Typography is the unheralded fine art of commercial layout. Of the tens of thousands of graduates of art schools, all are taught type as well as design and illustration, but only a handful, often relatives of printers or book designers, emerge with a genuine love for type.

Every creative organization should have at least one person who not only knows how to use typography but loves to work with it, for only that person will appreciate the infinite subtleties that go far beyond specifying type.

Sure, type must be selected and must fit the message to the available space, and anyone can be trained to count characters, use a Haberule, or otherwise "spec" type—but that has nothing to do with designing with type.

*Type Has Style*    Each and every typeface has been designed to convey a feeling which is somewhat different from all other types that had ever been designed before it. The simplicity of Futura has given way to subtler shadings of Univers, Helvetica, and Optima. The classic readability of Caslon has been joined by varieties of Baskerville, Bodoni, and Roman. There is an infinite variety of stylistic faces: the heaviness of Cooper Black, the playfulness of Kaleidoscope, the starkness of Stymie, and the stylistic games of playful Mediterranean faces like Memphis, Karnak, Cairo, and Delta.

For an advertisement or mailing piece, a typeface must be selected that, overall, conveys the positioning selected for the project. It must have the flexibility of providing the shadings necessary for subheads, captions, emphasis, or parenthetical comments. Of course, it must also be easy to read.

You can choose more than one face if you really know what you are doing, but mixing and matching typefaces is as dangerous as trying to match slacks and jacket instead of buying a suit. Sometimes separates come out fine and sometimes they look awful; but you can't go wrong wearing a suit.

Within each typeface there are usually light and bold styles, regular and italic (cursive and/or noncursive versions), and an infinite range of sizes. There was a time when typography was ordered only by point sizes, and you were limited by those precise sizes. Now, with photo-typesetting, you can ask for any line width you want, and can even condense or expand a typeface to your needs. Hand lettering can also create a variety of very worthwhile special effects.

*Leading*    Just as important as the selection of the type is the spacing between lines, called "leading." If you order an 8 point type and have no space between lines, it is set "solid" or "8 on 8."

This is usually somewhat difficult to read (except for some typefaces which are "small-bodied," with oversize ascenders and descenders). As mentioned above, the eye supposedly reads reflected light, the white space around type, not the type itself. Therefore the spacing between lines may contribute more to readability than the size of the type. As a result, I would usually prefer 8 on 9 to 8 solid or even 9 solid. Incidentally, the phrases refer back to the days when all type was cast in metal, and the "on" was the base slug which dictated the spacing.

The size of type to choose for text copy is relative to the surroundings. In a publication like *TV Guide,* which uses fairly small faces, you can safely use 6 on 7 for body copy. In newspapers or a large brochure, a larger face is usually more appropriate.

Age is an important determinant. Children like large type, and older people, whether they admit it to themselves or not, may have difficulty reading conventional type sizes and would prefer not having to get their reading glasses. Many advertisers whose propositions are aimed at older people go out of their way to keep typefaces large.

Another key factor is motivation. If the headline and initial subhead are so interesting that the prospect wants to read the rest, the size will be irrelevant. In fact, in earlier direct marketing ads, it used to be customary to drop type sizes down every few paragraphs.

Condensing a typeface can often save space more effectively than going down to a smaller type size or cutting out leading.

Simplicity is the byword of good type design. A safe way to design an ad is to pick a readable book face and use the boldface for the headline and all subheads. Using italic may work for captions, or you could use a smaller size. The body copy, subheads, and coupon copy could be the same size, with any insert panels a size smaller. You can't go wrong with this kind of design.

The opposite approach is to mix a half-dozen faces and present the reader with a hodgepodge of clutter and confusion. One agency I worked in gave no consideration to cleanliness in typography. If, as a copy-writer, I underlined a word in a headline, it would show up underlined (which is what I wanted) but also bolder, larger, capitalized, and in italic. If the ad was in color, it would also be red. The overall effect of this kind of overdoing it was, in a word, *CONFUSION.*

To be readable, lines of type can't be too long or too short. One rule says thirty characters is the minimum and fifty the maximum for each line. The question is more complex than any rule, and really requires good judgement about what is readable and important and what is inviting to read.

### Rules on Using Rules

Nothing can do as much good, or as much harm, to an advertising or direct-mail layout as a simple border. Lines can separate elements, combine them, isolate them to an irrelevant corner, or dramatize them. They can focus attention, or they can distract.

The illustrations below show some basic kinds of rules. I'll review these first and then discuss how to use them in layouts.

A. Bold solid line ▬▬▬▬▬

B. Fine rule ————

C. Framing border ══════

D. Vertical rule |

E. Styling rule

F. Dashed rule ----------

    A. Bold solid lines are a powerful aid to cohesiveness. They bring elements of a layout together into a unified whole and help them stand out on a page filled with competing layouts. However, care must be taken to be sure that what stands out is not just a busy blob of diverse elements surrounded by a heavy border. What readers perceive first should still be a headline or illustration calculated to stop them. This always requires establishing a relationship between the border and headline type. The rule is: *Border rules should be as wide as the thickest section of the headline typeface.* Heavy rules used within a layout are almost always divisive, breaking up the flow of the reader's attention. For use within a layout, fine rules or framing borders are usually better.

    B. Fine rules are best used within a layout to separate various copy elements or illustrations. Fine rules can be used relatively liberally, providing they do not become a crutch for the layout artist. Good typography and spacing should provide a logical flow of the selling message as part of the intrinsic design of the layout, even without the addition of rules. The rules should strengthen the layout, not be the layout.

The relationship between type and fine rules is the opposite of the relationship given above for bold rules: *Internal rules should be as wide as the thinnest section of the adjoining typeface.*

C. Framing borders combine at least two thicknesses of rules to center attention on one side of the border as opposed to the other. When a heavy and light line are combined, the combination seems to direct one's attention to the side of the rule where the line is lightest, or thinnest. This type of rule was used extensively in the earlier days of advertising when type was set in hot metal and mats or electrotype plates pulled directly from a locked-up chase; only illustrations required engravings. As production technology developed, such rules could be drawn by hand rather than set with lead rules, but only Book-of-the-Month Club, to my knowledge, has continued to make extensive use of this device.

Perhaps because they are not used extensively, framing borders are a valuable tool to consider when planning a layout. Often the addition of framing borders is all that is needed to focus attention on an important but otherwise unnoticeable copy or visual element.

D. Vertical rules are often used between columns of copy or product listings, to add a "contemporary" look to a long-copy advertisement. Theoretically, such rules should help keep readers from "jumping across" to the adjoining column when you want them to read down. They are valuable either when vertical column spacing is too tight and more separation is needed or when it is too loose and more cohesion is needed. Same firms—Quality Paperback Book Club for instance—use them as part of their design format.

E. Styling rules are valuable where an advertiser is building corporate identity for a multiproduct advertising program. I first encountered the use of such rules at Sussman & Sugar. They prepared unique rules for each of their clients, including Simon and Schuster and Random House.

Consider graphics for such borders. One of the most famous contemporary borders, and the most ingenious, is the grassy or floral borders used by Doyle Dane Bernbach for O. M. Scott. This border has even been adapted for all television advertising and product packaging for this company. A tennis magazine uses a border simulating tennis balls. Certificate borders always imply value.

F. Dashed rules, the standby of direct-response advertisers, are traditionally used to surround the coupon in an advertisement. They are supposed to suggest cutting with scissors, and with the help of a convention which was established in childhood with paper dolls,

they do just that. Advertisers whose positioning permits some cor-
niness or cuteness have been known to add a drawing of scissors
at such a line.

A variation is the dotted line, meant to suggest both tearing and
signing on the dotted line, by weaker conventions. Both of the
original conventions are no longer strong, and thus the devices are
only styling variations today, not really conventions.

Even the dashed line should bear some relationship to the type. It
should be no thinner than the thinnest part of the typeface it en-
closes and no thicker than the thickest part.

## Designing Coupons

In Chapter 13 I suggested that writers work on the coupon first, as a
way of crystallizing the basic purpose of the advertisement. Although
I do not give the same advice to art directors, the design of the coupon
should nevertheless be assigned a great deal of importance.

I have seen too many art directors work out the placement of headlines, copy blocks, and illustrations and leave a blank area for the
coupon. As the coupon is likely to be torn out for later use, and at that
time become a self-contained selling piece and response form, it must
contain the basic elements and positioning of the overall message.

Within the borders of the coupon or reply card, there should be a
simple restatement of the basic offer, possibly combined with a spur
to action. "Mail this card today to get your free copy" is the right kind
of headline, as opposed to just "Mail this card."

The ordering copy and the address should be simple, legible, and
to the point, without crowding. Small type inspires distrust, and this
is not the place to use a "type squeezer" or "shoehorn."

The "name, address, city" part of the coupon should be easy to fill
out, leaving enough space for long surnames and addresses.

Options or credit card information should also be designed with
great care. The placement and positioning of these elements in the
layout will materially affect the response.

For instance, if a credit option is built into the ordering paragraph
and a cash-enclosed option is separate, you might have a 3 to 1 or 4 to
1 ratio for the credit responses. If the options are treated equally, after
the order paragraph, the response will switch to 2 to 1 for credit or
perhaps come in evenly. Presenting the options "( ) Check enclosed"
and "( ) Bill me later" forces a decision. Otherwise inertia pushes people
to the option that does not have to be selected. The same principles
apply to presenting options such as "large size" and "small size" or
other trade-ups.

Telephone ordering options can be highlighted with a small drawing of a telephone or with a large telephone number, if telephone ordering is desirable for the particular proposition.

In a mailing piece, long commitments or credit terms can be contained in a stub or flap. This makes the ordering portion as simple as possible and yet still makes all sales and legal data visible at the time the coupon is filled out.

Don't be afraid of complicated coupons. The trick is to take the elements, experiment, and find a way to simplify them. At one point Columbia Record Club invited readers to accept a long commitment; select a music division; write in the six-digit numbers of thirteen records; fill in their telephone numbers; choose cartridges, cassettes, tapes, or records; pick the first selection at a special discount; and use a "gold box" if they saw the offer on television—all within a standard-size coupon.

## FIRST-AID KIT FOR ART DIRECTORS

Here are a few suggestions for art directors who are on the firing line, and for those who have to judge the art director's work.

### How to Spot a Bad Layout

- The message doesn't stand out from other ads.

- The image is contradictory to the theme of the copy.

- The mood is completely inappropriate for the medium.

- The ad blends in perfectly with the publication.

- It reminds you of another mailing piece you liked or didn't like.

- It's another expression of the latest fad.

- It's static. People look at one phrase or illustration and never "get off the dime."

- It's too busy. Readers jump from point to point contrary to the flow of the message.

- The ad calls attention to itself; it's designed to win awards rather than sell.

- Everything is important, or nothing is important.

- The ad is hard to read; the type is too small or crowded.

## Improving a Bad Layout

If a layout is finished and doesn't look right, here are ways to improve the ad or mailing piece.

- *Exaggerate or emphasize something.* Emphasize the headline, the illustration, the coupon, even the body copy. Take it "out of proportion" and deliberately throw the design "off balance." Balance is static; we need motion, action, and dynamism. Taking one element and filling 40 or 60 percent of the printed area with it will give you a whole new look.

- *Add people.* A spokesperson, a delighted customer opening a box and seeing your product, or a picture of a satisfied user can help a bad layout. People are interested in people.

- *Put the product in use.* Take it out of the package and show it being used. Add diagrams, sequence photos, or anything that will make the product come alive.

- *Change the typography.* Start all over and get an entirely different mood by working with different typefaces. Simplify the type and work within one family exclusively, or add one contrasting face for emphasis. Warm the ad up with a serif face and a cursive italic, or modernize it with a sans-serif face and a noncursive italic.

- *Pull the ad or mailing together.* Use white space at the exterior, use borders or background tints with consistent line spacing, or try to get a clearer flow of ideas from one point to the next.

- *Break the ad up.* Isolate the important elements with internal space and internal rules, or make the copy more inviting to read with bolder subheads and minor illustrations, with indents and handwritten annotations.

- *Follow Thoreau's advice.* "Simplify. Simplify. Simplify." Take a complicated headline and isolate one pertinent phrase. Take a headline with lead-ins and subheads and put in one long, simplified headline phrase. Take optional elements and isolate them with different faces, panels, or tints. Talk to the writer and share your problem, and see if copy can be cut to give you the space you need to simplify, simplify, simplify.

## CHAPTER FIFTEEN

# DIRECT-MAIL FORMATS

Format is the critical design element in direct mail, requiring the economical integration of creative and production processes to produce maximum communications impact.

In Chapter 14 we discussed design and layout principles which apply to any form of communication: a simple newspaper ad, a full-color magazine spread, a computer letter, a full-color brochure, a simple buck-slip insert, or the supers on a television commercial.

In direct mail, the art director's job increases a hundredfold, for the creative possibilities are multidimensional. The direct-mail art director not only has to know all the disciplines and technology of the general advertising art director but also has to understand what can be done with paper; printing; computer forms; personalization techniques; and the flexibilities and limitations of envelope fabricators, label affixers, and processes for collating and inserting mail.

In direct mail you have the space you need to use every trick in the book of direct marketing psychology. You can dramatize and personalize, and you can provide incentives. You can take advantage of the play instinct with scores of involvement devices. You have all the space you need to ask for the order on the most complex or expensive purchase, to explain commitments, to ask for credit information. Direct mail is unlike space advertising or broadcast in that you do not have to fit your message into the format; you can fit the format to your message.

## CONSIDERATIONS IN DIRECT-MAIL FORMATS

The essential considerations in every direct-mail design project include response stimulation, personalization, involvement, and economy.

## Response Stimulation

No matter how you stop the reader—with curiosity, self-interest, a powerful offer, a dramatic benefit—the payoff is asking the reader to send in the reply card. My recommendation here is similar to what I recommend in other media: Work out the reply card first.

Ease of response is the first consideration. You want to make it as easy as possible for the prospect to fill out your coupon and mail it. Preaddressing the name and address with a computer or label not only facilitates response but ensures that you will retrieve key codes, account numbers, or other data.

Incentives for fast response should be visible right on the response card, including any premiums for fast action or offer expiration dates. You should work on the assumptions that your prospect might not mail this card for a few days and that the rest of the mailing will have been discarded by that time.

Like all other pieces in a direct-mail package, the reply card should be capable of standing alone and should provide sufficient incentive to make the sale even if nothing else is read. See the discussions of coupons in Chapters 13 and 14 for further examples.

Even if a card can be a self-mailer, it usually is worth the extra cost to also provide an envelope. If the offer involves confidential or financial services or asks any kind of personal question, such as age, an envelope is essential.

Often the response card is the lead insert: the first piece visible through the envelope window and the piece personalized with the prospect's own name. This piece will be seen first. Therefore it is necessary to emphasize the positives about the offer and to obscure any negatives (such as price) until the prospect has had a chance to read the other sales pieces in the envelope.

In other cases, the reply card may be nested inside letters and brochures and may not be the first thing seen at all. It is then necessary to help the prospect find the card. To accomplish this, you have to refer to the card, and so it should have both a name and a color. For instance, "Send the reply card now" gives no help in finding the card in a complicated mailing. Consider, instead, "Send the red super-value certificate. . . . "

Many of the involvement devices to be discussed below are intended to facilitate response, as are some personalization devices.

## Personalization

Only direct mail, with the help of computer data and related high-speed printing technology, can facilitate the infinite range of personalization available today. It is one of this medium's most unique capabilities.

*Sorting*   Sorting is the simplest segmentation that can take place when address labels are prepared, permitting a message to be selected depending on demographic, geographic, or psychographic data. This personalization consists simply of inserting a different preprinted letter depending on the list or adding a special buck slip to address a type of prospect. For example, a magazine might include a special insert for people who once subscribed, or a slip announcing that a forthcoming issue will have an important article on a subject which, according to the list the prospect is on, should be of particular interest.

*Name Reference*   The next phase of personalized direct-mail design is the computer fill-in of the customer's name in the body of a letter, on the reply card which shows through the window envelope, or in other inserts.

These techniques usually involve the use of a window envelope to permit the addressed material to show through. It would ordinarily be difficult to match the personalized inserts with computer-printed envelopes, except in small quantities. A patented process of the Kurt Volk Company permits a very businesslike outer envelope with the name computer-printed on the outside, and with personalized letters and response cards inside. This technique is made possible by preprinting the computerized portions on a continuous form and then fabricating the envelope and its inserts in one piece. There are several very useful variations of this format.

*Multiple Personalization*   It is possible to design a form which permits the letter or an invitation to be produced on the same form as the response device. Most computer letter formats permit a maximum length of 22 inches and a width of up to 18½ inches. With various side-by-side or front-to-back folding, bursting, and slitting available, it is possible to easily and inexpensively assemble a 6- by 8-inch personalized letter with a 3- by 6-inch response form. Such a simple format enables the printing of six sets on each form sheet. More complex formats are cut out of this same size. They cost more because of slower output and larger size per unit.

One outstanding multiple format developed for Skandinavisk Press used a 5½- by 7½-inch four-page letter, a 3¾- by 5½-inch response slip, a 3⅛- by 5½-inch guarantee, and a 3⅛- by 5½-inch lift letter—all personalized with the prospect's name and all printed out of a single 10⅝- by 16½-inch form and machine-collated with five other inserts.

In designing such multiple formats, it is important for the artist to realize that the width of the computer area is less than the total width of the form—usually only 13.2 inches at 10 characters per inch. This demands another design refinement. Personalized information may have to be limited to one side or the other on half the form.

*Computer Cost Factors*    It is also important to recognize that computer firms charge by the number of lines printed. A fully typed 8½- by 11-inch letter can only be run at 1000 per hour. The same letter in a two-up fill-in runs at 10,000 per hour. Of course costs are affected. Both figures are for an IBM Series 360/370 and an IBM 1403 printer.

*Electronic Letter Writing*    In the mid-1970s a variety of exciting new techniques were developed which took the art of personalization to new heights.

First Mead Digit, then Response Graphics, IBM, Itel, Xerox, and others developed various types of nonimpact printing. Some worked by ink jet, spraying very tiny dots on a page at high speed to form letters, lines, or images.

The first applications were the use of new and larger typefaces. Suddenly it was possible to put the prospect's name on the letter in inch-high capital letters, facsimile handwriting, or colored type. Suddenly you could print sideways or upside down, and thus open up new kinds of trick folds and seams to get special effects and new formats.

There was an explosion of creativity in personalization. Even more significant were the economic factors. Some of the new techniques could be attached to a printing press, permitting personalization, printing, folding, and assembly to take place in one high-speed motion—52,000 letters an hour, fully "typed" 8½ by 11 inches high. The ink jet, laser, and electrographic processes now permit great economy as well as unlimited creative flexibility.

The best way to utilize these new techniques is to work very closely with graphic designers, printers, and computer houses who have the equipment available. They can show you the work others have done with their process and help work out your own format problems. Good suppliers are an important part of your direct marketing team.

The various exhibits at DMMA conventions and the International Symposiums in Switzerland should be seen by everyone involved in design and printing. They are dazzling displays of formats and applications by printers and others who are deeply committed to and involved with the direct marketing industry. It is unfortunate that those who would benefit the most—artists and production people—are often not sent by their companies.

*Noncomputer Personalization*    While the computer offers an infinite variety of sorting possibilities and letterlike or posterlike personalization, it is possible to get these effects in a simpler, more old-fashioned manner.

For years, *Business Week's* control package was an invitation format with the prospect's name handwritten. Avis scored a major direct-mail breakthrough using an outer envelope with the prospect's name written in by hand. One unique format for business mail uses a facsimile rubber-stamped routing form and the prospect's initials penciled in along with others.

## Involvement Techniques

Why do direct marketers make their mailings so complicated? Because it works!

With the exception of high-level business-to-business mailings, the devices of direct mail are repeated because they are successful. In some cases they are so successful that they are soon overused. A direct-mail user can outflank the marketplace by going back to once-successful ideas as easily as by coming up with new ones.

*Transfer Effect*   The purpose of involvement devices is more than keeping the reader interested. It is also used most effectively to transfer reader attention from one component of a mailing to another. If the prospect will first see the response card, it is a good idea to point out that there is a label or stamp which must be found on the letter in order to get a premium or activate the offer. This will generate readership of the letter. Or the other way around, having a seal on a letter which is to be transferred to the order form is a way of directing the prospect to the order device.

One application is the inclusion of "early bird bonus stamps" in Publishers' Clearing House contest mailings. The stamps, which are found on the same sheets as the magazine selections, are a way of encouraging entrants to handle and look at the offered magazines before responding.

Virtually anything can be included in an envelope or made visible through it. Virtually anything can be affixed to a letter or other mailing element for the prospect to peel off, punch out, or otherwise get involved with. Any of these devices can, in turn, be personalized by the computer. Here are some ideas:

- *Business cards.* For personal services, questions, warranties. Try them with a pseudohandwritten note printed on the back.

- *Carbon copies.* Of a previous letter. "Why haven't you answered?"

- *Checks*. A legitimately redeemable check or money order is a sure attention-getter, but see your lawyer first.

- *Coins*. A penny for your thoughts, or "Ten records for a dime, and we'll even give you the dime. . . . "

- *Collectables*. An Indian penny. Facsimile Confederate money. A foreign postage stamp.

- *Facsimile photographs*. A child to help. A baby seal to be saved. Very effective if the photo is emotional.

- *Gifts*. A packet of seeds or spices. A pencil. A bookmark. A key chain.

- *Information*. Local police and fire numbers. A veterans' benefits guide. A map. A calorie counter. A metric guide. You name it.

- *Numbers*. Serially numbered application forms, perhaps to indicate exclusivity. Often used in contests.

- *Peel-offs*. Reusable gummed labels to transfer the address of any tokenlike symbol from one location to another.

- *Perforated stamps*. Easter Seals for fund raising. Book covers for a club selection.

- *Postage stamps*. To pay for the reply postage.

- *Punched holes*. To look through, giving the impression of a computer card, bingo card, or what have you.

- *Samples*. Recipe file cards. Fabric swatches.

- *Seals*. Notary seals, certificates, etc., to indicate reliability.

- *Tokens*. To be punched out and placed in or on the order card to accept an offer.

- *Yes or no symbols*. A way of asking for an immediate decision.

## Economic Considerations

Check with production specialists before proceeding to finished layouts. Production advice at this critical point can save the embarassment of producing a mailing which has to be inserted by hand because there isn't clearance for automatic inserting equipment, or which wasted a client's money by using an inefficient paper size.

Everyone in this business has made the mistake at least once of not providing enough clearance for machine labeling or inserting. An even more painful experience is watching a high-speed press print a brochure with literally tons of unused wastepaper, paid for by you or your client, being trimmed off and baled to be sold as scrap.

Paper comes in standard sizes, depending on the type of paper and the press it will be printed on. Some standard sizes are book paper, 25 by 38 inches; bond paper, 17 by 22 inches; cover stock, 20 by 26 inches; newsprint, 24 by 36 inches; coated paper, 25 by 38 inches; and offset paper, 25 by 38 inches.

Flyers, brochures, and letters are usually cut out of these standard sizes and can be figured by folding or cutting such a sheet accordingly. Sometimes an extra insert can be printed without added cost by using paper that might otherwise be trimmed off and thrown away. One project I saw would have permitted four additional pages in a brochure without extra cost, just by using the full paper size.

On large-quantity press runs, paper companies can often prepare a special "mill run" of exactly the size and weight of paper you need, providing the quantity is large enough and you have the time to wait for it.

Art directors should familiarize themselves with paper for another reason as well. Interesting effects can often be added just by changing paper. Kraft paper portrays one feeling, bond paper another. Newsprint is good for sale brochures. Coated stock is essential where color is important. Specialty papers such as check safety papers can be very useful when conveying value concepts.

Envelopes also come in standard sizes. With rush jobs, weeks can be saved by using a stock envelope and printing a message on the face of it in simple type. Designing windows in unusual places or odd sizes requires special press runs. Usually the printing of the copy and art you provide is one job, and the subsequent conversion of the paper into envelopes through die cutting and fabricating is another. This is like two printing jobs in a row, and is usually the critical-path item in a direct-mail job. Any envelope house, such as Transo or U.S. Envelope, will be happy to provide you with a complete directory of their envelope styles and sizes.

*Mailing Weight*   As postage is always one of the highest costs in a mailing, the total weight of a package is critical, particularly in first-class mail, where tipping the scale over the 1-ounce mark practically doubles the cost of the postage.

It is imperative that actual paper samples be cut to size and carefully weighed to determine mailing weight before the job goes too far. Often a slight change in paper weight or the trimming of a size will make an enormous difference in total cost.

In bulk third-class mail or nonprofit mail the weight is not as serious, because the minimum weight is about 3 ounces, with costs going up in intervals of about half a cent for each fraction of an ounce. Check with your postmaster or letter shop for the latest postage rates.

*Working with Suppliers*    Many pieces have to work together. The mechanical paste-up. The computer specifications. The mailing lists. Paper and printing. Computer processing. Binding and collating. Subcontracting such as envelope fabrication. Sorting. Mailing. Getting the mailing to the post office. If there's any field where Murphy's Law applies, it is in the execution of direct mail: "Anything that can go wrong will go wrong."

Probably the best economy is to work with reliable suppliers. Unless you have printing specialists on staff or as consultants, let one firm— an agency or printer—coordinate the entire job from providing you with mechanical specifications to getting it in the mail. This way it's their responsibility, not yours, if the pieces don't fit or everything doesn't arrive on time.

In short, to save money on direct mail: (1) make sure it works; (2) design it economically; and (3) let professionals coordinate the printing, computer, and lettershop processes.

## ELEMENTS OF THE MAILING PACKAGE

### The Response Device

Everything in your direct-mail package—every thought, word, and picture—is there for one purpose: to get the reply card returned to you with an affirmative acceptance of your proposition.

The format can be anything from a complex order form to a simple inquiry card. Usually a response card is about the size of the envelope, in order to permit it to be preaddressed with the address showing through a window in the envelope. It should be large enough so that it doesn't shift around and obscure the address. It should be small enough so that it easily fits the reply envelope without having to be folded.

Often a tear-off stub or flap at the side or bottom of the form will help solve the size problem. A flap can be useful to cover information that you don't want seen right away, such as complicated ordering information or a credit application, or it can contain essential sales points or immediacy incentives.

**Sweepstakes, stamps, expirations, certificates, coupons. These subscription agent mailings are very complicated and very successful.** (Source: *Publishers Clearing House, Port Washington, New York.*)

Involvement devices can be placed on the stub—a gummed stamp, sticker, punched-out token, or any of the various devices listed above. The reader is usually invited to attach the device in a specific location on the response card. The purpose is to call attention to the reply card, or to transfer interest from one piece in the mailing to another.

*Implied Value*   When the offer is the primary sales device, it is helpful to give the order form (or the token or stamp to be affixed to it) implied value. This can be achieved in several ways.

- Gift certificates or check-paper formats
- Borders such as those found on money orders or stock certificates
- Official-looking layouts, with punched holes, authorizations, or rubber stamps
- Engraved moneylike images, indicated by choice of typefaces and decoration elements
- Notary seals, ribbons, gold embossing, signatures
- Money orders, traveler's checks, bank checks, and passbooks, all of which by convention have implied value

*Other Images*   Try making the response card look like something other than what it is. If a sweepstakes is involved, dramatize the entry concept. If the product is in limited quantity, make the response card look like a reservation certificate.

Business-to-business correspondence should be on a restrained level. A simple white response card and a stamped envelope are very classy, or you can include a carbon of your letter and ask the recipient to initial it and return it.

*Label Transfer*   A simple, dignified device that adds to ease of response and offers a measure of involvement is the address label transfer. If you order lists supplied on address labels with a wax-finish backing so they can be easily peeled off, the prospect can take the peel-off label off the letter or catalog cover and place it on the response card. *Consumer Reports* uses a unique double-response card with a one-year offer on one side, a three-year offer on the other. The prospect is involved by being asked to place the label on one side or the other.

Location in the envelope also has a bearing on results. The response card can be the first thing seen or the last. Some very successful mailings have had reply devices attached to the top or bottom of a computer-printed letter, to help generate readership for both. In other cases, where the letter is really trying to "pass" as a personal letter, the reply device should not, of course, be attached to it.

## The Outer Envelope

The outer envelope is the headline of direct mail. Half the battle is to get the envelope opened—and much direct mail never is opened.

Imagine an envelope that would be difficult to open, offered no reason to open it, and aroused no curiosity or interest of any kind. Such envelopes do exist—the products of dull design, poor thinking, and sloppy execution. They offer every turnoff short of "Junk mail—don't bother to open this."

Fortunately, most people do open most of their mail. The problem is not just to get it opened but to arouse enough interest or curiosity to read the contents. You want your mailing to be the one that's "saved for last," the one that a prospect wants to read because of the promise it holds forth to satisfy basic needs or interests. Here are some of the ways to accomplish your ends.

*Preselling*   The obvious approach is preselling. It consists of putting the offer—or what would be the headline in an ad—right on the front of the envelope.

"Save 50% on *Time*" is a surefire headline, if the prospect already wants *Time*. If a simple offer statement is so effective, a simple turnaround document or double-postcard format will do the trick. In some cases, with presold products to core lists, it's all you need, and you can dispense with practically everything else.

"Stop Smoking Fast" is another example of preselling which either reaches prospects or turns them off instantly. With a really good appeal, getting to the point right from the beginning can work. More often, subtler appeals are necessary in addition to or instead of direct sell on the envelope.

*Curiosity*   The most curiosity-arousing envelope of all is the one that looks like a real business letter or a note from a friend. If you use a first-class stamp and a typewritten address, there is an excellent chance you'll get the letter opened.

You can also use headlines to build curiosity. Any headline that raises a question, ranging from "Do you make these mistakes in English?" to "Fifty stocks to avoid this year" will get people to read further.

An incomplete statement will also get readership. Start telling a provocative story right on the outer envelope, and then just when it gets most interesting, you can . . . (Continued inside).

See what I mean? Curiosity pressures you to want to know the balance of the sentence.

A quiz will also do it, such as "Which should you buy?"—a *Consumer Reports* package which was mailed to over 20 million homes.

*Audience selection* can lend itself to interesting formats as well. One package for *Self* included a plastic mirror showing through the envelope, dramatizing the kind of person being looked for as a prospective subscriber.

The type of mailing list the prospect is found on can lead to interesting concepts. For instance, a mailing to engineers for a pocket calculator presented unique diagrams and formulas that would be of interest to that audience. Another to architects dealt with blueprints and diagrams.

For Lanier, we did a series of mailings geared to specific types of industries. Only a few pages and the envelope show-through changed from mailing to mailing, but to each reader the message appeared to be designed for the one particular industry.

*Personalization*    The address label itself is a form of personalization, and showing the address through an envelope window can add an element of curiosity.

A larger window can disclose a larger, bolder name, with the help of the new computer printing techniques. It can also disclose a longer message which also mentions an address, a personal fact, or even the name of a neighbor.

You can show an initial through a window, recreate a signature, or let a personal message show through. A mailing for Avis's Wizard Weekend suggested weekend drive ideas near the prospect's own home, as selected by computer zip codes.

Any aspect of personalization mentioned anywhere in this book can be adapted for use on an envelope or to show through it.

*Involvement Devices*    You can use any type of token, stamp, number, or device, as listed earlier, to show through a window in an envelope, and any type of gift or enclosure can be referred to on the envelope. The simple addition of "Valuable Savings Stamps Enclosed" can increase the rate of opening, and therefore the rate of response, very substantially.

*Implied Value*    There are many ways to indicate that the contents of an envelope are of value. One obvious way is to say so. Another is to use very fine paper, an interesting colored stock, or a very professional (perhaps engraved or embossed) envelope. However, don't expect to

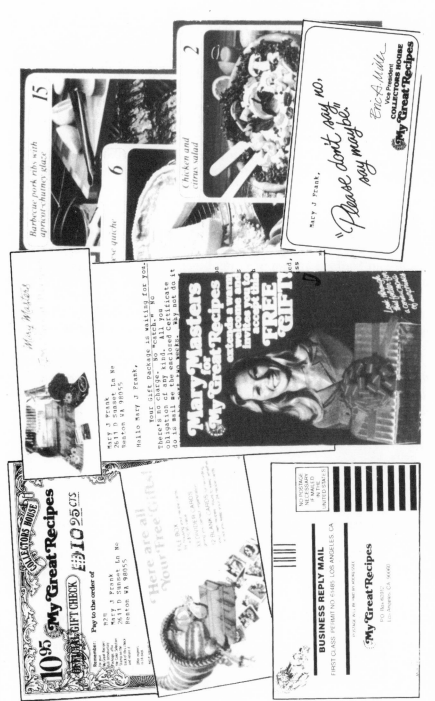

**Personalization is the key to this My Great Recipes card file solicitation—a format used all over the world. The prospect's name appears — in four different pieces.** (*Source: Collector's House, a subsidiary of Skandinavisk Press, Malmo, Sweden.*)

combine such images with bulk mail, unless the indicia are handled very well.

Kraft paper can imply that the contents are of value. So can a seal. European direct marketers have reported fantastic results with facsimile wax-sealed envelopes.

Value can be added in other ways also: rubber stamps referring to valuable contents, or stickers with added messages. One account executive invented the pseudolabel flap-seal—a portion of the gummed flap which is designed and die-cut to look like a seal. Because it is ungummed, it flaps up and looks like a real label sealing the envelope.

A show-through of something that looks like it might have value— a certificate, coin, or stamp—is of course another way of suggesting value. Value can also be just stated, as in "Free Recipe Cards Enclosed."

*The Official Look*    You can use the power of convention to make your mailing look like an official communication, providing the overall effect isn't misleading. If your client is a bank, you can be sure that the kind of envelopes in which statements are usually mailed will get attention. Another effective technique is to use officialese language: "Notice of Price Increase" or "Nontransferable."

*Adding Urgency*    An expiration date is the ultimate urgency appeal. It can even be computer-printed on one side of an oversized address label. Let it show through to boost results. Another way to add urgency is to make the format look like a teletype or wire. Or you can use headline typefaces and copy styles, as in "NEW PRODUCT SLASHES COPIER COSTS!"

*Transparent Envelopes*    Polyethylene envelopes are the closest thing to the disappearing envelope. They hide nothing, except those areas you may want concealed under a printed area of the polyethylene covering.

Materials are not inserted into these envelopes in the usual sense. Instead, the printed polyethylene is wrapped around the collated materials and fabricated into envelopes at very high speeds. At one time polethylene envelopes were actually less expensive than paper envelopes, but rising oil prices have increased the cost of polyethylene until they are now slightly more costly. However the increase in response, where the look is promotional, is well worth it.

For a four-color circular use a clear polyethylene envelope to let it show through. It will cost less than printing similar-color art on the outer envelope.

Use of transparent envelopes for certificates or other enclosures of obvious value makes them visible immediately, adding to the pulling power more effectively than merely describing the enclosure.

## Envelope Sizes

Envelopes come in many sizes. Twelve sizes of so-called official envelopes are usually available in stock from most suppliers, including monarch (3⅞ by 7½ inches), check (3⅝ by 8⅝ inches), the popular No. 10 (4⅛ by 9½ inches), and the more interesting No. 14 (5 by 11½ inches) which accommodates a letter folded in half down the center.

Booklet envelopes come in an even wider variety of 32 standard sizes, including the popular 6 by 9-inch size. Many suppliers even have standard sizes or dies with various window configurations which can be imprinted quickly and inexpensively.

These standard sizes are very handy for test runs or small printing jobs. In larger quantities and with proper schedules (see Chapter 17), it is possible to design anything you want without any real cost disadvantage.

Convention is a vital consideration in envelope size selection. People are accustomed to certain sizes of envelopes being associated with bills, checks, invitations, personal correspondence, and business correspondence. They also expect matters of importance to arrive in No. 10 or 9- by 12-inch envelopes.

Oddly enough, the most-used direct-mail size is one that has no associations except with direct-mail promotions, the 6- by 9-inch envelope. It is an efficient size and the largest that most Phillipsburg inserters can accommodate, but I prefer to use almost anything else. In fact, I have never come up against a 6- by 9-inch package that I wasn't able to beat, given the opportunity. I think it is a size that says "advertising" and puts the reader on guard. A squarer size has some interest. A 5- by 7½-inch envelope is unusual. A 3¾- by 6¾-inch envelope can contain items folded to form a very thick and apparently valuable package. Almost anything is better than a 6- by 9-inch envelope, in my opinion, and yet, because it is the easiest to work with, design for, and produce, it will probably always be the most commonly used size.

## The Letter

*How Long Should a Letter Be?*   Long enough to do the job. How many pages should it have? As many as are needed to tell the story.

There have been successful letters on one side of a monarch-size page and other successes—like Tom Collins' classic fund-raising appeal for George McGovern—which ran for a dozen pages.

True, the usual sizes are two and four pages, but this may be the result of failure to try alternatives rather than of careful testing. As the letter is one of the least costly segments of a direct-mail package, you should not skimp on it. (A two-color, four-page letter can cost between 3 and 5 cents, depending on quantity.)

*What Size Should a Letter Be?*   Convention determines size in most cases. Business letters should be standard business sizes and should be printed on one side only with each page separate, as if it came out of the typewriter. Consumer mail can be odd-sized just to be more interesting. It can be monarch size to resemble a personal letter, or it can be 5½ by 8½ inches with a handwritten message to make it resemble an informal note. It can be in the form and size of memo paper, telegrams, or anything that fits the positioning chosen for the promotion.

*What Should a Letter Look Like?*   First of all, it should be readable. Readability requires either that it look personal, with the prospect's name appearing on it, or that it look interesting. To get readership, use a headline in handwriting or giant typewriter type, or add a drawing or photograph.

Most of all, readability means that it cannot look like a dull letter with flush paragraphs. Some sentences should be indented, some should be underlined, and others should be annotated with handwritten marginal notes.

Formal paragraph rules can be thrown out the window. Instead, present your story in neat eyefuls of smaller readable paragraphs.

*Why Imitate Typing?*   A question that comes up frequently is whether imitation typing really fools anybody, and if it doesn't, why bother?

The real issue is not whether typewriter faces deceive the reader, but whether they suggest a letter by convention. The spirit of the letter format is that it is a one-on-one communication between two business executives or between a merchant and a consumer.

I have seen letters typed on IBM Executive typewriters that looked so perfect that they no longer seemed personal. Letters set in book or sans-serif typefaces look even less like letters. The suggestion, dictated by convention, is what is important. Deception is not the issue at all.

Once upon a time, when most typewriters used reusable ink ribbons, letters had to be printed in halftone or a fine-line process in order to simulate the irregular appearance of being typed through a ribbon. Today, with carbon-ribbon machines becoming more prevalent, simple offset reproduction adequately suggests typing.

Of course, computer letters or typed fill-in letters have to be carefully matched. The only way to do this is to type the body of the letter with the same computer printer or typewriter that will be used for the fill-in. Special care should be taken to match the typewriter ribbon as well as the typeface.

The illusion of personalization is sometimes broken by advertisers who illustrate a letter as if it were an ad or who use clever devices like rebuses. While I doubt that such devices are desirable, I don't know of any which have been split-tested against convention-based letters.

## The Brochure

The first question to ask is whether you need a brochure at all. I know of many successful mailings which omitted a brochure, and there have been some split-run tests of "brochure" versus "no brochure," where "no brochure" was the winner. However, I have never seen a successful mailing which left out the letter.

Whether or not a brochure is helpful really depends on the nature of the proposition and how well the brochure is done. If the proposition is an intangible, like a newsletter on tax avoidance or an appeal for a contribution, the brochure may have little to add. For a philanthropy a brochure might actually appear "slick" or "wasteful" and be a clear negative factor.

The brochure is usually one of the most expensive parts of a mailing, costing between 5 cents and 25 cents, depending on size, quantity, and complexity. The brochure is also the most expensive part of the total mechanical production cost. If a brochure costs 15 percent of the total cost of the mailing, that mailing without the brochure can do 10 percent worse and still break even, with a better return on investment.

*When Is a Brochure Needed?*   A brochure is needed most often when the sales message requires illustration, amplification, or accreditation. A brochure is the television of direct mail. Like television, it offers immense credibility, because words can lie but the eye cannot be fooled. It offers the prospect a chance to "see for yourself" the beauty of the product offered and how it will look at home, garden, or office. It provides space to diagram the most complex of working parts or the most elaborate of details. Unlimited except by the imagination of the artist and the skill of the photographer, it can make its presentations in full size, in color, and with dimension—from broad perspective to the finest close-up detail.

*What Goes in a Brochure?*   Once you've decided you need a brochure, you should include, in one way or the other, every selling point that you listed in your general copy platform. Don't worry about duplicating points in the letter. In fact, use the letter as a checklist to be sure that every major point has been mentioned again. In direct mail, each piece must stand alone. Let it do the whole selling job as if the prospect will read no other piece, which may be true.

Use the largest broadside area or brochure spread for the most impressive illustration—usually the finished product, whether a set of encyclopedias, a mature garden, or a completed project that your house plans or craft kit will build. The illustration can show a choice—the wide range of books, records, toys, or doll clothes you can choose from with this initial offer. Or it can show the "exploded" contents—pages from a magazine or book, materials in a correspondence course, the pieces in a set of mechanic's tools or a build-your-own-computer kit.

The opening pages or folds should be used to make the basic appeal. If the tactic chosen is to stress the offer, then this would be the place to dramatize the savings, the discount, or the premium. Even the simplest free trial offer can be dramatized, with an impressive certificate warranting the return privilege.

If the mailing is benefit-oriented, then show the benefit. In a book club, dramatize the relaxation of reading with pictures of people sitting with books on the beach or before the fire. Beyond that, bring to life the romance, adventure, excitement, or practical help that the books it offers contain. For as intangible a product as insurance you can dramatize the comforts of worry-free retirement, the security of knowing that the family home is secure or that junior will, indeed, graduate from college "no matter what."

*What about Format?*   "Brochure" is a term that usually describes a four- or six-page printed and folded sales message. A booklet is eight or more pages glued or stapled together. A broadside is larger than a brochure in that it is designed to unfold into a flat sheet, usually both vertically and horizontally. Flyers, pamphlets, circulars, inserts, and stuffers are all smaller items that usually unfold to a piece no larger than the letter.

Each has its own advantages. The smaller pieces are economical. The booklets and brochures are reserved, businesslike, and highly credible. The broadside is the heavy artillery of direct mail. It achieves a sense of dramatic impact that is not possible with any other format.

The principle involved in broadsides is the same as that involved in wide-screen motion pictures. If the visual image is wider or higher than viewers' focal range, so that they have to move their heads in order to see the whole picture, it is perceived as more realistic than if they see the edges, margins, or other reminders that it is only a picture.

*Apparent-Value Inserts*    Consider the possibility of making the booklet or brochure an element of apparent value in itself—something that would merit your saying something like "Helpful Booklet Enclosed' on the outer envelope.

For instance, a computer kit brochure can be labeled "Instruction Booklet: Step One." Such information has further value in that it dramatizes the simplicity of building the product.

A cookbook's brochure can include some sample recipes. A fashion catalog can include a color coordination guide. A vitamin brochure can include an article on nutrition. A grouping of several items can be presented as if it were a catalog.

Avis prepared a "confidential proposal," and Marriott Hotels did a "meeting planner's kit." Both were basically sales booklets with their own apparent value. In the case of Marriott, we were eventually able to offer the "kit" as the premium in a two-step promotion.

## Other Inserts

Other than the letter, a brochure, the reply card, and the outer envelope, what else do you need to make a mailing effective? Nothing, actually. These pieces give three or four repetitions of the main selling points, and should be capable of making the sale all by themselves.

However, for many mailers, the more inserts the better. The only requirement is that each insert have a raison d'être—a reason for being. An insert should not be just another piece of paper, but should have an obvious message or function.

*The Lowly Buck Slip*    I don't know how the buck slip got its name—maybe because it is often the size of a "buck"—but I do know it can make a big difference in results. Sometimes it's used to stress a point that may have been buried in the copy, like "Remember, you'll get a free tote bag. . . ." Or it can offer a special premium that may have been an afterthought: "Reply by X date and we'll also send you a mystery gift worth at least $10 in catalog value. . . ."

A buck slip may also contain news. "This widget has just been granted the seal of approval of the . . ." or ". . . selected for use in the space shuttle." It can give a correction: "We regret that we are out of the blue carrying cases described in the enclosed brochure; however, we will send the case to you in your choice of. . . ." It might be a trade-up or referral offer: "Buy three and you'll also get . . ." or "Give us the names of three friends and we'll send you a. . . ."

No doubt buck slips began as a way of adding information or sales appeal at the last minute, after a mailing had already been printed. But the occasional addition of such slips proved so effective that they are now deliberately planned in many mailings, as a way of stressing major points that might already be mentioned several times in a letter or brochure. Like the postscript of a letter, they are often read first. If you use buck slips, be sure they are self-explanatory and do not presume prior readership of the letter or other parts of the mailing.

*The Second Letter*    The "second" letter also been called the lift letter or publisher's letter. It has become an effective though now overused supplement to many mailings, particularly in the magazine subscription field.

As originally used, the second letter was a simple note from the publisher with a headline such as "Please read this only if you have decided to say 'No' to our offer." It went on to dramatize the no-risk aspect with copy like, "For the life of me, I can't understand why anyone would not send for. . . ."

With sweepstakes mailings, second letters often reiterate the message "No purchase necessary." With insurance mailings, they stress an inexpensive introductory offer.

Today scores of variations have sprung up. Some publishers put the second letter in a sealed envelope. Others have it sticking out of the reply envelope. National Liberty Insurance uses an interesting variation: a single folder printed as if it were an envelope and held together with a spot of glue.

A new variation is the double lift letter, or basically two separate lift letters which may or may not be joined together. One is for people who have decided to say yes, the other for people who have decided to say no. Naturally, curiosity will lead both groups to read both letters.

*Versioned Inserts*    Often it is too costly to prepare different versions of a mailing piece for different mailing lists. One way to take advantage of customized appeals without losing the benefits of large-quantity printing is to add customized inserts, with variations depending on list segmentation. These can be geographic in nature, referring to local conditions, local service availability, or local dealers. They can also be demographic, with special notes relating the product or service to people likely to be young or old, wealthy, or homeowners.

These inserts can be related to the mailing lists and the known interests of prospects, indicated by what they have bought or subscribed to in the past. For a magazine, the insert can relate to a specific article coming up in a future issue. For a craft tool or book, it can zero in on the person's field of interest: making planes, trains, dolls, etchings, or what have you.

*Selection Aids* The purpose of a selection aid is to make it easy to express a choice of one or more items offered in the mailing. It also has the effect of becoming an involvement device, and it gives you a second chance to list the products available.

In its simplest form, the selection aid can be an itemized order blank. All the customer has to do is check off the items desired or indicate quantity.

Marboro Books used to list the number of each book offered so that customers would have only to circle the numbers to order the books. I remember this device well because one of my first jobs included assembling and proofreading those lists of numbers.

Sol Blumenfeld once developed a record club mailer in which the gift records were 1 cent each and could be ordered by placing pennies in slots underneath photographs of the desired selections.

Book clubs, record clubs, and magazine subscription firms routinely use sheets of gummed stamps, illustrating the selections and including the order numbers and a value comparison. Merchandisers could develop such a device for catalog sales. A department store mailer could present each item on its own sheet with a gummed, perforated order stamp that need only be affixed to a preaddressed order form.

*Testimonial Flyers* Customer testimonials, a celebrity endorsement, a report of a testing laboratory, or other proof that your offer is sincere and valuable is often worth a separate insert.

Testimonials can be selected geographically, as in "What other Texans say about this offer." Endorsements can be in the form of a second letter.

## The Reply Envelope

It does pay to have a reply envelope, even when the offer can be mailed back on a card, but this is the only simple aspect of dealing with reply envelopes.

First of all, even with restrictive postal design requirements on business reply mail, there is room to make the envelope interesting. Typefaces, reverses, patterned paper, colors, and borders all are tools which can provide a sense of design and value even with strict adherence to postal requirements. The company name and the way the envelope is addressed can help the sale as well. There seems to be no objection to adding a line like "Special-Offer Department" or "Rush Service, Please."

On envelopes other than business reply mail, the only additional requirement is that you must fit the reply envelope into the outer envelope and make it large enough to get your order form into it without difficulty.

The reply envelope can be "red hot" to stimulate action with color, or yellow to imply telegraphic urgency. It can have a stamp affixed, or no stamp at all.

An interesting and effective development is the double reply envelope, used particularly with sweepstakes offers. One envelope is boldly marked "No" and addressed to the contest judging company. The other is similarly marked "Yes" and addressed to the mailer's fulfillment center.

Another way to accomplish the same end is to provide a window in the reply envelope so the selection of yes or no shows through, allowing for easy sorting in the mailroom.

Some reply envelopes build in an action-now buck slip, designing it as a perforated tear-off slip at the flap or inner edge of the envelope. Even a business reply envelope can be designed this way, as the stub will have been removed before the envelope gets to the post office.

Of course, a reply envelope doesn't have to be only an envelope. This term might include a Mailgram or telegram blank for the ultimate in immediacy.

Another possibility is to try to generate telephone response. Use a separate slip of paper to prominently display the phone number and the hours to call.

One trick is to provide the number on a gummed label to place near the phone or in an address book or, for business mail, a Rolodex card.

### Postage

The largest expense of most mailings is postage, and the choice of bulk, first-class, or nonprofit mail is worth consideration. The difference in rates is substantial, and more important, so is the difference in weight requirements.

*First-class mail* offers the ultimate in importance, and is often worth the added expense for business mailings or where fast results are needed. The basic rate, 18 cents at this time, is applicable only to 1 ounce. The slightest additional fraction requires another 17 cents. It is not difficult to take an elaborate mailing with a booklet over the 2-ounce line and even up to the 3-ounce rate. Even $2^1/_{16}$ ounce will require 52 cents of postage per piece.

First-class mail does move faster. It has priority in the post office, and it usually travels by air. If the piece is not deliverable, it will be forwarded or returned without added cost but also without the new address which would allow you to clean your list.

For 1-ounce mailing on a $260 per thousand package, the difference between 18 cents and 10.4 cents adds 7.6 cents, or $76 per thousand, to the cost of mailing. This adds almost 30 percent to the total cost, and would thus require 30 percent more response to justify the expense. Even with the added delivery of the forwarding service, and the added importance conveyed by first-class mail, most large-scale consumer mailings will not justify this cost differential. The added cost is often worthwhile, though, in business and professional mailings.

One caution: If you are going to use first-class mail, make it look like first-class mail. Use stamps (for consumer mail) or postage meter indicia (for business mail) rather than printed indicia. Keep the envelope simple, except perhaps for a pseudostamped "First-Class Mail." Otherwise the extra postage will not be noticed by the customer or the Postal Service, and the added cost will be completely wasted.

Green diamond first-class borders or red-and-blue airmail borders can be added to the envelope, even though they no longer have any postal significance.

*Third-class (bulk) mail* is the key delivery system used in the direct-mail industry. Despite rates which are disproportionately high to enable the Postal Service to subsidize newspapers, franked mail, and individually hand-addressed mail, it is still the most effective communication system available to American business.

The reason for rates lower than first class are many. First, it is standardized, and mail must be the same size and weight for convenient machine sorting. Second, it is presorted by zip code and can be handled in bulk, with entire trays or bags already tagged by the mailer for delivery to sectional centers. Third, it is paid for in bulk by the pound and needs less handling and bookkeeping. Fourth, most important, it is deferred, low-priority mail, which is permitted to sit around until time is available for handling it, after the individual mail and newspapers have been delivered.

At this writing, the minimum per-piece (minimal sorting) weight is 10.4 cents. More important, that covers a weight of up to 5.04 ounces. The rate is 33 cents per pound; 5.333 ounces requires 11 cents. As an illustration, for the 18-cent cost of 1 ounce at the first-class rate, you can mail 8.7 ounces by bulk mail.

The sorting requirements are complex, but any good mailing house already has them worked out, and most mailing-list merge programs will deliver labels in zip code sequence with header labels by batch to facilitate counting and sorting according to the latest postal requirements.

The most common (read "unimaginative") way to use bulk mail is to put a little square in the upper right-hand corner and include the required wording ("Bulk Mail/U.S. Postage Paid/Permit #____") and the name of the company or city. However, there are many alternatives. The same information can be designed into a facsimile postage-meter imprint, complete with circles simulating a postmark and a red eagle simulating the meter imprint. In one German mailing I admired, the indicia were placed in such a way that they looked like the cancellation on a commemorative stamp.

There is no reason to limit yourself to printed indicia. Postal meters and precanceled bulk-rate postage stamps can be used instead. Most mailers can accommodate these requests and can affix stamps by machine for a nominal added charge.

*Nonprofit Rates*    Legitimate nonprofit organizations like charities, churches, and foundations can enjoy the kind of rates that all direct mailers should be paying—20 cents per pound at this writing, or 19 cents a pound with a permit imprint. Up to 2.8 ounces costs only 3.5 cents. The first-class rate of 18 cents would mail up to 12 ounces at the nonprofit rate.

The catch is that the organization has to be authorized, and the penalties are stiff for any misuse or misrepresentation of this privilege. However, many organizations—Consumers Union, Smithsonian, and others—support major magazines with the help of this nonprofit rate. They can successfully mail millions of pieces at response levels that would bankrupt a company paying the regular bulk-mail rate.

The effect of this lower rate is so important that organizations have been known to restructure their activities in order to qualify. For example, *Ms.* magazine, which started out as a profit-making institution, completely revised their ownership and now operate as the Ms. Foundation for Education and Communication.

Nonprofit mail can also be mailed with meter imprints and precanceled nonprofit rate postage stamps.

*          *          *

This chapter has dealt with the physical aspects of taking a marketer's themes and a writer's words and getting them to the prospect. This physical process of format selection, design, printing, and letter-shop work is often lumped together as execution. Creatively, it is a direct marketer's version of origami. We cut a sheet of paper, fold it, and print it to create a fascinating variety of envelopes, letters, flyers, inserts, tokens, stamps, ad infinitum. This chapter has described what has been done and is being done. The real excitement lies ahead, in your hands: what can be done.

## CHAPTER SIXTEEN

# PRODUCING TV COMMERCIALS

Chapter 7 discussed broadcast as a medium, as well as the distinctly different ways in which radio and television can be used for direct response and support. This chapter will discuss the creative specifics of writing and producing commercials for both of these media and both of these purposes.

This chapter assumes that strategy, tactics, and copy platforms have been prepared as for print media or direct mail. All the basics apply equally well to broadcast. Our purpose here is to define the differences, offer advice, and explain the steps necessary to convert a script into an on-the-air communication.

## DIRECT-RESPONSE CRITERIA

The purpose of a direct-response commercial is to generate an immediate order or inquiry. Unlike general broadcast advertising which aims to impart awareness or a positive attitude, it must not only stop the reader and leave a positive impression, but it must also convey enough sales argument and ordering information to generate a letter or phone call from the viewer.

In the early days of direct-response broadcast, little consideration was given to the attitudes being created toward the product, the company, and direct marketing generally. Consequently, broadcast direct marketing developed an image of loud, tacky, amateurish, and sometimes dishonest commercials for poor-quality records and fragile kitchen appliances.

Today the immediate objective of getting an answer must be tempered with the longer-range goal of building credibility for the industry and the sponsor. This will pay off in the short range too, as each airing of a commercial is building awareness and attitudes that may lead to a response at the next airing.

Most of what we will discuss here applies to television, although the principles are also applicable to radio and to cable stations.

## Length

Without any question, the first attempt at making television direct-response work should be in the 120-second format. Occasionally, shorter lengths have worked, especially for magazines and other well-known products, but the fact is that we have never seen a 60-second spot work where a 120-second spot hasn't, and we have seen many 120's work where 60's haven't.

As 20 seconds must be devoted to the phone number or address segment, there are only 100 seconds for the basic message in a 120-second format. If you cut the commercial to 60 seconds, you are not cutting the selling message in half but reducing it by 60 percent, from 100 to 40 seconds. There is no question but that 120 seconds is the length to work with.

The only time to even try a shorter length is when a commercial is so successful that you need the shorter length to get onto stations that won't take a 120, or when your product has unique programming requirements that make placement flexibility more important than the length of the message.

## Length Requires Pacing

The 120-second length makes pacing an essential creative requirement. A message must begin with a stopper: a diver jumping off a cliff at Acapulco, a display of fireworks, a tiger's roar, an airplane taking off.

The first objective is to stop the prospect from getting up and going for a snack or visiting the washroom. In the AIDA formula, attention is the first requirement, then interest, followed by desire and action.

The pacing of a 120-second commercial requires a pulsing of high and low involvement points. You can't keep the viewers in a continuous state of excitement. You have to bring up their interest, pay it off, bring it back again, and pay it off again—usually five or six times in one announcement.

Doubleday's commercial for the Military Book Club stops viewers with an aerial battle, pays off with stock footage of the importance and excitement of World War II, builds them up again with an incredibly low-priced book offer, pays off with the book's contents, restates the offer and backs it up with offer justification and guarantee, and then backs it up again with a premium followed by ordering information.

## Credibility Requires Sincerity

Because we are usually asking someone to order a product they have never seen, from an advertiser they have never done business with before, credibility is an absolute requirement.

There are many ways to build credibility. The obvious ones are to state why a product is a good value, well-built, and backed by a reputable company. But remember, most communication is nonverbal. No matter what you say, the tone or mood of the message will do more to establish or destroy credibility than any of the words in the script.

The announcer must look reliable and sound sincere. This is no place for a flashy sports jacket or the bravado of most used-car commercials. (I don't believe used-car commercials are the right place for such devices either, but that's another story.) The setting, the music, the rates at which scenes change and the camera moves—all must contribute to credibility.

## Action Requires Immediacy

Credibility might ordinarily lead you to a relaxed, soothing pacing of the commercial. The challenge is that we also are trying to get an immediate action, and that requires a sense of urgency. The announcer must deliver the message in a manner that sounds both sincere and slightly breathless, as if the offer being made is a once-in-a-lifetime opportunity. The skill required to accomplish this is the reason why some announcers demand premium rates while others find it hard to get work at all.

## Cost Relationships

How much should a TV commercial cost? It is possible to spend anywhere from $10,000 to $50,000 on a 120-second spot. Usually, $15,000 to $30,000 will do the job very nicely.

The cost should be related to the size of the schedule and the type of programming. To compete for attention with an old movie requires much less talent and gimmickry than going up against prime-time programming and major packaged-goods advertisers, as the general agencies must do with their shorter commercials.

A typical first-time television test might involve $25,000 in time and

1. (SFX: THE SOUND OF A SIZZLING PLATTER. UP THEN FADE BACK) ANNCR: (VO) Listen...

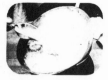

2. these are...

3. the sounds....

4. of Bon Appetit... magazine.

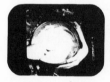

5. (SFX: PARTY SOUNDS) MALE: (VO) Look at this food...

6. FEMALE: (VO) Marion, you must have been cooking all day...

7. MALE: (VO) Here goes the diet...and who cares?

8. MALE: (VO) Okay...who wants an...end cut? (SFX: PARTY SOUNDS OUT)

9. (SFX: WIRE WISK BEATING RHYTHMICALLY IN METAL BOWL)

10. ANNCR: (VO) Bon Appetit magazine

11. is fabulous recipes...

12. made easy...

13. (SFX: PARTY SOUNDS FADE IN) FEMALE: (VO) Cathy...you made that??? (incredulous)

14. FEMALE: (VO) It was a snap with this recipe...

15.(SFX: CHOPPING SOUNDS)

16. ANNCR:(VO) Bon Appetit magazine

17. is new ways with old favorites.

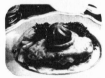

18. MALE: (VO) You know, I've never been crazy about chicken...(admiringly)... but this...!

19. ANNCR: (VO) It's elegant make-ahead party casseroles that are thrifty and simple to prepare.

20. (SFX: CORK POPPING FROM CHAMPAGNE BOTTLE)

**Two-minute direct-response commercials like this one for *Bon Appetit* magazine provide ample time to attract attention, dramatize product and benefits, and ask for the order.**     (Source: Reprinted with permission of Knapp Communications Corporation, Los Angeles, California.)

21. ANNCR: (VO) It's know-how about... wines...for cooking... with dinner... or dessert.

22. (SFX: SUGAR SHAKING OUT OF A SILVER DISPENSER) ANNCR: (VO) With Bon Appetit...

23. you can expect... the unexpected.

24. (SFX: POP CRACKLE OF FLAME) ANNCR: (VO) Flaming salads....

25. (SFX: RUNNING WATER OR WATERFALL)ANNCR: (VO) Freezing soups...and reliable recipes that make it all faster and easier.

26. (SFX: SOUND OF FOOD PROCESSOR UP AND THEN FADE DOWN AND OUT)

27. FEMALE: (VO) Great dip! Was it hard? FEMALE: (VO) Not with the processor recipes in Bon Appetit.

28. ANNCR: Here's a sound that can save you over $9.00 off the newsstand price of a year of Bon Appetit --

29. that's even $3.00 less than the basic subscription price.

30. Dial 800-453-9000 toll free...(SFX: TOUCH-TONE DIALING SOUND AS EACH NUMBER IS SPOKEN AND APPEARS ON SCREEN)

31. for 12 beautiful monthly issues of Bon Appetit magazine at only $8.95...

32. and, with your paid subscription, you'll also get this sensational book with complete plans for three perfect parties...

33. from a romantic dinner for two...to an elegant party for twelve...

34. to a gala buffet for thirty. It includes everything you need to know to plan, prepare, shop, even decorate.

35. Call 800-453-9000 to reserve your free copy... of Blueprints for a Perfect Party

36. and get a full year's subscription to Bon Appetit at 50% off the newsstand price. The phone call is free.

37. (SFX: PARTY) WOMAN: (VO) It's her menus...

38. so original!

39. MAN: (VO) She should open a restaurant...really!

40. FEMALE: (VO) (confidential) Her parties are always fabulous....

$10,000 in ad agency creative fees. Adding much more than $30,000 for the production of the commercial is unnecessarily increasing the downside risk.

If the commercial is a new one for a product line which has already been proved effective in direct-response broadcast, and there is a likelihood that a million dollars or more will be spent on the schedule, then the opposite is true, and no expense should be spared to make the commercial as effective as possible. If another $25,000 will increase response even 5 percent, it will pay off on even a $500,000 campaign.

The extremely successful commercials produced for Time-Life's Wild West and other libraries are all on the higher side of the cost spectrum, and all have been worth it.

To keep costs under control, the writer should be aware of basic economics. It's expensive to have large casts with speaking parts, or hordes of extras. Distant locations or complicated sets add to the cost. Night shooting can more than double a commercial's budget. Most important, stay away from the big-name production houses who look down their noses at direct-response television and its cost realities. There are plenty of very fine production houses in New York and elsewhere that can give you what you want at reasonable cost.

## Asking for the Order

If you are going to ask people to remember an address or a telephone number, then give them every possible assistance.

First of all, use both the visual and aural senses, by stating the address or telephone both verbally and on the screen. Second, repeat it in both ways. Third, if possible, repeat it again.

Twenty or thirty seconds should be devoted to the actual presentation of the address or phone number, broken up by a premium sell or a basic offer resell.

Advance warnings help, particularly on radio when there is no visual reinforcement of the number. "Get your pencil ready" may be a cliché, but it's one that works.

It's a good idea to plan a commercial so that these ask-for-the-order segments are self-contained. You may want to test a new price later, change the phone service, or work out per-inquiry deals with stations that want to insert their own local telephone service instead of your 800 number.

It's possible to edit the commercial so that the closing and any supers of price or phone number can be changed later without having to reshoot the entire commercial.

## Offer Modification

Often you cannot use the same offer in broadcast that was developed for print or direct mail. However, the reverse is true: A proven television offer can often be adapted for other media.

As discussed in earlier chapters, an entirely different strategy must often be developed to make the broadcast medium successful—perhaps even pulling for inquiries rather than orders, or changing the basic proposition completely.

*Multiple add-ons* are effective. "If you act now, we'll also send you this . . . and this . . . and if you call right now, even this." Sets of knives, dishes, towels, tools all look impressive when the camera pans the merchandise or as additional elements are added.

*Simplified responses* are necessary. If you ordinarily give prospects a choice, you may want to offer only one version on television. You can always tell them about an alternate when they call in the order.

*Qualified inquiries* can be obtained by selling an item representative of your main product line. The Doubleday commercial mentioned earlier, for instance, sells a World War II book for a low price, not to profit from the sale of books, but to get names which can be converted to club membership.

## SUPPORT BROADCAST CRITERIA

### Length

Support commercials are not expected to make the sale at all, and need little time to ask for the action, which is to look for an ad or letter. Consequently, they need much less time than direct-response commercials and can be handled well in 30-second and even 10-second formats. For some complex propositions, 60's may be used as well. The 10's, however, are usually used only in combination with the 30's, as an added reminder of a message that is being presented in the longer format. They don't provide enough time to do very much on their own.

### Variety

When there is a high frequency of support commercials, it is usually advisable to have a few different versions in order to avoid fatigue. Usually these commercials are on the same theme but use a different example or setting. Publisher's Clearing House, for instance, used a series of interviews with prize winners for their direct-mail support campaign. The subject matter in each interview was different because of the interviewee, but the theme—demonstrating that people really do win contests—was the same.

Television in support of a catalog mailing, for example, could present a different item in each commercial, but the main theme would be the value of the forthcoming catalog.

## Cost Standards

It would seem that a support commercial should be much less expensive to produce. After all, if 120 seconds costs $30,000, shouldn't 30 seconds cost one-fourth as much? Logically, yes, but it's not always true.

It's possible for support commercials to cost even more than longer response commercials. The main reason is the difference in quality required. Support commercials are placed against the best programming in the day parts they are up against. The adjoining commercials for packaged-goods products will be first-class, highly creative, well-executed commercials. You aren't up against the local furniture dealer or other direct marketers, so you've got to be good. Being good costs money.

## Credibility versus Immediacy

Because you are not asking for an order or response, credibility is not as much of an issue as it is with direct-response commercials, but immediacy is more of an issue.

In most cases, the medium that is being supported is a direct-mail piece that is timed to arrive within one or two days of the commercial. It can also be a newspaper preprint or a *TV Guide* advertisement which is appearing the same weekend the commercials are running. The prospect has to get that publication or look for that mailing piece, and act on it. There is no way to write down a phone number and call when you get around to it.

As a result, direct-response commercials can go all the way to put stress on immediacy. This is the place for the breathless enthusiasm, the proclamations of "big news," the thrill of presenting a wonderful offer.

## Support "Offers"

In its simplest sense, the immediate "offer" is simply "Look in your mailbox" or "Look in this Sunday's paper." However, the need to make a sufficient impression to get the message across is as important here as in giving the phone number on a response commercial.

If you are supporting a mailing, marketers agree that it is essential to actually show the mailing piece. If it is a preprint or other ad, you must show the ad and name the newspaper. "Look in your Sunday newspaper" isn't enough, particularly as there may be several news-papers in any one station's viewing area.

The newspaper should be identified by name in a super or closing panel. One economy is to have your announcer say "in your Sunday paper" but have the super show the specific newspaper's name. You can change visuals at will, but changing the words the announcer says will require all kinds of extra fees.

### The Transfer Device

The most important innovation in support advertising in recent years is the transfer device. Attributed to Lester Wunderman, this device offers a premium "just because you are watching this message" if the viewer will place a secret mark on the card in the ad or mailing.

This ingenious device, in one move, provides play appeal, imme-diacy, involvement, and a way of directing attention not only to the advertisement but right to the order form.

Transfer devices have become a mainstay of support commercials. Doubleday offers maps. Time-Life offers posters; their Home Repair Library commercials offer a handyman's apron; their magazines offer an extra issue or a free book. Record clubs offer an extra record. The premium possibilities are endless.

To add involvement, extra play appeal is added by directing people to turn an S on the card into a dollar sign, or to circle the correct plane or animal, or to write a number in a box. As a plus, the transfer device can be used to measure the relative effectiveness of different commer-cials. One ad asks people to circle the panda, and the other asks them to circle the polar bear. The transfer device should be particularly ef-fective with mail-order catalogs—a support application which I predict will become one of the most important in direct marketing broadcast.

Transfer results cannot be "read" in the classic sense. The commer-cial has to be evaluated on the combined effect of the media being supported and the support costs independently of the number of people who use the transfer device. However, the consensus is that commer-cials with transfer devices outpull those without them, and that support broadcast, properly bought and well created, is an important and worth-while investment for direct marketers.

## WRITING A TELEVISION COMMERCIAL

All the steps and disciplines outlined in Chapter 13, The Art of Copywriting, go into the writing of a television script, but the dimension changes radically. If we liken an advertisement to a drawing, then a direct-mail piece is like a sculpture and a commercial is like a motion picture.

You have infinitely more than words to create with. The 90 percent of communications that words on a printed page fail to convey all come into play on television. You have a setting for mood. There's a narrator whose personality and sincerity can come across in dress, posture, and tone of voice. You have realism, motion, and emotion—the ability to bring words to life. In addition, you have sound effects, music, lights, and special effects to add allure, excitement, and entertainment value.

However, all this is no substitute for the sound thinking that has to go into any kind of direct marketing selling in any medium.

### Timing the Script

First, take the time you are allotted—whether 30 seconds for a support commercial or 120 seconds for a response commercial—and set up a matrix on a blackboard or a sheet of paper.

Draw a line representing the length of the commercial, and divide it into segments, as if it were a ruler. But your unit of measurement should be seconds, not inches. Then break out the main components of your commercial—the must ingredients—and see how long each of them will run. For instance:

| | |
|---|---|
| Opening | 10 |
| Subject sell | 20 |
| Product sell | 20 |
| Offer sell | 20 |
| Guarantee | 10 |
| Restatement | 10 |
| Phone | 5 |
| Premium sell | 10 |
| Phone | 5 |
| Immediacy copy | 5 |
| Final phone | 5 |

Here's a different combination:

| | |
|---|---|
| Opening | 10 |
| Problem | 20 |
| Solution | 10 |
| Testimonial 1 | 10 |
| Testimonial 2 | 10 |
| Testimonial 3 | 10 |
| Product sell | 20 |
| Phone | 10 |
| Premium | 10 |
| Phone | 10 |

These are not formulas, just examples of how to approach this problem. The contents might consist of examples, demonstrations, case histories, applications, exhibits—any of the most graphic materials available to make the point.

Arrange the blackboard or paper in time segments, such as a frame for every 3 seconds. If you use this measure, draw forty lines across the page—one for each 3 seconds.

Then draw a line down the page, dividing it into two horizontal sections. Label the left-hand column "Video" and the right-hand column "Audio," and start writing your storyboard.

Under "Video," describe what pictures will be on the screen. Examples are an announcer, a product shot, a close-up of a product detail, some footage of the product in use, a picture of the factory where it's being tested, or a home or office where it's being used. Include any words you want to show on the screen.

Under "Audio," write your text: the words the announcer will be saying on camera or off, the statements of others, sound effects, musical effects that you know you want. The video and audio should work together and reinforce each other.

Once the first draft is done, read it out loud, with a stopwatch. You'll probably discover that it's way too long. That's where the 10 percent inspiration gives way to the 90 percent perspiration—the careful, calculated selection of what can fit and what can't.

Every visual image needs a few seconds to be comprehended, unless it's part of a flurry of images designed to create an impression rather than be seen individually. Every phrase can be measured in seconds, every word in fractions of seconds. Rigorous selection of what goes and what stays is critical. The writer must play Solomon, and decide which copy point can stay, which must go, and which favorite slogan or play on words has to be sacrificed for nuts-and-bolts copy.

The temptation will be to cut down on those terribly uncreative phone numbers at the end, or to plan for an announcer who can talk faster—which is fine ifyoudon'tcareifanyoneunderstandsanything. In broadcast, the essence of creativity is choice.

### Video Techniques

Once the basic script has been worked out, there's room to indicate some of the wide choice of effects that are available. Usually, the writer thinks, at first, in terms of home movies, with announcers and scenes following each other. However, the skills and facilities of the production company can give you any effect you have ever seen in a television show or motion picture, including all the effects listed below.

*Close-ups*   You can indicate exactly how close you want to get to a person or product. You can show a room full of people, close in on one of them, and then focus on something the person is holding.

   In the jargon of the production industry, the group would be a long shot or a medium shot, the single person would be a medium close-up (MCU), a shot of the person's face would be a close-up, and the focus on something in a hand would be an extreme close-up (ECU).

*Panning*   Panning is moving the camera sideways, to follow action or simulate it.

*Zooms*   If you know what a zoom lens is, the term "zoom" speaks for itself. You can bring the scene closer (zoom in) or move back from it (zoom out). This technique lets you set a scene and focus on one person or object. In reverse, you can start with a close-up that arouses curiosity and pull back to show what it is.

*Freezes*   Stop the motion with a freeze when you want to call attention to something. It's a good way to relate an exciting scene to its photograph in a book.

*Dissolves*   One scene fades out, the other in—a much smoother way of changing scenes than the abrupt "cut."

*Superimpositions*   More commonly called a "super," a superimposition is the placing of one image on top of another—usually a written message appearing at the same time as photography. It's often a phrase under or across an image.

*Split Screens*   You can show two images at once on a split screen, or four on a quartered screen. The images are combined in the editing stage and can be used to add a feeling of motion to an otherwise static still shot.

*Other Special Effects*   I don't think there is anything you can think of that can't be simulated by the technicians in a good production house. You can make images larger or smaller, add type, change backgrounds, speed scenes up, or slow them down. If you've seen it on your home television set, there's someone who can do it.

   Now that we've covered what you can do, let me add a word of caution, particularly to those producing their first commercial. Just because you can do anything doesn't mean you should. Too many good scripts are ruined because they get "gimmicked up" with flashy technique which distracts from the main theme. Don't use dissolves and pans and floating panels if there's no real reason to.

## Audio Techniques

There are three audio techniques which should be used together, in the proper balance: voice, music, and sound effects.

*Voice*   The announcer's voice, or on-screen dialogue, will be the primary delivery vehicle for your message. How it's said is as important as what is said. The tone can convey enthusiasm or boredom, sincerity or duplicity. The manner of delivery cannot be specified in the script, except with occasional instructions such as "with enthusiasm." Voice is an essential consideration in casting, direction, and editing.

*Music*   Music offers almost as wide a range of communication as voice, except that it reaches the emotions instead of logic. No one will ever remember your musical backgrounds, behind the voice or as fill-in between spoken passages. They will remember that the commercial was soothing, thrilling, gentle, or powerful. All these ideas—setting the tone for your message and conveying aural images to your product—depend on the music selected.

Most direct marketing budgets will not be able to afford original scored music, but there is an enormous range of stock music available, particularly in New York and Hollywood, to meet virtually any need. A skilled director can select from available music tapes to give your commercial any feeling you want.

*Sound Effects*   Since the earliest days of radio, sound effects have been developed to convey any image: the creaky door for suspense shows; horses galloping and livestock sounds for westerns; bullets ricocheting and sirens in the distance for detective shows; plus bells, explosions, traffic sounds, or anything you can think of.

Sound effects can suggest an off-camera happening very inexpensively. Do you want an announcer to bring a kitchen gadget to a home by helicopter? Do it this way: "*Whirring noise.* BOY: Look, ma, it's a helicopter. *Pilot makes entrance.*"

Want Santa Claus to make an entrance? You can get bells, reindeer hoofs, and the sound of Santa sliding down the chimney.

All these sounds are available on tape, and it's very simple to arrange to hear the ones you want and get permission to use them for reasonable fees.

For one commercial we used old newsreels, but the sound tape had a news commentary and so was unusable. We had to use stock sound effects to put the original sounds back in. For another, we simulated the sounds of cooking, food preparation, sizzling steaks, blenders, and party sounds, to bring *Bon Appetit* to life on television.

## PRODUCING A COMMERCIAL

In print advertising or direct mail, it is customary to treat production as if it were simply an execution process—setting the type that has been indicated, ordering the illustrations specified, and assembling the pieces into mechanical paste-ups for later printing.

In television, the creative process is only half done with the completion of the storyboard. Television production is a highly subjective process requiring artistic talent, skill, and experience to translate the storyboard into the message that will appear on the air. A professional producer is essential, regardless of the budget, the length, the medium, or any other variables.

### Choosing a Director

A full-service advertising agency will have worked with production companies or free-lance directors, and can help recommend one based on their past experiences. Because of the volume of production work they handle, they will usually have some "clout" to assure the best prices and other arrangements.

If you are trying to produce television on your own, there are several ways to go.

The local television station will usually know some independent producers and directors, and may even do television production themselves. Their prices are usually unbeatable, but their productions are usually very poor. The problem is that stations are geared to simple news shows or local interview-type programs and don't have the exacting standards of commercial production houses.

Production firms are set up in business to work for companies requiring professional production of documentaries, training films, commercials, and other expressions of the cinematic arts. There are very large ones and very small ones.

The larger firms may have commission representatives who do a wonderful selling job, and they may have one or two chief executives who have a fine reputation, but the only people who count are the producer and director they plan to assign to your project. Many of these companies may consider a direct marketing commercial a crass, unartistic venture, or they may resent having to work with budgets that don't permit taking the entire crew to Rome for a 3-second segment. The result is that your particular project may be delegated to a very junior manager who is learning the craft on your job.

A smaller firm usually is run by the principals who serve as both director and sales representative. You'll be working with the top people, but their crew may be assembled for each job. They may have technicians who have never worked together before, like the "pick-up musicians" who compose the bands that play at weddings. However, there is no reason why even a free-lancer can't rent the same facilities and assemble the same quality crew as a larger production firm.

My choice is usually a small, independent production company. The criteria should not be size, however, but the extent of experience and involvement in low-budget television production.

*Screening the Reel*    Usually a director seeking your business has one presentation and one only: a reel of work they've done for others. When you call a director you find in a directory or through referral, you'll be invited to a "screening."

Watching such a screening takes skill in itself. It is a classic caveat-emptor situation. First of all, take notes as you watch the work. You may be particularly impressed by some of the projects because of "big-name" clients or big-dollar budgets. Such projects are included to impress you. After the screening, refer to your notes and ask the director:

- Did you make this film at this company or when you worked for someone else?

- Who was the producer? The director? Are they still with you? Are they available for my projects?

- What was the budget? Is it comparable to the one I have in mind?

Then ask yourself these questions:

- What did I like about the reel? The acting? The special effects? The music? The humor or story line?

- Are the things I liked relevant to my project?

- Did the commercial come across as a well-integrated, continuous, consistent message, or were there good parts and bad?

- Do the producer and director seem enthusiastic about my project, or are they acting like they are doing me a big favor?

Once you've seen enough reels, you'll develop clear-cut standards of your own for comparing reels. Choose two or three companies you like best, discuss the specifications generally, and then ask for an estimate on your job.

## Getting an Estimate

Always, without fail, get more than one company to estimate, and always put the specifications in writing and make them identical for all bidders.

Begin by reviewing the storyboard, which should be self-explanatory but usually isn't. If you're showing a kitchen set, are you providing it? Can the studio find a kitchen that generally fits the scene? Or do you have such specific requirements that a set will have to be built to accommodate your needs? Obviously, the costs will be entirely different in each case.

Will you shoot on film or videotape? With union or nonunion talent? These factors will also make a big difference. The bid should ask the production company to specify exactly what the crew will be and whether the actors are figured on the basis of scale or above-scale fees.

Many of the questions and specifications about your particular commercial will arise in discussions with one director or the other. Directors can be very helpful in suggesting ways to cut costs or add creative strength to the finished product. The willingness and ability to make such suggestions should definitely be a factor in your final decision, even if the most helpful director's bid is a bit higher. Price should certainly not be the only criterion. In television production especially, you get what you pay for.

The proposal should also indicate, and make a commitment to, the shooting schedule and the completion date. Problems should be anticipated, such as what happens if bad weather spoils an outdoor shot, or who's responsible if the actor turns up drunk and can't work while the rest of the crew still has to be paid. That's what "contingency allowances" are for.

There are two ways to get such bids: cost plus and completion bid. Cost plus means that the director gets a flat fee or a percentage of costs of what actual charges come to. This gives you a great deal of flexibility if you want to "play Hollywood" and get several takes on each scene, but it also means that you are signing a blank check because you have no way of knowing what the finished cost will be.

The most responsible bid is the completion bid, in which the director quotes a price on the finished product regardless of problems. Reshoots, editing problems, and uncooperative talent are their problem and expense. Directors may skimp when it comes to reshooting a scene, but this probably won't happen because they too want to produce something they can be proud of.

## Film versus Videotape

Almost every producer and director will have a strong feeling about the choice between film and videotape, and there are pros and cons to each. You should be familiar with both media even if you decide to leave the choice to the producer or director.

Advertisers with large budgets generally use film to do their shooting. Most directors are comfortable with this mode, and so are their camera operators and other technicians.

The equipment is more readily available, less bulky, and more portable. You don't need to rent expensive mobile control units if you're shooting indoors.

The most important advantage, however, is that film is easier to edit. The director can edit film on an inexpensive viewer and can utilize all kinds of optical effects in the lab.

Videotape is more generally used by direct marketers. The advantage is that it is instantaneous. "Takes" can be played back while still on the set, and problems can be spotted and scenes reshot without having to call back the talent and crews. Special effects—"chroma-key" combinations of scenes, superimposition of text over photography—are much simpler to arrange.

The problem is the cost of the equipment needed to edit videotape. Editing facilities must be rented, complete with technical support, by the day or hour. Editing has to be done within a tight frame, and creative people, clients, and others concerned with the finished product have to stay at the studio until the editing is completed, so that it can be done in one continuous process.

If very fine quality is required, as in food or cosmetic commercials, the slight extra cost of 35mm film instead of 16mm film or videotape might be significant. Film may also be advantageous where outdoor or location shooting is required.

## Union versus Nonunion

Many direct marketing commercials are made on a nonunion basis—and they look it. I don't recommend nonunion labor. There are small savings involved, but only on the cost of the talent, which is usually one of the smallest parts of the production budget.

The technicians cost the same. The camera operator costs the same.

The sets and costumes and props cost the same. The film or tape and equipment costs the same. The music and titles cost the same. The director's profit markup is the same in both cases.

The only savings is on talent. Nonunion actors can often be "bought out" so residuals don't have to be paid on repeat commercials, and they can be persuaded to shoot a dozen different newspaper names or phone numbers at the end of the commercials. The problem is that production firms who have signed with SAG or AFTRA may not hire nonunion talent.

I strongly recommend the use of union talent. The actors may be the smallest part of the overall production budget, but they are the most important influence on the quality of the finished product. It is the actor who provides image, positioning, sincerity, realism—all the non-verbal communication which composes 90 percent of the message.

The better actors simply won't risk appearing in a nonunion project or working with nonunion actors. If they are professionals, they are working in other jobs and expect to continue in the business. They have too much at stake if they lose their union cards. Only amateurs, who have nothing to risk, will take the chance. Experience in several casting sessions indicates clearly that nonunion actors cannot compare with the caliber of union talent available.

The union's red tape is complicated; even they won't deny it. Union-recognized production firms may also charge a bit more. But it's worth it to get the right talent.

## Radio Production

Everything I've said about television applies to radio, except the obviously visual aspects. Sound studios and radio producers work the same way and should be interviewed and asked for estimates in the same way. They will always use tape, of course, as film isn't appropriate and discs are now obsolete.

The key difference is in the creative aspects, where sound effects become more important and the creative challenge is more difficult.

Some radio commercials are done live, of course, but this is very risky. If you listen to monitored tapes from live announcers in several cities, you'll be amazed at the differences in the style and the quality of the delivery. The only exception is live announcements on a personality show, where a well-known announcer will deliver the script in a style that implies a personal endorsement of the product. In such a case, provide fact sheets and product samples to encourage improvisation.

## The Shooting or Recording Session

Once the director takes over, the advertiser's main concern is to respond to the queries, copy revision requests, and schedules set by the director. This is no time for second guessing. The director is in charge—at pre-production meetings and casting sessions, on the set, and in the editing room.

That doesn't mean you have to abdicate responsibility. It does mean that you should respect the authority-responsibility structure and work exclusively through the director.

It is sheer disaster to have agency or client personnel on a set making suggestions to lighting people or camera operators, and it is worse yet to allow them to offer friendly advice to an actor who may be fighting off stage fright.

Be there, at everything. Watch, listen, scan the takes if they're on tape. Listen to the sound playbacks in either medium, but keep quiet. Pass your comments along at appropriate times, preferably in note form, to the director.

If there's a serious problem, ask to speak to the director privately. Never embarass a producer or director in front of their staff and associates, or they will have to resist your suggestion in order to save face. This is the time for protocol, courtesy, and strict observance of the channels of communication.

Try to confine your comments to your interests: your concern for getting the message across in accord with the general marketing strategy. Try to resist the temptation to play movie mogul. Sure, shooting a commercial is a new experience for many advertisers. It should be a fun experience as well, but let's remember that, in direct marketing, the fun that counts is counting coupons.

## CHAPTER SEVENTEEN

# PRODUCTION PLANNING

It is not necessary for every direct marketer to master the arts of production. The fine craft of planning, buying, and supervising the graphic arts aspects of print advertising and direct mail is the subject of dozens of books in itself. What every direct marketer should have, however, is an appreciation of the problems faced by production managers and their graphic arts suppliers, and how to work with them to achieve the optimum combination of time, cost, and quality.

The principles in this chapter apply to any type of production process—from a simple black-and-white ad for a newspaper to a complex full-color magazine ad with bound-in insert card or the most complex direct-mail campaign. I therefore encourage the reader to read the examples as principles, not as specifics which apply only to the media mentioned at the moment.

## THE TIME-COST-QUALITY TRIANGLE

Imagine a triangle with the words time, cost, and quality each written on an edge. If you press one side, the other bulges out. If you press two, the remaining one may stretch to the bursting point.

The same principle applies to the graphic arts, and probably to most other production endeavors as well. If all three dimensions are reasonable, then there is an equilibrium. If unreasonable demands are placed on one or the other, something has to give.

Want it super-cheap? No problem, if you give the production supervisor the time to shop around and get the bids from unknown suppliers, or to send it off to a printer in Taiwan.

Want top quality? Then be prepared to use the best suppliers and the slower processes, and allow enough time to check proofs carefully at every stage.

Want it yesterday? Anything is possible, if you are willing to pay for it in one of the other "currencies." If time is the only criterion, a multilith machine at a local duplicating shop can do it while you wait. (For political campaigns, I have sent a telegram to myself, opaqued the name and address, and used it as art to have thousands reproduced on yellow paper and mailed out the same night.)

If you need both speed and quality, financial printing houses have the staff and equipment standing by on three shifts to handle rush jobs. They'll get out your color brochure in forty-eight hours or less, but be prepared to pay far more than what the same job would cost at a commercial printing house.

Your production manager, printers, and letter shops can do anything you want, but understand that the time-cost-quality interrelationship is a law of nature. All the haggling, screaming, bargaining, or cajoling in the world isn't going to change the interrelationship.

## CONTROLLING COSTS

Each side of the cost-time-quality triangle has its own problems and opportunities. There is no trick in getting "the lowest costs." There are tricks in getting reasonable costs without sacrificing the other two considerations. These tricks involve (1) planning the job, (2) defining it, (3) getting estimates, (4) avoiding errors, and (5) avoiding rush work.

### Planning the Job

Whether you are working on a simple black-and-white ad for a newspaper, a multipage magazine ad with bind-in card, or a multi-million-piece printing run, the problems are the same, and so is the first step—planning.

It is too late to begin production planning after the layout is complete. The time to begin is after the writer and artist have worked out rough layouts, and before either finished copy is written or final layouts are completed. That is the time to bring in the production specialist or supplier.

In the simplest advertisement, the production specialist should have the responsibility for determining exact sizes and the kind of halftone that is acceptable for the publication. (Halftones vary from 60 to 120 screen; the lower the number, the coarser the illustration.) In a complex mailing piece the production specialist is responsible for knowing paper sizes, envelope formats, inserting requirements, and what you can and cannot do with computer personalization.

Here are some general planning areas to be considered:

*Plan for Changes* If you have different versions for testing or different markets, plan them in advance. It is usually not necessary to start from scratch with each version. If you confine changing areas to the black plate, different versions can be prepared on press at lower cost than making and setting up a whole new set of plates. If only an address or other element changes, then an overlay on the mechanical will be less costly than new mechanicals and will save on platemaking as well.

*Check Paper Specifications* Review paper specifications with publications and printers, to be sure halftones are prepared correctly, ink won't show through, and your job will be cut out of the available paper with minimal waste. Even the paper's grain direction is important, especially for neat folding.

*Plan for the Future* If you expect that color separations will be reused for other versions, do what publishers do when preparing books that will be printed in different languages. Order a "floating fifth" film from the color separation house. This is a second black film containing all text matter, while the original black film contains the black part of halftone illustrations. When printing, the two sets of film are combined into a single black plate, but the text can be changed without reshooting the expensive halftone areas.

*Avoid Printed Dating* More than one disaster has been averted by keeping dates off the printed area of an insert card or mailing piece. If an expiration date is mentioned in print in several places, you're up a tree if the lists come in wrong, the season turns bad, or one of the other elements is delayed. It's much better to imprint the date as part of the computer addressing or on a tickometer, referring to "the date indicated" in letters and other parts of a mailing. Then you can always remail later by simply changing the expiration date.

*Make Dummies* Take the time to cut out blank paper representing each piece of a mailing. Fold and insert it the way you want it. Errors, such as folders that open up and jam the inserter, or reply coupons that don't fit in the reply envelope, will be readily obvious and can be corrected before mechanical paste-ups are started.

*Check with the U.S. Postal Service* Always check for postal acceptability and new regulations. Don't presume tolerance, understanding, or common sense. An extra fraction of an inch on a reply card can increase your business reply postage costs. An error in postal indicia can lead to the refusal of an entire mailing. Go by the book, or they'll throw it at you.

## Defining the Job

Once you've worked out everything, write down detailed specifications; don't count on a layout's being enough.

Bob Jurick, president of Fala Direct Marketing, prepared the following lists of questions that should be asked by sales representatives when writing up orders for printing, computer, or mailing services.

### GENERAL PRINTING SPECIFICATIONS

1. *Name or subject matter of the job.*

2. *What is the quantity?*

3. *What is the size?* If a book or booklet, number of pages and the trim size of the page. Does it bleed?

4. *What is the paper stock?* a. Brand name if required. b. If brand name, can an equivalent sheet be used. c. What weight sheet. d. What finish is required—gloss, vellum, smooth, etc. e. If a book or booklet, is there a separate cover. If a separate cover, what stock, weight and finish. f. Color of stock.

5. *How many colors—how many sides?* a. If two colors, are they two colors, not black or black and one color. b. If two colors on two sides, are they the same two colors. c. If four colors, is it four flat colors or four color process.

6. *What type of art?* a. All line, ready for camera. b. Bendays—how many and what size. c. Halftones—how many, what size, square or silhouette.

7. *If process color—a.* Size of process area or areas. b. What art will be supplied for process areas—chromes, wash drawings, continuous negatives. c. If chromes, what size and are they all in the same focus. Are they separate units or assemblies? d. Do the process areas print on one or two sides.

8. *What is the approximate ink coverage,* in percent—50%, 80% 100%.

9. *What kind of proofs are required?* a. Blueprints. b. Color keys (or chromalins)? c. Press proofs.

10. *What type of binding?* a. Saddle stitch. How many wires? b. Type and number of folds. c. Perfect bind. d. Stitched or pasted? e. Die cut. f. Embossing.

11. *What type of packing.* Skid, cartons, pallet, banded? Moisture-resistant? How should cartons be labeled?

12. *Delivery.* Where? Is delivery additional? Date of delivery. Receiving department hours?

13. *Are over-runs acceptable?* If so, the normal 10% or less?

## GENERAL COMPUTER SPECIFICATIONS

1. *What type of job?* What is the quantity? Computer letter, list maintenance, labels.

2. *How is it to be run?* Impact, ink jet, laser? On continuous form or cut sheets?

3. *If computer letter*—a. Match fill-in—how many lines. b. Full computer letter—how many lines. c. Should everything be spelled out, abbreviated or exactly as on tape if tape is supplied, (i.e., Ave., St., State, etc.). d. If prefix is not on tape, what are the rules for Mr., Miss, Mrs., Ms.? Should we look up female names on table? e. Type style—standard courier, wide courier. f. Proof and artwork information.

4. *Computer forms information*—a. One-up or two-up. b. Trim size of letter, excluding pin holes. c. Weight of stock, color. d. One or two-sided printing. e. Bindary—perforations, die-cuts or tip-ons.

5. *If labels*—a. One-up, three-up, four-up or five-up. b. Type of stock—regular Cheshire, gummed, pressure sensitive. c. Should match code, source code or other information be printed on label.

6. *If list maintenance*—a. How will client submit changes. b. How often is list to be updated. c. Will list be used for rental. If so, should test tapes of various quantities be kept "hanging."

7. *Tape information.* a. How many bits per inch (1600, 800, 556, etc.) b. What track—nine or seven. c. What is the blocking factor. d. What is the record size. Is the field fixed or variable? e. Are tape layout sheet, explanation of codes, sample printout or "dump" available?

8. *Tape information—if conversion required.* a. How much information will go onto tape—codes, dollar amounts, references, dates, etc. b. What purpose will the tape be used for—letters, labels, etc. c. Will the client be doing "dupe" elimination. d. Will the list be used for rental.

### GENERAL MAILING SPECIFICATIONS

1. *What is the quantity?*

2. *When will material be received and what is mail date?*

3. *Envelopes.* a. Size? Booklet or open end? Preprinted indicia? b. Window or closed? (If window, open or cellophane?) c. Paper or polybag?

4. *Number of inserts.* a. Sizes of each. b. Pre-folded for machine inserting, (i.e., no accordian gate or open end folds). c. Order of inserts—from flap to front.

5. *Addressing.* If labels, what kind—Cheshire, pressure sensitive, gummed. b. If labels, what is labelled—envelope, BRC, etc. c. If computer forms, to be burst and trimmed. Size of forms—number up, trim size. d. If typed address—what font? On what piece? What is the source—directory, cards, galleys, handwritten.

6. *Mailing.* a. Is list provided in strict zip code sequence? b. How many lists? Sizes from smallest to largest? c. Class of mail—first, third, bulk? d. Is indicia pre-printed? e. To be metered? f. If stamps, what kind—regular, commemorative, bulk rate, non-profit, United Nations?

7. *Bursting and folding.* a. Size of full finished sheet. b. Number up—one or two? c. Number of folds and type of fold?

8. *Shipping.* a. Where? b. How—what carrier? c. Packed in cartons? Who supplies? d. Is shipping included in price?

9. *Incidentals.* a. Tipping, stapling, clipping. b. Keying. Separately or while labeling? How many different keys? Size and position of each key.

### Getting Estimates

Once the specification sheet is prepared, getting estimates is simple. Specification sheets are simply attached to a "request-for-bid" memo and given to various suppliers.

Ideally, three suppliers should be asked to bid on each part of each job. One should be a tried-and-true supplier who helped you plan the job. Another should be an alternate supplier who is sometimes used by your firm. The third should be a new supplier who has been soliciting your work.

Unless the savings are substantial, the supplier who has been working with you and helping you should get the job. It's only fair. The alternate supplier should get occasional jobs or parts of the overall job because you don't want all your eggs in one basket. New suppliers should be tried occasionally to keep prices where they should be. If the job is exceptionally important or difficult, you won't want to work with new suppliers, but if they brought in a low bid, add them to the list for future bidding and break them in on simpler jobs.

It isn't cricket to play one supplier against the other, telling what another's bid is. You'll drive the prices down in the short run, as a hungry printer will meet your bid; but you'll pay for it in quality short-cuts, last-minute additional charges, or by putting the supplier out of business. Most likely, you'll also suffer by not getting the job out on time.

If you get a printer to do a job for less than cost just to keep the presses busy, your job is the one that will get "bumped" if a normal-profit job comes along while yours is in progress.

*Other Bidding Methods*    There are other ways to go, if you have a trained production person on your staff or acting as a consultant.

Some advertisers place their printing on a cost-plus basis—a fixed-percentage profit margin over the actual costs of the job. To do this, however, requires that you know estimating and be able to calculate press time, setup time, ink coverage, bindery, and letter-shop functions in the same way that the supplier's own estimator does.

Other advertisers act as their own printing brokers, buying the paper directly, dealing with the separators and platemakers, and buying press time (including labor) from printers around the country. Some firms regularly canvass printers or letter shops for idle machine time, to make deals that will save significantly. Here again, you have to have trained personnel who can manage the entire job through each individual graphic process, and you have to be willing to take the full responsibility for the finished job.

*Purchase Orders*    Award the job in writing, with the specification sheet appended and all details of price, overruns, delivery, etc., worked out in detail.

## Avoiding Errors

There are two ways to avoid errors. One is to check everything yourself. The other is to be sure that the client, or the senior executive in your own organization, sees and approves every detail at every stage.

*Proofreading*    Don't count on proofreaders. They check the various stages against the original copy. If the copy is wrong, the finished job will be wrong too.

A proofreader once "corrected" Barbra Streisand's name to "Barbara" at the last minute, causing understandable consternation at her record company. To avoid problems like this, a proofreader must be given a detailed list of "do's and don'ts," including spelling of proper names, styles for numbers, grammar and punctuation policies, and preferred usage.

Whenever anything is corrected, don't just check the one area that contains the correction. I once saw a piece of copy prepared on a word processor that retyped a revised paragraph and plugged it into an entirely different piece of body copy. On the revised copy the changed paragraph was perfect but everything else described an entirely different product.

*Getting Approvals*   The most critical obstacle to cost control is revisions, whether made by agency, designer, or client. The way to avoid unnecessary revisions is to be sure to obtain all approvals at each and every step of the creative and production process.

A copy change on a press proof can cost thousands of dollars; on a blueprint, hundreds; on a mechanical or type proof, about $25; on typed copy, nothing. Obviously, the earlier changes are made, the less they will cost.

Be sure that everything is checked. Don't count on a client or a senior executive to know what to look for. If a layout isn't clear, or a mechanical paste-up is confusing, be sure to point out exactly what illustration goes where, what color backgrounds will be, and any concerns you may have about the quality of the finished product.

I once saw a $30,000 printing job rerun because a client company president didn't realize that computer letters are not as neat as a secretary's hand-typed letters. I saw another job rejected because an executive didn't like the very subtle perforations on a Letterlope format. The fact that no one else was bothered by these characteristics is irrelevant. The clients were not made aware of these details and had not been asked to sign off on samples as well as mechanicals. If they had, the projects would not have become a victim of what has been called "the expectation-realization gap."

## Avoiding Rush Work

Overtime costs money, and overtime for unionised typesetters, engravers, and printers costs more than overtime for writers and artists. If you must rush a job, put the pressure on the early stages and the approval process, not on the very costly graphic arts stages.

Schedule your job carefully, as described below, and then stick to the schedule. "Walk through" approvals and corrections, rather than using mail or messengers, and be sure that everyone concerned knows the effect on timetables. It's amazing how often it is precisely the same people who insist that a job be finished on a certain date also keep making changes or delaying approvals.

Each approval process should have a deadline, just as any other step does. The approver should be notified that delays past a due date will result in extension of the final deadline or perhaps even missing a deadline.

If the basic schedule is adhered to, most rush work will involve last-minute changes or catching up on steps that fell through the cracks. Planning, specifying, and avoiding changes will be the best way to avoid rush jobs.

## CONTROLLING TIME

When submitting a project for approval, I always make it a practice to submit a timetable as well as an estimate of costs. In some ways, the timetable is more difficult to control than cost.

### Time Requirements

Table 17-1 shows some timing allocations, a composite of schedules used by various graphic arts suppliers and ad agencies. It is important to note that no two were the same.

While any of these steps can take less time under rush conditions, these are reasonable guidelines for careful cost and quality control. They add up to six to eight weeks for preparing a color ad for a magazine, half that for a black-and-white ad, and between five and six *months* for direct mail, depending on whether or not it is computerized.

These are optimum schedules, within which costs and quality can be carefully budgeted and controlled. Unfortunately, such schedules seem to be the exception rather than the rule. The need to get a new product on the market before competition does, or to wait for results of a previous mailing before sending out the next, often requires that time allocations be reduced substantially. My experience is that they can be cut in half with great difficulty but without too serious an effect on cost and time. A bigger cut than that can require severe quality risks or "crash" costs necessitated by night and weekend work.

**TABLE 17-1**
**OPTIMUM PRODUCTION TIMING**

| | Black-and-white ads | Color ads | Ads with cards | Labeled mailings | Computer mailings |
|---|---|---|---|---|---|
| Orientation and planning | 2–4 weeks | 2–4 weeks | 2–4 weeks | 2–4 weeks | 2–4 weeks |
| Copy and rough layout | 2–4 weeks | 3–5 weeks | 3–6 weeks | 3–6 weeks | 4–6 weeks |
| Comprehensive layouts | 3 days | 5 days | 5 days | 7 days | 10 days |
| Approval and revisions | 5 days | 7 days | 7 days | 7 days | 7 days |
| Typesetting and mechanicals | 7 days | 10 days | 14 days | 14 days | 16 days |
| Mechanical approval and revisions | 3 days | 4 days | 4 days | 4 days | 7 days |
| Color preparation, engraving, and proofing | 5 days | 10 days | 10 days | 15 days | 15 days |
| List order and delivery | | | | 4–5 weeks | 4–5 weeks |
| List preparation, including merge | | | | 3 weeks | 4 weeks |
| Printing, including computer forms | | | 3 weeks | 4 weeks | 5 weeks |
| Envelope conversion | | | | 1–4 weeks | 1–4 weeks |
| Labeling or computer printing | | | | 5 days | 10 days |
| Inserting and mailing | | | | 10 days | 10 days |

Note: These optimum schedules include scheduling and waiting time. On tightly scheduled projects, most of these steps can be cut in half if suppliers with available time are prescheduled. Very complex projects or mail quantities over 1 million pieces may take more time during the last two or three

## Critical Path Scheduling

Critical path method is a business planning technique originally developed as part of a process called Program Evaluation and Review Technique (PERT). It has been used to plan complex research and development (R&D) projects like the space program and major construction projects. In its most advanced usage, every step is programmed into a computer, progress is reviewed, and "critical dates" are called to the attention of appropriate managers.

Basically, the critical path method involves placing a time factor on each phase in a process, figuring what are the necessary preliminary steps for each, and laying the phases out in the indicated sequence.

This is sort of a "backward timetable," beginning with the finished project and working back step by step, perhaps plotting the time factors with lines on a sheet of graph paper.

Figure 17-1 is an example of this process applied to a complex direct mailing on a sixteen-week schedule. Note that this project was completed in four months only because several steps were conducted at the same time, so that lists and mechanicals would both be ready on the same date.

Different companies will have entirely different schedules, and so there is no way to prepare one standard schedule for everyone. For instance, large corporations might require a week for legal approval. Regulated companies might need four weeks to get the National Association of Securities Dealers (NASD) or other officials to pass on a simple letter. Companies with in-house computer facilities might be able to cut time on list processing. If only house lists are being used, the four or five weeks waiting for delivery of rented lists can be cut to a week or so.

## Ways to Save Time

There are many ways to either shorten a schedule or, at least, prevent a job from getting behind schedule. Here are some that may be helpful.

*Use Good Suppliers*   A rush job is no place to use untested or out-of-town suppliers. Use people you can count on.

*Count Everyone In*   Let everyone—client, staff, and supplier—know what the deadline is and why it's important. If possible, bring all these people together in a "starter" meeting so that all of them will know what is expected and how their part of the job affects everyone else. You'll be amazed at what shortcuts they can work out if you let them talk to each other directly.

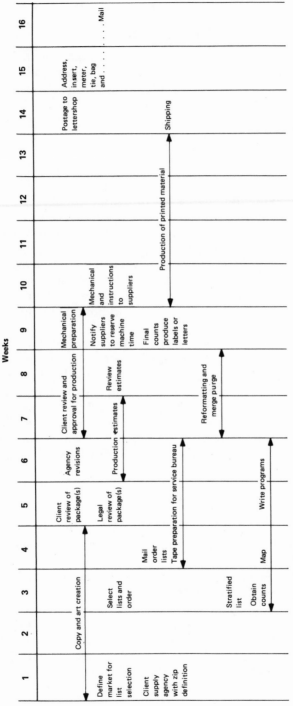

**Weeks**

| | 1 | 2 | 3 | 4 | 5 | 6 | 7 | 8 | 9 | 10 | 11 | 12 | 13 | 14 | 15 | 16 |
|---|---|---|---|---|---|---|---|---|---|---|---|---|---|---|---|---|

Copy and art creation

Define market for list selection

Client supply agency with zip definition

Select lists and order

Client review of package(s)

Agency revisions

Client review and approval for production

Mechanical preparation

Mechanical and instructions to suppliers

Postage to lettershop

Address, insert, meter, tie, bag and . . . . . . Mail

Mail order lists

Legal review of package(s)

Production estimates

Review estimates

Notify suppliers to reserve machine time

Final counts produce labels or letters

Tape preparation for service bureau

Stratified list

Obtain counts

Map

Write programs

Reformatting and merge purge

Production of printed material

Shipping

Times will vary depending on the complexity of the marketing effort, the availability of decision making people and the promptness of decisions.

**Figure 17-1.** This direct marketing production flowchart was created by Shirley Stevens of American Family Publishers for a specific mailing. This format is a convenient way to plan any promotional project. (*Source: Shirley Stevens, "Direct Marketing Production Flow Chart," Direct Marketing Manual, Direct Mail Marketing Association, New York, Manual Release No. 4007, April 1978.*)

*Order Lists Immediately*   Ordering lists is often the critical path on any job. As soon as you know the format and the lists you want, place your order with your list broker.

*Get Interim Approvals*   Don't hold everything up for minor copy revisions. Ask for an OK to proceed with preparing color artwork, for instance, or envelopes. These can be done while other parts of a mailing are still being revised.

*Order Paper Early*   Place the paper order as soon as the format has been approved, even if some copy and art elements are still being worked out. Paper is the most costly and least flexible part of the production process.

*Get It Right the First Time*   It seems contradictory, but rush jobs are precisely the time to slow down and be extra careful. There's no time to redo anything, or to fold or insert by hand; everything has to be planned carefully. Make dummies. Check with the mailing and computer firms. Be sure everything is right from the beginning.

*Consolidate Corrections*   Don't take time correcting type errors or mechanical adjustments before showing them to your client. Just mark the changes you want to make on a tissue overlay and ask the client to add corrections. You'll save time and money by doing them all at once.

*Be Mobile*   You can pick up days just by eliminating the need to send proofs back and forth for approval. Go to the printer or other supplier, and take your client or boss with you. If everyone knows the timing of the job, you should get full cooperation.

*Arrange Batch Deliveries*   On large jobs that have to go to a binder, envelope fabricator, or computer printer, don't wait to ship all copies at once. Send the first million as soon as it's ready, to let the next processor get started. Send the rest in agreed-upon increments.

*Pin Down All Interim Dates*   Be sure that delivery dates—and sometimes even the time of day—are indicated in writing and pointed out to each supplier. "As soon as possible" and even "rush" are meaningless. If suppliers have a specific time to aim for, they are more likely to make it, and will be less likely to "bump" your job for some larger customer's rush job.

## CONTROLLING QUALITY

Presuming that the layout of the ad or mailing represents what you are really looking for, the problem of quality control in the production process is one of fidelity—being faithful to the original design.

### Typesetting

Fidelity begins with the type-specification process, a task sometimes delegated to a member of a production department or outside art studio staff. However, it must be done under the direction and with the approval of the art director who designed the original layout. The wrong choice of type faces, sizes, or spacing can completely alter the feeling of a layout.

A frequent problem is that copy might turn out to be too long, especially if lawyers or others have added long phrases that were not in the original copy. The wrong solution to this problem is to "make it fit," with illustrations reduced, spacing omitted, and type set small and crowded. It doesn't take much to impair the entire body language of the ad or mailing. A better solution is to sit down with all parties concerned, including the copywriter, and make deliberate choices about what can be cut or omitted.

### Type Proofs

The readability of the finished product will be no better than the quality of the type proof. It's easy to spot broken type. It's not as easy to pick out the results of a poorly pulled proof if the type is set from linotype. or a bad print if from phototype. Either way, it is a lot easier to be fussy at this stage than when the ad is in mechanical, film, or plate form.

If the proof isn't clear and sharp, if the edges of type are blurred or rounded, then ask for a new proof right away. Don't try taking a bad proof through the various production processes. Quality can't be gained, only lost. Sharpness goes downhill from that first type proof, so insist that it be right.

### Illustrations

If you're using photography, go to the photography session and look at all the details that the photographer might miss. The chances are that the photographer will be concentrating on lighting and composition. You should look at how the model is dressed and posed, whether your production is displayed at the best possible angle, whether the background is distracting, and whether the props set the right image. The photo will be no better than the negative at the moment the picture is taken.

Cropping and retouching usually can't add quality that's not in the photo. You can remove some defects or mask out an error, but the best bet is to get the picture right at the beginning.

If you're using artwork, then have it drawn oversized and insist that it be right. Revise it as many times as you have to, until you know it's what you want. This is no time to spare the artist's feelings.

Be sure to get a photostat and look at any artwork in the size that it will actually appear. Embarrassing details can suddenly show up when a 35mm chrome or contact print is blown up to a larger size. An oversized painting that looks exciting can lose all its detail and blur together when printed in a smaller size.

## Mechanical Paste-Ups

The mechanical stage is very important. This is where all the pieces fit together into camera-ready art. It's the last practical opportunity to make simple revisions or catch typographic errors.

As stated in previous chapters, spacing is very important. It can usually be easily adjusted in the mechanical stage, but more can go wrong than right. Strictly speaking, the mechanical stage is an executional one, and although it is a skilled and professional craft, it is usually not an additive process. Fidelity is the objective. The art is avoiding loss of fidelity. For instance, if photostats of type are ordered, those stats can lose a degree of sharpness from the original type proof. They can never make it sharper.

The mechanical should be prepared and checked with fidelity in mind. Any approval authorities should be cautioned that this is the last stage at which changes can be made without stopping the progress of an entire job.

## Photographic Processes

Color separators, Velox makers, and platemakers have the common objective of converting the mechanical paste-up into a form that can be turned into press plates and printed at a newspaper, magazine, or printing plant. The processes vary according to the end use and the artwork provided, but the objective is the same: fidelity.

The way to get what you want is to be sure that everyone knows what that is before starting. You have to supply good artwork and clear instructions. For instance, if you are shooting gold coins and want a

# Rapp & Collins INC.

A DOYLE DANE BERNBACH COMPANY • 475 PARK AVENUE SOUTH, NEW YORK, N.Y. 10016 • (212) 725-8100

# Direct Mail Production Estimate

| Client | SKANDINAVISK | Date | 6/25/79 | Approved By | | |
|---|---|---|---|---|---|---|
| Job No. | 2046 | Title | Introductory-My Great Recipes | DM | AE | Client |

**Job Description**
1. 4PP Letter: 11x7½ 4/4 50# offset fold to 5½x3 3/4
2. Certificate & Stamps: 5½x7½ 4/2 " " 5½x3 3/4 Die-cut perforations/perforations and spot gum
3. Lift Letter: 11x3 3/4 2/2 folds to 5½x3 3/4
4. Triple guarantee: 5½x3 3/4 4/4 50# offset
5. Outer envelope: 6½x5 3/4 4-color 70# offset window cello patch
6. Business reply envelope: 5 9/16x4 2/C 24# W.W.
7. Brochure: 16½x11 4/4 70# coated fold to 4x5½ and bleed

**Production Schedule**

| | | | Mechanicals To Printer | 7-17 |
|---|---|---|---|---|
| Copy & Layout | 6-25 | | | |
| Dummy | 6-27 | Proofs | 8-1 |
| Mechanicals | 7-12 | At Lettershop | 8-20 |
| | | Mail Date | 9-3 |

**Mailing Information**

Sort and bag by carrier route code. Mail third class.

**Preparation**

| Photography | $ 2,500 |
|---|---|
| Retouching | 500 |
| Illustrations | 1,125 |
| Mechanicals | 2,000 |
| Photostats | 200 |
| Typesetting | 2,000 |
| Photolettering | 1,000 |
| Assemblies | 850 |
| Props | 1,000 |
| Lettering | 800 |
| Dupes | 1,000 |
| Copy Prints | 350 |
| Tax | 1,066 |
| **Total A & M** | 14,391 |

| *to be decided | Contingency | 2,159 |
|---|---|---|
| | Production Fee | 2,921 |
| | Creative Fee | |
| | **Total Preparation** | 19,471 |

**Comments:**
- One computer form/run together
- 50,000 and 150,000 run in combination
- Additional cost for programing, etc., if needed
- First class could be 28¢ each based on weight

**Printing & Mailing**      60,000

| Quantity | First Cl | Bulk | |
|---|---|---|---|
| ☐ Form  ☒ Computer  * | 4,800 | 4,800 | |
| Letter | | | |
| Brochure | 11,260 | 11,260 | |
| Outside Envelope | 5,800 | 5,800 | |
| Reply Envelope | 1,380 | 1,380 | |
| lift letter* | 2,400 | 2,400 | |
| triple guarantee* | 1,200 | 1,200 | |
| *order form/cert/stamps | 2,400 | 2,400 | |
| Paper | | | |
| Separations | 15,000 | 15,000 | |
| Finishing | | | |
| Binding | | | |
| Shipping | | | |
| **Total Printing** | 44,240 | 44,240 | |
| Labeling or Addressing 12 lines | 2,100 | 2,100 | |
| Affixing or Metering  computer | | | |
| Inserting | | | |
| Sort, Tie, Bag, etc. | | | |
| **Total Mailing** | 2,900 | 2,900 | |
| **Total Printing & Mailing** | 49,240 | 49,240 | |
| Contingency  15% | 7,400 | 7,400 | |
| Mailing Lists | 5,705 | 5,705 | |
| ☐Dup. Elim. ☐Zip Elim. ☐Purge | To be determined later – if needed  cost additional | | |
| Postage ☐First ☐Bulk | 9,000 | 5,040 | |

| | Total | 71,345 | 67,385 |
|---|---|---|---|
| | Agency Fee | 12,600 | 11,900 |
| | Preparation | 19,471 | 19,471 |
| | **Grand Total** | 103,416 | 98,756 |
| | CPM | | |

All estimates are based upon current costs and normal schedules. Any changes in specifications, paper prices, or working schedules may be reflected in final costs.

A typical production estimate form. This one combines mechanical costs with printing and mailing.

specific tone of gold, then be sure to show the photo processors a sample. They are not mind readers. If two photos of the same coin start with different colors, the finished printing job will look the same way. High-quality photo processors can work miracles, but only on request.

Usually the only adjustments that are necessary are color specifications, within very narrow ranges. Some minor adjustments can be made, through lightening or darkening one of the color-separated positive films, or by expensive dot etching; but the color of the proof and the ensuing printing job can be no better than the artwork you provide.

One helpful hint: Be sure the engraver knows what kind of paper the job will ultimately be printed on. Insist that press proofs be pulled on the stock specified. Degrees of finish and absorbency can dramatically affect the fineness of the screen and the mix of the colors selected.

### Printing

It would take years to teach an advertiser everything a printer knows about achieving quality. All you have to understand is that by the time the job gets on the press, the printer's options are very limited.

Quality begins with the typesetting, the artwork, the mechanical, and the photo processing. By the time the piece gets on press, all that can be adjusted is the impression, the speed, and the color. Yet it is always the printer who gets blamed if the job doesn't look right.

*Impression* is a function of the make-ready process, in which the pressure between the printing cylinder (whether letterpress or offset) and the base cylinder behind the paper being printed is adjusted slightly.

*Speed* can affect the ink application and how fast the printed sheet passes through a drying station.

*Color* can be lightened or darkened on press, but it's better if it starts out right in the proof stage.

*Other Processes*   If quality is the supreme requirement, then consider—when first planning the job—using letterpress or gravure printing instead of the more common offset lithography. These processes are sometimes used when printing illustrated books, photography magazines, and fine art reproductions. The differences are dramatic, and the costs are not excessive. The problem is that most printers have converted to the higher-speed offset process, and letterpress and gravure printing are no longer widely available.

*Mailing Lists*   The simplest process should be placing orders for the mailing lists you previously selected. Unfortunately, because there are so many sources and subsuppliers involved, such orders are frequently mishandled. I recently ordered ten lists for a test of a new product which included both sex select and sectional center zip select. Over 40 percent did not meet specifications and had to be reordered.

Lists should be "dumped"—printed out on paper—as soon as they arrive so you can spot-check to see if they fit specifications. It's a mistake to wait until they are all ready to be merged for labeling or computer printing, as it can then be too late to have incorrect lists rerun as you requested.

Computer Printing   Here too, many things can go wrong. For instance, most computer printers print through ribbons. The darkness of the finished printing can be very different depending on the ribbon and type chain used and on how the pressure of the printing device is set. This will affect whether or not fill-ins match the type that was originally provided, presumably by the same computer printer.

Also, there are different typefaces in computer printing. Some are narrow, some are wide, and some are entirely different faces. If you want your job to look the way you expect it to, be sure that you match the computer fill-in to the rest of the job.

Shipment   Here's another apparently simple process—but what disasters can take place! Be sure to specify whether a job is to be banded, in cartons, or stacked on skids, and choose how you want it shipped. I've shared many anxious moments with production managers waiting for news that a magazine insert, last seen on a loading dock in St. Louis, finally arrived at the publication only hours before final closing.

Shipping and freight are not to be taken for granted and should be considered, planned, and executed correctly. Any shipping instructions to suppliers should be sure to include not only when something should be shipped, but how.

Letter Shop   What can go wrong in a letter shop? Plenty. For one thing, there have been plenty of horror stories about mailing the wrong insert to the wrong list. For another, it's easy to completely omit one of the pieces of a mailing.

Careful written instructions and clear insert coding must be provided. Each and every piece should have a code number clearly visible without unfolding the piece. And your inserting instructions should clearly list the sequence, the facing, and the nesting of the various pieces. A sample package, stapled together so the sequence will not become confused, should be provided as soon as printed samples are ready.

A Phillipsburg inserter stacks one piece on top of another. A Pitney-Bowes inserter nests one inside another. Inserting equipment can have six, eight, ten, or even fourteen "stations," each inserting a single component. The more stations you need, the more costly the inserting will be and the more difficult it will be to find a supplier with the right equipment.

Also, if you don't want your mail date delayed, be sure to send the letter shop a certified check to cover postage. They can't mail until the Postal Service has been paid. If postage is affixed on-line, the entire process will be held up.

*Mailing Checks* How do you know the mailing went out on time and the way you wanted it? The final test is to see how and when it arrives in the mail.

Always "salt" a list with names of some of your key executives, and be sure they are merged into the list at the computer house, not at the letter shop.

A mailer once inserted the "salt names" by hand, including an awful error. Fortunately, the automatically inserted part of the mailing was correct, but the reverse happens more often, so be sure the names are mixed in so they get the same treatment as the bulk of the mailing.

It's a good idea to include some people in other parts of the country, so you can get an idea of the Postal Service's delivery at the time of the mailing. It will make a difference when you're trying to read results if you discover, for example, that your mail still has not been delivered on the other coast.

## SUPPLIERS ARE PEOPLE TOO

Choosing graphic arts suppliers is more than a matter of getting three bids and picking the lowest one. You might save 5 or 10 percent with such strict purchasing procedures, just as you might save a small part of the 15 percent commission by not using an ad agency, but these economies can cost you 50, 100, or 200 percent or more where it really counts—in response rates.

Of course, get competitive bids; but put service, cooperation, and creative contribution into the mix when you make your final decision.

Your suppliers are not servants, and they are not the enemy. They can and should be part of your team, involved in the creative process at as early a stage as possible. The contributions they can make are enormous.

For instance, an engraver can suggest a fine white line between two illustrations to avoid expensive premium services, or can show you how to prepare a scaled assembly of illustration elements or to work with Veloxes. An engraver who is willing to work with you can save you much more than the difference between suppliers.

A printer can suggest a slight change in sizes that will make better use of paper sizes, or can help you develop a format that will do a better job of presenting your particular message at a better price.

A computer firm may have stock programming that can save you both time and money. A mailing house can make subtle suggestions, such as widening an address window or changing a fold, that can facilitate inserting.

Too many marketers simply prepare their specifications and send them out for bids, without making suppliers part of the process. Three different printers, for example, might vary 5 or 10 percent in price; but one of them may show you how to combine two elements in the package and save 25 percent of the total cost. Isn't *that* the real economy?

The way to build a relationship with your suppliers is to make them part of the team and to let them know that they will have your work as long as they keep their prices in line. You want your account to be important to them, and it won't if they have to low-ball their bids to get each and every job. My suggestion is to take bids on every job from new suppliers but to change suppliers only when you can save at least 10 percent. In that case, *change* suppliers, don't rotate them or play one against the other. When you find good ones, be good to them as long as they're good to you.

## CHAPTER EIGHTEEN

# BACK-END PROMOTIONS

The many kinds of new business efforts discussed in previous chapters are sometimes referred to as front-end promotions. The equally vital techniques for making these customers, once acquired, profitable buyers of our products and users of our services are called back-end promotions.

In direct marketing, back-end promotions are particularly vital. Each new customer usually represents a sizable investment in advertising cost and sometimes in a premium. Customers don't have to walk out of the store to abrogate this investment. They don't even have to make a negative decision. The effect is the same if they simply do nothing. Our hard-won customers—even those with the best intentions—start to fall by the wayside from the very first contact.

Perhaps they simply inquire but don't buy. That's understandable. But what about the customer who orders and decides not to keep our product? Or the one who, worse yet, keeps it and doesn't pay for it? Then there's the one-time buyer, who takes advantage of our initial offer and never makes a purchase that gives us enough margin to make the whole effort worthwhile.

## HARNESSING INERTIA

One principle that helps us understand the dynamics of customer behavior at the back end is inertia. *Webster's New Collegiate Dictionary* defines "inertia" this way: "a property of matter by which it remains at rest or in uniform motion in the same straight line unless acted upon by some external force." Inertia is a human characteristic as well, and it can work for you or work against you.

**349**

Inertia is your ally if your proposition is a "club" with negative option, or a series of publications or products sold on a "ship-till-forbid" basis. It is your ally in the travel field if your customers have your company's reservation number in their pockets or by their phone, or in banking, if they have authorized any type of automatic investment, sale, or savings—particularly with payments charged to an existing checking or charge account.

However, inertia is a formidable obstacle to be overcome for most marketers. Imagine this scenario. A male customer returns from a hard day's work, greets his family, kicks off his shoes, and collapses into his favorite chair to look at the day's mail. He has magazines he would enjoy reading, a letter from an old friend, a bill that demands attention, and an assortment of mail from both local and national advertisers. One of them is yours.

Your letter asks him to buy something that he has somehow managed very well without for most of his life, to decide which of several models or subscription terms is right for him, to calculate not only the price but shipping costs and sales tax, to remember his size, to find his charge card or write out a check—right at that moment. Lotsa luck!

Some might say "If people want my product, they'll go to the trouble to write a letter or deal with a complicated order form." In theory that's correct, but inertia gets in the way. No matter how good your deal, you will lose business because some people will put it off until later, and then just never get around to it. In most cases, "later" means "never."

## OVERCOMING PROCRASTINATION

All this brings us to another important principle that should be kept in mind when planning back-end promotions: procrastination. The need for immediacy or urgency, more fully discussed in Chapter 12, Creative Tactics, applies just as much to the back end—but with greater opportunities for effective application. Expiration dates, limited supply, impending price increases, and special introductory offers all have greater credibility with a previous customer than with a front-end prospect.

## EFFECT ON ALLOWABLE MARGIN

Chapter 20, Mail-Order Math, explains the concept of allowable margin: the portion of the selling price available for a combination of advertising (new-customer acquisition cost) and for contribution to advertising and overhead. The importance of back-end improvement is obvious after one has done some final projections this way.

Let's postulate a product with a $100 sales cost and a $40 allowable margin. In this example, the back-end figures include existing conversion, collection, return, and unit sale experience. Imagine that we can devise an offer to sell some type of accessory costing $30, with a $15 margin and a $5 back-end cost per order, to one-half of our customers. This might be, for instance, a "bounce-back" promotion (explained below). In this case, the supplementary contribution is $10 per order on one-half the orders, or a $5 overall addition to the new order margin (the total contribution divided by the total number of customers). If our new-member advertising cost was $25 before, leaving us a $15 contribution per new customer, the effect of the back-end improvement—an additional $5 margin—goes directly to the promotion's bottom line and gives us a $20, instead of a $15, contribution per new customer. This one-third increase in profitability is the result of the back-end promotion.

Another way to look at this is to calculate what improvement in cost per order you would have needed to get the same result. In our example, the new-member advertising cost would have had to be improved by 20 percent—from $25 to $20—in order to get the same result. For instance, a 4 percent direct-mail response rate would have had to become 5 percent.

One reason this is so important in understanding direct marketing is that there are business propositions that appear to be patently unprofitable, unless you understand the dynamics of the back end. There are magazines that lose money or, at best, break even on the first year's subscriptions, making their entire profit on advertising or renewals. There is at least one company selling incredibly low-priced maps or books, whose real aim is to amass sizable lists for promoting their other products and for renting to other direct-mail users.

The balance of this chapter will be devoted to describing a score of possible back-end promotions. Almost all of them are adaptable, at least in theory, to virtually every type of product or service. The creative grid technique, discussed in Chapter 12, is one way to apply these ideas to your own situations.

## RESELL EFFORTS

The primary objective of this technique is to reduce returns by customers. It is used most often with shipments of high-ticket mail-order merchandise purchased on impulse.

In its simplest form, the resell effort can simply be a restatement of the basic appeals that motivated the customer to purchase from the original advertisement, commercial, or mailing piece. The less considered the purchase, the greater the need to resell at the point of delivery.

For example, one company advertised a revolutionary way to rid one's backyard of mosquitos and other insects without electrical grids and the noisy sound of bugs being zapped all night long. This was certainly an appealing item. However, the item delivered was basically an electric fan which sucked in slow-flying insects and dropped them in a tray of water to drown. Where the original appeal presented the idea of relaxing in your hammock without annoying insects, the focus now was on the instructions which indicated a need to periodically empty the water tray filled with assorted bug carcasses. Ugh! Of course return rates were high.

A resell insert can change the focus back to the ultimate benefit to the customer. It should restate guarantees and dramatize the manufacturer's offer to try the product for a reasonable amount of time before deciding. It might use a kind of peer pressure to tell, perhaps in letter form, how many people have ordered and reordered the item. A few testimonials certainly help delay the decision to return a purchase.

If an item requires complicated assembly or operating instructions, care should be taken—even at the expense of rewriting the instructions completely—to make the use of the item as easy as possible.

If an item was sold as a prestige-giving asset, perhaps with some type of club membership or air of exclusivity, this should be carefully restated and consistently presented.

No matter what imagery was involved in motivating the original purchase, it should be carried through consistently in every aspect of this first impression: the shipping package, the wrapping, the bills or shipping documents. It is amazing how often a well-presented product advertised in a sophisticated magazine is fulfilled in a battered manila shipping envelope with tacky, uncoordinated inserts.

If you must generate additional income by accepting package insert enclosures from other companies, then at least be fussy and accept only those whose offers and appearances enhance your own product. Bargain offers of pantyhose, no matter how meritorious in their own right, simply have no place in the initial shipment of a Zubin Mehta recording to a new member of the classical division of a mail-order music service.

Resell involves not only the communications included with the product, but the entire first impression.

## TRADE-UP PROMOTION

"Here's the shirt you asked for, sir," says the clerk in the haberdashery store. "Let me show you a beautiful tie that will go perfectly with it."

"As long as you're buying such a fine car," the automobile saleswoman says, "I'm sure you'll want the deluxe radio with stereo, tape player, signal seeker, and CB radio."

Trade-ups have long been accepted in retailing, but they have still to gain general acceptance in the direct marketing field. Yet they represent one of the easiest profit potentials for most ongoing propositions.

The front-end application is simple. "Check this box and we'll send you the deluxe edition for only $5 more." The deluxe edition might mean only a better binding, an extra section, or stamped initials.

The back-end application isn't so simple. It often means devising accessories, companion pieces, or refills of some kind. Encyclopedias offer yearbook subscriptions. Products offer large economy sizes. Services offer an extra premium for a longer term.

Perhaps one of the most innovative examples of a trade-up offer is the way sophisticated magazine advertisers are using direct-response television combined with inbound telephone. The two-minute announcement offers an introductory subscription at half the newsstand price: "One year for only $12." The customer calls an 800 number, and the telephone operator takes the necessary information—name, address, city. Then comes the trade-up offer: "Instead of the one-year offer, ma'am, I can enter your subscription for two years for $20—a savings of 58 percent."

In magazine circulation promotion, this technique is sometimes called "renewal at birth." The trade-up effort can range from an elaborate mailer or bill insert to a simple line on the invoice: "Check here for greater savings. . . ."

There are trade-up applications for virtually every product or service, and because they usually enjoy a "free ride" with an invoice or shipment, they are as close as one ever gets in this business to a sure thing.

## COLLECTION LETTERS

When you are selling on credit, sometimes the sale is the easiest part of the marketing problem.

*Convention*   The mainstay of any collection effort is, of course, the invoice. It should look like an invoice and be worded like an invoice—not like a colorful promotion piece. An effective mail-order bill is often a computer-printed invoice, complete with account numbers, computer codes, the exact amount, and if possible, a due date.

An initial invoice can include some gentle references to memberships in national credit bureaus, or a reminder that promptness counts when building a credit reputation. In my opinion, it should always include an addressed reply envelope, though not necessarily one with postage paid by the addressee.

Convention is the governing force here, as in any kind of direct-mail layout. People expect a bill to look a certain way, and if it meets their expectations, it will be treated like their other bills.

Graphically and typographically, even a bill and a payment envelope should maintain the imagery selected for the initial promotion. Even an invoice can look elegant, newsy, personal, or businesslike.

*Progression*   Subsequent bills traditionally take on added urgency. A gentle "Please pay" in handwriting or a "Past due" in a formidable rubber-stamped impression will always have a place in any series of collection letters. Friendly notes with a message like "Have you overlooked our invoice?" or "Is there anything wrong?" are always appropriate.

Flattery can get you somewhere in collection letters: "This may be a small amount to you, but it means a lot to us" is an effective theme.

Later in a progression of collection letters, the threatening approach has become routine, meaning overused. "Before I turn this account over to our collection manager . . ." is followed by a change in stationery, signature, and tone: "Please be advised that . . ."

I prefer a more sincere approach, with handwritten letters, perfumed notes, or a touch of humor. Most severe collection approaches are no longer legal or, more to the point, effective. A really heavy threat usually won't bring in enough money at that late stage to be worth the bad will created. Let the outside collection agencies or lawyers do the threatening. When all else has failed, you may as well turn the account over to collection specialists and let them do their thing in their way—which is much more powerful than the roughest letter you would want to produce yourself.

*Immediacy*   The urgency principle applies in collection letters as in any other kind of promotion. Letters can have the deadline theme, as in "Last chance to renew without interrupting your subscription," "Last chance to reinstate your subscription," or "Last chance to pay and maintain your present excellent credit rating with us."

Billing letters are designed to collect money as their primary purpose, but there is another objective as well. That objective is to collect the money without endangering the basic customer relationship.

Notations such as "If you have already paid this invoice, please disregard this request" may reduce the level of correspondence somewhat, but there is still a lot of annoyance if customers receive bills for accounts that have already been paid. Many companies skip a full month after the first bill to give customers a chance to make payments before getting the next bill. In this way, the prompt payers—the largest and most valuable group of customers—are spared the annoyance of getting the second bill at all.

## CONVERSION EFFORTS

How do you turn an inquiry into a sale? A trial subscription into a full-term one? An unused credit card or charge account into an active customer? A catalog request into a catalog sale? A simple kit buyer into a steady customer? The answer: every way you can.

Conversion is the payoff effort to every type of two-step promotion. Traditionally, the first response, sometimes called the acknowledgement package, is an all-out effort to make every point you have to, in every way, to make the sale now or never. This is where the blue-chip brochures, broadsides, samples, letters, and testimonial flyers come in—and usually pay off. This is the first impression, the opening curtain, the grand climax, and the finale all rolled into one.

Your prospects asked for this package, in one way or another. They have identified themselves as prospects. They are almost sure to open the package and at least look through it. You have their names and perhaps other information which makes it possible to highly personalize your communication. With a high order ratio expected, you can afford to do it right. This is no time to hold back.

Presuming you have pulled out all the stops, your marketing problem here is not just to overcome buyer concerns but to deal with your real obstacle: procrastination.

The recipients who don't want our product or service, perhaps because of cost, aren't going to be persuaded to buy something they don't really want—no matter what you do. The presold prospect who has just been waiting for the specifications and an order form will buy it if you send a bundle of mimeographed pages. The real target is the person in the middle—who needs your product but can live without it, who would like to have it someday but has more pressing needs, who definitely wants to buy it but has put aside the order form to fill out and mail "someday."

For this prospect, you need "the works": facts, proof, guarantees. What is even more important, you have to overcome inertia. The key to making the conversion effort work is to provide effective motivations for acting now rather than later.

- A shoe company offers a free wallet with the first order from its catalog, sent to a customer acquired with a low-priced item advertised in a Sunday newspaper supplement.

- When filling a customer's initial order, a photo processor includes a coupon good for a 50-cent credit or a free enlargement.

- A car rental company offers a free roadmap book the first time their newly issued credit card is actually used.

- Political and philanthropic fund raisers provide a moral incentive to act now, in the form of an immediate need—funds for a major television campaign; to finance a special effort in a key state; to get a tractor to a needy village in time for harvest; to feed a particular hungry child whose name, background, and photograph are enclosed.

- In one of the highest-unit sales efforts around, a precut home fabricator offers preseason specials—for each season. (I've seen price discounts, offers of free insulation, and bonus garages—all for acting now, this season, rather than the next.)

If the acknowledgement package is too heavy to go by first-class mail, a fast, simple letter is usually in order, thanking the customer and promising the requested information. This is sometimes called a "keep-warm letter."

However, even with every possible device in the initial acknowledgement package, only 40 to 60 percent of the potential business will be derived from the order form it contains. The initial package should be only the beginning of a series of communications designed to remind and resell the customer.

The main purpose of these mailings is to restress urgency and to make an order form available at the time when, because of personal finances, biorhythm, astrology, or change of mood, the prospect is finally ready to take the plunge and follow through on the interest expressed when the inquiry or trial originated.

Follow-ups can take many forms, but all should be aimed at combating inertia. They can include carbons of the original letter, reminders of special-offer deadline dates, and announcements of new special offers with new deadlines. To make each mailing look different, they should usually stress different points. One might have a testimonial emphasis, another might dramatize the guarantee, and still another might be a sincere letter from a company officer.

How many efforts should a conversion follow-up series include? As many as you need to do the job. As long as the allowable margin continues to exceed the order cost, try another mailing. You can always cut back if the last one doesn't pay out. Even then, it will probably pay to send it to inquiries from one source if not another. Usually my clients end up with between six and eight mailings in this type of series. Some companies, with large lists and sophisticated analysis methods, have refined follow-ups to a point where they will vary the eventual number of follow-ups according to the source. High-quality leads will justify more efforts than those from less desirable sources.

Table 18-1 shows a typical mailing series—a composite of several successful ones. It's a good starting point for your own experimentation with conversion techniques.

If the value of the order is high enough, this series may be supplemented by telephone calls following up the letters at key points and making the same offers. The calls—starting with introductions such as "Did you get our letter?" and service offers such as "Do you have any questions?—can be effective if they are done well. However, care should be taken so that resentment about the telephone intrusion doesn't hurt overall response. Phone selling will show a quick lift in directly attributable sales, but it could depress the overall return depending on the script, the skill of the caller, and the sensitivity level of the typical customer.

**TABLE 18-1**
**TYPICAL CONVERSION SERIES**

| Effort | Theme | Offer |
|---|---|---|
| 1. On receipt; first-class mail | Thanks; information on way | None (this is a keep-warm letter.) |
| 2. On receipt; bulk mail | Basic acknowledgement | Premium for fast action by date |
| 3. Two weeks | Carbon copy | Premium reminder |
| 4. Four weeks | Testimonial | Premium expiration |
| 5. Eight weeks | Letter from president | Premium extension |
| 6. Twelve weeks | Guarantee | Easy payment or low down payment |
| 7. Sixteen weeks | New premium announced | New premium |
| 8. Twenty weeks | Benefit theme | New premium reminder |
| 9. Twenty-four weeks | Questionnaire (Include referral request.) | Premium expiration |
| 10. Thirty weeks | Last chance | Prices not guaranteed later |

What happens after letter No. 10? Do you write the name off and dispatch it to direct marketing limbo? No, just move it into a general file of previous inquiries to be solicited all over again, once or twice a year. House lists including such names as former customers, inactive members, and subscription expires always, without exception, become the most effective and profitable mailing list for subsequent promotions. Each name goes full circle and becomes ready for the whole gamut of front-end approaches.

## RENEWAL SERIES

Whether you have a home repair service, a term insurance policy, a membership of some sort, or a periodical subscription, renewals are the key to profitability.

In magazine subscriptions, one of the most demanding of all direct marketing fields, the first attempt to convert a trial offer to a full-rate subscription is called a conversion because the introductory offer is customarily at a lower price than the ongoing renewal rate. Perhaps 50 percent of initial subscribers "convert," and 80 percent of those who have already converted "renew."

The same type of ratio applies to any renewal effort. Because the expected response rate is so high, it is once again economically feasible to devote a major effort to this process. As in conversion or collection efforts, it is not uncommon to use a six- or eight-letter series over a period of months.

However, unlike conversion efforts, the major efforts in renewals are usually not at the beginning of the series but toward the end. Inertia is already on your side and the writer should presume an intent to renew rather than dramatizing the need to make a decision. A major sales effort presumes nonrenewal and a need for a decision. A simple invoice or reminder presumes that no change in the inertia-driven status is expected.

The most effective opening renewal notice is, therefore, the simplest. Most publishers today use a "turnaround document," a simple notice and card designed to mail back to the publisher. To be consistent with the convention theory discussed in Chapter 14, I prefer that such cards be as official looking as possible.

One technique is to ask the customer how many years of renewal or how many refills they want, or whether they want the plain or deluxe edition this year, rather than asking for a yes or no decision. This technique is based on one of the earliest examples of sales psychology: Coca-Cola's advice to restaurants to ask whether a customer wants "a large or small Coke" rather than "Do you want something to drink?" It is now accepted practice to invite a current member or subscriber to choose the "large or small" renewal without featuring the negative alternative. After all, the negative choice can be expressed by not responding at all.

Many companies combine renewal and billing efforts by asking for renewal only with payment, at least in the first few mailings. Later in the series, they offer the "Bill-me-later" alternative. This is one of those details that differs from one client to the next and should be tested, analyzed, and modeled financially.

A typical series begins about four months before the expiration of the series, unless the subscription was so short that only a few months have gone by since the first issue was received. After the first renewal effort, skip a cycle—that is, wait two months instead of one—before sending out the next effort. So many renewals are received on the first effort that you want time to get the responses before sending out the next mailing, which will then be a substantially reduced quantity. Perhaps 25 percent of the total response will come in from that first mailing, and avoiding a second bill will save the cost of answering a great many letters from people telling you that they have already paid or renewed.

The subsequent renewal efforts can then get a bit more urgent, with specific references to forthcoming expiration dates, missed issues, or possible reinstatement. Toward the end of the series, it is sometimes advisable to resell the benefits of the product all over again, to use sincere appeals, to devise questionnaires, or to otherwise dramatize the basic selling themes of the proposition.

As with conversion efforts, the length of the series may vary according to source. The economic analysis determining whether more letters are justified will show different results when different groups of members or subscribers are reviewed.

Some interesting experiments have been conducted with early-response incentives. The classic renewal series might offer a full-price renewal at the beginning of the mailing series and switch to a special introductory offer when the name gets placed in the expire file. Some companies have tried the reverse. A special incentive is offered for early renewal, justified by "saving us the trouble and expense of sending more notices." The approach is a very interesting one, though few publishers have used it. I suspect that the cost of sending the incentive to all subscribers (even those most eager to renew) might not be justified by the added renewals. Also, the added renewals at the beginning of the series may simply be accelerated responses that are offset by lower response later on.

For example, a premium or discount may cost $1 and result in a 10 percent increase in response. The effective premium cost of the increased response is $11, because the same premium has to be given to the original ten customers who would have responded anyway as well as to the one additional customer.

It is a shame that renewal efforts, like billing and conversion efforts, are so often considered routine. Some companies use professional creative sources for their front-end material but feel that this type of letter is so simple they can handle it themselves. Yet the truth is that such back-end efforts demand the same care and expertise as any other part of the promotional effort, because the net effect on profitability is usually greater than the result of a slightly increased front-end response.

One additional approach to renewals can be to build the renewal process into the proposition. There are three ways that this is being done which might apply, in principle, to other businesses as well.

One is the book club bonus-books system, in which the membership continues after satisfaction of the initial commitment. An offer such as "One book free for every two you buy," is generally dramatized with bonus coupons.

The second is the automatic shipment authorization, where the publisher of an annual—say an encyclopedia yearbook—has built into the original agreement an authorization to ship and bill the product each year. Usually the customer is granted the option of returning the book without further obligation or shipments.

The third is the automatic renewal technique, where the original offer guarantees "the lowest rate available" for future renewals, and builds in the order for renewal. The only problem then is billing. At the time of this writing, one major advertiser has used such an offer without a material decrease in initial responses, which will be successful if the renewals hold up a year later. However, it will be some time before we know whether this hidden renewal order is actually honored a full year later.

## REACTIVATION TECHNIQUES

An attempt to keep a former relationship active or to reinstate it is a form of renewal, but it is actually closer to the front-end promotion in theory and practice. Every front-end creative and offer approach can be used in attempts to reinstate former relationships, with the single addition of reminding the customer of the previous contact.

One client, Avis Rent-a-Car, had millions of "Wizard Reservation Numbers" but found that a large percentage were completely inactive.

The gamut of programs we developed ranged from free gifts with the next rental to simply reissuing the stickers bearing the numbers. (The numbers were originally sent on labels with instructions to affix them to a credit card, but the labels were discarded when the cards expired.)

Another interesting example was RCA Music Service's mailing which referred, in giant ink-jet type showing through an envelope window, to the previous date and type of music: "To Mrs. Jones—our 1968 classical music member." This type of "We've missed you" mailing is used by many large mailers. Reactivation efforts are so profitable that this technique belongs in any direct marketing program.

## REFERRAL PROMOTIONS

Prospect lists are valuable assets to any company, and list building is an important activity to be included in a marketing plan. List-building activities come in many forms, but the most common are member-get-member (MGM) and get-a-friend (GAF) offers.

In the simplest form, you ask customers for a list of friends who might like to receive a catalog, learn about your service, or receive news about your activities. Such a request can be minimal—a simple slip of paper or a message on the back of an invoice form—or it can be a separate insert or brochure.

One common theory is the "birds-of-a-feather" idea. Good customers tend to send in names of other potentially good customers. Bad customers tend to send in names of other potential bad-pay buyers. Therefore, requests for names are often included only in package inserts, mailings to converted buyers, or early-stage invoices—never in dunning letters or initial conversion packages.

More ambitious programs actually recruit present customers as salespeople to some extent. Record clubs often enclose a brochure which a club member can give to a friend. Such brochures contain the basic offer and an order form or membership application. The only difference is that there is a space for the recommending member's name and address. The sponsoring member is usually offered some type of free gift or credit for recommending the new member.

Because the brochure has to contain the entire sales story and an application or order form, it is usually a multiple-page pamphlet. It is possible for the same brochure to have a detachable flap containing the offer to the sponsoring member.

Some political candidates use mailings to their core supporters, asking them to each get five or ten new contributors by distributing envelopes and pamphlets which are enclosed. This is a notably successful technique if there is genuine enthusiasm for the particular candidate. This same idea is often effective for religious fund raisers.

Incentives to sponsoring members may include just about anything. I've seen bonus books or records, gifts matching those given to the new member, simple premiums, contest entries, and silver dollars. The gift can be as much as you are willing to pay for a new customer or member, less the allocated costs of the brochure.

## CROSS SELLING

You are an insurance agent with a list of people who have bought life insurance. How do you sell them accident insurance, property insurance, and retirement plans?

You are a bank with a large number of checking account customers. How do you sell them savings accounts, Christmas clubs, traveler's checks, and home mortgages?

You run a neighborhood gas station and have taken the trouble to get addresses of customers who come to you for gas. How can you sell them auto repairs, tires, and oil changes?

These are just a few of the many types of cross-selling opportunities. They exist in virtually every field. If you have a basic list of customers who are satisfied with their previous dealings with you, but you don't have a second product to promote, it is often worthwhile to develop a new product, or act as a retailer for someone else's product, in order to take advantage of the tremendous opportunity that cross selling offers.

The basic principle to utilize with cross-selling promotions is, once again, inertia. The present relationship is a bond to build upon, which is a far easier process creatively than establishing a new relationship.

The application of this principle demands that you start with the present customer relationship, not only by reminding the mail recipient about it but by making the new offer appear to be a continuation in every way: in name, copy style, graphics, and offer structure.

One of the best cross-selling case histories I know was created for a large New York banking institution. As automobile and other loans were paid off, the bank sent out highly personalized mailings inviting customers to continue to make the same monthly payments as before, but as deposits to their own savings accounts instead of as loan payments.

The mailing piece included a computer-printed letter, a computer-filled account form, and a series of coupons bearing the customer's name, account number, and the amount of the previous monthly payments. This mailing, tailoring the savings-account product to the present relationship by utilizing the familiar payment coupon format, is an excellent application of both the inertia concept and the principle of convention.

Another example, also in the financial field, is the growing tendency of investment solicitors, including such prestigious firms as Merrill Lynch and Dreyfus, to dramatize the liquidity of their investment vehicles by issuing checkbooks for instant access to funds. Merrill Lynch has since gone a step further by issuing Visa cards offering not credit but instant access to the holder's entire net worth deposited with Merrill Lynch.

A simpler example of cross selling is one used by Time-Life Books. This enormous, highly sophisticated organization produces "libraries" of books on various subjects—animals, boating, history, cooking, and so forth—all sold by ship-till-forbid subscription. Once a relationship has been established with a subscriber to any one of these libraries, that subscriber is cross-sold other libraries, single books, magazine subscriptions, or other products of the Time, Inc., family.

In the simpler efforts, statement stuffers describing one library are inserted with shipments and invoices for others. A unique technique of Time-Life is to make a cross-sell offer on a perforated extension of the billing invoice. The necessity for handling the extension when paying the bill assures its being noticed and relates it directly to the customer's present point of contact with Time-Life Books.

Cross selling presumes, of course, that your product and service have been well received. I know of one converse example: a photo-finishing concern which changes its name periodically to attract customers who declined to do business with it again under its original name.

## REORDER SOLICITATIONS

Giant corporations like Fingerhut and Sears devote the bulk of their marketing activity to sending catalogs and mailing pieces to their vast, scientifically segmented mailing lists. Merchandising departments are constantly looking for new items and analyzing previously used ones. Mailing lists are segmented by type of purchase, unit sale, type of product, and original source, to enable them to vary the frequency and scale of the promotions sent to each group of customers. Price-oriented buyers are sometimes sent only sale catalogs. Buyers of certain types of merchandise are offered specific specialty catalogs with in-depth offers of auto repair accessories, uniforms, western wear, home workshop tools, home improvement materials, and other merchandise categories.

The number and scale of catalogs has evolved over years of testing and ranges from simple flyers to full-color volumes of over 1000 pages, localized for various regions, and seasonalized for spring, summer, winter, and pre-Christmas.

On another scale, many smaller companies have a fall catalog as their most important and profitable effort. Unless they have segmented active buyers who merit year-round promotions, or they have seasonal merchandise, they can barely sustain one more catalog in the spring season. When a second catalog isn't profitable, it can often be revitalized by drastically changing the format, adding a sale theme, or restricting the size of the mailing compared to the pre-Christmas effort.

Of course every "free-ride" opportunity should always be taken advantage of. Statement stuffers—four- to eight-page flyers enclosed with bills—are often extremely profitable, as are bounce-back solicitations enclosed with merchandise shipments. Some types of companies (photo finishers, for example) have built their entire back-end business on bounce-backs enclosed with processed film. Often their promotions include some type of extra incentive: coupons good with the next film-processing order sent in by a certain date, credit certificates representing unprocessed prints, opportunities to conveniently enter a contest or sweepstakes, and most often, frequency bonus certificates.

These certificates can be used in virtually any kind of business. They involve enclosing some type of value voucher with each shipment, or some type of card which has to be punched or validated in some way. When five certificates are saved, or the card is completely punched, they may be redeemed for another item free.

Back-end promotions require a strong commitment to positive thinking. If you are sending out your first catalog, don't get discouraged if the results seem disappointing. That's only a starting point. Take the result figures apart, piece by piece. Some lists or list segments were probably profitable even if the overall mailing wasn't. Some items in the catalog or some pages probably did well even if the total result was in the red. Find your strong points and build on them, even if they steer you into an entirely different product line or market than you originally intended. A little objectivity can go a long way in direct marketing.

## LEAD SELLING SYSTEMS

All the principles discussed above also apply to using leads. Converting inquiries by direct mail is a two-step proposition. In such a case, the lead selling effort is basically the conversion system outlined previously.

More often, leads are used because the second step is not only by mail but through some type of personal selling. Once a lead is obtained, it is turned over to a telephone or field selling organization for further contact. This contact, in turn, can go directly for the sale, try to establish an appointment in the home or office, or invite the prospect into a sales office.

The simplest type of lead selling system is the one used by Dictaphone for their dictating equipment. The lead, once obtained, is simply transcribed onto a multiple-part document and turned over to a local independent dealer. The dealers are expected to report on the disposition of the prospect (sold, no interest, bought other), but no added preselling support is given to the dealer at all. This can be effective only in those rare situations (so rare I don't know of one) where management believes that all members of their sales organization—in all parts of the country, new salespeople and old—are consistently effective at following through on leads and turning them into sales.

An effective lead selling system, in my experience, should sell the prospect as well as the salesperson or dealer. I recommend that a conversion-type series of letters be sent to the prospect independently of contacts by the sale force or dealer.

These mail efforts can be designed to persuade the prospect to visit the dealership or call the salesperson for an appointment, or simply to keep interest in the product or service alive until the salesperson gets there.

International Gold Corporation had been giving dealer names to phone inquirers without any follow-up at all when I was invited to design a new Krugerrand marketing system. The one I put in provided for capturing the names and addresses of callers and forwarding the name to not one but three dealers, who then had to compete to make the sale. A five-letter follow-up series was sent to the prospect, not only selling the inquirer on the basic proposition, but asking for the order on behalf of any of the three recommended dealers. All any dealer had to do was give a telephone price quote and arrange for delivery once the check was received. In this case, our confidence level in the dealer organization was relatively low, necessitating a particularly high degree of preselling.

Even sophisticated sales organizations have conflicting priorities, varying confidence levels, and conflicting motivations. Salespeople have to be sold on following up leads. A very dramatic example of this occurred when two different offices of a major business equipment company followed up the same type of leads. One office was enthusiastic about leads and followed up every one by telephone sales call;

the other was skeptical and put in a minimal effort. The conversion rate in the enthusiastic office was 300 percent greater than in the other.

Salespeople and dealers are basically human beings, and like any other human beings they don't want to be rejected any more than they have to. This simple psychological fact results in what we call "pre-screening." This is what happens when a salesperson sorts through leads and decides, "This company isn't large enough," "This title isn't that of a decision maker," or even "This handwriting indicates someone I'd rather not have to do business with."

When I was vice president, marketing, of LaSalle Extension University, in the years before government regulations crippled the correspondence school business, I had inherited a system in which inquirers were mailed a school catalog and everything else was left to the salespeople, who eventually converted about 15 percent of the leads sent to them. In the meantime, in rural areas where we had no sales representative, a mail-order conversion sequence was signing up 10 percent of those leads completely by mail, without having to pay a substantial sales commission.

Our new system gave the lead to salespeople for only sixty days. They had this initial period to make their sales on a protected basis. After that, we cut in the mail-order sequence, with monthly letters, brochures, and a variety of premiums and trial offers, just as we had done in the rural areas. The result was amazing. We picked up an additional 5 percent conversion in mail-order sales even after the sales force had supposedly "worked" the lead. Amazingly, the average salesperson's conversion ratio increased from 15 to 20 percent. Counting the mail-order conversions, we were now getting 25 percent conversion instead of 15 percent. You can imagine the phenomenal effect this had on the bottom line. It seems salespeople increased their efforts for two reasons: one, they could no longer procrastinate because they would eventually lose their protected exclusivity, and two, they didn't want to be embarrassed by the mail-order department's turning up new enrollees from leads they had supposedly worked.

Did salespeople resist this new system? Sure. But only until they found that, despite their worst expectations, they were making more money. Also, we were able to sell them on the idea by demonstrating that the higher total conversion would make it possible for us to significantly expand the lead-procurement budget and provide each salesperson with a greater flow of leads than before—which we did. This simple change in the back-end follow-up system helped LaSalle grow threefold in only two years.

An ideal lead system should be flexible. Too few leads discourages a dealer or salesperson. Too many results in the leads being "burnt off"—not given the full attention they would deserve if the salesperson had more time for each lead. New computer systems make it possible to issue leads to a sales territory automatically, to adjust lead flow according to past conversion experience for individual dealers or salespeople, and to adjust territories by spilling over surplus leads to salespeople in adjoining territories. Ideally there should also be an early warning system for the sales and marketing managers if any territory is getting too few leads. With timely information territories can be revised, salespeople can be transferred, and supplementary lead-generation systems can be activated to provide leads in a dry area.

## SPECIAL SITUATIONS

There is no way to anticipate every situation that may arise in the course of running a direct marketing business, but here are three unusual ones that might be of help to some readers of this book: handling credit turndowns, out-of-stock situations, and dry-run testing. Inevitably a certain number of new orders other than prepaid orders have to be turned down because of credit risk. This may be by virtue of the customer appearing on a bad credit index or because of probability, as indicated by zip code experience or other factors. Some companies just ignore the order; others send brutally frank letters. My own recommendation is to try to save the situation by tactfully switching the credit request to a cash order.

When turning down a credit order, first of all attribute the turndown to lack of credit information rather than to bad credit information or zip code probabilities, either of which is bound to create ill will and useless correspondence. Then, instead of a cold turndown, offer a special cash deal. One record club, declining to send the advertised "6 records for $1" offered a no-strings-attached plan that let the customer select one free record for every one purchased, on a cash-with-order basis.

A common situation with catalog houses and other mail-order vendors of products is the out-of-stock situation. FTC requirements now specifically spell out standards and procedures for notifying customers if an item can't be shipped within thirty days and giving them an opportunity to cancel the order. These procedures should be followed to the letter not only because it is the law but because it is good business.

Even thirty days is too long to keep customers waiting when they have ordered something they want for themselves or as a gift. Don't substitute an item or send a different size or color, without explicit authorization from the customer, and don't keep customers on the string waiting for suppliers to replenish inventory. A prompt, no-nonsense letter explaining the situation is in order, along with a reply card giving the customer the option of waiting, canceling, or selecting an alternative. Where possible, a substitute should be specifically recommended. Where the unit sale is large enough, a phone call might be in order, followed up by the required FTC written notice and response card.

Dry-run testing is another problem faced by some advertisers. Current regulations make it impossible to solicit payment for a product that is not yet ready to ship. Yet there are times when we want to test various factors before the product is complete—sizes, packaging, premiums, and most often, prices.

We recently planned a Knapp Communications dry-run test for *Bon Appetit's* "Wine Journal" and were able to determine whether or not to offer a leather-bound trade-up edition, whether we should offer a premium, and which of several price levels would be most effective.

Such offers should be clearly labeled as preview or prepublication offers, and no prepayments should be accepted. If credit card charges are solicited, it should be made very clear—and scrupulously arranged for—that no credit charges will be processed until the item is ready to ship. Also, though this is not necessarily a legal requirement but certainly an ethical one, these test orders should be fulfilled, when finally ready to ship, at the lower of the new price or the price originally offered.

*    *    *

As you can see by the wide variety of techniques presented here, there is as much room for creativity and strategic planning in back-end promoting as in more glamorous and highly visible front-end promotions. This type of program is not an adjunct to a good marketing program; it is an integral and vital part.

## CHAPTER NINETEEN

# FULFILLMENT

The mailing piece is attractive and inviting. You open the envelope and find yourself involved in an offer of a product that will make your job easier or your life more satisfying. Eagerly, you mail in the coupon. Like most customers, you then impatiently wait . . . and wait . . . and wait.

Finally, weeks later, a battered-looking carton arrives. Your name is misspelled. You break your fingernail opening the carton. You rustle through a mass of yellowed pages from an old newspaper, and there it is—broken!

Maybe it's not even what you ordered. The instructions may be in pidgin English. Sometimes the item doesn't come at all, but a polite postcard arrives six weeks later to tell you that it has been out of stock or not available in your size all along.

Whether you keep this item or not, or whether your return or refund is handled efficiently or not, you've already lost your enthusiasm for the product, for the company, and probably for buying by mail at all.

Avoiding this all too common scenario is what fulfillment is all about. Fulfillment should be concerned, but too frequently isn't, with not only fulfilling the order but also fulfilling the customer's expectations. This subject is, technically, a matter of operations rather than marketing, but it can dramatically influence return rates, collections, reorder rates, and the entire future of direct marketing.

Good fulfillment practices, including prompt shipment, can significantly affect conversion and acceptance rates. Fulfillment expenses, including order processing, shipping, and service functions, are always a material expense, whether handled in-house or by an outside supplier. Fulfillment problems can get your company in trouble with the Better

Business Bureau, the DMMA Ethical Standards Committee, the Postal Service inspector, the press, and the law. More important, it is unfair both to your customer who trusted you and to your fellow direct marketers whose reputation will be tarnished along with yours.

## FULFILLMENT PROCESSES

Each fulfillment process involves a complicated decision-making process. There are many trade-offs. One is the standard of customer service you set as your goal.

Direct marketers aim for a high level of personalization, promptness, and performance—the three Ps of fulfillment. At each phase these must be weighed against the realities of time and cost, expressed in added personnel, inventory risk, computer capability, and the expenses of communicating with your customer by mail and telephone. Let's look at each step individually.

### Opening Mail

Most firms count or number the mail first, to establish a control against loss. If there's cash involved, a "caging" process takes place, in which remittances are removed and the amount noted. The money is handled under supervision within a security area and deposited each day. Even outside fulfillment suppliers deposit payments in their customer's banks on a daily basis.

Often the mail is sorted into types: payments, orders, general correspondence, returns. Advertising responses are sorted or counted so that daily counts by key numbers can be supplied to marketing personnel. If the volume is large, the sorting and counting process can be helped by using different sizes or colors of reply envelopes, bold tag marks on envelope edges, windows with code number show-throughs, or optically scannable imprints on the envelope faces.

Large fulfillment operations also use very ingenious machinery which slits open envelopes and exposes the contents for easy removal. Other machinery can imprint checks with source and amount, generating deposits which are quickly processed by the bank as well as efficiently recording and controlling cash intake.

### Handling Telephone Orders

For most types of mail-order propositions, the ring of the telephone is becoming as important as picking up the mail. The growth of telephone usage brings with it both problems and opportunities.

Toll-free WATS lines are the usual technique for providing such service, but the costs are high and getting higher. Marketers must not only provide for enough lines to handle the normal flow of inbound phone calls, but must also provide for skilled and trained operators on all shifts.

To take full advantage of this medium, the phones should be answered day and night, seven days a week, whenever people are likely to be reading your message in their mail or in publications. Some companies use answering machines during off-hours, but this is obviously not as effective as a sales-trained operator.

If your message is offered on television, it is usually uneconomical to handle the inbound calls yourself. The intensive peak demand for inbound lines would result in expensive idle capacity most other times. Outside phone services are geared to handle peak usage at advantageous rates.

The telephone contact is an opportunity to make a positive impression for your company by the way the phone is handled. A courteous, efficient operator can do a lot to inspire trust. While on the phone, the operator can offer special trade-up offers or sell related items.

Some particularly sophisticated companies have an on-line inventory system which lets the operator know, on a CRT terminal, whether an item is in stock and when it can be delivered. If it is not available, alternate colors or sizes or replacement items can be recommended. With credit card orders, the entire transaction can be confirmed and entered on the spot.

Inquiries and orders entered by telephone operators can be forwarded to order-entry departments in various ways. Handwritten inquiry slips leave room for error in handwriting interpretation. The best way is to have the operators immediately enter the customer's name, address, and all relevant data on something that can go directly into a computer—an optically scannable typed list, or a magnetic disk, tape, or cartridge in a word-processing system.

## Entering and Processing Orders

Theoretically a mail-order sale can be fulfilled by copying the customer's name and address onto a shipping label, but even the simplest proposition needs data—which ads pulled best or which proved to be the most profitable. Then there is the mailing list. We need to keep a list of customers so we can mail them other offers or rent out the list. And what about credit? We must send bills, see who paid and who didn't. For magazine subscriptions, clubs, continuity programs, no number of clerks with green eyeshades can handle the job.

A company large enough for a computer can take the initial data and prepare it for keypunching or other entry methods to put the information on a master tape or disc. Other companies can hire outside computer services or fulfillment firms to do the job for them.

It's a lot more complicated than newcomers imagine. The order must be edited—examined for completeness and clarity. It may have to be coded in some way. Then it is put into a form where it can be compared with lists of former customers, lists of bad credit risks, lists for verifying zip codes, and other data. Codes are counted, and reports are compiled and perhaps even analyzed, depending on the sophistication of the system. The customer file is then used to send out acknowledgments and to generate shipping documents, invoices, statements, and offers of other items. Payments are recorded, and so are returns. All along the way reports are generated that tell management whether the customer, the promotion, the product, and the business itself are sound and healthy.

However, not everyone starts out on such a scale, and not everyone wants to deal with the complexities of the computer. Some companies still use a ledger card system in which the original order is set up on a Scriptomatic card, an Eliot stencil, or some similar system. One copy of the label is posted onto the top of the card, and all entries are then entered—sometimes manually—on the cards as they come in. Such systems can work and can help some new companies get started, but I would suggest that the first step for any company that expects to handle more than 5000 customers a year is to line up a computer or fulfillment firm to handle this work. If you choose a computer firm, it should be one that specializes in this type of work, so that the software—systems, techniques, programs—are already in existence.

For even smaller companies, or start-up situations, a very simple and effective system is to use Avery gummed or peel-off labels. These labels, which are available in different sizes in stationery stores, require typing each customer name on a master list. After that any duplicating machine can make additional sets of labels for additional mailings. When an address changes, you just type a label and paste it over the old one on the master list. If you want to drop someone, just cross out the name. The various pages of labels can be sorted in any way that is convenient—by date of order, product, source, alphabet, or state. Labels can be affixed to simple index cards or Rolodex cards for cross referencing.

## Maintaining Lists

The heart of any system is the mailing list. Everything that comes in or goes out is part of some sort of list, and as I have already pointed out, a list is likely to be a company's greatest single asset.

The fulfillment list is more complicated only in that it carries more data: source codes, shipments, payments, returns, items ordered, and dates of transactions. Even the simplest system should be capable of quickly determining whether you want to make new offers to the customer (depending on credit), what the customer has bought, and when. Recency, frequency, and unit sale data will be vital in eventual segmentation. At the very least, you need enough data to prepare a statement of account if a customer demands one.

If you plan to rent the list out, it will be necessary to be able to tag test rentals, so that the same names are not used for every test mailing and you can omit the tested names when a customer rents the list again. You may want to retain data that may not be necessary for your own operation but that makes the list more rentable to others. For instance, renters will definitely expect you to know how old the name is (when it was put on your list), whether it is active or not, and how recently it has been active. They can also make use of source information. Direct-mail-sold names are generally more responsive to direct-mail offers. Catalog mailers prefer "catalog buyers." Mailers may want to select one group or the other on the basis of which names came in on a sweepstakes offer and which did not.

One giant mailing list omitted millions of birth dates which were available—a terrible waste of irreplaceable data that would have been of great value to list renters.

List rentals can be a very profitable source of income. Direct marketers should plan their systems to handle rentals in a manner that will render the type of fast, reliable, accurate service they would want when they rent lists from others.

### Shipping Orders

Presuming you have hand-addressed, duplicated, or computer-generated the shipping labels, the most important action remains: shipping the customers what they ordered.

Shipping is a separate function from order entry and processing. The label may be created at one building and the merchandise shipped from warehouses close to the customer, or "drop-shipped" directly by a supplier. If outside suppliers are used, separate firms may be used for fulfillment and shipping.

In a warehouse, there are several major functions. One is receiving: keeping track of shipments that are coming in, spot-checking quality merchandise, verifying quantities, and getting the incoming merchandise to the right section of the warehouse.

Inventory control keeps track not only of everything that comes in but also of everything that is supposed to come in. Late orders have to be followed up and the appropriate party notified when quantities appear to be low. Inventory systems, to be effective, cannot confine themselves to tracking the inventory as it is shipped, but must include a sophisticated forecasting function based on the expections of new promotions. Reorders must be placed while there is still time to get additional merchandise. Customers must be promptly notified that the item ordered is not available, so that they will be still inclined to order something else.

Once in the warehouse, the merchandise must be clearly marked and assigned locations so it can be found again. I have seen desperate warehouse managers frantically tearing open cartons because a shipment couldn't be found. Marking cartons clearly and storing them so the markings are visible can save your sanity.

Often the main bulk of merchandise—books, printed material, or whatever—is in cartons or on skids in one area of the shipping facility; a more modest quantity is on shelves in a more compact area closer to the shipping area. It would take too much time for order pickers to go through the entire warehouse to find a single item. Instead, a pick rack keeps some of each handy to minimize walking, searching, and time wasting. Some larger firms have more complex systems with pick areas for different lines of merchandise, multiple documents, and high-speed belts or conveyor systems. The principle is the same: Minimize walking to increase orders picked per hour.

Once the order is assembled, it goes to a packer. The packer checks the items picked against the shipping document and, if correct, places it in a bag or carton. For most companies, pickers and packers are the heart of the shipping process.

The labels are affixed; the cartons are sealed. Then they are weighed and postage or a UPS sticker is affixed. Some larger warehouses have postal facilities right in the warehouse to receive and sort the packages.

The invisible part of a warehouse operation is administration—the managers, personnel people, and security guards who keep the whole thing together behind the scenes. Unless you've been involved in warehouse management, you can't imagine the variety and complexity of problems that are handled by administrators.

Much of this discussion does not apply to items such as single books, file card sets, or magazines. These can be mass-packaged on automated equipment with automatically affixed labels.

## Customer Service

Theoretically customer service should be an unnecessary function. If everything went right all the time, there would be no need to handle complaints, inquiries, replacements, and special problems. The cost of maintaining a customer service department is one of the incentives to get it right in the first place—to hire the right people to prevent fires instead of putting them out.

Correspondents are, basically, the human beings who read customer mail; make note of problems for management attention; and direct the computers or other systems to make an adjustment, accept a return, correct an address, or reship a damaged item. Oh yes, they also do correspondence.

Once upon a time this meant they wrote personal letters to customers. This still happens, but very rarely, in the case of complex adjustments or explanations, or in companies where a highly personal approach is part of the image to be maintained. More often the correspondence is a form letter, a preprinted postcard, or at best, standard paragraphs on a word-processing system.

More and more, customer inquiries come in by telephone. Customers expect the person answering the phone to have instant access to their account record and instant authority to make a required adjustment.

At Capitol Record Club I used to make it a point to accept one or two calls a day from callers who demanded to talk to the president. After they got over the shock of learning that they really did get through, I was able to learn a great deal about what was important to our customers and how an incorrect shipment or unanswered letter can cause enormous anger and distrust. I recommend that any executive concerned with customer service spend some time dealing directly with customers in this way, in order to find out what kind of feelings lie behind the cold statistics in customer complaint reports.

## FULFILLMENT-GENERATED REPORTS

In other chapters we have discussed the role of reports, results, and statistics in evaluating promotions. The reports generated within the fulfillment process evaluate everything else: the quality of the customers generated by promotions, the value of the customer base as a whole, the acceptance of the company's product, reactions to its service, forecasts to indicate expense levels that will have a profound effect on profitability, and the intrinsic health of the entire business.

Any business, large or small, simple or complex, should record the kinds of data listed below in some type of regular reporting or review system. The data should be examined by the highest levels of management, by all relevant operating departments, and by consultants, ad agencies, or other suppliers in a position to influence the operations. Not all these kinds of data will be applicable to all businesses, of course, but they are included here as a checklist for your own operation.

## Sales Information

What's selling, to whom, and with what kind of promotion. Regular reports must be produced and examined in varying degrees of detail and at varying frequency, depending on company needs.

## Inventory Data

What's on order, what's needed, what's overstocked, and how much it all represents as cost of goods. Some companies obtain this data monthly, some weekly, some on a real-time basis with instant updating on a computer terminal.

## Returned or Refused Merchandise

A cost factor, an inventory factor, and most important, an indication of promotional overselling or product deficiency. Alternatively, if the returns are for incorrect shipments or poor arrival condition, you know you have to review your picking and packing operation.

## Work in Process

Orders waiting entry. Correspondence waiting answers. Shipments stacked up in the warehouse. Promotional mailings held up. These reports will measure the efficiency of operating departments and the likelihood of customer dissatisfaction.

## Customer Service Reports

Tabulations of complaints, inquiries, unfilled orders, and damage claims, to help point out problem areas for future correction.

## Credit and Billing Information

If you're selling on credit, you have to track the percentage of customers turned down. You have to know how many are paying, and how many are not, what credit cards are being used, and how many customers are being turned over to collection departments.

## Quality Control

Spot checks should be made of all operations and departments to determine how well work is being done, in addition to other reports which indicate how fast. Computer programs should be checked. Work in process should be sampled and reviewed. Dummy orders should be put through the system and compared with the service being offered by the competition, which should be similarly monitored.

Reports should be compiled on everything for the information of department heads and management. Error rates should be recorded, as they are usually more significant when expressed as a trend than in themselves. An increase in error rate is a cause for concern in any function.

### Productivity and Employee Reports

As fulfillment operations are often personnel-intensive, cost controls depend on the proper utilization of employees. Work loads must be forecast by department, and employees must be reassigned or staff levels revised to meet changing demand requirements.

In addition, the output of employee work groups or individual employees has to be monitored in order to identify exceptional producers or those who may need additional training.

### Continuity Reports

Organizations selling on a continuity, club, or subscription basis need many additional reports, including acceptance rates by cycle, renewal rates, commitment status, attrition rates, and sales projections.

This list does not include the financial and budget reports that would ordinarily be produced by the accounting department, or the reports prepared by the analysts in the marketing group. However, all reporting will depend on these fulfillment reports as input data for reliable financial projections.

### Report Design Considerations

In setting up a direct marketing company's reporting system, there is one standard that is paramount: usability. Reports must be in a form that genuinely helps those who must use it, and that quickly indicates the significant trends, events, and exceptions that require management action.

The definition of usability depends on the level of management. Operating foremen and department heads may need every detail that pertains to their department. Interfacing departments and senior management may need only highlights.

Some sophisticated reporting systems include comparisons with previous months, previous years, annual budgets, and variances for each—for every single expense line. Other reports turn everything into trend lines, or relate each action to a plan or a profitability standard. Some reports come in such detail that it takes pages of computer print-outs to present everything, every week or month. You've seen reports like these—stacked up unread on the tops of filing cabinets or on win-dowsills.

As one step toward solving this problem, every department circu-lating a report should have the automatic responsibility for preparing a one-page summary, in simple language, of changes, exceptions, var-iances, good news and bad.

My suggestion is that a key management assistant be delegated to prepare executive summaries of every available report—looking for the information that should be called to the attention of management. This is an excellent role for an executive trainee. There's no reason why, if dozens of people are involved in the preparation of reports, at least one shouldn't be assigned to reading and summarizing them.

## FULFILLMENT PHILOSOPHY

Fulfillment is an operations process with a profound effect on marketing results and an impact on profitability. The standards of fulfillment practice within a given organization are subject to a series of strategic decisions which, in total, derive from a company's philosophy.

This philosophy must be consciously and deliberately chosen by top management, not left to the sometimes myopic preferences of line man-agers. Let's look at some possible extremes, as a framework with which to define commonsense midpoints.

### "Stop the Deadbeat"

Not a year goes by when I don't find that a zealous credit manager has guided ever-obliging programmers and customer service personnel on a course of "throwing out the baby with the bath water."

If credit is the priority, the philosophy begins with the offer. No credit at all is permitted. Merchandise is shipped only after checks have been received, deposited, and cleared. The weeks this adds to shipping time materially increase returned merchandise. More impor-tant, orders and reorders are materially decreased from a credit prop-osition.

Under this policy a customer's claim that an item arrived broken might become the subject of lengthy correspondence, or a claim that a billed item never arrived would be looked up, invalidated, and turned into a collection process.

### "The Customer Is Always Right"

The opposite position is preferable in terms of short-term expense reduction and long-term corporate reputation. In this philosophy, account look-ups are minimized, returns are accepted without checking shipping dates, and credits are issued on the customer's word.

The problem is that there are always some bad apples in the customer barrel who will take advantage of this policy. However, depending on the relative costs of products and fulfillment practices, it may actually be less costly to overlook the abuses and concentrate on pleasing the 99 percent who are the bread-and-butter customers.

### "Cost Efficiency Uber Alles"

Let the engineers and cost accountants reign supreme and you'll have a different emphasis—cutting costs ahead of all else.

Maximum efficiency in managing operating costs is important, of course, but it should not be attained at the expense of customer service. Daily batches are more efficient than continuous processing, and weekly batches are more efficient than daily ones. This reasoning can lead to filling orders once a month.

Personal letters and phone calls are costly, both outgoing and incoming. One company, after finding that customers objected to having collect complaint calls refused, solved the problem by having their phone number unlisted. Very efficient! But is it smart?

Manpower planning finds peaks and valleys a nuisance. It's a lot easier to let a backlog of orders, payments, returns, and entries stack up so personnel are fully utilized. One company built a wall to hide unprocessed returned merchandise from visiting management, rather than hiring the people to process the returns. No, this is not a joke. I've seen the wall.

### "A Rolling Stone Gathers No Loss"

"Keep it moving. Get it out. The customers are waiting." This should be the cry of every supervisor and department head.

Fast order turnaround and shipping materially increases customer satisfaction and sales levels. Slow handling leads to correspondence, refusals, and returns. Slow handling of correspondence leads to more correspondence, with increasing levels of anger and annoyance.

Every marketer should read through aggravated complaints and letters to government regulators. They almost always begin with a phrase like "I've written three times and no one answered." Often there has been some kind of form response—but one so vague, so impersonal, so noncommittal, that the customer did not even realize it was a reply.

Computers were originally introduced as a way to improve customer service. Today, they are more often the excuse for slow, inaccurate service. Don't blame computers; they do only what we tell them. If our service is not what we'd like, it may be because we have not set standards, defined policies, and established correct criteria. Systems designers and programmers, like copywriters, can be infinitely creative in meeting objectives and solving problems; but someone has to tell them what is wanted.

The place to begin good customer service is in the original advertisement or mailing piece. Don't make promises you can't keep or guarantees you can't fill. Make the coupon clear and easy to fill out, with plenty of space so your customer can print clearly.

Screen out the deadbeats before they get on your books. Screening by maintaining deadbeat lists or using outside services is cheaper than collection efforts. Offers which require some payment will knock out the professional coupon clipper, and quality media and lists will usually produce quality business.

Go after the right customers in the first place, and treat them right in return. Good service is good business.

## CHAPTER TWENTY

# MAIL-ORDER MATH

In earlier chapters I have described direct marketing as both art and science, but it is first and foremost a business. As in any business, the fundamental objective is profit.

In direct marketing each individual promotion can be evaluated in terms of profit or loss. Each mailing list, advertisement, or TV schedule can be examined as if it were a subsidiary business, and decisions made to expand that business or close it down.

## THE BASICS

### Cost per Response

CPR can refer to cost per lead, cost per member, cost per subscriber, or any variation that is relevant for a particular business, but the formula is always the same. Simply divide the cost of the ad or mailing piece by the number of responses.

Promotion cost ÷ number of responses = cost per response

There are some refinements that should be remembered. If you are doing a direct-mail test campaign in small quantities, be sure to base your evaluation on what the campaign would have cost in quantity rather than on the higher cost of the small test campaign.

Also, if you are testing in a relatively less efficient season, estimate what response you would expect in the better season when you would run the full campaign.

## Allowable Margin

Allowable margin (AM) is what is left after you pay for the product, ship it, and write off any credit losses. In its simplest form, it is the amount of money available for profit and overhead after you deduct every expense except advertising.

For example, let's say a widget costs 50 cents to make, 25 cents to package, and 25 cents to ship. The $1 total is subtracted from the selling price. If the selling price is $2, the AM is $1.

If, in addition, 10 percent of those ordering the product fail to pay for it, then that 10 percent is deducted, making the allowable margin only 90 cents.

Many advertisers add in a charge per unit for administration or overhead before figuring the margin. In such a case, the AM is profit before advertising cost.

## Profit per Response

Deducting the cost per response from the allowable margin gives the profit per response (PPR). If the figure is positive, you have a successful mailing; if negative, an unsuccessful one. The allowable margin concept, not used in ordinary accounting practices but a traditional approach in direct marketing, provides a simple rule of thumb for planning and evaluating promotions.

## Return on Investment

ROI is the common standard by which all business decisions are eventually evaluated. In direct marketing, the out-of-pocket expense consists of all the money placed at risk—cost of goods, shipping, postage, and advertising cost—divided into the profit per response. On a calculator, divide the margin by the larger investment figure and move the decimal point two places to the right; the difference will represent the percentage return on investment.

## SOME VARIABLES

The previous examples are the basic parameters, with examples applicable to simple mail-order propositions. Here are some more factors which everyone in this business should be familiar with.

## Conversion Rates

If you are offering a free booklet and then converting the lead into a sale, you will be concerned with conversion rates. The same term applies to a credit order, a trial subscription, or a membership. These transactions are not considered sales until they are actually paid for.

If you have 1000 inquiries and 200 of them become buyers, you have a conversion rate of 20 percent. As an algebraic equation, this would be expressed as

$$\frac{\text{Buyers}}{\text{Inquiries}} = \frac{\text{conversion rate } (X)}{100}$$

This kind of simple equation is resolved by cross-multiplying, 100 times buyers equals $X$, the unknown conversion rate, times inquiries. You then divide both sides by the number of inquiries in order to isolate the unknown $X$ factor. But it is not necessary to use this equation.

On a calculator, simply enter the smaller number of buyers and divide by the larger number of inquiries, then move the percentage point two places to the right. If your calculator has a percent key, you press that instead of the equals key, and the two places will automatically be moved over for you.

## Renewal Rates

Renewal rates are determined in the same manner as conversion rates. The term is generally used in analyzing the profitability of a subscription or service sold on an annual basis. Typically between 40 and 60 percent of first-year subscribers renew for the second year. Of these subscribers, perhaps 80 to 90 percent will renew in subsequent years. In the circulation field, they are then called renewed renewals, or RRs.

## Attrition Rates

If you are selling a proposition on a continuity basis, or a club which requires a purchase every month or cycle, you will have to deal with attrition. This is the number or percentage of "starters" (initial customers or subscribers) who drop out at the end of each cycle by canceling, failing to meet a purchase commitment, or not paying. Typically 50 percent or so will not "convert" by making the first purchase, dropping off by 5 or 10 percent in subsequent cycles—that is, as a percentage of those who survived the previous attrition.

## Units per Response

In calculating profitability, take into account the number of units per sale. This can vary substantially, and can make the difference between success and failure. Usually a single unit offer which has a gift appeal will produce anywhere from 20 to 50 percent more units than orders— a factor to be considered when projecting or analyzing profitability.

## Average Take

In a catalog or club, you know that not everyone will buy from every mailing. If you expect 20 percent of your customers to make a purchase, the average take is 0.2. If half, then it is 0.5. One major club with a tight definition of "active member" and strong incentives for multiple purchases enjoyed an exceptional 1.2 "take" per cycle.

## Name Value

All financial projections should provide an allowance for the value of a name—either for future sales as part of a company's house list or as a contributor to list rental income. This factor is an estimate of the net value as a name only. You cannot include the entire profit because future promotions will require both product and promotion investments.

Such house lists are worth at least twice what an outside rented list would be worth and can be presumed to be rented internally at twice what you would pay to rent an outside list. The balance of the name value is an estimate of the number of times you or your list broker believe such a name would "turn" times the net income, after brokerage and computer costs.

## Time Value

Some advertisers plan to break even the first year and then make their profits in subsequent years' reorders or renewals. Continuity plans and clubs make large up-front investments with the intention of pulling ahead months later as additional purchases are made.

The value of the money tied up in advertising and premium investments should always be taken into account in long-range planning. Whether you're borrowing money from a bank or simply not having it available to invest yourself, the current interest value of money is a factor to be considered. If interest rates are at 10 percent, then $1 invested now has to return $1.10 a year later just to break even. All long-term planning should be weighted for this time value factor. Tables exist for the value of a dollar in the future as opposed to the present at various rates. Similar tables show when it might be more profitable to take 90 cents now rather than $1 later—the reverse consideration. Your banker or accountant can supply such data easily.

## CATALOG SPACE ANALYSIS

If you are mailing out a catalog or any type of multiple-item proposition, you will want to analyze not only the total proposition but also the profitability of each individual item in the catalog. This involves treating each page or fractional page unit as if it were an advertising promotion of its own.

Divide the cost of the entire catalog by the number of pages. For instance, if the catalog costs $90,000 and has 48 pages, of which 3 pages are used for covers and ordering information, then each page is worth $90,000 divided by 45, or $2000. Similarly, a half-page is worth $1000, a quarter page $500, and a tenth page $200.

When calculating the profitability of each item, the cost of the space has to be added to the cost of goods and to shipping and overhead costs.

If an item is very profitable, you will want to not only repeat it in future catalogs but also enlarge the space used to feature it. If an item is unprofitable, you can either drop it or reduce the size of the space allocated to it.

What products will be successful will vary widely depending on the positioning of the catalog merchandiser and the lists used. The results per item are examined individually and by category to guide future selections and spacing. It is important to look for patterns—product type, price range, style, uniqueness, or markup percentage—to find the unique key to each catalog's profit potential.

Often it pays to do a separate calculation of this type for major list categories. It could be desirable to produce segmented catalogs with different merchandise for different list categories.

## ANALYSIS MODES

The simplest report is a list of media in inverse order of cost per response, or a list of copy tests with "percent lift" indicated next to each.

The simplest profitability study involves taking the difference between allowable margin per unit and cost per response per unit, multiplying it times the total number of orders received, and indicating the total profit or loss.

**TABLE 20-1**
**TEST VERSUS ROLLOUT COSTS**

| Test package | Quantity | CPM | Response | CPO |
|---|---|---|---|---|
| Test | 10,000 | $600 | 4.2% | $14.29 |
| Control | 100,000 | $270 | 4.2 | 6.43 |

The simplest reports, unfortunately, are usually not enough. In Tables 20-1 to 20-4 are some examples of other reports prepared by Pierre A. Passavant (copyright 1979 DMMA) and provided by the Direct Mail Marketing Association.

*Test versus rollout costs* The sample in Table 20-1 relates rollout costs to test costs, which is simply a matter of restating the cost per order as it would be if the package were mailed at a quantity price.

*Conversion rates* Table 20-2 would apply equally well to any medium. In this analysis line 3 represents a cost per inquiry calculated from a magazine's cost per thousand circulation and a response rate. For magazines it would be simpler to divide the space cost by the number of responses and get the same figure, without having to refer to circulation or response percentage. This example would be more applicable to direct mail, where a cost-per-thousand figure would appear on line 1 and a response rate on line 2.

Line 4 takes into account the cost of the mailings designed to convert the inquiry into a sale, multiplying it by the number of mailings in line 5. This case indicates only four packages at an average cost of $400 per thousand. Telephone conversion costs might also be added in at this point, along with the costs of a computer firm to handle the incoming mail.

Line 6 combines the cost of acquiring the lead (line 3) and converting it (line 5) to produce combined cost of inquiry and conversion series.

**TABLE 20-2**
**CONVERSION RATE IMPACT (TWO-STEP EXAMPLE)**

| | |
|---|---|
| 1. Inquiry magazine ad CPM | $18 |
| 2. Response to ad | 0.3% |
| 3. Cost per inquiry | $ 6.00 |
| 4. Cost per conversion effort | $ 0.40 |
| 5. Four conversion efforts | $ 1.60 |
| 6. Total cost of inquiry and conversion | $ 7.60 |
| 7. Cost per order | |
|     10% conversion | $76.00 |
|     15% conversion | $50.67 |
|     18% conversion | $42.00 |

Line 7, then, is merely a projection of what the eventual cost per order would be at various conversion rates. You can see how dramatically changes in the conversion rate affect the CPO. Increased conversion effort costs are usually insignificant compared with the profitability of increasing the percentage rate, which is why six- and eight-part conversion series, with added telephone efforts, have become commonplace in this type of promotion.

*Direct-mail P&L*   Table 20-3 includes every factor applying to the profitability of a direct-mail promotion, presuming a simple cash offer with half of the customers electing to pay by credit card and the others by check. It also indicates a 5 percent customer correspondence factor, 10 percent returns, and 3 percent bad debt.

Note that this analysis shows the P&L in terms of total dollars rather than unit costs. While CPR and AM figures are handy for planning, P&Ls should always be in terms of real dollars.

*Response rate–profit relationship*   Table 20-4 shows the relationship between various profit objectives and the response rate. The contribution per sale and the package cost are the same as in the preceding example. Note that only a 16 percent increase in response rate—from 2.4 to 2.8—is needed to produce a 100 percent increase in profit.

## Back-End and Front-End Analysis

When testing offers or significant media categories, it is very important to determine or at least estimate what changes in quality might take place—the effect on collection, payment, conversion, renewal, member life, returns, etc.

An offer can be "hyped" with a sweepstakes or an exceptional premium only to find out that the incremental customers pull down the overall allowable margin and thus lower profit rather than raising it. More often, an added response rate up front more than compensates for back-end deterioration. Either way, it is essential that back-end performances be monitored and that basic offer changes be postponed if possible until performance data is available.

## SEGMENTATION ANALYSIS

In the most elementary form of segmentation analysis, direct marketers evaluate individual lists, publications, or stations, not entire campaigns. In any campaign, some media perform better than others. It is axiomatic that in future seasons we will expand our usage of those which did well, seek others like them, and drop those that did poorly.

TABLE 20-3
PROFIT AND LOSS WORKSHEET FOR DIRECT-MAIL PROMOTIONS (100,000
PACKAGES COSTING $250/M AT 3.2% RESPONSE OR 3200 ORDERS)

|  |  | Unit value | No. of units | Total dollars |
|---|---|---|---|---|
| 1. | Cash selling price | 29.95 | 3200 | 95,840 |
| 2. | Deferred payment price | — | — | — |
| 3. | Plus shipping/handling | 1.75 | 3200 | 5,600 |
| 4. | Average gross order value | 31.70 | 3200 | 101,440 |
| 5. | Minus returns (10%) | 31.70 | 320 | 10,144 |
| 6. | Average net sale | 31.70 | 2880 | 91,296 |
| 7. | Cost of goods per sale | 7.49 | 2880 | 21,571 |
| 8. | Cost per unrefurbished return | 7.49 | 64 | 479 |
| 9. | Order receipt and processing |  |  |  |
| 10. | Business reply postage | 0.18 | 3200 | 576 |
| 11. | Order process and customer setup | 1.50 | 3200 | 4,800 |
| 12. | Credit card fee at 3½% | 1.11 | 1600 | 1,776 |
| 13. | Credit check | 0.75 | — | — |
| 14. | Installment billing | — | — | — |
| 15. | Customer service | 7.50 | 160 | 1,200 |
| 16. | Shipping and handling | 1.75 | 3200 | 5,600 |
| 17. | Returns postage | 1.50 | 320 | 480 |
| 18. | Returns handling | 0.50 | 320 | 160 |
| 18A. | Returns refurbishing | 0.75 | 256 | 192 |
| 19. | Bad debt (3%) | 31.70 | 86 | 2,726 |
| 20. | Collection effort | 1.00 | 86 | 86 |
| 21. | Premium | 1.00 | 3200 | 3,200 |
| 22. | Promotion (CPO) | 7.81 | 3200 | 25,000 |
| 23. | Overhead | 3.80 | 2880 | 10,956 |
| 24. | Total expenses |  |  | 78,802 |
| 25. | Profit before taxes |  | 2800 | 12,494 |
| 26. | Profit % to net sales |  |  | 13.7% |

TABLE 20-4
EVALUATING THE EFFECT OF RESPONSE RATES (ASSUMING $13.02
CONTRIBUTION PER SALE AND $250 PER THOUSAND PACKAGE)

| Campaign objective | Profit per net sale | Available for promotion ($13.02 − $ profit) | | Promotion response needed ($250 ÷ promotion per order) |
|---|---|---|---|---|
|  |  | Per sale | Per order (10% returns) |  |
| Breakeven | 0 | 13.02 | 11.72 | 2.1% |
| 5% profit | $1.59 | 11.43 | 10.29 | 2.4 |
| 10% profit | $3.17 | 9.85 | 8.87 | 2.8 |
| 13.7% profit | $4.34 | 8.68 | 7.81 | 3.2 |

The criterion is profitability, and using CPR and AM, we can quickly tell which are likely to perform satisfactorily in the future.

In Chapter 10, Testing, there is a discussion of statistical validity, which must always be considered when planning future campaigns. This pertains to the margin of error that should be considered when drawing conclusions from one season's efforts in anticipation of the next season's.

List all the media sources in inverse order of cost per response— those with the lowest CPR first. For those on top of the list, look for additional media with similar audience characteristics. For the ones on the bottom, drop them or find a new proposition to appeal to them. For those in the middle, proceed cautiously with test extensions. For many years, this simple process was the key to planning future media campaigns. Then came segmentation, in progressively more complex forms.

*Internal segmentation* is the analysis of a medium by its built-in categories. The results of a magazine ad or one in the *Wall Street Journal* can be related to its geographic editions. Perhaps a national ad is marginal, but by using only the best three-fourths of the circulation, it might turn out to be very profitable. Some larger advertisers use different propositions in different geographic editions of Sunday supplements to place the most profitable ones in each area, while still enjoying the economies of a national buy.

A run-of-station buy on a television station may also be marginal, but a breakdown of the results by different day parts might show that it would be very profitable if you bought weekend only, nighttime only, or whatever the proposition called for.

Direct mail is especially sensitive to internal segmentation. With both house lists and rented lists, it is possible to break down results into a wide variety of segments—recency of purchase, size of purchase, type of purchase, original source, and demographic data. Credit card and insurance companies usually have available age, income, marital status, and similar data as well.

Any available characteristic can be analyzed in terms of relative responsiveness. Either assign key numbers in advance to predetermined segments or arrange with a computer house to analyze respondents in comparison with the characteristics of those mailed to.

There is room for imagination in defining segments. One client suggested converting birth dates into astrological signs and looking for patterns according to the supposed characteristics of different signs. Another suggested an age, or age-of-children, breakdown, on the theory that people at different points in the life cycle will have different purchasing proclivities.

*External segmentation* refers to the analysis of characteristics that are not intrinsic attributes of the media. Generally applicable to direct mail, this has become a valuable tool for more sophisticated direct marketers.

There are many degrees of external segmentation. The simplest is the identification of areas of the country which produce either less than acceptable response rates or, in another dimension, acceptable member quality. In its purest sense, this would involve tracking the number of pieces mailed to a particular zip code and determining whether the response from the individual zip code was ultimately profitable. Unfortunately such samples tend to be much too small to analyse in this pure sense.

At one time, such analyses were done by state. When zip codes came in, some companies started analyzing profitability and quality by sectional center. Both of these are very gross parameters. The most scientific application of this approach is cluster analysis, as popularized by Claritas and now available from several companies, including Comselect and Magi. Their refinements group zip codes together according to the latest available census data, as updated by commercial projections of population trends. In this way zip code responses, mailing quantities, and eventual pay-up rates are assembled into patterns according to any and every type of data available in the latest U.S. Census.

Not only the obvious parameters, such as age, income, education, and home ownership, can be included but also less obvious ones. *Field & Stream*, for instance, was found by Claritas to be most effective when they sent their mailings to zip codes with a high incidence of freezer ownership.

Zip code analysis is not the only method of external segmentation. It would be possible to match lists according to individual-name telephone book data, such as length of residence, single- or multiple-family occupancy, and ethnic last-name indications.

Knowing the characteristics provides a tool for the refinement of list purchasing beyond gross list selection. Desirable areas can be selected or undesirable ones purged when the initial list buy is made. In print media, tougher credit standards can be applied to zip code clusters that are likely to produce poor-quality business.

The added cost of a select or suppress factor when buying lists is very little compared to the savings involved.

## Decile Analysis

An extension of segmentation analysis, decile analysis is the practice of breaking the lists of a mailing program into ten segments, each representing 10 percent of the total, and then listing them in descending order of profitability.

This type of analysis generally lists each segment individually and then on a cumulative basis. Fixed costs such as overhead and mechanical production are not allocated, but assigned as a lump sum at the beginning. In this way, you can readily determine the optimum mailing quantity.

If you mail too small a percentage of the total, the fixed costs will not be offset. If you mail too large a percentage, you'll be reaching down into the less profitable segments of the total.

The risk/return ratio is also obvious in such an analysis, as there is a point where the next 10 percent of advertising investment would yield a much smaller percentage in profit increase, a factor to be considered in terms of overall objectives.

Decile analysis properly refers to a report breaking the total into ten parts, but the practice and the name have been applied to breakdowns of 20, 50, or more segments as well.

## Dimensional Analysis

In a hypothetical analysis of ten lists, list categories, or lists arranged by profitability (see the discussion of decile analysis above), it is presumed that some will do much better than others. Though the overall result may be good or bad, within that result some lists are exceptionally good and others very poor. Another possibility is that all may be good or bad, but with relative degrees of performance.

The usual practice has been to draw a line somewhere and decide which lists or groups are worth mailing to in the future and which are not. However, if each list, or mailing as a whole, is further broken down by zip code clusters or some other external factor, it is highly probable that the line drawn to designate which lists are to be mailed in the future and which omitted will be diagnonal rather than horizontal.

Imagine that a cluster analysis or state grouping indicates that some parts of the country or demographic groups do 25 percent better than the average and others 25 percent worse, and that these groups are shown across the top of a report. Down the side, you have the lists themselves, the SIC codes for a business list, or the decile groupings or list categories. If these percentages are applied to the lists, individually or collectively, depending on what kind of valid data is available, this additional result factor will be overlaid on top of the list results. This type of grid analysis can usually be made by combining list results with a zip code analysis.

The chances are that even the best lists will have some areas that would be better omitted, and that even the worst lists will have some segments or parts of the country that are mailable. Many lists which would have been marginal producers can now be certain of producing a satisfactory profit.

It is theoretically possible to refine mailing-list results on a three-dimensional base, using a computer to compare and weight results for additional factors—say the lists themselves, zip code clusters based on demographics, and regional criteria based on other geographic factors such as size of market, area of the country, or weather (for a gardening or recreational product). House lists can similarly be refined based on recency, frequency, and unit sale—the three most important characteristics of customer lists.

## ACCOUNTING PRACTICES

Direct marketing is like any other business in that the rules of conventional accounting hold true despite all its uniqueness. Below are some considerations that the direct marketer will want to learn more about from an accountant or tax adviser.

*Inventory Valuation*   What you put in stock ties up capital and is often subject to taxation. Drop-ship or installment shipping arrangements might be desirable.

*Year-End Tax Treatment*   If advertising is expensed rather than capitalized, it might be possible to reduce current-year taxes by sending out mailings at the end of one year—an expense—and taking the resulting sales in the next year. This would defer taxes and make available more capital for mailing.

*Capitalized Advertising*   If showing earnings is your objective, as with a publicly held company, it appears reasonable to capitalize advertising costs, making them a current-year asset in the year they are paid for, and then write off the expense during the years when the income is produced. This would be most applicable to programs with long-term customer relationships.

*Reserves*   Holding reserves is another accepted practice, to allow for inventory write-off, returns, or bad credit, thus reducing current-year tax obligations.

*Hidden Assets*   One of the great frustrations of direct marketing executives is the extent to which major corporations fail to recognize the real strengths of a direct marketing business.

For instance, a direct marketing firm's greatest asset is its mailing list, which should be computed at a value based on the capitalized value of its list-rental income and internal solicitation potential. If a direct marketing company is sold, its list is the asset most in demand. Yet most companies fail to give it any value in computing assets or profits.

Similarly, control of key media positions, such as options on back covers or insert card positions, is a substantial hidden asset. So are fulfillment software that works smoothly, result data that guides a company in its marketing decisions, and trained, loyal personnel. Direct marketers accommodate figures to accounting methods; perhaps someday accountants will develop an appropriate method of valuing the industry's greatest assets.

*       *       *

Other mathematical subjects are covered in the discussions of various media and testing. The reader is urged to read the chapters described below, which include other examples of mail-order math and economics.

Chapter 2 includes examples of offer testing and pricing comparisons. Chapter 6 reviews print-media buying practices and the quality factor. Chapter 7 discusses the math of broadcast support advertising for preprints and direct mail, as well as the role of the penetration factor. Chapter 18 includes an example of the effect on profitability of back-end promotions.

This chapter was not meant to be a course on algebra, statistics, accounting, economics, or business math, for excellent books are available on all these subjects. What I have tried to do here is to give the reader the basics and an idea of the more sophisticated approaches that are available.

To acquire more advanced knowledge of the math and finance of the direct marketing field, I suggest that readers enroll in the DMMA's course on math and finance, taught by Pierre Passavant and offered in major cities throughout the country. For information, write the DMMA Education Department in New York City.

## CHAPTER TWENTY-ONE

# THE FUTURE

"Greater than the tread of mighty armies is an idea whose time has come," reads a liberal translation from a work by Victor Hugo. Direct marketing is such an idea.

Once the mystique-shrouded preserve of entrepreneurial wordsmiths, direct marketing is today a tool of sophisticated marketers, a venture of giant corporations, a beacon for courageous venture capitalists. It has never had greater recognition, greater acceptance, or greater success—and yet it is just beginning.

## CORPORATE STRATEGIES

The profitable utilization of direct marketing within modern corporations requires—even demands—understanding, flexibility, and creativity. Discussed below are some of the ideas and attitudes which should be understood in order to succeed in this field.

### Market Orientation

Most companies take a retail product and hand it to a marketing manager with the order, "Go and sell it." It doesn't work that way in direct marketing. The consumer comes first. The economics of the marketing method require different formats, pricing, and positioning. The ideal approach is to have the direct marketing manager determine what can be sold and then go to R&D or manufacturing with the reverse request: "Go and make it."

## Willingness to Take Risks

Traditional managers turn pale at the idea of developing three or four business concepts, offering them on a limited basis, and knowing that only one will be successful. "Which one will work?" they demand. "Who knows?" replies the honest manager, soon to be unemployed. Yet this is the right way to enter this business.

No amount of planning or research will give an absolute answer to the consumer's buying intentions. Just when we think we have consumers psyched out, they have a nasty way of reminding us that they are unpredictable. Risk taking must be built into any direct marketing process.

## Management Positioning

Invariably, direct marketing propositions that are managed by business development managers or product managers within packaged-goods marketing departments will not succeed. As is plain throughout this work, direct marketing requires a different discipline, a different way of planning, and a different, more entrepreneurial type of management.

The most successful companies are those owned by related companies which understand the reasoning behind multiple products and leveraged risk taking (such as producers of books, records, toys, films, and magazines) and those which are established as relatively autonomous subsidiaries.

If this field is to be properly positioned and effectively utilized, a direct marketing manager should be on a line with managers of any other aspect of product distribution. A direct-mail manager should report to marketing on an equal level with advertising, sales promotion, and public relations.

## Loss-Leader Philosophy

In direct marketing we evaluate the profitability of a customer relationship, not just the first sale. It is logical planning to set up a business which loses money on the first transaction—offering free books, low-priced film processing, free catalogs, or premiums—in order to "buy" a name for subsequent mailings.

Too many infant direct marketing subsidiaries have been shot down by trigger-happy auditors who failed to incorporate this philosophy into their profitability analysis.

## Long-Term ROI

Financial planning must be long-range. Magazines, for instance, traditionally lose money on their first-year subscribers, making their circulation profits two or three years down the line as renewals come in. A book or record club financial plan presumes that many members will not repay their acquisition cost (advertising expense plus premium cost) until several purchases have been made. In some propositions, this may not take place until the following year.

## Accounting Flexibility

I once managed a division of a company that was tax-reduction-oriented. All advertising was expensed as it appeared, as were all gift and premium costs. There was no allowance for the value of the customers brought in, although they would produce profitable sales in future months and years.

The company was then bought by a publicly held company which wanted everything to look good for investors. Suddenly reserves were eliminated and all advertising costs—going back for years—were capitalized over an optimistically estimated three-year average customer life. Millions of dollars in paper profits were thus created.

Neither extreme is appropriate. What is correct is a sensible recognition of the unique financial profiles of direct marketing companies, accompanied by reports which accurately reflect the true condition of such a company.

## Rocking the Boat

Another reason why major companies don't enter the direct marketing field, or don't succeed if they do enter, is the common advice, "Don't rock the boat."

The downside risks of taking a chance or recommending something new are just too great in many large corporations. If a middle manager sticks his or her neck out and suggests taking a risk, the chances are that success will merit a pat on the back and a modest salary increase, while failure will lead to dismissal.

To overcome this, major companies must seek out potential entrepreneurs in their ranks and bring them together in a separate department with a radically different environment. Whether this environment is a new-product unit or some kind of think tank is not the point. What is essential is that progress be measured in terms of solid creativity, ambitious planning, and dynamic leadership away from the influence of the don't-rock-the-boaters.

## Where to Start

If you are a business executive considering bringing your company into direct marketing, permit me to offer some advice on where to start—and where not to start.

Do begin by building on your company's strengths. These may be your good name, a publishing or manufacturing capability, a unique product franchise, your access to a unique mailing list or medium, or even in-package or on-package promotional capability.

One client chose to enter the direct marketing business with a product line not previously associated with their company, with a low profit markup and no prior production experience. They had no list, no computer facility, and no fulfillment capability.

If this client had begun where they already had strength—in the product area where they had production capability and an established name—they might be in the direct marketing business by now. They held back because they were concerned about offending their dealer organization—a common fear, but an exaggerated one. Columbia Records is a good example. Their introduction of a mail-order club business turned out to be additive; the retail and direct marketing businesses grew together.

If you're going into the direct marketing business, do it right—or don't do it at all. Make a commitment by getting the best people, the best advisers, and the best agencies. Go all the way. Appropriate the money for the development, research, and testing of every potential approach. Plan on a long-range investment from the very beginning.

## STRATEGIES FOR THE INDUSTRY

As direct marketing is growing, so are its problems. Its acceptance, popularity, and growing sophistication are all both opportunities and problems. Here are some problems I'm concerned with and some suggestions for the future.

### Attracting New People

It is imperative that direct marketing be popularized so that young people will make a conscious choice to enter this field while still in college. At this time, the great bulk of direct marketers are people who stumbled into the field by accident. My own company includes several former secretaries who had opportunities to move into creative or account work and have done a splendid job, but the field is growing too fast to depend on chance to build the ranks of qualified specialists.

Most college marketing departments either do not teach direct marketing at all or confine their teachings to direct mail as a medium. College professors trained in packaged-goods marketing hire teachers from the same discipline and continue the pattern of exclusion.

The DMMA Educational Foundation, under the direction of Richard Montesi, is working to interest universities in this field. At the present time about thirty colleges and universities offer at least one full-credit undergraduate or graduate course in direct marketing.

Everyone in the field, and particularly people who owe their success to it, should make it a point to work in some way to teach other people, to talk to marketing professors at their alma maters, and to provide trainee spots for college graduates. A good source for entry-level positions are students who have participated in programs like the Lewis Kleid Collegiate Training Institute, a week-long training program for outstanding college seniors. The program is sponsored and conducted by the DMMA Educational Foundation.

## Raising Academic Standards

Even those universities that do offer direct marketing training usually confine their coursework to one lesson in a general advertising course or a series of lectures in an adult education program.

There is a need, and an opportunity, for a university to offer courses on direct marketing leading to B.B.A. and M.B.A. degrees specializing in this discipline. As far as I know, there is no such curriculum anywhere in the country. Such a curriculum would include relevant courses on administration, management, statistics, computer systems, economics, and other subjects.

Within the industry, there is already more emphasis on advanced technology. The DMMA Marketing Council offers advanced lectures on applications of mathematics, computer systems, and psychology to various direct marketing subjects, and is publishing a series of bulletins on these subjects.

## Cleaning Up Our Own Act

There are very, very few rotten apples in the direct marketing field, but those few are an embarrassment to the entire industry. Anytime a customer gets a product that wasn't ordered, is defective, or is not as advertised, the entire industry is damaged. Anytime a direct marketer goes bankrupt, leaving customer orders unfilled and unrefunded, all of us lose another customer.

The DMMA Ethical Standards Committee has started working on these problems, but more must be done. Just as stockbrokers have set up programs to insure the assets of those who buy stocks through them, and just as manufacturers arrange for the Underwriters Laboratory to certify absence of fire hazards, so must direct marketers work together as an industry to find a way to assure the public that they can buy from us with confidence.

## Improving Service

The occasional service delay is problem enough. Far more serious is the fact that the standards of service in the industry are set far too low.

Blaming our problems on the Postal Service has become an excuse. Efforts to develop alternative suppliers must continue, and we must redouble our efforts to get the Postal Service to understand our requirements and economics.

In the meantime, the inefficiencies of postal delivery do not excuse slow delivery but demand faster turnaround on order processing to make up for postal slowness.

I would like to see the industry create a "10 Club," with a standard of perfection that, with apologies to Bo Derek, would not be all appearances. A direct marketing "10 Seal" could be issued to companies which agreed to send an order to a customer within ten days of receipt, to allow ten days for a customer to return an item for any reason at all, and to guarantee that refunds would be processed and paid within ten days.

## Mailing List Availability

In Sweden a direct marketer buys mailing lists from the government-owned postal system. Such lists are segmented by individual income tax information and provide the most highly refined selectivity possible: age, income, family composition, etc. The United States government, instead of helping to refine the mailing system, looks for roadblocks to hinder it.

Consumerists should support direct mail because it offers an opportunity to answer questions and explain details that television and newspaper advertising have no room for. Privacy advocates should want to support further refinement of mailing lists so messages would be sent to those who are most likely to be interested. Without the mailing list system, we would be obliged to send our mailings to everyone. If anything, the government should be helping us to refine mailing lists by providing more timely, more accurate, and more relevant census data.

List refinement does not lead to invasion of privacy. After all, no one is forced to read a letter.

## New Technology

We are on the verge of very exciting developments in communications. Active testing is already under way, attempting to apply cable television, interactive television, and phone/television hookups to direct marketing.

New products and services will emerge—research services that can display anything in the library on your home television screen. Tax, budget, and financial services will enable you to pay your bills by telephone, balance your checkbook on a home computer, and get computer analysis of your investments on your home television screen.

New developments and experiments are reported every day, and direct marketers are actively vying to be among the first to use these methods. I predict that the next generation will take these new techniques for granted, just as we presume that television has always been with us.

The challenge for direct marketers is to be flexible enough to adapt our methods and our way of thinking to these new fields—to marry the disciplines of the early copywriters to the electronics of these pioneering methods.

If there is a lesson to be learned in direct marketing, it is that nothing remains the same. By the time this book is printed, there will be new developments, new changes, and new refinements.

My purpose here is to give you the background to look at the forest instead of the trees and to understand the principles which underlie this field as of this moment, so that you can apply them to the opportunities that face you at the time you read these words.

Keep your mind open. Keep learning. Keep trying. You can add your own lessons and experiences to this still-infant body of knowledge. In direct marketing, the excitement of discovery awaits us all.

# INDEX